Economic Integration
in the Soviet Bloc

**PRAEGER SPECIAL STUDIES IN
INTERNATIONAL ECONOMICS AND DEVELOPMENT**

Economic Integration in the Soviet Bloc

WITH AN EAST GERMAN CASE STUDY

Heinz Köhler

**Associate Professor of Economics
Amherst College**

FREDERICK A. PRAEGER, *Publishers*
New York · Washington · London

The purpose of the Praeger Special Studies is to make specialized research monographs in international economics and politics available to the academic, business, and government communities. For further information, write to the Special Projects Division, Frederick A. Praeger, Publishers, 111 Fourth Avenue, New York, N. Y. 10003.

FREDERICK A. PRAEGER, PUBLISHERS
111 Fourth Avenue, New York 3, N.Y., U.S.A.
77-79 Charlotte Street, London W.1, England

Published in the United States of America in 1965
by Frederick A. Praeger, Inc., Publishers

Library of Congress Catalog Card Number: 65-24729

Printed in the United States of America

To my parents

Arthur O. and Gertrud A. Köhler

The present study was begun as a doctoral dissertation on "East Germany's Economic Integration into the Communist Bloc" at the University of Michigan and in that form finished in early 1961. Subsequently, my interests were drawn to a similar study of other Soviet bloc countries which showed that national differences in the postwar chain of events were few and that there was an almost unbelievable similarity in the type and timing of economic changes in all satellite countries. Indeed, many a chapter could have been almost literally lifted from the original East German study and, *mutatis mutandis*, been inserted with identical conclusions into a study of integration of any other bloc country. In all of these countries there have been noticeable changes in the structure of the economies. The original impetus for this development came, furthermore, in several instances (East Germany, Hungary, Rumania) clearly from quantitatively significant reparations demands by the Soviet Union. These demands were weighted so heavily in favor of investment goods that they must have contributed to the decision to concentrate on the expansion of industry as against agriculture and investment goods industries as against all others. As a matter of fact, there frequently is clear-cut evidence, on an industry by industry basis, how heavy or low Soviet demand was followed by relative expansion or contraction of the corresponding production. The system of Soviet corporations, which was even more widespread in the early postwar time than the collection of reparations, similarly influenced economic structures, quite independently of and in addition to changes sought for ideological reasons by the new Communist regimes.

Both the political and economic changes were reflected also throughout the Soviet bloc in changes of the regional and commodity composition of foreign trade. None of the present bloc countries, before World War II, had exchanged a signifi-

cant portion of its foreign trade volume with other (future)
bloc countries; they all reoriented their trade to this area
starting in 1948, achieving by 1951 their present substantial
trade involvement in the bloc. The commodity composition has
typically changed also to reflect the increasing importance of
industry, but the over-all importance of foreign trade, compared to output, has usually not changed very much. It is quite
true, of course, that the Council for Mutual Economic Aid, especially since the mid-1950's, has been heralded as an important instrument of bloc economic integration. Its work is,
therefore, discussed in great detail in this study.

However, because of the great national similarities, it
was decided to analyze the process and status of Soviet bloc
economic integration by revising and enlarging upon the original East German study, letting it stand as an exemplar of
postwar economic history in the bloc.

I am indebted to many persons, too numerous to mention,
who were kind enough to give their advice on specific subjects.
I am also grateful for valuable suggestions received from Pro-
fessors Morris Bornstein and Wolfgang F. Stolper, both of the
University of Michigan, who read a very early version of parts
of this book. Professor Stolper has been particularly helpful in making available an excellent collection of source materials without which this study would have been truly impossible.

An earlier version of CHAPTER 7 was published as an article in *Kyklos*, 2, 1963. I am thankful to the publishers of
this journal who gave their kind permission to reprint it here.

For the original study, which was the starting point for
this book, I was assisted by a generous fellowship from the
Ford Foundation. Similarly, I have since been assisted gener-
ously by Amherst College in the procurement of source materials. Most of all, a grant from the American Council of Learn-
ed Societies has materially aided in the revision and consider-

able expansion of the original study. For all this aid I am
very grateful. However, the conclusions, opinions, and other
statements in this publication are mine and are not necessarily those of the supporting institutions or of those who gave
me their kind advice.

Special thanks are due also to Mrs. Mildred Buzicky who
did an expert job of typing and retyping patiently many tables
and a once almost illegible text, filled with foreign words.
She also assisted bravely in the tedious task of proof-read-
reading.

Heinz Köhler

Amherst, Massachusetts
July 15, 1965

CONTENTS

Page

PREFACE   vii

LIST OF TABLES   xv

LIST OF ABBREVIATIONS   xix

INTRODUCTION   1

Chapter

1. SOVIET REPARATIONS POLICY IN EAST GERMANY   5

    A. The Legal Basis for Reparations   6

    B. The Forms and Magnitude of Reparations

        1. Removals From the Wealth of East Germany   10

        2. Deliveries From Current Production   17

        3. The Use of German Labor   23

        4. Summary and Evaluation   24

    C. Consequences of the Reparations Policy

        1. Slowing Down the Rate of Growth   31

        2. Structural Changes   38

            Footnotes   43

2. EAST GERMANY'S COMMERCIAL FOREIGN TRADE RELATIONS

    A. The Resumption of Trade and the Creation of
        the Foreign Trade Monopoly   51

    B. The Volume and Regional Distribution of
        Foreign Trade   54

        Footnotes   75

3. THE COUNCIL FOR MUTUAL ECONOMIC AID

    A. The Founding and Structure of CMEA   79

    B. A History of CMEA

        1. Attuning Foreign Trade Plans: 1949-54   85

        2. Coordinating Production and Investments:
            1954-57, an Idea Takes Hold   88

        3. Coordinating Production and Investments:
            1958-65, the "Decisive Step Forward"   101

    C. A Survey of Alleged Specialization Decisions   127

    D. Summary   140

        Footnotes   145

Chapter   Page

  4. INTERNATIONAL TRADE THEORY IN THE SOVIET BLOC   158

      A. Criteria For Measuring Direct Economic
          Profitability

          1. Simple Price Comparisons   160

          2. Indicators of Profitability   166

      B. Foreign Trade Pricing   182

      C. Theory and CMEA Decisions   186

      D. An Evaluation   189

          Footnotes   191

  5. MEASURING EAST GERMAN ECONOMIC INTEGRATION   196

      A. The Distribution of the Labor Force   197

      B. The Distribution of Investments   202

      C. The Structure of Output   210

      D. The Structure and Importance of Foreign Trade

          1. The Trade Structure with the Rest of the
              World as a Whole   213

          2. The Trade Structure with the Communist Bloc   223

          3. The Trade Structure with Individual Com-
              munist Countries   237

          4. The Importance of Foreign Trade   246

          Footnotes   259

  6. EAST GERMANY'S BALANCE OF PAYMENTS

      A. The Balance of Trade   264

      B. The Service Balance   284

      C. Unilateral Transfers   295

      D. The Capital Balance

          1. Capital Movements with Albania   301

          2. Capital Movements with Bulgaria   305

          3. Capital Movements with Czechoslovakia   307

          4. Capital Movements with Hungary   307

          5. Capital Movements with Poland   308

          6. Capital Movements with Rumania   309

          7. Capital Movements with the U.S.S.R.   309

Chapter   Page

        8.   Capital Movements with Communist Asia   312

        9.   Capital Movements with Non-Communist
             Countries   313

       10.   Summary   326

    E.   The Balance of Payments as a Whole, 1950-63   327

         Footnotes   334

7.   EAST GERMANY'S TERMS OF TRADE   345

    A.   The Calculation of Gross Barter Terms
         of Trade

        1.   Methodology   346

        2.   Results   349

    B.   The Calculation of Net Barter Terms of Trade

        1.   Methodology   355

        2.   Results   355

    C.   Conclusions   357

         Footnotes   359

CONCLUSIONS   363

Appendixes

    A.   THE EAST GERMAN INDUSTRY CLASSIFICATION   368

    B.   A NOTE ON EXCHANGE RATES   369

         Footnotes   374

    C.   BASIC PRINCIPLES OF THE INTERNATIONAL
         SOCIALIST DIVISION OF LABOR   377

SELECTED BIBLIOGRAPHY   396

LIST OF TABLES

Table   Page

1. Reparations delivered to the Soviet Union from East Germany, by type and years, in million RM/DM-E, at current prices, 1945-60   25

2. Indices of real reparations from current production, of real GNP (West German definition) and real reparations as a percentage of real GNP, East Germany, 1945-60   34

3. East German commodity exports to selected trading partners, 1936 and 1946-63, in 1,000 rubles, at current prices f.o.b. East German border   61

4. East German commodity imports from selected trading partners, 1936 and 1946-64, in 1,000 rubles, at current prices f.o.b. border of seller   66

5. Distribution of East Germany's labor force, by industries, in per cent of total industrial employment, 1936 and selected postwar years   198

6. Distribution of East Germany's gross investment in industrial plant and equipment, by industry groups, in per cent of total, in real terms, 1936, 1944-55   204

7. Distribution of East Germany's gross investment in industrial plant and equipment, by industries, in per cent of total, at current East German prices, 1950-57   206

8. Percentage distribution of East Germany's commercial commodity exports to all areas, by sectors, 1936 and selected postwar years   214

9. Percentage distribution of East Germany's commodity imports from all areas, by sectors, 1936, and selected postwar years   224

10. Percentage of East German commodity exports going to the Communist bloc, by sectors, selected years   228

11. Percentage of East German commodity imports coming from the Communist bloc, by sectors, selected years   230

12. Percentage distribution of East Germany's commercial commodity exports to the Communist bloc, by sectors, selected years   232

Table   Page

13. Percentage distribution of East Germany's com-
     modity imports from the Communist bloc, by
     sectors, selected years   234

14. Commodity composition of East German trade with
     Albania, in per cent of total exports and im-
     ports   238

15. Commodity composition of East German trade with
     Bulgaria, in per cent of total exports and
     imports   239

16. Commodity composition of East German trade with
     Czechoslovakia, in per cent of total exports
     and imports   240

17. Commodity composition of East German trade with
     Hungary, in per cent of total exports and im-
     ports   241

18. Commodity composition of East German trade with
     Outer Mongolia, in per cent of total exports
     and imports   242

19. Commodity composition of East German trade with
     Poland, in per cent of total exports and im-
     ports   243

20. Commodity composition of East German trade with
     Rumania, in per cent of total exports and im-
     ports   244

21. Commodity composition of East German trade with
     the Soviet Union, in per cent of total exports
     and imports   245

22. East German export ratios (exports divided by
     production) for selected commodities, in per
     cent, selected years   247

23. East German import ratios (imports divided by
     the sum of production plus imports) for se-
     lected commodities, in per cent, selected years   252

24. Percentage distribution of the uses of East
     German real GNP   256

25. East German commercial exports by selected in-
     dustries, 2nd half-year 1951, at foreign
     trade DM, internal prices, and foreign trade
     rubles, in millions. PAG and exchange rate
     of foreign trade ruble values to internal
     price values   268

Table   Page

26. Translations of 1951 reparations from current
     internal prices into foreign trade rubles,
     in millions   269

27. East German commercial exports at internal
     prices and foreign trade rubles, in billions,
     1950-56, and the implied real exchange rate   271

28. East Germany's commodity reparations in foreign
     trade rubles and internal prices, 1950-60,
     and a comparison of the implied real exchange
     rate with the official exchange rate   272

29. Distribution of East Germany's balance of trade
     by selected trading areas, 1950-63, in 1,000
     rubles   276

30. East German service reparations in millions of
     internal prices and foreign trade rubles,
     1950-58, and exchange rates for non-commer-
     cial transactions   285

31. East German commercial service imports and ex-
     ports, 1950-63   289

32. East German exports and imports of selected
     services (technical document exchange, fairs
     and exhibitions, expert and student exchange,
     tourism), in 1,000 rubles, 1950-63   290

33. East German exports and imports of postal and
     communications services and of services con-
     nected with diplomatic missions, in 1,000
     rubles, 1950-63   292

34. East Germany's interest income, 1956-63, in
     1,000 rubles   296

35. East Germany's interest payments, 1950-63, in
     1,000 rubles   298

36. Example of methodology for the calculation of
     interest payments and principal amortization,
     first Albanian credit, in 1,000 rubles   306

37. Capital exports (credits granted by East Ger-
     many), annual drawings, 1951-63, in 1,000
     rubles   315

38. Capital exports (credits repaid by East Ger-
     many), annual repayments, 1950-52, 1955-63,
     in 1,000 rubles   318

Table   Page

39. Capital imports (credits granted to East Ger-
    many), annual drawings, 1950-51, 1953-63,
    in 1,000 rubles   321

40. Capital imports (credits repaid to East Ger-
    many), annual repayments, 1956-63, in 1,000
    rubles   324

41. East Germany's balance of payments, 1950-63,
    in 1,000 rubles   328

42. A sample of East German commodity imports and
    exports in constant 1955 West German foreign
    trade prices, quantity indices of imports
    and exports, and gross barter terms of trade,
    1950-63   350

43. Value and price indices of East German commer-
    cial commodity exports and imports, and net
    barter terms of trade, 1950-63   356

44. East German exchange rates   372

LIST OF ABBREVIATIONS

AAK	Aussenhandelsabrechnungskontor
AEG	Allgemeine Elektrizitäts Gesellschaft
AH	Der Aussenhandel (journal)
BB	Bonner Berichte
BMfgF	Bundesministerium für gesamtdeutsche Fragen
ccm	cubic centimeter
c.i.f.	cost, insurance, freight
cm	centimeter
CMEA	Council for Mutual Economic Aid
Č.S.S.R.	Czechoslovak Socialist Republic
DAHA	Deutscher Aussenhandel, Anstalt des öffentlichen Rechts
D.D.R.	Deutsche Demokratische Republik
DHG	Deutsche Handelsgesellschaft
DIW	Deutsches Institut für Wirtschaftsforschung
DM	Deutsche Mark
DM-E	East German Deutsche Mark
DM-W	West German Deutsche Mark
DVIA	Deutsche Verwaltung für Interzonen- und Aussenhandel
DW	Die Wirtschaft (newspaper)
DWK	Deutsche Wirtschaftskommission
f.o.b.	free on board
g	gram
G.D.R.	German Democratic Republic
GIH	Gesellschaft für innerdeutschen Handel
G.m.b.H.	Gesellschaft mit beschränkter Haftung
GNP	Gross National Product
GRT	Gross Register Tons
HICOG	(U.S.) High Commission for Germany
H.P.	Horsepower
HVIA	Hauptverwaltung für Interzonen- und Aussenhandel
IWE	Informationsdienst West Wochenbericht (Berlin-West)

JDDR	Jahrbuch der D.D.R.
kg	kilogram
kV	kilovolt
kw(h)	kilowatt (hour)
l	liter
MAI	Ministerium für Aussen- und innerdeutschen Handel
MAM	Ministerium für Aussenhandel und Materialversorgung
Mat.	Materialien zur Wirtschaftslage in der sowjetischen Besatzungszone
m.b.H.	mit beschränkter Haftung
MIAM	Ministerium für innerdeutschen Handel, Aussenhandel und Materialversorgung
MW	Megawatt
ND	Neues Deutschland (newspaper)
PAG	Preisausgleich
PI	Presse-Informationen
RGW	Rat für Gegenseitige Wirtschaftshilfe
RM	Reichsmark
RM/DM	Reichsmark until and Deutsche Mark after 1948 currency reform
SAG	Sowjetische Aktiengesellschaft
S.B.Z.	Sowjetische Besatzungszone
SED	Sozialistische Einheitspartei Deutschlands
SHD	Statistisches Handbuch von Deutschland 1928-1944
SJDDR	Statistisches Jahrbuch der D.D.R.
SKK	Sowjetische Kontrollkommission
SP	Statistische Praxis (journal)
SPD	Sozialdemokratische Partei Deutschlands
t	ton
tdw	ton dead weight
U.d.S.S.R.	Union der Sozialistischen Sowjetrepubliken
U.K.	United Kingdom
U.N.	United Nations
U.S.(A.)	United States (of America)

U.S.S.R.	Union of Socialist Soviet Republics
VE	Verrechnungseinheit
VEB	Volkseigener Betrieb
VEH-DIA	Volkseigene Handelsunternehmen--Deutscher Innen- und Aussenhandel
VEV	Volkseigener Verlag
VS	Vierteljahreshefte zur Statistik
VVB	Vereinigung Volkseigener Betriebe
VzW	Vierteljahreshefte zur Wirtschaftsforschung
WMW	Werkzeugmaschinen und Metallwaren
WW	Wirtschaftswissenschaft (journal)
ZK	Zentralkomitee

Economic Integration
in the Soviet Bloc

INTRODUCTION

The following study is concerned with the efforts at economic integration in the Soviet bloc, as exemplified by the case of East Germany. The period considered is from the end of World War II to mid-1965, but, whenever possible, postwar data are compared to prewar magnitudes. When referring to East Germany, this author considers that area of Germany which ultimately was occupied by the armed forces of the Soviet Union, i.e., the area of the Soviet occupation zone of Germany, including the Soviet sector of Berlin. This is the same territory which in 1949 was proclaimed an independent political unit, called German Democratic Republic or G.D.R. The Soviet bloc is defined as all Communist countries in Europe and Asia.

CHAPTER 1 deals with the immediate result of World War II, the exploitation of the conquered German territory by the Soviet Union. The Soviet reparations policy in East Germany is discussed in detail. The author considers the legal basis for reparations, the forms and magnitudes of reparations deliveries, and the consequences of this policy for the East German economy.

When using the term "exploitation," furthermore, the author does not necessarily wish to imply disapproval. The utilization of the East German economy by the Soviets for their own purposes was only one episode of World War II and its aftermath. The destruction inflicted upon the Soviet Union by the German invaders was another. It lies beyond the bounds of economics and of this study to consider questions of war guilt and related matters and to decide whether Soviet actions in postwar Germany might not have been fully justified in light of German actions in the war-time Soviet Union. This author is inclined to believe that the postwar exploitation of East Germany might well have been a justifiable form of restitution but the purpose here is simply to determine what actually did happen.

CHAPTER 2 deals with East Germany's commercial trade re-

lations, especially the volume and regional distribution of
such trade.

CHAPTERS 3 and 4 take up the central concern of the book.
The past fifty years have brought about enormous changes in
Eastern Europe. The Soviet Union has been transformed from
one of the economically backward nations to one of the world's
foremost industrial giants. In the middle of this century we
find ourselves at the beginning of another intensified struggle to break out of the bonds of economic stagnation. Dozens
of old and new nations are tempted to and invited to follow
the path blazed by the Soviet Union, which has already overtaken the early pioneers of the Industrial Revolution. Even
though propaganda will distort what has happened, will hide
the failures, and will ignore the sacrifices, the fact remains that one country has made enormous economic progress in
an unprecedented short time. It is the confidence gained from
this experience that leads Soviet leaders again and again to
predict that also the U.S. will be overtaken, and without the
need of military conquest, will find herself an odd, backward
remnant in the New World of the future. In the past, the Soviet leaders claim, their success was based on the introduction of socialist central economic planning emphasizing heavy
investments. This will continue to be true. But they also
believe that Soviet bloc economic growth can be even further
accelerated by a bloc-wide international division of labor promoted via the Council for Mutual Economic Aid. The goals of
this international Communist organization and the history of
its actions are described in detail in CHAPTER 3.

CHAPTER 4 deals with the theoretical aspects of determining international specialization within the Communist orbit.
The theoretical discussion in East Germany as well as in the
other Communist countries about the desirability of and criteria for determining an international division of labor is

described and evaluated.

CHAPTER 5 attempts to measure the degree to which East Germany has been integrated economically into the Communist world. The distribution of the East German labor force and of investments and output are investigated. The commodity structure of foreign trade is reviewed, and a measure of East Germany's foreign trade dependence is considered. This has not always been an easy task. Though official statistics have become increasingly plentiful since the mid-1950's, many data are still missing from systematic accounts. Even official data frequently are too ambiguous to be of use without further information. Such information, therefore, has been compiled from literally thousands of Soviet bloc sources: daily newspapers, weekly and monthly publications, records of speeches by government officials, and so on. As a result, the account is as up-to-date as possible, though less so than we might wish.

It is, of course, impossible to present a readable account of events while including all sources. Much detailed information has been relegated to the footnotes gathered at the end of each chapter. The bibliography lists, in addition, the sources most heavily relied upon, but without specific detail. There is also available from the author a *Supplement*, listing the sources to Tables 3 and 4, to section D of CHAPTER 6, explaining the methodology of CHAPTER 7, and presenting a detailed discussion of the puzzling apparent inconsistencies in Communist foreign trade statistics. As a result, any interested scholar can, if he wishes, follow the author's reasoning step by step and check his conclusions.

Utilizing the material collected in connection with the previous chapters, the author also was able to estimate a balance of payments for East Germany from 1950 to 1963 and to calculate East German terms of trade for the same period.

This is presented in CHAPTERS 6 and 7, respectively.

A number of appendixes are designed to spell out in detail some of the technical points and basic information involved in this study. APPENDIX A, for instance, elaborates upon the East German industry classification employed. APPENDIX B presents a brief account of the role of Soviet bloc exchange rates. APPENDIX C, finally, contains a translation of the most important joint statement on integration made to date by the member countries of the Council for Mutual Economic Aid.

CHAPTER 1 SOVIET REPARATIONS POLICY IN EAST GERMANY

East Germany's economic integration into the Soviet bloc, as her close political ties with this area, can be understood best as a consequence of military and political events of the last phase of World War II. The military success of the Red Army brought the East German area physically under the control of the Soviet armed forces, while the conferences at Yalta and Potsdam enabled the Soviet Union to retain legally that position of control.[1] Therewith the foundation was laid for the future political and economic development of this area under the guiding hand of the Kremlin.

Economically, as well as politically, this development differed markedly from what happened in the western zones of occupation. At Potsdam, the Soviet Union had agreed official-ly to the continued <u>economic</u> unity of Germany as a whole. She had also cooperated in the establishment of an Allied Control Council as an instrument, among other things, for the realiza-tion of this goal. In fact, however, the Soviet Military Ad-ministration in Germany, from the very beginning of the Con-trol Council's work, stood accused of arbitrary interpreta-tions of Council directives and of displaying bad faith in gen-eral by the generous use of her veto power. Eventually, in March of 1948, the Soviet Union caused the Council's demise by boycotting its sessions entirely.

Whoever may have been most responsible for the failure of this joint Allied undertaking, a uniform occupation policy failed to materialize, and East Germany's fate differed sig-nificantly from that of the rest of Germany. In particular, East Germany's foreign economic relations in the early postwar period were determined almost exclusively by Soviet demands on the East German economy for restitution. This became the first step in the direction of economic integration with the Commu-nist world.

The Soviets, as well as the East Germans, have been extremely hesitant to publish any data on reparations. A sufficient number of classified East German documents have, however,
reached the west, via the special routes existing in the unique
German setting, to shed considerable light on this subject. In
this chapter, an attempt will be made to reconstruct the important aspects of this particular part of postwar history.

The Communist press, with great vigor, skill, and consist-
ency, has depicted the Soviet Union as East Germany's greatest
benefactor. As will be shown here, quite the contrary is true.
There can be no doubt that, at least until 1953, the overrid-
ing Soviet goal in East Germany has been to take reparations
in all forms and ways imaginable.[2] This one-sided utilization of East Germany's economic potential in favor of the Soviet Union, furthermore, was as severe as could be designed
and tolerated. The enormous extent of Soviet exploitation (by
any standard) will now be discussed in detail.

A.   THE LEGAL BASIS FOR REPARATIONS

The agreements among the Allies of World War II constituted the legal foundation upon which Soviet reparations demands were based. According to these agreements, Germany was
to pay in kind for the losses caused by her to the Allied nations in the course of the war. Such reparations were to be
received in the first instance by those countries which carried the main burden of the war, suffered the heaviest losses,
and organized victory over the enemy.

When the end of German resistance could be foreseen with
certainty, the first detailed discussion of the reparations
question took place at Yalta (February 3-11, 1945). The content of the talks among Churchill, Roosevelt, and Stalin did
not become known to the public until a speech of Molotov, the
Soviet Foreign Minister, at the Moscow four power conference

on March 17, 1947.[3] The three leaders unanimously agreed to
extract reparations from Germany in kind and in the following
forms:

a) Removals within two years from the surrender of Germany or the cessation of organized resistance from
the national wealth of Germany located on the territory of Germany herself as well as outside her territory (equipment, machine tools, ships, rolling stock,
German investments abroad, shares of industrial,
transport, and other enterprises in Germany, etc.),
these removals to be carried out chiefly for the purpose of destroying the war potential of Germany.

b) Annual deliveries of goods from current production
for a period to be fixed (the Soviet Union proposing
twenty years, H.K.).

c) Use of German labor (without any definite plans, apparently, as to where and for what, H.K.).

No agreement was reached at Yalta, however, on the magnitude of reparations to be imposed. The Russians proposed to
collect goods worth $20 billion at prewar prices. They demand-
ed half of this amount for themselves, the rest to go to the
other Allies. Churchill and Roosevelt counselled moderation on
this point. The U.S. was at least willing to accept the Soviet
proposal as a basis for discussion within the Allied Reparations Commission which was to meet in Moscow, but the U.K.
would not even agree to that.[4]

The discussion was continued, after the Allied victory
over Germany, at the conference at Potsdam (July 17 - August
2, 1945). The final protocol on reparations, unlike the one of
Yalta, dealt only with dismantling of industrial installations.
There was no mention at all of deliveries from current production and the use of labor as forms of restitution. It soon became apparent that this was more than a technical detail. The
way was open to a number of different interpretations of the
Yalta and Potsdam agreements, and this practice soon became a
major cause of friction between the Western Allies on the one

hand and the Soviet Union on the other.

The western powers argued that the Potsdam agreement had
replaced all previous ones, including that of Yalta. They held
deliveries from current production, as well as the use of German
labor, to be illegal, since these had not been explicitly sanc-
tioned by the Potsdam protocol. In view of the experience after
World War I, they saw in the removal of capital the ideal way of
avoiding the mistakes of the past. Germany, so the argument
went, would never again become a threat to the world, if she was
disarmed not only militarily, as after World War I, but also in-
dustrially. The Potsdam agreement clearly embodied such a goal
in its provision to limit German industrial capacity to the
needs of a peacetime economy that could exist without assistance from the outside and provide an "average European standard of living" for the German population.

The Soviet Union, on the contrary, saw in the Potsdam
agreement a mere supplement to that of Yalta. The Potsdam protocol, by not repudiating the Crimean declaration, the Soviet
leaders felt, had implicitly confirmed it in all its aspects.
They were unwilling to renounce any of the forms of reparations
envisaged at Yalta. At the Moscow conference of early 1947,
Molotov even proposed to discard the Potsdam limitations on German industrial capacity in order to facilitate reparations deliveries from current production. Since such capacity increases
were to be made possible with foreign assistance, presumably
from the U.S., the western refusal to yield on this point is understandable. "We cannot accept . . . a procedure," said Mr.
Marshall, then U.S. Secretary of State, "which in effect would
mean that the American people would pay reparations to an ally."[5]

The Allies of World War II were equally divided on other
details. As to the magnitude of reparations, the Soviet Union
repeated her request of $10 billion at prewar prices for her-
self. She specified, in addition, that all deliveries were to

come from the area of the four occupation zones of Germany
rather than Germany within her 1937 borders. Hence German assets abroad and deliveries from areas east of the Oder-Neisse
Line would not enter the official accounting. The Soviet
Union agreed, however, to satisfy Polish reparation demands
out of her own share. She officially acknowledged, at the
time of the Potsdam conference, receipt of $300 million of
reparations. The western powers rejected this as much too low.

The Western Allies preferred not to fix in dollars the
amount of reparations to be collected. It was felt that such
amount was already implicitly determined as the difference between the values of the actual capital stock and the one "desired" for the operation of the peacetime economy envisaged at
Potsdam.

The final outcome of the Potsdam talks was a compromise.
Each ally was to satisfy his reparation demands from his own
zone of occupation. The Soviet Union was to receive, in addition, 25 per cent of the western zones' industrial "war capacity" and all German assets in Bulgaria, Eastern Austria, Finland, Hungary, and Rumania. Ninety per cent of the deliveries
from West Germany, however, were to be paid for by shipments
of East German raw materials to the Western Allies.

As mentioned above, the Potsdam agreement gave theoretical
recognition to the treatment of Germany as a single economic
unit. There is good reason to believe that the Allied rift
over forms and extent of reparations was a major reason pre-
venting the realization of this goal. Since agreement on reparations failed to come about also at subsequent international
conferences, the Soviet Union unilaterally proceeded to impose
her demands on her zone of occupation in the forms she preferred. For this reason alone, she could not and would not co-
operate in upholding Germany's economic unity.

The Soviet Union has never wavered in her demand for $10

billion of reparations at prewar prices and, as will be shown below, has extracted them from East Germany in all the forms envisaged at Yalta. For the first eight years of occupation, this certainly must be regarded as the prime goal of her policy in Germany.

B. THE FORMS AND MAGNITUDE OF REPARATIONS

1. Removals From the Wealth of East Germany

The Western Allies, as well as the Soviet Union, pursued policies resulting in a reduction of Germany's capital stock. As shown above, the western powers did not recognize the legality of any other form of restitution. But even in this case, where actions were similar, basic views diverged. The western powers wanted primarily to destroy Germany's war potential, the Soviet Union to collect all types of goods needed badly for reconstruction at home. As a result, her dismantling operations went far beyond expectations of the Western Allies in magnitude, as well as composition. Furthermore, a large part of the goods thus removed were never entered in the reparations accounts, but taken under the victor's right to "military trophies."

a. The Trophy Campaign

The gathering of "war booty" began immediately after occupation. This in itself is to be expected. It is even recognized as legitimate activity by international law. Since such operations were carried on to the very end of 1946, however, one is probably justified in accepting western charges concerning the too generous use of the "trophy" label by the Soviets in order not to burden the reparations accounts.

It has been reported that special "trophy units" were organized within the Red Army. They were responsible for delivery to the Soviet Union of specified quantities of various commodities from East Germany, as well as certain "liberated" ter-

ritories, such as Czechoslovakia and Poland.[6] Unit commanders
were personally responsible for the success of the operations,
which may be one reason for the waves of physical violence frequently accompanying these early removals from Germany's wealth.

Apart from the equipment and stores of the German military,
the trophy campaign also engulfed agricultural and industrial
inventories, such as stores of grain, potatoes, and all types of
semi-finished and finished industrial products. Many industrial
installations were dismantled under the trophy gathering operations. Large proportions of the animal population and the stock
of agricultural machinery became subject to sequestration. Forests were cut down at an unprecedented rate, the lumber being
claimed as booty. Other sectors of the economy were equally affected. Large-scale removal of telephone lines and exchanges
and of the rolling stock and signalling equipment of railroads
are cases in point. Hospitals, university laboratories, and mu-
seums were favorite targets, as were the homes of the civilian
population.

The total value of the commodities taken in the trophy campaign has been estimated by German sources from RM 2-8 billion
at current prices.[7]

b. Official Dismantling

The official collection of reparations by dismantling industrial installations occurred simultaneously with the trophy
operations. There are indications that the Soviet Union proceeded in accordance with a plan of her own, which she never expected to be approved by her Western Allies. She certainly never attempted to implement the plan embodied in the Allied Control Council's list of restricted and prohibited industries.[8]
This plan, moreover, was ready only in March of 1946 after long
negotiations during which Soviet dismantling teams had gone a
long way in creating accomplished facts.

Soviet dismantling activities were guided by the needs of

the Soviet economy for all types of industrial equipment due to
four years of the most bitter warfare. East Germany was ideally
suited to provide such equipment.

It must be emphasized that East Germany, contrary to beliefs
sometimes expressed, was not the breadbasket of Germany, providing nothing but agricultural surplus to the industrialized western regions of the country. She was, indeed, largely self-sufficient in food production, but she was also highly industrialized. In 1936, East Germany was the home of 24 per cent of the
German population, yet the area produced 27.8 per cent of Germany's industrial output.[9] In particular, East Germany produced
23.3 per cent of Germany's basic industry output, 26.8 per cent
of the food, drink, tobacco industries' output, 28.0 per cent of
the output of the metal-working industries, and 33.0 per cent of
that of the light industries. These data suggest some weakness
in the basic industries, and this is confirmed by a more detailed breakdown. In terms of total German output of the respective
industries, the East German percentage share of metallurgy output in 1936 was only 13.2; it was 19.8 for mining, but 26.8 for
energy, 29.5 for chemicals, and 31.9 for building materials. A
similar breakdown by individual metal-working industries shows
little variation around the over-all share of this industry group.
The lowest percentage was 24.2 for electro-technical output, the
highest 32.6 for fine-mechanical and optical production. Within
the light industry category, the spread ranged from 21.1 per
cent for glass-ceramics to 37.4 per cent for textiles.

By 1944, 25 per cent of the population living within Germany's 1936 borders lived in East Germany, yet 28.9 per cent of
the same area's total industrial output originated there. East
Germany then produced 24.5 per cent of German basic industry
output, 25.5 per cent of German output of the food, drink, tobacco industries, 30.1 per cent of metal-working industries'
output, and 35.3 per cent of that of light industries. More-

over, the East German share in total German output had increased for almost all individual industries, in particular for mining to 23.8 and for fine-mechanics and optics to 43.2 per cent.
The share of East German machine building reached 33.4 per cent
of German output. No industry's share declined by more than
1.3 percentage points. In short, there was certainly no decline during the war in East Germany's role as the supplier of
a significant portion of German industrial output.

The real volume of this output, moreover, increased substantially from 1936 to 1944. This was largely made possible
by stepped-up investments in industry. In relation to such a
growth in capacity, war damage to German industry must be termed insignificant. In spite of the destruction through bombing
and ground fighting, various sources estimate total German industrial capacity, even at the close of the war, to have been
at the very least equal to that of 1936, but possibly 50 per
cent larger.[10] War damage was most severe in other areas, such
as housing and transportation.

Western estimates of the damage inflicted by the war on
East German industry show an over-all loss of industrial capacity, in terms of the 1936 capital stock, of about 17 per cent.
War damage was, however, considerably lower in the basic industries. It ranged from only 3 per cent of capacity in coal mining to 8 in metallurgy and 15 in the chemical industries. In
the metal-working industries, on the other hand, damage was
above the over-all industrial average, ranging from 15 per cent
(machine building, fine-mechanics and optics) to 21 per cent
(vehicles, ships, aircraft). Damage in the light industries,
finally, was generally below 15 per cent of 1936 capacity.

These estimates differ sharply from those of East German
writers. The East Germans consistently report that by the end
of the war in East Germany "the greatest part of industry had
been destroyed." Further, we are told: "The bombing squadrons

of the British and American imperialists destroyed the factories because already during the war they wished to create the
greatest possible obstacles to peaceful reconstruction after its
end, for already then they did not count on the continued existence of capitalism in Germany's east."[11] The propagandistic
purpose of such an evaluation is obvious. It makes possible to
claim that Soviet dismantling operations were of minimal impact,
since there was supposedly nothing left to dismantle. On the
other hand, the "efforts of the working class" and the "generous help of the Soviet Union in reconstruction" can be all the
more extolled.

   But the truth is not such. The Red Army won a prize asset
in East Germany's large and highly modern capital stock. Industrial capacity was at least equal to, and possibly 50 per cent
above, that of 1936. In light of the appalling wreckage inflicted upon the Soviet Union by the German invaders, it is of
little wonder that East German industry became the object of
feverish activity of dismantling crews almost immediately. One
can clearly distinguish six waves of dismantling, first growing
and then weakening in intensity.

   The first one, in the spring of 1945, was characterized by
extreme hurry on the part of the dismantlers. From Berlin a-
lone, 460 of the larger plants were taken before the Western
Allies entered the city. Within the Soviet zone of occupation[12]
the following were chief targets: coal mine installations,
railway repair shops, power plants, and highly developed technical plants, such as Zeiss (optics) at Jena, Ohrenstein und
Koppel (locomotives) at Potsdam, and the great electro-technical works of AEG and Siemens-Halske.

   A second wave followed in the fall of 1945. The Potsdam
agreement had specified in the meantime which industrial
branches were subject to dismantling. Yet the primary objects
of this particular phase of dismantling lay clearly outside Ger-

many's "war potential," as defined at Potsdam. Involved were
in the main sugar factories, breweries, installations for the
production of building materials, textiles, and paper, as well
as railroad tracks all over the Soviet zone of occupation.[13]

In a third wave, from the spring to the late summer of
1946, more than 200 plants were removed. They had been carefully selected earlier and almost exclusively were part of the
chemical, textile, shoe, and paper industries. It was announced in May of 1946 that no more dismantling would occur after
completion of this operation.[14]

Nevertheless, in the fall of 1946, another and fourth wave
of dismantling activity set in. It was thorough and sudden,
lasting to the spring of 1947. Though power stations and printing installations were affected to some extent, armament factories were hit most severely. In spite of all Allied agreements,
such factories had been spared this fate until then. Frequently, they had been reconstructed or enlarged to produce for the
Soviet Union. The sudden reversal of policy probably can be explained by the reopening of international talks on disarmament,
which were also expected to lead to an international control of
disarmament in Germany.

A fifth wave of dismantling in the fall of 1947 returned to
the old pattern. It affected the installations of coal mines,
briquette factories, power plants, and more railroad tracks,
bringing to 32 per cent the portion of the total track taken.[15]

In the spring of 1948, dismantling occurred for the last
time. Compared to earlier such occasions, it was a minor event,
affecting only a few electro-technical and synthetic rubber
works (Buna Werke Schkopau).

Western experts have made a number of (admittedly rough)
estimates of the over-all effect of dismantling operations on
East Germany's capital stock. They deem it quite conceivable
that half of 1936 industrial capacity was lost on account of

trophy and dismantling campaigns. Moreover, the loss in individual industries, in particular the metallurgical, chemical, and metal-working industries, might have approached two thirds of 1936 capacity. In other basic industries and in the consumer goods industries, however, the loss was closer to 25 per cent. Even cautiously interpreting such data, one may reach the following conclusions:

(1) the combined effects of war-time investments, war damage, trophy campaign, and official dismantling reduced East Germany's capital stock almost certainly below its 1936 level, possibly to one half, (2) by far the larger part of this reduction occurred after the war through the actions of the occupying power, and (3) dismantling and capacity decrease were strongest in the basic and investment goods industries.

Western experts unanimously agree that the value of dismantled installations amounted to a minimum of RM 5 billion at current prices.[16]

It is doubtful, however, that there was any comparable gain to the Soviet economy. Conditions surrounding dismantling operations frequently bordered the chaotic. Such operations were guided by special dismantling teams, which were completely independent from the Soviet military in Germany. They could and did choose any object to their liking, and they utilized the services of local Red Army units and the civilian population. Such untrained personnel undoubtedly damaged much of the equipment already during the process of dismantling. Packaging was highly inadequate and was done inexpertly. Not only were the items protected insufficiently against the influences of the weather, but the mix-up of parts and the loss of blueprints made oftentimes future use impossible. In addition, transport difficulties were almost insurmountable. The German railroad system, depleted by war and dismantling itself, could not handle the sudden flow of goods towards the east and was on the verge of

complete breakdown. As a result, dismantled equipment was a-
bandoned to rust on railroad sidings, and the trails of these
actions were visible for many years. Hence it is conceivable
that the Soviet Union, if anything, gained little more than the
scrap value of the dismantled portion of East Germany's industry.[17]

2. Deliveries From Current Production

Long before the major waves of dismantling had spent themselves, East Germany was burdened by extremely high deliveries
from current production.[18] These took a number of different
forms which will be discussed below.

The Soviet Union, presumably to assure deliveries in accordance with the plan, secured for herself tight control of
the East German economy by the establishment of *Sowjetische
Aktien-Gesellschaften* (Soviet Corporations), hereafter, in accordance with East German usage, referred to as SAG. Their
establishment followed Order No. 167, issued on June 5, 1946,
by the Soviet Military Administration in Germany. Entitled "On
the transfer of enterprises in Germany into the property of the
U.S.S.R. on the basis of reparations demands of the U.S.S.R.,"
it affected 213 enterprises.[19] These had originally been ear-
marked for dismantling, but were then to remain in Germany and
to be owned by the Soviet Union.[20] Soviet generosity was given
as the official reason for changing the original plans. The
Soviet Union wanted to "preserve jobs for the German working
class" by leaving the plants on the spot.[21] Western observers
have pointed out the unnamed advantages of this arrangement to
the Soviet Union, such as utilizing the skilled German labor
force, saving the costs of dismantling and re-assembling, avoiding the large losses of equipment in transfer to the Soviet
Union, and utilizing buildings and other equipment in Germany
which could not have been dismantled and would have to be built

in the Soviet Union. The arrangement was preferable also from
the East German standpoint, however, for all these enterprises
eventually were returned to German ownership.[22]

Until their return, however, the SAG were operated as
branches of Soviet corporations domiciled at Moscow. They
were managed by Soviet citizens who appeared as nominal share-
holders. A large network of auxiliary companies also began
operating in Germany at that time. They undertook such tasks
as the transportation of SAG production to the Soviet Union
and its distribution there and the export of SAG output on
Soviet account.[23]

Most western estimates agree that from one quarter to one
third of East German output originated in the SAG during the
years of their existence and that less than a third of this
output remained in East Germany.[24] The SAG predominated in
the basic and metal-working industries and frequently held a
monopoly in certain strategic products, such as gasoline, and
some non-ferrous metals and steel products. Output in the SAG
sector of the economy grew faster than anywhere else, since
the SAG had first claim on the supply of labor and materials
and were not hampered by bottlenecks. Even the official organ
of the East German Communist Party, *Neues Deutschland*, on the
occasion of the return of the last of the SAG, termed them "the
very heart of the economy and the most productive of all
plants."[25]

There is little doubt that the only reason for their existence in the first place was the securing of deliveries to the
Soviet Union of currently produced goods. These deliveries will
now be discussed under four headings: (a) official direct deliveries to the Soviet Union of commodities, excluding uranium;
(b) official direct deliveries to the Soviet Military Administration in Germany, which were in part used by the Red Army in
Germany and in part also shipped to the Soviet Union; (c) unof-

ficial indirect deliveries to the Soviets via their private
purchase of German goods; and (d) uranium shipments to the
Soviet Union, which is the only type of delivery still prevail-
ing in 1965.

a. Direct Deliveries of Goods to the Soviet Union

From 1945 to the end of 1953, a significant portion of
East Germany's current output went to the Soviet Union under
the official label of "reparations." Though this has never
been admitted publicly, it follows from internal East German
statistics, which were top secret, but became available to the
West German Government and were then published by it. The annual deliveries of this type are given in row 2 of Table 1. In
terms of current prices, they increased in size from 1945 to
1947 and then fell gradually until 1953. These deliveries were
abolished as of January 1, 1954. On the occasion, East Germany
was lauded for having "conscientiously fulfilled her obligations in the past."

Since data of sufficient detail are available, it is also
possible to look at the composition of these deliveries to the
Soviet Union. The Soviet demands emphasized the products of
the basic and metal-working industries. This displayed the
same preference as in dismantling and the selection of enterprises to be transferred into Soviet property. While deliveries from the basic industries fluctuated between 23 and 33 per
cent of the total during the 1945-1953 period, there was a
clear-cut tendency for the products of the metal-working industries to provide an ever-increasing share of the total, rising
from 43 per cent in 1945 to 58 per cent in 1953. Until 1952,
light industry products provided roughly one fifth of all deliveries. Their share declined in 1953 to about one tenth.
Deliveries from the food, drink, and tobacco industries, while
never being of great significance, declined steadily in rela-

tive importance since 1945 from 6 to 1 per cent.

Within these broad categories, it is interesting to note that chemical industry products provided roughly one fifth throughout, but there was a significant increase, from the beginning to the end of the period, in deliveries of heavy machinery and the products of the electro-technical and fine mechanical/optical industries. While products of these industries provided 19.2 per cent of all deliveries in 1945, they provided 45.7 per cent in 1952 and presumably a comparable percentage in 1953. Textile deliveries, on the other hand, never even reached 5 per cent of the total, though this was a traditionally strong industry in East Germany. The extremely weak ship-building industry, however, provided even 6.6 per cent of the total in 1950.

b. Direct Deliveries of Goods to the Soviet Military Administration in Germany

In addition to commodity deliveries discussed under (a) above, significant quantities of goods were delivered to the Soviet Military Administration in Germany. In part, these goods were used by the Red Army in Germany, but some were shipped to the Soviet Union or exported by Soviet trading companies on Soviet account. Though officially not labelled as such, these deliveries, in their economic effect on East Germany, were identical with reparations. They are treated that way in this study, though legally "occupation costs" may belong in a different category.

The magnitude of these annual deliveries is known and given in row 3 of Table 1. These deliveries were only abolished on January 1, 1959. Their composition did not differ much from that of official reparations discussed above. The basic and metal-working industries again provided the largest share of such deliveries. Deliveries from the basic industries fluctuated between 22 and 30 per cent of the totals, those from

the metal-working industries showed an upward tendency over the
years from 34 per cent in 1945 to 43 per cent in 1953, the last
year for which detailed data are available.

The share of the products of the consumer goods industries,
however, was significantly higher than in the case of direct
deliveries to the Soviet Union. This obviously reflects the
needs of the Red Army in Germany. But even here the share of
these consumer goods deliveries declined over the period for
which data are available, from about 40 per cent in 1945 to 27
per cent in 1953. Within the other industry groups, one no-
tices, compared to reparations in the narrower sense, a significantly greater share of pharmaceutical and general machinery
products. This again reflects special provisions for the military, weapons being classed under general machinery. As in the
case of deliveries to the Soviet Union, there was a marked increase in the later years of deliveries of electro-technical
products to the military.

Combining the data on deliveries discussed under (a) and
(b) above, the following summary judgment for the 1945-53 period can be made. Roughly three quarters of all deliveries to
the Soviet Union and the Soviet Military Administration in
Germany came from the basic and metal-working industries (71.8
per cent in 1945, 68.7 per cent in 1946, which was the lowest
figure for the period, and 82.8 per cent in 1953, which was
the highest). The rest came from the consumer goods industries. Many of the relative shares of individual industries
were quite stable over time, varying by fewer than four percentage points. The only exceptions were the increasing
shares of deliveries of the chemical industries (13.1 per cent
in 1946, 19.0 per cent in 1952, about 25 per cent in 1953), of
heavy machinery (from 4.2 per cent in 1945 to 13.6 per cent in
1952), and electro-technical goods (from 6.6 per cent in 1947
to 18.9 per cent in 1952). On the other hand, energy and min-

ing delivered 7.0 per cent of the total in 1946, only 2.1 per cent in 1952, other than heavy machinery 17.2 per cent in 1946 and 10.0 per cent in 1952, and the food, drink, tobacco indus- tries 9.0 per cent in 1945 and 2.8 per cent in 1952.

c.   Unofficial Purchase of German Goods

In addition to the deliveries discussed above, certain amounts of goods were taken from the East German economy in various other forms. From funds available to the Soviet au- thorities, Soviet officers and men stationed in East Germany were paid salaries which could be spent in so-called free stores, established in November of 1948. These stores also sold consumer goods to the German population without ration- ing coupons, but at extremely high prices compared to those of rationed goods.

West German experts have estimated total goods sold to Soviet troops in this way during 1949-53 at DM-E 1,057 million at current prices. Assuming equal distribution over the years, this would amount to DM-E 211.4 million per year, a reasonable figure considering the number of Soviet troops in East Germany (see row 4, Table 1).

Furthermore, the Soviet corporations, returned to German ownership in 1952 and 1953, were depleted of all types of in- ventories. These were bought by the Soviet Union just prior to the return of the SAG. West German experts believe the value of these goods to have been DM-E 1 billion at current prices. Assuming a positive correlation between the value of inventories and that of the enterprises themselves, one can probably assign DM-E 500 million each to the years 1952 and 1953, for, according to official statements, the value of the SAG returned in the two years was about equal (see row 5, Table 1).[26]

d.   Deliveries of Uranium to the Soviet Union

Data on the Soviet uranium mining operations in East Germany are shrouded in a tight veil of secrecy.   Nevertheless,
the following has become known.

The search for uranium was begun in the summer of 1945 in
the Erzgebirge Mountains along the Czech border.[27]   Originally, these operations were directed by several small Soviet enterprises.   They soon merged into one company, the SAG Wismut,
which was administered separately from the other SAG in East
Germany by the Central Administration of Soviet Property
Abroad and the Soviet State Corporation Med in Moscow.   All
costs of the company were to be paid from the German budget
and acknowledged as reparations receipts.   The mines were
leased by East Germany to the Soviet Union until 1999.

All deliveries of uranium until the end of 1953 have to
be regarded as reparations.   On January 1, 1954, the status of
the Wismut Company changed.   While all the other SAG became
German property, the uranium mining company was transformed
into a joint Soviet-German enterprise.   From this time on to
the present (1965), the East Germans have been reimbursed partially for the costs of uranium mining.   Total output has always been shipped to the Soviet Union, hence part of these
shipments can be regarded as commercial exports, part as reparations.[28]   Estimates by this author of the magnitudes involved are given in row 6 of Table 1.

3.   The Use of German Labor

The Soviet Union has also made use of the third major form
of restitution envisaged at Yalta, the services of German labor.   This has been done largely by transporting thousands of
civilian "specialists" to the Soviet Union from East Germany
and by retaining hundreds of thousands of German prisoners of
war in the Soviet Union for several years after the war had

ended.[29] It is impossible to evaluate in exact economic terms
what has happened in this area, and the deep injury inflicted
upon human beings by this particular kind of restitution certainly goes far beyond the bounds of economics.

There are, however, also certain services that were rendered to the Soviet Union within Germany. These are services
rendered in connection with the deliveries of commodities described above, as the services of transport, packaging, insurance, dismantling, etc. Estimates of the value of these services are given in row 8 of Table 1.

4. Summary and Evaluation

Table 1 affords an over-all view of the absolute magnitude and relative importance of the various forms of reparations. No attempt was made to include the value of the booty
gathered in the trophy campaign, since the author regarded
these estimates as the least reliable ones. A number of
other forms of restitution, however, are also excluded from
this final accounting. These are, for instance, the value of
German services performed in the Soviet Union, the value of
German patents taken over and of German assets seized abroad,
and reparations deliveries from West Germany.[30]

As the table shows, the volume of reparations in current
prices was practically unchanged from 1945 to the end of 1953.
At that point, direct deliveries to the Soviet Union ceased
(except for uranium), and the total volume declined significantly. Another decrease occurred in 1957, when occupation
costs were reduced, and in 1959, when they were abolished.

In all years, except 1945 and 1946, when most of the dismantling took place, reparations from current production provided the bulk of deliveries. Total deliveries, from 1945 to
1960, amounted to about RM/DM-E 63 billion at current prices.
From then to 1964 at most another billion (of uranium) has

Table 1.   Reparations delivered to the Soviet Union
from East Germany, by type and years, in million
RM/DM-E, at current prices, 1945-1960.[a]

Type	1945	1946	1947
Capital Stock			
1. Official dismantling	2,300.00	2,300.00	200.00
Current Production			
2. Direct to Soviet Union	2,294.66	2,995.21	3,692.10
3. Direct to Red Army	746.96	871.71	979.68
4. Indirect to Red Army	-	-	-
5. SAG Inventory	-	-	-
6. Uranium[a]	-	96.00	413.00
7. Subtotal (2-6)	3,041.62	3,962.92	5,084.78
Labor			
8. Services in Germany	290.16	378.04	485.06
Total	5,631.78	6,640.96	5,769.84

Sources:

Row 1:   See page 16 above.   The distribution over the years was
assumed according to the discussion in the text.

Row 2:   This information was brought to West Germany by a ref-
ugee from the East German Reparations Office (*Amt für
Reparationen*).   It was published in Anonymous, "*Die Reparationen der sowjetischen Besatzungszone in den Jahren 1945 bis Ende
1953*," *BB* (Bonn: BMfgF, 1953), *Anlagen* 1 and 3.   The 1953 figure is a plan figure, but there is no reason to believe that it
was not fulfilled.   According to *Die Sowjetische Besatzungszone
Deutschlands 1945-1954* (2 vols.; Bonn: BMfgF, 1954), II, page
251, the East Germans had to agree that any part not sent by
the end of 1953 would still be delivered in 1954.

Table 1 continued

	1948	1949	1950	1951	1952
1.	200.00	-	-	-	-
2.	3,657.81	3,481.59	3,012.25	2,570.38	2,385.59
3.	948.17	925.57	911.39	1,069.45	1,153.31
4.	-	211.40	211.40	211.40	211.40
5.	-	-	-	-	500.00
6.	647.00	763.00	1,081.00	1,594.00	1,434.00
7.	5,252.98	5,381.56	5,216.04	5,445.23	5,684.30
8.	501.11	493.21	477.42	497.14	519.86
	5,954.09	5,874.77	5,693.46	5,942.37	6,204.16

Row 3:   Data for 1945-1953 same source as for row 2, but
        Anlagen 2 and 3. Data for 1954-58 were estimated from
Deutsche Finanzwirtschaft, 19, 1959, p. 373. This source contains data on actual payments of occupation costs. It was
assumed that 90 per cent of such funds were used for the purchase of commodities delivered directly or indirectly to the
Red Army, with 10 per cent being used for services. Note that
for earlier years payments of occupation costs exceed deliveries to the Red Army. This can be explained by the fact that
the Soviet authorities generally used funds collected under
various headings (such as reparation payments, occupation
costs, SAG profits, currency issue) quite arbitrarily for various purposes and not necessarily for the purpose they were of-

Table 1 continued

1953	1954	1955	1956	1957	
-	-	-	-	-	1.
2,028.75	-	-	-	-	2.
997.16	1,440.00	1,440.00	1,440.00	720.00	3.
211.40					4.
500.00	-	-	-	-	5.
1,275.00	876.00	750.00	709.00	406.00	6.
5,012.31	2,316.00	2,190.00	2,149.00	1,126.00	7.
456.00	160.00	160.00	160.00	80.00	8.
5,468.31	2,476.00	2,350.00	2,309.00	1,206.00	

ficially paid for. Hence it is quite conceivable that direct
deliveries of goods to the Soviet Union continued after 1953,
being paid with occupation cost funds. If this should be so,
such deliveries would be included in row 3. Sources for rows
2 and 3 are also the sources for the industry breakdown of
deliveries, as discussed in the text.
Row 4: Same source as row 2. See also page 22 above.
Row 5: *Ibid.*
Row 6: Estimated by the author from a variety of sources
        based on reports of former Soviet and East German ura-
nium mining officials who fled to the west. The data represent the total costs of the uranium mining operations, exclud-

Table 1 continued

	1958	1959	1960	1945-1960
1.	-	-	-	5,000.00
2.	-	-	-	26,118.34
3. }	540.00	-	-	15,240.40
4. }				
5.	-	-	-	1,000.00
6.	350.00	292.00	250.00	10,936.00
7.	890.00	292.00	250.00	53,294.74
8.	60.00	-	-	4,718.00
	950.00	292.00	250.00	63,012.74

ing the amounts for which the East Germans (after 1953) were
reimbursed. See *Supplement*, Chap. I, pp. 27-31.
Row 7:   Sum of rows 2 through 6.
Row 8:   For 1945-50 same source as row 2, p. 16, and Anonymous,
         "Die sowjetischen Entnahmen aus dem Produktionsaufkom-
men der Sowjetzone im Jahre 1951," Mat. (Bonn: BMfgF, not
dated), p. 3. For 1951-53 estimated at 9.5 per cent of rows 2,
3, 5, and 6, the percentage having held for the preceding
years. For 1954-58 compare explanation to row 3.

Notes:

Dash (-) means amount was zero
[a]Uranium deliveries from 1961-64 were probably equal to 1960.

been delivered. Until 1953, when according to Communist claims
deliveries ceased, more than RM/DM-E 53 billion of commodities
had been delivered and of services performed.[31]

We can now compare the above estimates of East German reparations actually delivered with the original Soviet demand of
$10 billion at 1938 prices and the official Soviet acknow-
ledgements of reparations receipts.

This author estimates that total reparations deliveries,
as given in Table 1 above, amounted to $19,305.56 million at
1938 prices for the 1945-60 period. Uranium deliveries since
then would increase this figure by about one per cent. Of
this total $17,088.74 million had been delivered by the end of
1953. Total deliveries, therefore, were twice as high as
originally demanded by the Soviet Union.[32]

This estimate includes, however, types of deliveries
which the Soviet Union would refuse to count as reparations.
Indications are that the Soviet Union would consider only dismantling and direct deliveries from current production as
valid inclusions (rows 1 and 2 in Table 1). All other forms
of deliveries have either openly been kept out of the reparations account (as occupation costs), or have been ignored (as
SAG inventory and uranium), or have been denied (as the use
of German labor). If one accepted this Soviet definition of
reparations, this author would still estimate the magnitude
at $10,429.12 billion at 1938 prices for the 1945-53 period,
with no deliveries thereafter. In this case one would have
to conclude that the Soviet Union has indeed extracted from
East Germany all she had intended to. But, of course, there
is no reason to follow the Soviet definition, and it is still
true that reparations deliveries, more reasonably defined,
were about twice as large as officially demanded.

Neither one of the author's estimates has been confirmed
by the parties directly involved. While there has not been

any systematic public accounting at all, the official pronouncements that have been made by the East Germans and the Soviets
have been quite different.

The first official statement with regard to reparations
was made by the Soviet Commander-in-Chief at a spring 1946
meeting with leading administrative officials of the Soviet
Zone. He stated that reparations in the first quarter of 1946
had amounted to RM 300 million. From this one may infer a total of about RM 1,200 million for the year 1946 as a whole.

The East German budget plan for the fiscal period April
to December 1949 listed reparations payments as DM 1,034.74
million. From this one may estimate a total of DM 1,376 million for 1949 as a whole.

Another official statement was contained in a speech by
the late Heinrich Rau, then Minister for Economic Planning, on
January 18, 1950, before the provisional *Volkskammer* (parlia-
ment). He supplied information, such as reparations per capita,
from which magnitudes of RM/DM-E 1,400 million for 1948, DM-E
1,400 million for 1949, and DM-E 937 million for 1950 can be
calculated. All these statements, though much lower, even by
the Soviet definition, than the estimates given in Table 1, are
at least consistent with each other.

They differ appreciably from other official statements,
however. Reparations payments from the budgets alone (excluding payments for occupation costs) amounted to RM/DM-E 21,880
million from 1945 to 1953 inclusive, i.e., an average of
RM/DM-E 2,431 million per year.

Neither the East German officials, nor the Soviets have
ever explained these discrepancies between their official
statements on the real and monetary sides of reparations. Probably they cannot be explained without admitting fraud and de-
ception of the public by the government. There would presumably be no other explanation than to admit that actual deliver-

ies, paid with whatever funds, far exceeded what either of the parties involved was prepared to admit.

West German experts have pointed to a number of factors, in addition to the possibility of fraud, which may explain why actual deliveries exceeded acknowledged receipts. The Soviet quality control, when accepting reparations, was extremely strict and arbitrary. Without any reason, it has been alleged, part of the deliveries were regularly declared to be of second and third grade quality, and a significant reduction was made from the factory price (as it appears in Table 1). Secondly, Soviet officials bargained about the definition of 1938 prices, using frequently lower prices than actually existed in 1938. Finally, an original acknowledgement of receipt was sometimes withdrawn later on. The East Germans had to guarantee the arrival of commodities in the Soviet Union in perfect condition, but they did not have the slightest chance to protect such commodities once they had left German territory. Hence East Germany could not check and had to accept the veracity of reports concerning loss of commodities during transfer due to theft, accident, etc.

In terms of 1938 prices, the story is largely the same. The Soviet Union has officially acknowledged receipt of $4,292 million at 1938 prices from 1945 to 1953, with nothing thereafter. According to this author's estimates, this accounts for only 22.2 per cent of all deliveries from 1945 to 1960. Using the narrower Soviet definition of reparations, it would still only account for 41.2 per cent of actual deliveries.

C.   CONSEQUENCES OF THE REPARATIONS POLICY

1.   Slowing Down the Rate of Growth

Some of the consequences of the policy of massive exploitation, as described above, are more readily apparent than

others.   But they all combined during the postwar period to
seriously slow down East Germany's rate of economic growth.

Among the more apparent effects on East Germany is the
significant reduction of her capital stock by dismantling.   The
capital stock is a factor of production; it is to be expected
that by its reduction East Germany's output should be seriously
affected, and with it the living standard of her people. [33]

Furthermore, Soviet reparations policy also largely de-
prived East Germany of the means to repair the damage done to
her capital stock.   By demanding a large portion of current
production, concentrated, as these deliveries were, in the investment goods industries, investments in East Germany were
much lower than one would have expected given the actual volume
of output and the great sacrifices in consumption asked of the
population.

It is of interest in this context to test the real burden
of the reparations on East Germany.   This burden lay, of
course, not in their absolute magnitude, but in the share they
took of total output.

This share can be calculated from this author's estimates
of reparations in 1938 RM and the excellent study of East German GNP by Professor Stolper. [34]   The result is given in column
4 of Table 2 for the years 1950-59.   A similar calculation for
earlier and later years cannot be made, because of a lack of
meaningful GNP data, but one can make a good estimate.   It is
beyond doubt that, before 1950, real GNP was below the 1950
level, the more so the further back we go in (postwar) time.
It can also be seen from Table 2 (col. 2) that the real volume of total reparations from current production during 1946-49
was at least equal to, and at times (1947) considerably larger
than, the 1950 volume.   Dismantling accounted for up to 41 per
cent of reparations in 1945 and 1946, but never even 4 per cent
thereafter.   The conclusion seems inevitable, therefore, that

currently produced reparations probably took an increasing percentage of real GNP until 1947, slightly decreasing thereafter.
They may well have taken 33 per cent in 1947, then gradually
falling to the 1950 percentage cited in the table. As for the
period since 1960, there can be little doubt that reparations,
in the form of uranium deliveries, took a fraction of one per
cent of GNP.

On first sight, as has been pointed out by Professor
Stolper,[35] one is tempted to dismiss the pre-1954 estimates as
impossibly high, but further considerations lead one to accept
them as quite conceivable. If the Nazis took 15 per cent of
Danish GNP, Denmark being treated rather gently by them, why
should it not be possible for the Soviet Union to take as much
as a quarter or third in East Germany? On a less speculative
level, Professor Stolper's estimates of the uses of East German
GNP indirectly support this estimate of Soviet exploitation.[36]
His calculations show the following: In 1950, individual consumption accounted for only 30.9 per cent of real GNP, compared
with 60 per cent in 1936, while gross domestic investment held
about the same share as it had in 1936 (17.7 vs. 18.7 per cent).
This left in 1950 a very large part of real GNP for "other"
uses (51.4 per cent), which meant, of course, an export surplus, largely in the form of reparations, and the government
sector, as this term is understood in the west. The large relative decline in private consumption compared to 1936 had not
resulted in more domestic investment, but made possible the
payment of reparations. This situation improved gradually during the 1950's. By 1954, "other" uses accounted for only 31.5
per cent of real GNP, which must largely reflect the decline in
the real burden of reparations. Correspondingly, one or all of
the other shares must have increased since 1950. Indeed, the
relative share of consumption had reached 51.1 per cent, but
that of investment was unchanged (17.4 per cent). Thereafter,

Table 2.   Indices of real reparations from current
production, of real GNP   (West German definition),
and real reparations as a percentage of real   GNP,
East Germany, 1945-60[a]

Year (1)	Real Reparations Index (2)	Real GNP Index (3)	Reparations in per cent of GNP (4)
1945	77.8	.	.
1946	101.4	.	.
1947	121.6	.	.
1948	101.1	.	.
1949	103.2	.	.
1950	100.0	100.0	28.6
1951	97.8	111.6	25.1
1952	96.0	118.4	23.2
1953	79.8	124.2	18.4
1954	33.8	131.0	7.4
1955	30.8	135.8	6.5
1956	30.0	140.3	6.1
1957	15.5	146.4	3.0
1958	12.1	151.7	2.3
1959	3.7	163.0	.6
1960	3.1	.	.

Sources:

Col. 2:   Calculated by the author from Table 1, rows 7 and 8
          and price indices.   Includes all forms of reparations,
except dismantling.   Based on data in 1938 prices.
Col. 3:   W.F. Stolper, *op. cit.*, p. 418, col. 8, and for 1959
          from unpublished parts of the manuscript.   GNP data
in 1936 prices were adjusted to include uranium production as
calculated from Table 1, row 6, in 1938 prices.   See note to
Table 24.
Col. 4:   Calculated from same data as cols. 2 and 3.   German
          1936 and 1938 prices were roughly the same, making
the juxtaposition of real reparations in 1938 prices and real
GNP in 1936 prices a legitimate procedure.
[a]Dot (.) means "amount unknown."

however, while "other" uses continued to decline until at
least 1959, consumption's share rose to 54.3 per cent, somewhat below the 1936 share, but the relative share of investment climbed to an all time high of 39.4 per cent in 1959.
This, of course, can be expected in a Communist society obses-
sed with rapid economic growth.

It is clear from the context of Professor Stolper's study
that reparations may indeed have taken from 20 to 33 per cent
of output in East Germany during the first eight years after
the war.

We can now compare this evaluation with the official East
German statements on the subject. These statements have the
advantage of definitely giving minimum figures. So far as this
author knows, the East Germans have made announcements about
the burden of reparations in per cent of production for the
years 1948, 1949, 1950, and 1952. Heinrich Rau, in a speech
before the *Volkskammer* concerning the 1950 economic plan,
stated on January 18, 1950, that reparations (in the narrow
official sense) plus occupation costs in 1948 took 14.6 per
cent of industrial gross production.[37] Walter Ulbricht, Communist Party Chief, stated that in 1948 reparations plus occupation costs took 25 per cent of net production.[38] This surprising statement lends considerable support to the estimates
given above. Heinrich Rau also asserted in the same speech
that the corresponding figure was 12.4 per cent of industrial
gross production in 1949, and would be 6.3 per cent in 1950.[37]
If one assumes that in 1949 and 1950 the same relation of gross
to net production existed as in 1948, according to the Rau and
Ulbricht statements, this would amount to an acknowledgement
that reparations and occupation costs took in 1949 21.2 per
cent and in 1950 10.8 per cent of East Germany's net industrial
production. Finally, the 1952 economic plan equated the magnitude of reparations, apparently excluding occupation costs,

with 2 per cent of gross production.[39] Accounting for rounding
and assuming the same relation of reparations to occupation
costs as in 1950, this could mean 3.4 per cent of gross production for both categories combined. Assuming, furthermore, the
above relation of gross to net production, this could amount to
5.8 per cent of net production, probably of industry.

It is, of course, extremely difficult to evaluate such
East German statements on a subject about which the government
is very hesitant to say very much. Usually, if there are any
statements at all, they serve the propagandistic purpose of
proving how low the burden of reparations has been. Furthermore, these statements exclude reparation deliveries paid with
such funds as SAG profits, currency issue, and SAG purchase
funds. They probably also exclude uranium deliveries. Hence
the East German figures ought to be higher for these reasons.
It is also by no means clear what is meant by gross and net
production or by the term production itself. The multiple
counting in East German production data is well known. Conceivably, the gross as well as the net production figures given in
the above statements contain such multiple counting, which
would automatically make the percentage of reparations taken
appear relatively low. It has also been suspected that in making statements of this type the East Germans give reparations
in 1938 prices in per cent of production, however defined, but
expressed in current prices. The effect on the resultant percentage, given the secular rise in prices, is obvious.

All in all, we do not know how to interpret the official
pronouncements, but it is reassuring for our own estimates that
even the East Germans admit the taking of significant percentages of current production, at least for the years prior to
1950.

Because of the depressant effect on the level of investment of such a large share of reparations, East Germany's capi-

tal stock grew only slowly to its former level. Nothing can
demonstrate the resulting effect on output more dramatically
than a comparison of development of East and West German GNP.[40]
Setting the respective area's GNP of 1936 equal to 100, East
German real GNP in 1950 was 73.4, while West German real GNP
had already surpassed the 1936 level and stood at 117.2. By
1953, East German GNP had reached 94.6 per cent of the same
area's 1936 level, but West Germany's index stood at 151.9.
In 1956, East German GNP had barely surpassed the 1936 mark
(108.6 per cent), while West German GNP had almost reached a
level twice the prewar magnitude (194.7). In 1959, finally,
East Germany's index stood at 128.9, West Germany's at 240.7,
compared to 1936.

The significantly slower growth of East German GNP after
the war, furthermore, holds for total as well as per capita
GNP. Though other factors, such as the difficulties associated
with central economic planning, may help to explain East Germany's bad economic performance, differences in occupation
policies between East and West Germany must surely have been
the major factor.

Besides the effects of dismantling and the relatively low
rate of investment, there was another impact of the Soviet
policy which has hampered economic growth. This one concerns
another productive factor, labor. East Germany's population
is extremely hostile towards the Soviet Union and the Communist regime in East Germany. However understandable Soviet
actions may have been when looking at the war as a whole, i.e.,
including the harm done to the Soviet Union by the Germans, the
open exploitation of East Germany has been too apparent to the
Germans living there in order to be forgotten or forgiven soon.
Everyone was affected in one way or another by the trophy campaign; many were eyewitnesses of the dismantling operations
and had to help ship the products of their labors to the Soviet

Union. Even more significant, at least from a psychological
standpoint, almost everyone knew of friends or relatives held
back in the Soviet Union for many months or years. The resultant alienation of public opinion was simply enormous. It must
be held responsible for the significant movement of population
to the west and the tendency of East Germany's labor force to
decline continually. This became a major worry of East Germany's rulers by the late 1950's and resulted, in the summer of
1961, in the closing of the Berlin border. In spite of a natural increase, East Germany had lost almost 10 per cent of her
population between 1948 and 1960.[41]

2. Structural Changes

Significant structural changes have occurred in the East
German economy. They may be partly the result of the new political ideology and be one consequence of dismantling, but
they are probably also due to the preferences of the Soviet
Union as expressed in decisions on the composition of deliveries from current production. To the extent that such structural changes went against the natural resource endowment of
East Germany and tended to neglect important skills of the
labor force, they must have also contributed to East Germany's
economic weakness. Furthermore, the costs of unfavorable
structural changes were not eliminated by the cessation of uncompensated exports. Undoubtedly these changes must be regarded as one symptom of East Germany's economic integration into
the Soviet bloc. Such structural changes, by attuning the economy to Soviet demand, must have laid the foundation for the subsequent reorientation of East Germany's foreign trade towards
the east, as it will be discussed in CHAPTER 2.

Professor Stolper's study, referred to above, provides excellent data on the structure of the East German economy. Considering only six broad sectors of the economy (industry, agri-

culture and forestry, transport and communications, trade, construction, and services), the over-all structure of the East
German economy during the 1950-54 period, for instance, was
little different from 1936.   Though industry's share of real
GNP increased somewhat between 1950 and 1954 (44.2 to 51.8 per
cent), it was in 1954 only slightly above the 1936 share (which
was 48.5 per cent).   The importance of agriculture and forestry
was in 1954 only slightly below the 1950 and 1936 levels, which
were the same (somewhat above 17 per cent).   The shares of the
remaining sectors of the economy were almost constant during
the postwar period and equal to their 1936 relative positions.
The only exception to this was construction which seemed to be
in the slow process of regaining its prewar share of real GNP.
Its share was 4.1 per cent in 1954; it had been 6.2 per cent
in 1936.[42]

Within the industry sector, however, highly significant
changes did take place.   The author assembled for this purpose
structural data on the origin of GNP created in the industrial
sector during a number of important years.   It was possible to
break down data of real GNP originating in industry into 18
separate industries for the years 1936, 1946, and 1950 through
1954.[43]   Since it was desirable to establish whether structural
differences observed between 1936 and 1946 might not in fact
have come about through the events of the war years, the author
has also used a corresponding breakdown of 1944 industrial GNP,
which, however, was only available at current prices.   The 1944
data presented below are, therefore, not strictly comparable to
the data for the other years, which are all expressed in 1950
West German prices.   It was felt, however, that there would
still be sufficient comparability in a broader qualitative
sense to make the inclusion of the 1944 data worthwhile.

There were marked structural changes within industry between 1936 and 1944.   While there was only a slight decline in

the relative importance of all basic industries as a group
(they accounted for 25.8 per cent of GNP produced in industry
in 1936 and 23.5 per cent in 1944), the relative importance of
the chemical industry within this subgroup increased from 7.9
to 11.3 per cent. This obviously reflected the increased emphasis of a war economy on the production of such items as am-
munition, rubber products, gasolines, and pharmaceutical supplies. As one might expect, the relative share of the metal-
working industries increased dramatically from 27.0 per cent of
GNP produced in industry in 1936 to 46.5 per cent in 1944.
This occurred almost entirely at the expense of the light industries. Their share was depressed from 35.8 per cent of GNP
originating in industry in 1936 to 19.8 per cent in 1944, with
the largest decline in the textile industry (from 19.1 to 8.9
per cent). The food, drink, and tobacco industries, on the
other hand, just as the basic industries, declined only insig-
nificantly from 11.4 to 10.2 per cent of industry's contribution to GNP.

Such then was the structure of industrial output when East
Germany was occupied by the Soviet armed forces. Between 1944
and 1946, however, presumably as the result of dismantling, the
changes during the war years were more than reversed. Dismantling affected primarily the capital stock of the metal-
working industries. As a result, the 1946 shares of the metal-
working industries declined to an all-time low of 8.5 per cent
of industrial output. The capital stock of the other industries, and consequently their absolute level of output, was
affected to a lesser degree. As a result, the relative shares
of these industries within industry's total contribution to
GNP returned to, or even surpassed, the 1936 positions. In
1946, the basic industries provided 39.8 per cent of industrial
output (mostly mining and chemical products), the light industries again provided 35.8 per cent (with almost all individual
industries regaining their 1936 importance), and the food in-

dustries produced 15.9 per cent of industrial product.

By 1950, this abnormal situation had been partially corrected. The metal-working industries, as a group as well as
individually, had almost exactly regained their 1936 shares
in industrial production. The same was true for the food industries which had declined relatively somewhat since 1946.
The basic industry share, however, though declining to 37.9
per cent in 1950, was still considerably above its 1936 share,
while that of the light industries was again below the 1936
position.

Between 1950 and 1954, one can observe a clear-cut tendency of all major industry groups to approach the relative
positions they held in the 1944 war-time economy, rather than
those of peace-time 1936. This may, of course, show the impact of Communist ideology on the East German economy. It is
this author's contention, however, that it signifies primarily
the impact on the East German economy of the Soviet reparations
policy. A comparison of the output structure discussed here
and the data on the composition of reparation deliveries discussed earlier will clearly illuminate this point. It can be
seen immediately that the structure of reparation deliveries
from current production was quite different from the structure
of production as it existed in East Germany before the war, but
quite similar to what it had been at the end of the war. Between 1945 and 1953, about a quarter of reparation deliveries
came from the basic industries, and, in this case, about a
quarter of industrial output came from these industries in 1944
as well as in 1936. During the same period, however, between
41 and 54 per cent of reparations from current production came
from the metal-working industries, which had provided about the
same percentage of industrial output in 1944 (46.5 per cent),
but much less in 1936 (27.0 per cent). Similarly, about a
fifth of reparations from current output came from the light

industries, which, in 1944, had produced a fifth of industrial
output, but 35.8 per cent in 1936. In light of these considerations, it is not difficult to explain the subsequent developments. Reparation deliveries being an important part of total
output, the 1946 industrial structure was slowly adjusted to
the structure needed to satisfy the Soviet Union's demand for
current output. Production of the light industries, of second-
ary importance to the Soviet Union, was developed at a slow
rate. Their relative share, therefore, declined steadily and
significantly from 35.8 per cent in 1946 to 22.8 per cent in
1954. Thereby the low 1944 share had almost been regained.
Production of the metal-working industries, in which the Soviet
Union showed an extremely strong interest, was stressed, and
their relative share increased from 8.5 per cent in 1946 to
27.4 per cent in 1950 (the 1936 share) and to 32.4 per cent in
1954. The decline in the importance of the basic industries
after 1946 can be similarly explained.

Beyond that, several interesting correlations can be observed. For instance, there was the strong Soviet desire for
products of the chemical, machinery, and electro-technical industries (providing in 1952 19.0 per cent, 23.6 per cent, and
18.9 per cent of reparations from current production, respectively) and the increase in the relative importance of these
industries within the East German economy beyond their 1936
share of industrial output: In 1936, 7.9 per cent of industrial output came from the chemical industries, it was 10.0
per cent in 1946, and 13.5 per cent in 1954. In 1936, 12.2
per cent of industrial output originated in the machinery industry, it was 4.7 per cent in 1946, and 14.6 per cent in 1954.
In 1936, 3.6 per cent of industrial output consisted of electro-
technical products, the percentage was 1.1 in 1946 and 6.2 in
1954.

On the other hand, there was the low priority attached by

the Soviets for deliveries from the textile and leather industries (providing in 1952, for instance, 3.8 per cent of reparations from current production) and the relative decline of
these industries below their 1936 share: In 1936, the textile
and leather industries in East Germany produced 21.6 per cent
of industrial output, their share was again 21.4 per cent in
1946, but only 14.1 per cent by 1954.

FOOTNOTES

[1]Compare H. Kraus and K. Heinze, eds., *Völkerrechtliche Urkun-
den zur europäischen Friedensordnung*, (Bonn: Institut für
Völkerrecht an der Universität Göttingen, 1953), 1 and 8.

[2]Another goal was, of course, the establishment of a Communist
regime, but even its main task in the early years was to help
in securing reparations: Eleven German Central Administrative
Departments were established in July of 1945. They had only
limited powers over the state governments and were equally subject to complete Soviet control. Eventually, they dissolved
into Central Administrative Departments for the Interior, Jus-
tice, Health and Education, and the German Economic Commission
(*Deutsche Wirtschaftskommission*, DWK), Heinrich Rau becoming
chairman of the latter. The function of the DWK was expressed
in Order No. 32 of the Soviet Military Administration in Germany, February 12, 1948, as quoted in Bundesministerium für
gesamtdeutsche Fragen (hereafter referred to as BMfgF), *S.B.Z.
von A bis Z* (6th ed., rev. and enlarged; Bonn: Deutscher
Bundesverlag, 1960), p. 97: "The Economic Commission is
ordered to supervise the punctual realization, in accordance
with the predetermined plan, of commodity deliveries designated as reparations, as well as the satisfaction of the needs
of the Soviet occupation forces in Germany," and "the Economic
Commission will exercise its activity under the supervision of
the Soviet Military Administration in Germany."

[3]Compare Frederick H. Hartmann, ed., *Basic Documents of Inter-
national Relations*, (New York: McGraw-Hill, 1951), pp. 174-
75. See also Erich Klinkmüller, *Die Gegenwärtige Aussenhan-
delsverflechtung der Sowjetischen Besatzungszone Deutschlands*
(West Berlin: Duncker und Humblot, 1959), pp. 4-5; and Erich
Klinkmüller and Maria Elisabeth Ruban, *Die Wirtschaftliche
Zusammenarbeit der Ostblockstaaten* (West Berlin: Duncker und
Humblot, 1960), pp. 6-15.

[4]Compare Margaret Carlyle, ed., *Documents on International Affairs 1947-1948*, (London: Royal Institute of International Affairs, 1952), pp. 434-35.

[5]*Ibid.*, p. 441.

[6]One list of such goods, going all the way from forty thousand sheep to three thousand bathtubs, is reprinted in Vassily Yershov, "Confiscation and Plunder by the Army of Occupation," in Robert Slusser, ed., *Soviet Economic Policy in Postwar Germany*, (New York: Research Program on the U.S.S.R., 1953), pp. 1-14.

[7]See *Die Sowjetische Besatzungszone Deutschlands: 1945-1954* (2 vols.; mimeographed; Bonn: BMfgF, 1954), II, p. 247. Such estimates have mostly been made by East Germans who escaped to the west. The abbreviation RM refers to *Reichsmark*, the German currency unit in east and west until the 1948 currency reforms. Thereafter, the unit was renamed DM or *Deutsche Mark* on both sides of the Iron Curtain. Throughout this book, if there is danger of confusion, this writer refers to the East German *Deutsche Mark* as DM-E and to the West German *Deutsche Mark* as DM-W. In discussions of longer time periods, the symbol RM/DM signifies that the currency unit was RM for data before, and DM for data after the 1948 currency reform.

[8]It limited the basic industries to 55 per cent, the investment goods industries to 45 per cent, and the consumer goods industries to 80 per cent of their respective 1936 capacities. See Appendix A for a definition of these industries.

[9]Data for population for this and the following paragraph were taken from *Statistisches Jahrbuch der Deutschen Demokratischen Republik 1959* (East Berlin: VEB Deutscher Zentralverlag, 1960), p. 17. This source will hereafter be referred to as *SJDDR*. Output data were calculated from gross production data in million RM at current prices, as published in Bruno Gleitze, *Ostdeutsche Wirtschaft* (West Berlin: Verlag Duncker und Humblot, 1956), pp. 170-85.

[10]For the minimum estimate see Guy Roustang, *Développement Économique de l'Allemagne Orientale* (Paris: Sedes, 1963), page 16. Much more typical, however, are higher estimates, as in U.N., *Economic Survey of Europe Since the War* (Geneva: 1953), pp. 1-3 and 7. The latter estimates are based on the U.S. Strategic Bombing Surveys, which showed, for instance, an increase in the German machine-tool stock from 1938-45 by at least 33 per cent, but maybe as much as 61 per cent. During 1944, when air attacks were the heaviest, about 6.5 per cent of machine-

tools were damaged or destroyed, yet three quarters of even these were currently repaired. This situation is regarded as typical for all of industry.

[11]The statements in the text were made by Stefan Heymann, East German ambassador to Poland, in *Der Aussenhandel* (hereafter referred to as *AH*), 2, 1956, p. 36. More recently, an official government publication said the same: "While in West Germany, in spite of all damage done, industrial capacity at the end of the war exceeded that at the beginning, in East Germany the greatest part of industry was destroyed or heavily damaged." See *Handbuch der Deutschen Demokratischen Republik* (East Berlin: Staatsverlag der DDR, 1964), p. 354. Interestingly, Heinrich Rau, sixteen years earlier, had claimed that East German industrial capacity shortly after the war exceeded that of 1936 in spite of heavy war damage and reparations. See *Die Wirtschaft* (hereafter referred to as *DW*), 7, 1948, p. 212.

[12]It was customary in Germany to distinguish zones and sectors of occupation. The occupation sectors refer to occupied parts of Berlin, the zones to the occupied areas outside Berlin.

[13]One half of double track lines was taken, leaving East Germany with nothing but single track lines. This caused enormous transportation difficulties subsequently. See *S.B.Z. von 1945 bis 1954* (Bonn: BMfgF, 1956), p. 22.

[14]Statement by the Chief of the Soviet Military Administration in Germany, Marshal Zokolovsky, on May 21, 1946. A similar statement was made on January 16, 1947. *Ibid.*, p. 49.

[15]*Ibid.*, p. 58. Note that this statement is not inconsistent with note 13 above, since here all tracks, both double and single, are included.

[16]See *Die Sowjetische Besatzungszone Deutschlands 1945-1954* (2 vols., Bonn: BMfgF, 1954), II, p. 250; and Franz Rupp, *"Die Reparationsleistungen der sowjetischen Besatzungszone,"* Bonner Berichte aus Mittel- und Ostdeutschland* (Bonn: BMfgF, 1951), p. 36. The latter publication will hereafter be referred to as *BB*. According to the latter source, p. 9, the East German state governments had collected exact data on dismantling in their respective areas of jurisdiction, but these data were sequestered by the Soviet secret service in 1947.

[17]See the report of Vladimir Alexandrov, "The Dismantling of German Industry," in Robert Slusser, ed., *Soviet Economic Policy in Postwar Germany,* (New York: Research Program on the U.S.S.R., 1953), pp. 14ff. According to one estimate, only 18 per cent of dismantled equipment was reinstalled in the U.S.S.R. See *Basler Nachrichten*, 5-12-1946.

[18]Section 1.8 of the draft of East Germany's First Five Year
Plan (1951-55) read as follows: "It is the primary and unques-
tionable task of industry to guarantee the punctual and strict
fulfillment of reparation obligations towards the Soviet Union
and the Republic of Poland in regard to the planned quantity,
assortments, and qualities." In the final (November 1951) law
this paragraph was omitted. See Franz Rupp, *op. cit.*, p. 39.

[19]This is the most likely number. Sources vary between 200
and 235 enterprises, but this is due to certain arbitrary decisions as to whether several plants are counted separately
or not.

[20]This development had been foreshadowed by Order No. 124 of
October 30, 1945, "On the sequestration and provisional take-
over of certain property categories in Germany." It lead to
the division of the property of persons, previously accused
of being Nazi agents and war criminals, into three categories,
A through C. The fate of property in group A was to be decided by plebiscite. One such plebiscite, "On the punishment
of war criminals and Nazi leaders and for the breaking of the
power of monopoly capitalism," actually took place in Saxony on
June 30, 1946. Since 77.7 per cent of the voters favored na-
tionalization, no further plebiscites were held in the other
provinces, "the people's view being obvious." Group A property was then given to various governmental units, anti-Fas-
cist organizations (such as trade unions), and even sold to
private individuals. Property in group B was returned to the
former owners, who had been found innocent of the charges.
Property in group C was to be disposed of by the military government. This was done via Order No. 167 discussed in the
text. For more detail the reader may consult Anonymous, *"Die
sowjetische Hand in der deutschen Wirtschaft,"* BB (Bonn:BMfgF,
1952), pp. 11-13; and Anonymous, *"Die Stellung der SAG in der
Wirtschaft der Sowjetzone im Jahre 1951,"* *Materialien zur
Wirtschaftslage in der sowjetischen Zone* (Bonn: BMfgF, 1952),
pp. 5-6. The latter source will be referred to hereafter as
Mat.

[21]Marshal Zokolovsky in *Tägliche Rundschau*, 1-11-1947.

[22]No such return was envisaged originally. The value of these
plants was to enter the reparations accounts at the time of
take-over. Much has been written about the curious valuation
procedures used (at 1938 prices minus four to twelve per cent
depreciation per year since then), leading to an extremely
small figure. Because of the eventual return, however, such
accounting can be foregone here. In accounting for deliveries
from current production, however, goods bought with SAG profits
and the money paid by East Germany when "purchasing" the SAG

at the time of their return will be counted like those bought
by the Soviet Union with official payments from the German
budget.   Total net profits of the SAG from 1947 to 1953 have
been estimated at RM/DM 3.55 billion, or exactly 12 per cent of
production value.   Such profits were practically guaranteed to
the SAG because they were legally free from several types of
taxes and avoided all others by paying "rent" equal to profits
to the Soviet headquarters in Berlin, these rents appearing as
costs in the income statement.   The SAG, unlike German owned
firms, also enjoyed special pricing privileges.   The return
of the SAG to German ownership occurred in several stages.   As
early as February/March 1947, 74 plants were returned and 13
more during the rest of the year.   In May/June of 1950, 23
plants changed hands, 66 in June of 1952, 3 in August of 1953,
and 33 by the end of 1953.   The remaining uranium mining company *(Wismut)* became a joint Soviet-German corporation.   The
plants returned in 1950 were paid for with DM-E 500 million.
Those returned in 1952 were valued at DM-E 2,490 million, of
which DM-E 2,060 million had been paid when East Germany's remaining debt of DM-E 430 million was cancelled on August 22,
1953.   All other SAG were returned free of charge, the last 33
being valued at DM-E 2,700 million.

[23]A list of such companies can be found in Anonymous, *"Die sowjetische Hand in der deutschen Wirtschaft,"* BB (Bonn: BMfgF,
1952), pp. 60-65, and in J.P. Nettl, *The Eastern Zone and Soviet Policy in Germany, 1945-1950* (London: Oxford University
Press, 1951), pp. 225-31.

[24]One western publication claims to have a secret plan of East
Germany's State Planning Commission, dividing 1951 SAG production as follows: 61.4 per cent reparations, 9.0 per cent exports, 29.6 per cent East Germany. See Anonymous, *"Die Stellung der SAG in der Wirtschaft der Sowjetzone im Jahre 1951,"*
Mat. (Bonn: BMfgF, 1952), p. 15. The East Germans, on the
other hand, have "countered western press libels" by giving
this distribution of SAG production: 0.8 per cent reparations,
23 per cent exports, 76.2 per cent East Germany. See *Neues
Deutschland,* 11-4-1953. The East Germans usually agree, however, on the large percentage of total output originating in
the SAG. In 1950, the SAG are said to have produced 22 per
cent of total output, but 38 per cent of mining, 58 per cent
of chemical, and 36 per cent of electro-technical output. See
Vierteljahreshefte zur Statistik (hereafter referred to as
VS), 3/4, 1959, p. 94.

[25]Issue of January 8, 1954. The paper also claimed that all
SAG had been entirely rebuilt by the Soviets, since the plants
"were worth nothing after the ruthless management of the Fas-
cists and the bombing of Anglo-American terrorists."

[26]The SAG returned in 1952 were valued at DM-E 2,490 million, those returned in late 1953 at DM-E 2,700 million. Compare note 22 above .

[27]It had been known for decades that pitchblende deposits existed in this area. Pitchblende, an impure uraninite, is the principal ore of uranium and radium. Ore from this area had been used late in the 19th century by Marie Curie and her husband in the discovery of radium. Also, the town of Oberschlema in this area was a well-known spa which boasted of the healing qualities of its springs containing traces of radium.

Other areas of potential deposits, such as the Harz and Zittau Mountains, and the province of Thuringia, were investigated by so-called geologists' brigades over the next six years. Eventually, only two localities were found to have such deposits: (1) the Erzgebirge Mountains and the Vogtland area with centers at Aue, Johanngeorgenstadt, Falkenstein, and Schneeberg, and (2) Thuringia around Ronneburg. By 1954, three hundred shafts existed in these areas. Twelve processing plants produced uranium chloride which was shipped to the Soviet Union without exception. The areas involved became highly restricted and were closed to almost all traffic.

[28]The East Germans have boasted about the uranium exports "which contribute to a considerably more favorable condition of our balance-of-payments. It is obviously not useful to give data about this, since they would allow insights for the enemies of the socialist camp." See *AH*, 10, 1957, p. 350.

[29]At least 37,000 "Nazi agents, militarists, and war criminals" were deported to the Soviet Union, while about 10,000 physicists, engineers, and technicians signed "voluntary" five year contracts to work in the Soviet Union. The latter group went to the Soviet Union mostly in 1946 or 1950, and the persons involved took their families along.

[30]Apart from the difficulty of evaluation, these forms of reparations were excluded for the following reason. It has been reported that the Soviet Union delivered some raw materials to the East German SAG free of charge. These were then processed and re-exported to the Soviet Union as reparations. In this case the value of deliveries from current production, as given above, is overstated, for it should consist only of the value added to any free raw material deliveries. Since the value of such raw material deliveries is also reported to have been small, one may conveniently assume that they were at most equal in value to the goods removed during the trophy campaign and of German labor performed in the Soviet Union. If this assumption holds, an overstatement in one section of the repa-

rations account is made good by an understatement in another.

[31]This estimate of the real side of reparations is corroborated by statistics on the monetary side. The Soviets had the following sources of funds: (1) use of conquered RM notes and issue of occupation currency in 1945/46, RM 4,200 million (sometimes used directly for commodity purchase, at other times given as "credit" to the new local governments and repaid in goods), (2) SAG profits from 1947-53, RM/DM-E 3,550 million, (3) receipts from sale of SAG to East Germany from 1950-53, DM 2,560 million, (4) receipts from German budgets (in the early postwar period from local and provincial governments and the budgets of the central railroad and postal administrations, later all from the central government) until 1953, RM/DM-E 37,880 million. (Actually the Soviets did not receive the entire amount directly. They received part and paid the producers of reparations goods 1938 prices. The other part was paid directly by the government to the producers as a subsidy to bring total payments up to the value at legal current prices.) Hence the Soviets had funds, between 1945 and 1953, to purchase RM/DM-E 48,190 million of goods at current prices. (The Soviets were not affected by the 1948 currency reform, as all funds held at the time were exchanged for them only at the rate of 1:1.) The estimates in Table 1 show 1945-53 purchases of RM/DM-E 48,179.74, excluding dismantling, which would not have any monetary equivalent. See Anonymous, *"Der Aussenhandel der sowjetischen Besatzungszone Deutschlands,"* *Mat.* (Bonn: BMfgF, not dated), p. 21, Franz Rupp, *op. cit.*, p. 17, and the source listed for row 2, Table 1.

[32]The derivation of this estimate is based on a translation of data in current prices in RM/DM-E into 1938 RM with the help of price indices. 1938 RM data were then translated into dollars at the 1938 average exchange rate of RM 2.49/$. The price indices were derived as described in the detailed note to Table 24.

[33]The East Germans have blamed the difficulties arising from dismantling on the "disproportions" created by Germany's economic division.

[34]Wolfgang F. Stolper, with the assistance of Karl W. Roskamp, *The Structure of the East Germany Economy* (Cambridge, Mass.: Harvard University Press, 1960).

[35]Wolfgang F. Stolper, *op. cit.*, p. 5.

[36]*Ibid.*, p. 437 and (for 1959) from unpublished parts of the manuscript. Calculated from data in RM and 1936 prices, after adjustment for the inclusion of uranium production. See also

the author's article "On East Germany's Foreign Economic Relations," *Social Research*, summer 1962 and Table 24.

[37]Franz Rupp, *op. cit.*, p. 20 and *DW*, February 1949, Heft 3,
p. 74. The division between occupation costs and reparations
proper was given as follows (in per cent of gross production).
1948: 4.8 and 9.8 per cent, respectively, 1949: 4.1 and 8.3
per cent, respectively, and 1950: 1.9 and 4.4 per cent, respectively.

[38]Walter Ulbricht, *Der deutsche Zwei-Jahres-Plan für 1949-1950*,
p. 19. He said reparations in 1948 were 17 per cent of net
production, occupation costs 8 per cent. Production here presumably refers to industrial production and not, as in the
analysis above, to GNP, western definition.

[39]Bruno Gleitze, *"Stand der Entwicklung im mitteldeutschen
Wirtschaftsraum," Vierteljahreshefte zur Wirtschaftsforschung*
(hereafter referred to as *VzW*), 1, 1952, p. 58.

[40]The following data were taken from Wolfgang F. Stolper,
op. cit., pp. 418-19 and for 1959 from unpublished parts of
the manuscript. The indices were derived from GNP in 1950 West
German prices, GNP according to West German definition. East
Germany includes East Berlin, West Germany excludes West Berlin.

[41]It should be pointed out, however, that there has always
been a tendency for an east to west population movement in Germany, but the fact that this movement was accelerated in the
postwar time, rather than reversed, must speak for itself.

[42]The foregoing shares were calculated from data in 1950 West
German prices taken from Stolper, *op. cit.*

[43]All data, except for 1944, were taken from Stolper, *op. cit.*
and are based on 1950 West German prices. 1946 data are partly estimated, partly taken from unpublished parts of Professor Stolper's manuscript. 1944 data were calculated from
Bruno Gleitze, *op. cit.*, pp. 170-85.

2

EAST
GERMANY'S COMMERCIAL
FOREIGN TRADE RELATIONS

A. THE RESUMPTION OF TRADE AND THE CREATION OF THE FOREIGN TRADE MONOPOLY

With the unconditional surrender, Germany's foreign trade relations with other nations ceased. All power in this field passed to the supreme military commanders in the four occupation zones.[1] But as has been shown in the previous chapter, commodities in significant quantities began to flow almost immediately from East Germany in the eastward direction as reparations.

The revival of trade on a commercial basis, however, was a much more gradual affair. One of the major reasons for this suggests itself. Low output, coupled with large reparations, left little to be exported on a commercial basis. In addition, of course, the chaotic conditions of the early postwar period brought many forms of economic activity to a temporary standstill.

The economic structure of East Germany, however, made trade with outside areas an absolute necessity. Due to the weakness of certain basic industries, imports of coal, iron, and steel, for instance, were of vital importance. The production of many reparations goods depended thereon. For this reason alone, the Soviet desire to get foreign trade started again is understandable.

Until the currency reform in 1948, there was no attempt by East German governmental units to monopolize foreign trade operations. The Soviet Military Administration, ever since 1946, encouraged the development of foreign trade relations and made use of the initiative and the experience of private German entrepreneurs. It is true, of course, that these could do little more than take care of the business side of transactions, basic policy decisions being made by the Soviets. Every single foreign trade transaction had to be licensed by

the Department of Foreign Trade of the Soviet Military Administration in Germany. It also signed all trade agreements.
All foreign exchange was handled exclusively by a Soviet bank,
the *Garantie- und Kreditbank* in Berlin.[2]

On June 4, 1947, the first German governmental unit, the
German Administration for Interzonal and Foreign Trade (*Deutsche
Verwaltung für Interzonen- und Aussenhandel,* DVIA), entered the
foreign trade field. It had advisory capacity and acted as an
intermediary between German private firms engaging in foreign
trade (as well as some nationalized enterprises which began
operations) and the Soviet authorities. As time went by, the
DVIA received some freedom of action of its own, such as the
licensing of exports up to $5,000 per transaction. Its succes-
sor, the Central Administration for Interzonal and Foreign
Trade (*Hauptverwaltung für Interzonen- und Aussenhandel,* HVIA),
itself an integral part of the emerging East German Central
Government's Economic Commission (DWK), was authorized, in August, 1948, to license export transactions up to $20,000 and
imports up to $5,000 in value. East German writers hailed this
as a step practically eliminating Soviet control of foreign
trade,[3] but this was certainly exaggerated. Even open Soviet
control continued until March, 1954, when East Germany became
"completely sovereign" and the Soviet Control Commission (*Sowjetische Kontroll-Kommission,* SKK) was abolished.

At the time of the founding of the German Democratic Republic, the HVIA was dissolved and its functions were taken
over by the Ministry for Foreign Trade and Material Supplies
(*Ministerium für Aussenhandel und Materialversorgung,* MAM).
In November, 1949, it was renamed Ministry for Intra-German
Trade, Foreign Trade, and Material Supplies (*Ministerium für
innerdeutschen Handel, Aussenhandel und Materialversorgung,*
MIAM). Finally, in October of 1950, MIAM lost its inland supply function. It became the present Ministry for Foreign and

Intra-German Trade (*Ministerium für Aussen-und innerdeutschen Handel*, MAI). Since the founding of the G.D.R. the East German state bank (*Deutsche Notenbank*) has also taken over the functions of foreign-exchange and internal-currency accounting from the *Garantie- und Kreditbank* and the AAK, respectively. Hence all matters of foreign trade were officially in German hands by October of 1949.

In the meantime, since the currency reform of 1948, the stage was being set on a somewhat lower level of government for the complete monopoly of foreign trade relations by the government. Originally, the HVIA founded two state enterprises, one for foreign trade (*Deutsche Handelsgesellschaft m.b.H.*, DHG) and one for trade within Germany (*Gesellschaft für innerdeutschen Handel*, GIH). They competed with private firms and the nationalized enterprises (*Vereinigungen Volkseigener Betriebe*, VVB). In the middle of 1949, the DHG was renamed *Deutscher Aussenhandel, Anstalt des öffentlichen Rechts*, DAHA. On September 1, 1951, both the DAHA and the GIH were dissolved and succeeded by the People's Owned Trade Enterprises, German Internal and Foreign Trade (*Volkseigene Handelsunternehmen Deutscher Innen- und Aussenhandel*, VEH-DIA). From this time on, the state enjoyed in fact a complete monopoly in foreign trade.[4]

The VEH-DIA were originally grouped into 17 departments (*Fachanstalten*) according to the economic sector they dealt with. Their number has varied since. Twelve of these were left by 1960. They were the departments for chemicals, chemical industry equipment, electro-technical industry, glass/ceramics, wood/paper, invest-export (i.e., the export of complete factories), cultural products, machinery, food, textiles, transportation equipment, and WMW export (*Werkzeugmaschinen und Metall-Waren*, i.e., machine tools and metalgoods). These foreign trade enterprises in turn own thirteen other companies of the limited liability type, for which state ownership is not quite so obvious.[5]

Finally, there are a few allegedly private firms, such as the *Ultimex-Aussenhandelsvertretungen G.m.b.H.*, which are engaged in procuring embargo items from the west and the executives of which are said to be selected by the Central Committee of the Communist Party.[6]

All trade is carried on by these government enterprises within the framework of trade agreements negotiated at some higher level.[7] The East Germans prefer long term agreements on a governmental level, as is generally the case in trade of Communist countries. Much of the trade with western countries is carried on via banking agreements (between the *Deutsche Notenbank* and the respective state banks) or chamber agreements (between the East German Chamber for Foreign Trade and a similar organization in the partner country). The latter two approaches avoid the issue of diplomatic recognition of East Germany, though, of course, the East German Central Bank as well as the Chamber for Foreign Trade are pure government agencies.

To summarize, East German foreign trade was started again by private initiative which was encouraged, but also controlled, by the Soviet military government. From 1948 to 1951, while the Soviets transferred more and more of their controlling functions to the emerging East German government, there was a period of mixed private and governmental activity in foreign trade, though there was still over-all government control. Since 1951, there has been in fact, and since 1958 in law, complete governmental monopolization of foreign trade.[8]

B. THE VOLUME AND REGIONAL DISTRIBUTION OF FOREIGN TRADE

This section presents an attempt to establish what has been the volume and regional distribution of East Germany's foreign trade from 1946 through 1964, and how the postwar situation compares to the prewar era.

In particular, the following have been investigated: East
Germany's foreign trade with each of the Communist countries
and with four groups of western countries, the so-called anti-
imperialist areas, with which trade is being encouraged for political reasons; West Germany, trade with which is of particular interest because of many old ties in spite of the present
political rift; the other five members of the European Common
Market (Benelux, France, Italy); and a final group of western
countries comprising "all others."

The "Communist bloc" has been defined to include the following countries: in Europe, Albania, Bulgaria, Czechoslovakia, Hungary, Poland, Rumania, the Soviet Union, and Yugoslavia;
and in Asia, mainland China, Outer Mongolia, North Korea, and
North Vietnam.

According to East German usage, the "anti-imperialist
areas" are not always independent political territories, but
may include areas fighting for their independence, those having recently gained such status, or others having been politically sovereign for a long time. All these areas have in common, however, that they are economically underdeveloped, are
anxious for development, and, the Communists hope, are good
prospects for a Communist revolution. The East Germans, so
far as one can tell, seem to define this group of countries as
follows: in the Americas, all areas outside the U.S. and
Canada; in Africa, all areas outside the Union of South Africa;
in non-Communist Asia, all areas outside Formosa, Iran, Israel,
Japan, Pakistan, the Philippines, South Korea, South Vietnam,
Thailand, and Turkey. East Germany, even in 1964, did not have
trade relations with all the "anti-imperialist" areas thusly
defined, but she did with a large number of them.

The European Common Market is here defined to include the
European areas only, not associated territories outside Europe.

Before the estimates are presented, however, a few explan-

atory notes will prove useful. First, all trade data in this
study are expressed in terms of rubles, which may seem odd in
a discussion of East Germany's foreign trade. The internal
currency used in East Germany is, of course, German marks
(*Deutsche Mark* or DM), not rubles. All commodities and services have internal DM prices, just as there are such internal
ruble prices for goods traded within the Soviet Union. Prior
to 1950 and the definition of the East German mark and the
ruble in terms of gold, East German foreign trade accounting
was in terms of U.S. dollars, but such data have not been published systematically by the East Germans. Since there also
existed an official exchange rate of dollars per DM, one could
of course, translate such dollar trade data into DM. Only by
coincidence, however, would such a DM figure represent the
value of trade at internal prices. Internal prices are fixed
by governmental decree quite independently from foreign-trade
prices, and the magnitude of trade evaluated at such prices
would almost certainly differ markedly from a DM figure representing the foreign-exchange equivalent of the dollar value.
For this reason, trade at internal and valuta (or foreign-
trade) DM can be distinguished.

Since 1950, all East German foreign-trade data, when officially published, have been in rubles. These are based on
dollar world market prices translated into rubles at the gold
parity rate or they are foreign-trade ruble prices negotiated
originally in rubles by the partners. These ruble data, therefore, are not referring to domestic rubles and have nothing to
do with internal prices in the Soviet Union. Translating such
foreign-trade ruble data, at the official exchange rates, into
the various currencies used in the Communist countries will
give data in those currencies which have also nothing to do
with trade values at interal prices in those countries.

It is, therefore, best to use foreign-trade ruble data
as they are published for East German trade or as they can be

derived from a variety of sources. It would be of no use to
translate such ruble data into DM at the official rates of exchange, for the DM data so derived would have nothing to do
with exports and imports valued at internal German prices.[9]

Second, a methodological note is in order. The official
East German statistical yearbooks contain only some data on the
export and import of commodities, expressed, as stated above,
in foreign-trade rubles. For the years 1950 through 1963, such
information is given for trade with the rest of the world as a
whole, as well as separately for trade with the Communist world,
the non-Communist world, and West Germany (including West Berlin). Since 1953, more detailed information by selected countries is also given. All other data, such as those for years
prior to 1950 (including the prewar period) and the country
breakdown until and sometimes beyond 1952, were estimated by
the author. For the postwar years this was done with the help
of a large number of mostly Communist sources, such as journal
articles, speeches of government officials reprinted in daily
newspapers, etc. The most common procedure was the translation of index and percentage figures given in these sources into absolute data with the help of absolute data known for other
years. Naturally, special attention was given to the distinc-
tion of planned from realized magnitudes and similar potential
pitfalls.[10] The 1936 data on the magnitude and regional distribution of East German foreign trade were prepared for the
express purpose of making possible a meaningful comparison with
the postwar data. Therefore, all 1936 trading partners were
defined in terms of postwar boundaries. For example, the area
within the German Reich of 1936 that now is called German Democratic Republic (i.e.,the former Soviet Zone of Occupation plus
East Berlin) has been singled out, and its trade with all other
areas (whether they were German in 1936 or not) has been treated as foreign trade. This is exactly in line with postwar po-

litical realities. This means, for instance, that 1936 trade
of East Germany with Danzig and the German areas annexed by
Poland in 1945 has been regarded as trade with Poland; while
1936 trade with Estonia, Latvia, Lithuania, the northern part
of East Prussia, and with the eastern part of Poland annexed
by the Soviet Union after the war has been regarded as trade
with the Soviet Union. It was not possible, and was regarded
as unimportant, to make any adjustments for other small bound-
ary changes, as, say, between the Soviet Union and Finland or
Rumania. Similarly, 1936 trade with Japanese Manchukuo was
regarded as trade with "Communist" Asia. Detailed regional
statistics on internal German trade before the war made it possible to estimate East Germany's "foreign" trade with West Germany in 1936 directly, the same can be said for part of the
trade with "Poland" and the "Soviet Union" in postwar boundaries. So far as trade that was foreign in 1936 according to
1936 boundaries is concerned, one basic assumption was made,
viz. that the regional distribution of East Germany's foreign
trade (with areas that were not German in 1936) was identical
with that of total German foreign trade. Since only the East
German share of total German exports and imports is known, together with the geographic breakdown of this total, this was
the only possible assumption to make. But it must, of course,
not necessarily be true. It is quite possible, for instance,
that East Germany had a larger share of trade with Eastern
Europe than did West Germany, while West Germany might have had
a larger share than East Germany in trade with areas closer to
it. On the other hand, reasonable as such speculation may
sound, it could be wrong, and was therefore neglected.[10]

Third, a final comment shall be directed to the subject of
inconsistencies of foreign trade statistics. It is a well
known fact that the foreign trade statistics of different countries are frequently inconsistent with each other. The author
has, therefore, made an attempt to reconcile such inconsisten-

cies wherever possible. This investigation was confined, however, to East Germany's European Communist trade partners and
only one western country, West Germany including West Berlin.[11]
The East Germans define their exports and imports as all commodities that have crossed East German borders during the calen-
dar year. Exports include only commodities produced or significantly reworked in the G.D.R. (which excludes mixing, repacking, sorting), if these goods remain in the partner country.
Imports, similarly, include only commodities produced or significantly reworked in the partner country, if these goods remain in the G.D.R. Categorically excluded are gifts; technical documents delivered in connection with a program of scientific-technical cooperation; samples; goods destined for exhibitions, fairs, consignment (until realized); deliveries to be
returned (such as animals participating in races; films to be
copied; means of transport and equipment to be repaired; pack-
ing materials, containers and means of transport, if temporar-
ily used; etc.); personal effects of travelers and migrants;
postal packages; personal and official effects of embassies,
diplomatic missions, and consulates; gold used as a means of
payment; payments in foreign currency for technical aid; and
goods in transit. Most data, in addition, exclude improvement
trade (the value added to raw materials or semi-finished goods
delivered, reworked, and returned), repair trade (the value
added to goods repaired abroad and returned to place of origin),
re-exports (goods bought abroad and, even without having crossed purchaser's border, resold in unchanged form, including
mixing, repacking, sorting), provisions for aircraft and ships,
exchange of films, license fees, and costs of assembly and making blueprints.[12] The values of such exports as well as imports are defined f.o.b. border selling country.[13]

     The investigation revealed that almost all discrepancies
in the statistics reported by various trade partners in the
Communist bloc can be explained by differences in coverage,

valuation, or timing. The tables that follow are based entirely on East German data. The basic data are presented in Tables
3 and 4, all statements in the text are derived from them.

It becomes immediately obvious that the East German commercial foreign trade structure has undergone a significant regional change during the postwar period. In 1936, 17.8 per
cent of the trade volume was with the area that later became
the Communist bloc,[14] but even this percentage is largely accounted for by trade with areas then German (Poland of postwar
boundaries 12.7 per cent). Trade with countries now considered as "western" provided 82.2 per cent of the volume. Nearly two thirds of the entire trade volume was with West Germany
and West Berlin. This distribution was largely the same for
imports and exports, though the "bloc" countries provided a
slightly larger share of imports (19.1 per cent) than they received of exports (16.6 per cent).

In 1946, the situation was largely the same. Twenty-two
per cent of trade were with the later bloc countries of Poland
and Czechoslovakia (both areas within the Greater German Reich
of 1944, it will be noted), and 78 per cent of trade were with
western areas, mostly West German, the rest also being European
(Scandinavia, U.K., Austria, Switzerland). Though the total
volume of trade (exports plus imports) was significantly lower
than before the war, West Germany's share increased from 64.8
to 73.8 per cent. The continued trade orientation towards the
west was even stronger for imports than exports of East Germany
(83.5 versus 73.1 per cent).

The trade volume increased substantially in 1947 (it more
than tripled), but most of this increase was with western countries. As a result, though the trade volume with bloc countries increased somewhat (Bulgaria, Hungary, the Soviet Union,
and Yugoslavia becoming new partners), their share in East Germany's foreign trade reached an all-time low of 8.7 per cent.

Table 3. East German commodity exports to selected
trading partners, 1936 and 1946-63, in 1,000 rubles,
at current prices f.o.b. East German border[a]

Year (1)	Total (2)	Bloc (3)	Rest (4)	CMEA (5)
1936	6,070,416	1,006,211	5,064,205	946,935
1946	295,889	79,493	216,396	79,493
1947	955,992	56,987	899,005	47,960
1948	984,742	439,325	545,417	426,942
1949	1,714,356	1,001,835	712,521	978,200
1950	1,709,100	1,107,600	601,500	1,107,282
1951	2,850,780	2,249,700	601,080	2,166,523
1952	2,954,680	2,218,600	736,080	2,050,502
1953	3,869,968	3,051,128	818,840	2,781,199
1954	5,552,297	4,442,307	1,109,990	4,002,190
1955	5,483,586	4,131,761	1,351,825	3,697,200
1956	5,979,025	4,520,550	1,458,475	4,075,123
1957	7,243,029	5,438,252	1,804,777	4,930,913
1958	7,558,576	5,801,776	1,756,800	5,114,655
1959	8,485,611	6,554,486	1,931,125	5,925,464
1960	8,762,330	6,630,230	2,132,100	6,022,967
1961[bd]	9,101,065	6,812,186	2,288,879	6,375,817
1961[cd]	2,047,742	1,532,742	515,000	1,434,559
1962[ce]	2,136,381	1,661,481	474,900	1,598,685
1963[cf]	2,437,786	1,899,886	537,900	1,837,420

Source:

See *Supplement,* Chap. I.

Notes:

Col. 2 = sum of cols. 3 and 4; col. 3 = sum of cols. 5,
13, and 18; col. 4 = sum of cols. 19 - 22; col. 5 = sum
of cols. 6-12; col. 13 = sum of cols. 14-17.
[a]Data for 1964 were not available. All data include commercial uranium exports to the Soviet Union.

Table 3   continued

Year (1)	Albania (6)	Bulgaria (7)	Č.S.S.R. (8)	Hungary (9)
1936	255	13,455	39,291	23,461
1946	-	-	30,101	-
1947	-	1,590	27,133	1,299
1948	-	7,707	62,746	2,597
1949	-	24,823	81,810	9,024
1950	-	12,902	120,716	31,851
1951	5,980	33,130	180,421	88,747
1952	12,060	45,631	189,092	143,707
1953	11,964	79,708	226,457	170,414
1954	9,603	95,409	291,875	187,571
1955	24,602	85,013	375,334	184,475
1956	18,316	129,661	439,032	190,660
1957	17,713	119,166	562,190	252,925
1958	23,713	145,680	602,511	244,959
1959	27,760	202,837	686,129	345,977
1960	19,957	275,752	759,170	374,376
1961[bd]	15,564	334,547	915,644	397,342
1961[cd]	3,502	75,273	206,020	89,402
1962[ce]	2,612	57,372	195,369	101,187
1963[cf]	3,535	87,990	206,487	109,624

[b]Old rubles
[c]New rubles
[d]Includes improvement, repair, re-export trade, etc., of
    55.297 million old = 12.442 million new rubles for
trade with the bloc. See footnotes 12 and 13.
    [e]Includes improvement, repair, re-export trade, etc., of
    11.564 million new rubles for trade with the bloc.
    [f]Includes improvement, repair, re-export trade, etc., of
    14.913 million new rubles for trade with the bloc.

Table 3   continued

Poland (10)	Rumania (11)	U.S.S.R. (12)	Communist Asia (13)	China (14)
697,823	29,285	143,365	37,454	37,454
49,392	-	-	-	-
18,018	-	53	-	-
159,409	3,000	191,749	-	-
186,031	4,769	671,743	-	-
315,056	12,049	614,708	318	318
490,575	41,079	1,326,591	83,177	83,177
421,362	83,009	1,155,641	168,098	164,098
434,007	125,031	1,733,618	269,929	241,479
535,553	103,187	2,778,992	437,864	390,981
494,974	99,143	2,433,659	426,928	389,608
556,049	114,171	2,627,234	432,026	379,673
604,479	135,605	3,238,835	472,590	423,015
575,492	138,483	3,383,817	586,000	532,953
705,579	191,330	3,765,852	509,994	425,848
705,621	193,179	3,694,912	471,266	388,537
832,507	235,022	3,645,191	278,849	220,320
187,314	52,880	820,168	62,741	49,572
209,653	49,678	982,814	31,283	19,674
224,866	56,866	1,148,052	18,277	9,363

Table 3   continued

Year (1)	Outer Mongolia (15)	North Korea (16)	North Vietnam (17)	Yugoslavia (18)
1936	-	-	-	21,822
1946	-	-	-	-
1947	-	-	-	9,027
1948	-	-	-	12,383
1949	-	-	-	23,635
1950	-	-	-	-
1951	-	-	-	-
1952	-	4,000	-	-
1953	-	28,449	1	-
1954	-	46,826	57	2,253
1955	-	30,455	6,865	7,633
1956	313	33,234	18,806	13,401
1957	5,161	27,224	17,190	34,749
1958	11,350	22,063	19,634	101,121
1959	10,718	33,455	39,973	119,028
1960	18,955	18,933	44,841	135,997
1961[bd]	12,231	16,187	30,111	157,520
1961[cd]	2,752	3,642	6,775	35,442
1962[ce]	2,121	4,628	4,860	31,513
1963[cf]	2,409	3,269	3,236	44,189

Table 3   continued

| "Anti-imperi-alist" areas (19) | European Common Market | | Others (22) |
	West Germany and West Berlin (20)	Benelux, France, Italy (21)	
229,638	3,954,430	311,526	568,611
-	214,700	-	1,696
-	651,200	35,613	212,192
-	389,400	64,442	91,575
-	553,600	111,338	47,583
2,792	402,300	116,026	80,382
42,619	140,840	120,714	296,907
82,445	132,340	125,402	395,893
23,000	278,800	130,090	386,950
50,000	419,400	143,485	497,105
104,726	545,725	153,036	548,338
129,175	616,025	164,034	549,241
210,022	818,600	176,030	600,125
211,273	845,200	161,992	538,335
242,627	918,925	207,070	562,503
366,651	962,500	232,950	569,999
488,965	875,100	246,916	677,898
110,017	196,900	55,556	152,527
96,520	189,100	51,932	137,348
122,079	218,000	57,810	140,011

Table 4. East German commodity imports from selected
trading partners, 1936 and 1946-64, in 1,000 rubles,
at current prices f.o.b. border of seller.[a]

Year (1)	Total (2)	Bloc (3)	Rest (4)	CMEA (5)
1936	5,904,365	1,129,829	4,774,536	1,076,960
1946	259,042	42,820	216,222	42,820
1947	633,379	81,844	551,535	72,816
1948	1,065,505	489,174	576,331	457,397
1949	1,442,640	706,897	735,743	702,657
1950	2,022,550	1,425,550	597,000	1,425,550
1951	2,430,325	1,774,800	655,525	1,715,387
1952	3,091,100	2,320,400	770,700	2,200,345
1953	3,930,149	2,999,471	930,678	2,787,384
1954	4,383,612	3,234,362	1,149,250	2,961,275
1955	4,690,919	3,312,894	1,378,025	2,958,967
1956	5,334,851	3,853,368	1,481,483	3,487,402
1957	6,461,920	4,625,720	1,836,200	4,221,008
1958	6,719,514	4,765,214	1,954,300	4,218,002
1959	7,969,450	5,969,475	1,999,975	5,372,872
1960	8,678,873	6,415,673	2,263,200	5,785,332
1961[bd]	8,929,675	6,777,254	2,152,421	6,464,404
1961[cd]	2,009,182	1,524,882	484,300	1,454,491
1962[ce]	2,155,829	1,692,030	463,799	1,620,582
1963[cf]	2,085,046	1,597,024	488,022	1,533,660
1964[c]		1,804,637		

Source:

See *Supplement*, Chap. I.

Notes:

Col. 2 = sum of cols. 3 and 4; col. 3 = sum of cols. 5,
13, and 18; col. 4 = sum of cols. 19-22; col. 5 = sum
of cols. 6-12; col. 13 = sum of cols. 14-17.

Table 4   continued

Albania (6)	Bulgaria (7)	Č.S.S.R. (8)	Hungary (9)	Poland (10)
13	16,138	31,352	26,169	826,818
-	-	3,604	-	39,216
-	3,710	6,995	3,949	56,599
-	23,122	68,046	7,897	133,547
-	24,823	99,991	20,976	254,800
-	19,987	167,728	99,500	348,480
22	37,661	180,422	56,265	330,883
32	44,371	198,000	116,631	379,706
3,699	72,073	233,419	137,339	447,654
3,387	98,847	307,467	192,125	447,315
5,071	123,998	282,938	248,419	458,527
7,738	137,359	421,400	156,664	419,383
10,807	106,401	475,632	188,256	411,777
10,542	121,471	567,433	282,548	338,902
17,280	180,954	618,904	327,547	418,690
17,326	217,565	725,323	369,489	434,032
25,142	263,329	871,604	415,009	408,769
5,657	59,249	196,111	93,377	91,973
4,322	68,393	202,016	88,622	97,361
2,734	65,398	194,247	85,691	97,611
5,468		219,499	101,115	136,655

[a]Data for 1964 were only partially available from *DW*, 8, 1965, p. 13, and 9, 1965, p. 5. They are preliminary. All data exclude armament imports.

[b]Old rubles

[c]New rubles

Table 4   continued

Year (1)	Rumania (11)	U.S.S.R. (12)	Communist Asia (13)	China (14)
1936	25,860	150,610	31,800	31,800
1946	-	-	-	-
1947	-	1,696	-	-
1948	2,000	223,050	-	-
1949	3,180	298,887	-	-
1950	13,054	776,801	-	-
1951	30,239	1,079,895	59,413	59,413
1952	59,300	1,402,305	120,055	120,055
1953	59,726	1,833,474	212,087	212,087
1954	86,035	1,826,099	269,502	269,502
1955	151,556	1,688,458	347,033	346,592
1956	116,560	2,228,298	351,839	343,638
1957	84,227	2,943,908	380,491	354,164
1958	120,500	2,776,606	451,069	415,304
1959	131,265	3,678,232	499,441	447,326
1960	207,714	3,813,883	454,497	400,655
1961[bd]	201,053	4,279,498	205,463	160,324
1961[cd]	45,237	962,887	46,229	36,073
1962[ce]	39,144	1,120,724	38,777	28,739
1963[cf]	33,230	1,054,749	29,735	22,240
1964[c]	56,823			

[d]Includes improvement, repair, re-export trade, etc., of 64.81 million old = 14.582 million new rubles for trade with the bloc. See footnotes 12 and 13.

[e]Includes improvement, repair, re-export trade, etc., of 20.029 million new rubles for trade with the bloc.

Table 4 continued

Outer Mongolia (15)	North Korea (16)	North Vietnam (17)	Yugoslavia (18)	"Anti-imperialist" areas (19)
-	-	-	21,069	325,535
-	-	-	-	-
-	-	-	9,028	-
-	-	-	31,777	-
-	-	-	4,240	4,731
-	-	-	-	-
-	-	-	-	5,974
-	-	-	-	11,947
-	-	-	-	20,000
-	-	-	3,585	22,587
-	441	-	6,894	71,127
-	6,704	1,497	14,127	112,902
6,654	10,118	9,555	24,221	238,756
6,887	11,391	17,487	96,143	254,329
9,852	20,873	21,390	97,162	265,734
8,105	18,358	27,379	175,844	373,465
14,196	13,036	17,907	107,387	335,457
3,194	2,933	4,029	24,162	75,478
1,526	3,794	4,718	32,671	107,396
2,498	2,517	2,480	33,629	119,888
			57,842	

fIncludes improvement, repair, re-export trade, etc., of 18.446 million new rubles for trade with the bloc.

Table 4   continued

| Year (1) | European Common Market | | Others (22) |
	West Germany and West Berlin (20)	Benelux, France, Italy (21)	
1936	3,807,765	172,167	469,069
1946	194,600	-	21,622
1947	499,600	18,018	33,917
1948	436,000	90,515	49,816
1949	522,400	107,570	101,042
1950	387,200	133,277	76,523
1951	174,225	158,984	316,342
1952	183,400	184,691	390,662
1953	250,800	210,399	449,479
1954	415,000	190,082	521,581
1955	524,425	235,619	546,854
1956	584,725	221,920	561,936
1957	735,500	201,956	659,988
1958	760,500	239,469	700,002
1959	914,349	188,936	630,956
1960	825,800	275,550	788,385
1961[b]	786,200	351,880	678,884
1961[c]	176,900	79,173	152,749
1962[c]	172,700	52,159	131,544
1963[c]	172,800	55,306	140,028

The bloc held, however, a greater share of imports than exports (12.9 versus 6.0 per cent). West Germany was again the trading partner for almost three quarters of total trade volume (68.1 per cent of exports, 78.9 per cent of imports), other European countries for the rest (25.9 per cent of exports, 8.2 per cent of imports). Contrary to speculation by some, the regional distribution of East Germany's foreign trade, therefore, in the very first years after the end of the war, did not show an immediate alignment with the eastern world. One can easily explain why this was so.

First, as has been shown above, foreign trade was, until 1949, in the hands of the Soviet Military Administration which encouraged private enterprise in this area. Since before and until the end of the war most trade had been oriented towards the west, it is only to be expected that the resuming of old commercial ties should create the same kind of regional trade pattern.

Second, and maybe even more important, in spite of the common Communist denominator, the early postwar relations between the East Germans and the other East European nations never achieved more than the appearance of concord.[15] The social, political, and the economic barriers between East Germany and her eastern neighbors were almost impassable. There was a universal hatred of everything German. The transfer of the German minorities (or even majorities) was a concrete expression of such feelings. There was little inclination to accept postwar Germany as a friend, whatever its political complexion. East Germany was an underling, certainly not a partner. The chilly reception given to Grotewohl and Pieck (then Chairmen of East Germany's Communist Party) in the summer of 1948 when they visited Budapest, Prague, and Warsaw testifies to this. It should, therefore, not come as a surprise that economic contacts were confined to small transactions.

All this, however, changed since 1948. While the total
trade volume continued to rise, the share of trade held by the
Communist world suddenly jumped from 8.7 to 45.3 percent. In
1949, this share increased further to 54.1 per cent, in 1950
to 67.9 per cent, and in 1951 to 76.2 per cent. The shares of
the western world declined correspondingly. Both shares have
remained fairly constant ever since, while the volume of trade
has been rising continually and substantially. The Soviet bloc
share after 1951 fluctuated between a low of 73.2 per cent of
the trade volume (1955) and a high of 78.1 per cent (1962).
Preliminary data indicate a percentage of 76.3 for 1964. These
developments were practically the same for exports and imports
taken separately. After 1951, the bloc received never less
than 74.9 per cent of exports (1961) and at one time even 80
per cent (1954). The latest (1963) data show a 77.9 per cent
share. Similarly, after 1951, the bloc never delivered less
than 70.6 per cent of imports (1955), at times (1962) even 78.5
per cent. The latest (1963) data give a percentage of 76.6.
In short, from 1948 to 1951, East Germany experienced a complete
and apparently permanent reorientation of her trade relations:
away from the western world and towards the east.

Undoubtedly, there are a number of reasons for this sudden shift. The most obvious event that might have precipitated
the change was the blockade of West Berlin. It began on June
24, 1948, and by the time the western counterblockade was fully
in effect (September 15, 1948) absolutely all trade relations
with West Germany, apart from a few illegal transactions, were
disrupted.[16] This must have been a terrific blow for the East
German economy. West Germany had provided nearly 80 per cent
of her commodity imports in 1947, and trade was at about the
same annual rate until the imposition of the blockade. (In
spite of the fact that there was hardly any trade with West
Germany in the second half of 1948, West Germany still held

40.3 per cent of East Germany's 1948 trade volume.)   The East
Germans have never ceased talking about the "dangerous pitfalls
in trade with the capitalists."

Trade with West Germany resumed after the end of the
blockade of Berlin (May 1949), but relations to the present
(1965) have remained terribly chilly. West Germany's share in
East Germany's trade volume actually declined to an all-time
low of 5.2 per cent in 1952, then rose to 11.3 per cent in 1957
and has steadily fallen to 8.6 per cent in 1963. West Germany
was still (in 1963) East Germany's third largest trading partner (after the U.S.S.R. and C.S.S.R.) but the importance of
this trade, compared to prewar and early postwar days, was
small, indeed.

The relative importance of trade with all other western
countries has, furthermore, also declined somewhat after 1947,
but to a much lesser degree than in the case of West Germany.
It declined from 18.9 per cent of the volume in 1947 to 11 per
cent in 1950 and has been fairly close to 15 per cent since.
This may at first have been partly the result of western non-
recognition of the G.D.R. For this reason it was frequently
impossible, or at least rather difficult, to renew trade agreements which the Soviet Military Administration had previously
made with western governments on behalf of East Germany. The
western embargo against the export of certain strategic materials to Communist countries and the Korean crisis may also
have served to discourage trade with the west and to intensify
trade relations within the bloc.[17]

In addition to these events, making it very difficult for
East Germany to continue her traditional reliance on trade with
the west, there also seems to have been made around 1948 or
1949 a basic policy decision by the Soviet Union in regard to
East Germany's future. This decision was to integrate East
Germany economically into the Communist orbit. Since 1950, the

Soviet Union has been East Germany's principal trading partner,
substituting in part for the role held by West Germany earlier.
Some have seen in this only an expression of the Soviet desire
to further exploit East Germany via unfavorable terms of
trade,[18] but, as will be shown in CHAPTER 3, there was, for
whatever reason, a genuine desire to bring closer economically
the countries united politically under the Communist banner.
The outward expression of this was the founding of the Council
for Mutual Economic Aid in January, 1949, to which East Germany
was not admitted until late 1950.[19] It seems that even without
blockade and embargo the East German leaders would have undertaken a basic revision of their trade policy, the former events
just accelerating the inevitable.

In summary, the following can be said. The regional structure of East German foreign trade underwent a significant
change from 1948 to 1951. While in 1946 twenty-two per cent of
the trade volume was with the bloc area and 78 per cent with
the west, this relationship since 1951 was almost exactly the
reverse. This was due to a large decline in the importance of
trade with West Germany which was not made up by relatively
more trade with other western nations. In particular, the
trade offensive with the so-called anti-imperialist world,
which was announced in the early 1950's and received so very
much attention in the East German press ever since, has been
found to be little more than talk. Economically it was of no
importance. Trade with this area at its height in 1963 com-
prised only 5.3 per cent of the total trade volume, only
slightly more than in 1936 (4.6 per cent).

The largest trading partner in the Communist world since
1948, as well as over-all since 1950, was the Soviet Union. It
had been Poland in the Communist world and West Germany over-
all before these dates. Since 1951, the U.S.S.R. shared in almost half of the trade volume. Preliminary figures for 1964

show a percentage of 47.4. The second largest partner in the
Communist world was Czechoslovakia till 1947, Poland from 1948
until 1956, and Czechoslovakia since. Interestingly, distant
China has been the third or fourth ranking partner in bloc
trade from 1951 to 1960. In 1961, China trade dropped significantly, absolutely as well as relatively, presumably because of
the Moscow-Peking rift.

   With the exception of Poland, trade with every Communist
country was in 1963 (absolutely and relatively) more important
than in 1936. It will be remembered, however, that 1936 trade
with "Poland" was largely intra-German trade at the time. The
same was true for the "anti-imperialist" world since 1962. On
the other hand, trade with West Germany, the European Common
Market as a whole, and all other western countries was relatively less important than before the war. Absolutely, the trade
volume with these western areas was, however, higher for the
non-German partners of the European Common Market and all other
countries as a group.

   These statements, with only slight variations, are true
not only for the trade volume, but also for imports and exports
by themselves.

FOOTNOTES

[1]See the *Allied Proclamation No. 2* of September 20, 1945.

[2]This bank had branches throughout East Germany. It administered all funds for the Soviet military and did the bookkeeping
for reparations. In 1960, it was in the process of liquidation.
Foreign trade accounting in RM was done by the *Aussenhandels-
Abrechnungskontor G.m.b.H.* (Foreign Trade Accounting Office,
Limited), called AAK, founded in August of 1946. It operated
till the summer of 1949, paying exporters and billing importers
at legal internal prices. There never was any relation whatsoever between the Soviet bank mentioned above and the AAK.

[3]See Josef Orlopp, Chief of the HVIA, *"Entwicklung und Perspek-
tiven des Aussenhandels der Ostzone," DW*, 1, 1949, p. 13.

[4]A law to this effect was not passed until 1958, however. See *Gesetzblatt der D.D.R.: 1958*, Teil I, p. 69, of January 9, 1958.

[5]They are the *Bergbau-Handelsgesellschaft für die Ausfuhr und Einfuhr von Bergbauerzeugnissen m.b.H.* (mining); the *Deutsche Export und Importgesellschaft Feinmechanik/Optik m.b.H.* (fine mechanical and optical products); the *Deutsche Stahl- und Metallhandelsgesellschaft m.b.H.* (steel and other metals); the *Mineralöle Import und Export G.m.b.H.* (oil); the *Deutsche Genussmittelgesellschaft m.b.H.* (drink and tobacco); *Deutscher Buchexport und Import G.m.b.H.* (books); *Geschenkdienst und Kleinexport G.m.b.H.* (gifts and "small" exports); *Wiratex Exportgesellschaft für Wirkwaren und Raumtextilien m.b.H.* (textiles); *Polygraph Exportgesellschaft für den Export polygraphischer Maschinen m.b.H.* (printing machinery); *Deutsche Rauchwaren Export- und Importgesellschaft m.b.H.* (furs); *Büromaschinen Export G.m.b.H.* (office machinery); *Heim-Elektrik Deutsche Export und Import G.m.b.H.* (household electrical equipment); *Deutsche Kamera Aussenhandelsgesellschaft m.b.H.* (cameras).

[6]Compare *S.B.Z. von A bis Z* (4th ed., rev., Bonn: BMfgF, Deutscher Bundesverlag, 1958, p. 306, and 8th ed., rev., 1963, pp. 50 and 471).

[7]Some industrial firms and artisans have been allowed, since 1954, to carry on so-called own-transactions in foreign trade, presumably to take advantage of old commercial ties. But this has been a very minor and only effect of the New Course after Stalin's death, for even these transactions were limited to certain commodities and required the permission of MAI or the relevant VEH-DIA. Similarly, the effect on the organization of foreign trade of the New System of Economic Planning and Administration, introduced since 1963, is negligible so far. See below, p. 374, footnotes 2 and 3.

[8]For a detailed account of the organizational aspects of East German foreign trade, including all the relevant orders of the Soviet Military Government and East German laws, see various issues of *S.B.Z. von A bis Z* (Bonn: BMfgF). An abundance of articles on the foreign trade monopoly can be found in various issues of the East German magazine, *Der Aussenhandel*. It has for many years devoted an unbelievable amount of space to an extremely sterile discussion of the necessity of the foreign trade monopoly as a weapon in the class struggle and has exposed the "counter-revolutionary thinking" of many a "Titoist agent" on the subject. An impressive number of Communist party members have fallen into disfavor allegedly because of their heretical views on the foreign trade monopoly; see for instance the fate of Behrens (one-time Deputy Chairman of the

State Planning Commission), Benary (one-time department Chairman in East Berlin's Academy of Sciences), and Harich (onetime editor of an East Berlin journal), to name just a few.

[9]For a detailed discussion on foreign trade pricing and exchange rates, consult Chapter 4 and Appendix B.

[10]For detail consult *Supplement*, Chap. I.

[11]For detail consult *Supplement*, Chaps. I and IV.

[12]Only *SJDDR 1962* and *1964* give some regionally detailed statistics including the types of trade given in this sentence. Such data are partially included for 1961-63 in Tables 3 and 4 below. For the definitions given see *SJDDR 1964*, p. 381 and especially Staatliche Zentralverwaltung für Statistik, *Definitionen wichtiger Kennziffern und Begriffe für Planung und Statistik* (East Berlin: Staatsverlag der D.D.R., 1965), pages 260-62.

[13]This is also the definition on which the following tables are based, one exception being 1936 imports, which are defined c.i.f., since it was impossible to make the necessary correction in the basic data. This would, however, make no difference for East Germany's neighbors, where f.o.b. and c.i.f. evaluations are identical. Another exception is the inclusion in 1961-63 data for the bloc of some types of trade, usually excluded. See last footnote.

[14]This estimate is supported by two independent estimates, which are given without comment on their derivation: The 1936 percentage of trade with the later bloc area is given as 17 by U.N., *Economic Survey of Europe since the War*, (Geneva: 1953), p. 216; for 1937 as 15-20 by Karl C. Thalheim, *"Die Entwicklung der Wirtschaftsintegration im Ostblock," Osteuropa-Wirtschaft*, 1, 1956, p. 3.

[15]For an evaluation of this situation see, for instance, J.P. Nettl, *op. cit.*, pp. 282-294.

[16]The East Germans themselves have blamed the "western" blockade for the east-orientation of their trade. See Josef Orlopp, *op. cit.*

[17]Compare Nicolas Spulber, "Effects of the embargo on Soviet trade," *Harvard Business Review*, Nov./Dec. 1952, pp. 122 ff.

[18]This question is discussed in Chapter 7 below.

[19]It apparently took some doing on the part of the Soviet
Union to get East Germany accepted as a junior partner and to
divert the hatred of all Germany in Eastern Europe to the hatred of West Germany. The East German acceptance of the Oder-
Neisse line as a permanent border and the renunciation of the
Sudetenland probably helped considerably. Originally, the
East German Communists had maintained that "on the eastern
frontier question the Communist Party. . .will oppose any loss
of German territory. The . . .frontier is provisional and can
be fixed only at the Peace Conference with the help of all the
victorious powers." *Neues Deutschland*, 9-14-1946. The latter
source will hereafter be referred to as *ND*.

CHAPTER **3** THE
COUNCIL FOR
MUTUAL ECONOMIC AID

As was pointed out in CHAPTER 2, East Germany's trade reorientation towards the east was only partly the result of the
Berlin blockade and the western trade embargo. It was also
and primarily a matter of design independent of the above his-
torical accidents. It appears that during 1948, the Soviet
Union arrived at a high-level policy decision which strongly
influenced economic developments in the Communist bloc throughout the 1950's and is to have even more far-reaching effects
in the 1960's. This was the decision to bind together the
Communist countries economically as well as politically. This
decision has been put into effect within the framework of the
Council for Mutual Economic Aid, hereafter referred to as CMEA.
This chapter will deal in some detail with this organization,
its growth, and, incidentally, East Germany's involvement
therein.

A. THE FOUNDING AND STRUCTURE OF CMEA

Until 1945, Soviet Russia was the only Communist country
in the world. Her policy of "socialism in one country" found
expression in strong autarkic tendencies in the economic realm.
Though she could have fared better undoubtedly by wholehearted
participation in an international division of labor on the
basis of comparative advantage existing then, the Soviet leadership under Stalin tried to minimize the country's economic
dependence on others. Heeding the old advice of Adam Smith
that "defense. . .is of much more importance than opulence,"
the Soviet Union - undoubtedly for justifiable reasons - decided to produce directly at home what could have been obtained more cheaply abroad. The pursuit of autarky, in short, was
based on the decision to be safely poor rather than insecurely
rich.

This policy was continued by the Soviet Union for quite

some time after the end of the war, which led to the emergence
of a number of new Communist nations in Europe (and Asia).
Originally, these nations slavishly copied the Soviet pattern
of industrialization, as it had developed "under the conditions
of capitalist encirclement."[1] Their main concern was, accordingly, the setting up of centrally planned economies, self-sufficient within the national borders. However, what had been
costly - though possible - for the Soviet Union was suicidal
for the emerging satellites. Nevertheless, regardless of
their countries' raw material endowment, the new rulers attempted to develop their economies with a view to achieving
the impossible, economic self-sufficiency.[2]

Of course, there had to be some international economic
relations among the new Communist brothers-in-faith, but these
hardly went beyond the (reluctant) exchange of goods under annual agreements and the mutual giving of (small) credits, designed to bolster the establishment of Communism. Stalin him-
self saw the division of the world market into two camps as
"the most important economic result of the Second World War."[3]
But he failed to see the possibility of an integrated socialist world economy. And in those days, his word was the last.
Autarky became the aim for each of the Communist nations.
Imports could alleviate bottlenecks, and exports were the necessary evil to pay for them. Foreign trade was just a "safety
valve" of the national economic plan. Its optimum volume was
zero.[4]

Slowly the Communist leadership became aware of the fact,
however, that they should adjust their theories and actions
to the existence of a Communist world economy. A policy of
"autarky for the whole camp," rather than for its individual
units, was eventually seen as a promising alternative to the
earlier, narrower objectives. Ostensibly (according to Soviet
bloc economic historians), this new phase of official thinking

arrived with the formation of CMEA in 1949. In fact, it did
not arrive until several years later. The founding of CMEA
was rather an action designed to create a counterforce to the
Marshall plan.[5]

The decision to establish CMEA was made on January 21,
1949, in Moscow by Bulgaria, Czechoslovakia, Hungary, Poland,
Rumania, and the Soviet Union. Albania joined in April of the
same year, a Yugoslav attempt to do the same was turned down,
and East Germany became a member in September, 1950.[6] It was
immediately stated, however, that membership is open to all
(European) countries acknowledging the principles of CMEA and
willing to take part in the comprehensive economic cooperation
they call for. In May, 1956, China and Yugoslavia joined in the
work of CMEA as observers. North Korea and North Vietnam have
been observers since 1957 and 1958, respectively. Excepting
Yugoslavia, the observers voiced their readiness, in 1958, to
associate themselves more closely with CMEA, while Yugoslavia
disassociated herself at the same time. The closer cooperation
with the Asian countries, however, never materialized. With
the coming into the open of the ideological split between China
and the U.S.S.R. in the early 1960's, the Asiatic observers
have withdrawn increasingly, though not entirely, from the work
of the organization. Their only ally in Europe, Albania, withdrew completely in late 1961. In December of 1962, CMEA officially recognized that the Albanians had recalled their representatives, stopped paying dues, and communicated their lack of
interest in the organization.[7] Earlier in the same year (June),
the organization's statute was changed to allow non-European nations to membership, and Outer Mongolia was admitted as such.
Therewith, CMEA continued to have eight members: besides the
Soviet Union, six in Europe and one in Asia. In 1964, Yugoslavia, after six years of isolation from CMEA, once more took
up closer ties with the organization.

Just as its membership, the administrative structure of
CMEA was largely unchanged from 1949-62, but was altered then.
The highest organ has always been the Plenum, an assembly of
delegations from the member countries. It is supposed to con-
vene at least once a year, alternating between the capitals of
the member countries, with the leading representative of the
host country holding the chairmanship. The country delegations
are usually led by a high government official, such as the Foreign Trade Minister or the Chairman of the State Planning Commission, with other ministers and party functionaries as advisers.

The Plenum, after intensive study of all relevant factors,
makes recommendations to the member governments as to economic
policies to be pursued. Since "all activities of the Council
are based on the principles of mutual aid, complete equality of
each member country, mutual advantage, and non-interference in
internal affairs," these Plenum decisions are said to be not
binding on the members. They become so only after ratification
by each government concerned, and are subsequently realized via
bilateral or multilateral treaties. All actions are said to be
unanimous, and the official communiqués never fail to mention
the "atmosphere of complete unanimity, mutual understanding,
and brotherly cooperation and cordiality." Undoubtedly the latter is exaggerated, but it would be just as wrong to go to the
other extreme and assume that the formal veto power of each
member is always overridden by party discipline or sheer Soviet
pressure.[8] In recent years, for example, conflicts are known
to have existed on the question of economic integration, because members were reluctant to scrap some of their industries,
even if they were high cost and inefficient. And such reluc-
tance has in many cases resulted in national action contrary
to the wishes of CMEA.[9]

While the Plenum is not in session, the organization's

work is carried on by other organs. A Deputies' Council was
permanently located in Moscow until June of 1962. It met at
least twice a month to work out policy proposals to be considered by the next Plenum and to supervise the realization of
past decisions. As the name suggests, it consisted of deputies of the government officials attending the Plenum. Though
reports are not entirely clear, the Deputies' Council has apparently been abolished in mid-1962 at the time of the creation of an Executive Committee. It consists of deputies of
the chiefs of government of the CMEA countries and has apparently all the powers of the Plenum itself, i.e., it can, between plenary sessions, make recommendations and decisions on
all questions of economic cooperation.

The Deputies' Council did earlier and the Executive Committee does now direct the work of a Secretariat which is
also located in Moscow. There is a permanent Secretary with
assistants and a staff of advisers and experts from the member
countries.[10] They do administrative work and also represent
the organization at official functions. It was estimated in
1959 that "under a hundred" persons were then working at the
Deputies' Council and the Secretariat in Moscow.

A subordinate position similar to the Secretariat is held
by a Bureau for Comprehensive Questions of Economic Planning,
staffed with planning officials.

The work of other subordinate organs, such as the Standing Commissions for Economic and Technical-Scientific Cooperation[11] and various permanent or temporary committees, is also
guided via the Secretariat by the superior organs. The following is a list of Standing Commissions (including the time of
their creation and location of their headquarters) as of June,
1965. Their role will be discussed below.

1.   Agriculture Commission (after 7th Plenum, 1956; Sofia)

2.   Chemicals Commission (after 7th Plenum, 1956; Berlin)

3. Coal Commission (after 7th Plenum, 1956; Warsaw)
4. Electric Energy Commission (after 7th Plenum, 1956; Moscow)
5. Ferrous Metals Commission (after 7th Plenum, 1956; Moscow)
6. Foreign Trade (incl. Complete Factories) Commission (after 7th Plenum, 1956; Moscow)
7. Machine Building Commission (after 7th Plenum, 1956; Prague)
8. Non-Ferrous Metals Commission (after 7th Plenum, 1956; Budapest)
9. Oil and Gas Commission (after 7th Plenum, 1956; Bucharest)
10. Construction Industry Commission (after 9th Plenum, 1958; Berlin)
11. Economic Problems Commission (after 9th Plenum, 1958; Moscow)
12. Transportation Commission (after 9th Plenum, 1958; Warsaw)
13. Food Commission (originally Food and Light Industries Commission, after 10th Plenum, 1958; Prague - split after 18th Plenum, 1963; Sofia)
14. Light Industries Commission (originally Food and Light Industries Commission, after 10th Plenum; 1958; Prague - split after 18th Plenum, 1963; Prague)
15. Peaceful Uses of Atomic Energy Commission (after 13th Plenum, 1960; Moscow)
16. Coordination of Scientific and Technical Research Commission (after 16th Plenum, 1962; Moscow)
17. Standardization Commission (after 16th Plenum, 1962; Berlin)
18. Statistics Commission (after 16th Plenum, 1962; Moscow)
19. Foreign Exchange and Finance Commission (after 17th, Plenum, 1962; Moscow)
20. Geology Commission (after 18th Plenum, 1963; Ulan Bator)
21. Radio-technical and Electronics Industry Commission (after 18th Plenum, 1963; Budapest)

B. A HISTORY OF CMEA

1. Attuning Foreign Trade Plans: 1949-54

Relatively little is known about the first years of CMEA's work until 1954. This might well be due to the fact, however, that not much was done. The First Plenum met in Moscow on April 26 and 27, 1949. The official announcement summarized the purposes of the new organization. They were "to help exchange economic experiences and to foster mutual technical aid and mutual aid through the shipment of raw materials, food, machines, equipment, etc."[12] As subsequent years showed, this was indeed an exhaustive list of activities promoted by the Council. It involved nothing that could be compared with the massive unilateral aid program of the Marshall Plan. It dealt primarily with questions of trade, each nation exchanging its traditional products and, as was later criticized, thereby deepening the "disproportionalities inherited from capitalism."[13]

As a result of the Second Plenum in Sofia on August 25-27, 1949, there seems to have been some advance over the practices of earlier postwar years. Each nation now submitted long-term (1951-55) import and export plans to CMEA which attempted to fit these together and then recommended the signing of long-term bilateral treaties. During the years prior to 1949, not even such coordination of trade plans, drawn up by national planning boards in isolation, was attempted, and a nation planning to export to another Communist country frequently found no one was planning on such imports.[14]

Another concern of the Second Plenum was the fostering of mutual technical aid. The members agreed on the exchange of technical documents, delegations of experts, and the reciprocal training of specialists. Stretching the terms somewhat, one might go along with those who saw in this the first and faint beginnings of cooperation in the sphere of production. This cooperation in the technical-scientific field was heralded by

the Communists as a novelty completely unheard of in the capitalist world, where selfishness in the search for profit was
pictured as dictating the keeping secret of inventions and production methods and industrial espionage alone as able to
lift the veil of secrecy. The mentality of Communists was and
is described as quite different, however. Freely and free of
charge (except for the cost of printing or copying), they claim
to arrange the exchange of blueprints, patents, descriptions of
technical processes, results of research work, etc.[15] The medium for such exchanges are bilateral standing committees. Two
or three months before the meeting of such a committee, technical information requests are sent from one country to another
and these, in turn, go to various ministries. In its meeting,
the joint committee then discusses the ministry reports on the
feasibility of exchanging the desired information and the measures needed to implement the request. But here again the official image of reality is distorted, for it is known that not
all requests are granted.[16]

Nothing is known about the Third Plenum in Moscow on November 24, 1950, except that foreign trade and the signing of
long-term trade agreements were discussed. It was to be the
last full meeting until the spring of 1954. It is not known
with certainty what caused the interruption of CMEA's work.
According to remarks of a leading official of the Polish government (made to the author in a personal interview in 1962),
it may well have been the result of direct intervention by Stalin. He is reported to have very intensely distrusted the in-
tentions of the satellite regimes and feared that these countries' economic strengthening and cooperation might lead to the
formation of an anti-Soviet bloc, economically independent of
the U.S.S.R. Therefore, he discouraged any further steps in
the direction of bringing satellite countries closer to each
other economically, though he continued to encourage their in-

dividual dependence on the Soviet Union.

Though CMEA's main functions seem to have lain dormant, the organization was not entirely inactive, either. In July, 1951, the Secretariat recommended certain standards to be incorporated into all member country trade agreements. In 1953, a committee developed a standard nomenclature for foreign trade and foreign trade statistics. And outside the framework of the organization, the Council members tentatively tried deeper forms of cooperation. In 1952, several nations agreed to specialize in the fabrication of different types of steel beams and forms. In 1953, there appeared the first of the bilateral "industrial treaties" which specified articles one country would produce, but the other would not manufacture. The reasons behind such agreements lay in the unfortunate experience of several bloc countries which found their export markets in other bloc countries drying up, as the latter took up production of the imported items themselves. This, of course, constituted an implicit criticism of the work of CMEA, for within the Council the coordination of production, rather than of trade, was hardly considered a possibility, except for the case of ball-bearings where some sort of long-range production coordination did take place.

The criticisms of the Council's narrow interpretation of international economic cooperation became stronger as the years went by. National autarky had not been buried with the formation of CMEA. It became more and more apparent that problems remained, even though long-range trade plans began to be coordinated. The general feeling of dissatisfaction was expressed in many different ways, especially after Stalin's death and the "New Course" in economic policy. Some argued against any kind of industrialization in certain countries, others spread the "mistaken" theory of primacy of consumer goods production in a socialist world. And there were those who saw a great vision.

They contemplated a grand scheme of international division of
labor within the Communist bloc. They wanted to get rid of
"capitalistic disproportionalities," as well as to avoid new
ones, by coordinating the investment and production plans rather than those of trade only. Trade then was to express this
more basic coordination which would lead to specialization
among the Communist countries according to their comparative
advantage and an increase in output and living standards
throughout the bloc.[17]

2.   Coordinating Production and Investments:
1954-57, an Idea Takes Hold

It is this visionary idea that has ever since been slowly -
very slowly - transforming the Council of Mutual Economic Aid.
The Fourth Plenum, meeting again in Moscow from March 26-27,
1954, took up the challenge. It has been generally designated
as the beginning point of a new phase in the Council's activity. The Council was reported reorganized in a fashion not
publicized, but it is more likely that there was only talk
about expanding CMEA activities after the death of Stalin. The
Plenum directed its main attention towards the possibility of
coordinating the members' long-range economic plans for 1956-60,
which were being worked out at that time. In particular, it
was noted that emphasis on the rapid growth of heavy industry
had created disproportions in many countries with regard to the
sizes of the agricultural and raw material output on the one
hand and heavy industry demands for such output on the other.
Therefore, attention was drawn to the possibility of foregoing
investment in a branch of heavy industry in any one country, if
there already existed sufficient productive capacity from an
over-all bloc standpoint to satisfy over-all bloc demand.

As later comments abundantly show, there cannot have been
many practical results at this stage. Whatever actual coordination of production there was, seems to have been on a bilater-

al, short-run basis via industrial treaties mentioned earlier.
It has been reported, for example, that some such coordination
existed successfully between East Germany and Czechoslovakia
ever since 1954.

The Fifth Plenum was held in Moscow once more, on June 24
and 25, 1955. It made recommendations to eliminate parallel
investments and dealt in general with measures for the coordination of member countries' investment plans. Apparently, there
was enough progress by now that a series of bilateral treaties
for "mutual coordination of investment and production plans for
1956-60" could be signed.

The same subject continued to be under discussion at the
Sixth Plenum in Budapest from December 7-12, 1955. It examined
the system of existing industrial treaties and made recommendations for widening their scope. It made the first decisions,
it is reported, on a multilateral coordination of production of
the member countries, covering the 1956-60 period. Involved
were the production of passenger automobiles, trucks, tractors,
railroad cars, combines, and other agricultural machinery. The
question of standardization in machinery was also taken up.
There was special concern with a uniform beginning of all member countries' plans on January 1, 1956, since otherwise planning coordination would be more difficult. Finally, the Plenum considered the lag in agricultural output and the precarious raw material, energy, and metallurgical basis of industry.

These questions were immediately taken up again by the
next and Seventh Plenum in Berlin from May 18-25, 1956. This
meeting may well be called the apex in the developments of this
second phase of the Council's history, the transition to a
"higher level of cooperation in the coordination of production."
In the preceding months, 300 machinery experts from the member
nations had met, and from their work the Plenum made suggestions to the members for the division among them of the produc-

tion of 611 different types of items made by the machinery, precision mechanics, and optical industries.[18] It also recommended dividing research and development work on new machines. More specifically, the production coordination covered such items as diesel motors; metal cutting machines; forge-presses; road-building machines; railroad cars; automobiles; ships; agricultural machines; equipment for rolling mills, foundries, for the purpose of hauling, transporting, and hoisting, and for the energy, electro-technical, coal, oil, chemical, building materials, food, and light industries. This coordination was said to be multilateral and to cover the period "until 1960 and beyond." It was hoped that by avoiding unnecessary parallel production and making possible mass production, costs could be cut as well as quality improved in the machine building industry.

Furthermore, this Plenum was reported to have coordinated production in agriculture, and such industries as non-ferrous metals, oil and gas, chemicals, and some branches of light industry, notably in the areas of textiles, leather, and shoes.

To alleviate bottlenecks in coal, coke, iron ore, and energy, needed for the ferrous metals industry, the Plenum gave recommendations as to the development of Polish hard coal, and Krivoi Rog iron ore for the entire bloc, and took up the questions of exchanging electric energy among the members and developing the water resources of the Danube. A committee was appointed to make concrete suggestions.

Members also exchanged experiences in planning and economic administration to make them more uniform throughout the bloc.

Finally, a very important innovation was made which was said to be part of the reorganization begun at the Fourth Plenum. As then proposed by Polish and East German delegates, the Plenum instituted Standing Commissions for Economic and Techni-

cal-Scientific Cooperation. They consist of permanent delegations from the member countries, led by the minister in the
field in question and staffed with highly qualified experts.
Each Commission has a chairman and an international secretariat. Its purpose is, when applicable, to propose measures for
coordinating and specializing production, as well as research
and development, in its area of competence, to actually coordinate the investment, output and trade plans of its branch of
the economy, to enhance standardization, to improve quality,
and to organize scientific and technical-economic conferences
and exchanges.

From this time on, all the important CMEA work has really
been done in the Commissions. Sometimes they split into sections or form permanent or temporary work groups, but the work
of all these is always coordinated by the Commission Secretariat. All Commission decisions, however, are only carried out
with the unanimous agreements of all governments concerned.

Before the next Plenum, the first nine Commissions, as
given above, had been formed.[19] The following sections shall
report in some detail on the kind of work done by the Commissions.

The Agriculture Commission has synchronized research work
in the bloc, particularly concerning the breeding of seeds and
animals (questions like nutrition, artificial insemination),
animal and plant diseases, and weed killers. It has worked on
a uniform system of machines. The types of agricultural machines were reduced from about 1,000 to 400, covering 14 agricultural branches, through a systematic program of comparative
testing. The testing of agricultural machinery forms the basis
of specialization decisions. Specialization is recommended
only in those cases where machines fulfill the agrotechnical
needs of several countries. The Commission has not only been
concerned with the mechanization but also the electrification

of agriculture. Specialization decisions, covering periods to
1966, then to 1970, and now to 1980, largely concerned fruits
and vegetables (according to soil, climatic, and economic conditions) and seeds, with recommendations to the Machine Building Commission concerning the specialization of appropriate
machinery to mechanize horticulture. In particular in South
Eastern Europe, large areas were reportedly set aside for the
multiplication of flower and vegetable seeds, with corn and potatoes being of primary concern. In 1960, 700 types of East
German seeds were being tested by other CMEA countries, while
578 types from those countries were being tested in East Germany. In 1959, Bulgaria sent 31 types of seeds to other CMEA
countries and received 51. In the same year, the Soviet Union
provided 30,000 types. The Commission's concern with the output of oil seeds led to an investigation by the Chemicals Commission as to the possibility of substituting in technical uses
synthetic oils for vegetable oils. It also worked on problems
of storing, transporting and packaging agricultural products,
on the improvement of irrigation, and on fertilization (especially as to use of mixed and liquid fertilizers).

The Chemicals Commission has been one of the most active.
Like the Machine Building Commission, it had the task of coordinating production and research in a priority industry. Its
emphasis has been on developments in the production of synthetics and on agricultural "chemification." But it also has coordinated studies of working conditions in the industry.

The Coal Commission has introduced a uniform classification system and quality indices for coal and coke, and has investigated new methods of mechanized mining (e.g., automated
open pit mining, air conditioned deep-shaft mining). Other
projects have been the gasification of lignite under pressure
and the economics of the coal industry (labor organization, labor productivity, wages, working conditions). There also has

been promotion of internationally financed new mining projects.

The <u>Electric Energy Commission</u> made a detailed study of the energy output of all Communist countries from 1951-57 (and prospects to 1960, 1970, and 1980) and appraised probable technological developments, e.g., electricity produced by atomic power, until 1975. A joint Institute for Nuclear Research was founded in March of 1956 by the Council members and the Asian Communists. Its seat is in Dubna, near Moscow, with the Soviet Union making available freely "her research results of long standing, without charge."[20] By 1960, a 100,000 kw atomic power station was under construction in East Germany, and others were to be built in Czechoslovakia, East Germany, and Poland.

This Commission also dealt in detail with the so-called Danube project the Seventh Plenum had considered, which called for a joint utilization of the water resources of this river for electricity production and irrigation. Only in 1964 did Rumania and Yugoslavia on the one hand (Iron Gate project, hoped for completion 1971), and Czechoslovakia and Hungary on the other, agree on concrete steps to build hydroelectric power plants and dams.

The Commission also considered other cheap energy sources, such as low quality lignites, and the possibilities to mass-produce boilers, turbo-aggregates, pumps, armatures, high pressure pipes, and control and measuring devices. Further, it considered the construction of power lines (such as protection from corrosion). Most importantly, it has been concerned, since 1956, with the construction of an international high tension (220 kV or more) electricity network. The purposes of such a network have been reported to include the following: a) saving of costs through exchange of electric power in border regions, since it might be cheaper to supply a given place near the border from a short distance across it rather than from an internal source further away, b) mutual aid in cases of emer-

gency, such as the sudden breakdown of generating stations or
transmission lines, c) full utilization of generating capacity
from an international (bloc) standpoint.

The latter point is undoubtedly regarded as the most important and is based on the fact that generating capacity for any
given town, province, or county must be such as to meet the
peak demand made on it, e.g., during the evening hours. It is
also known, however, that for many hours during each day actual
use of this capacity is well below 100 per cent. Because of
the geographical expanse of the Soviet bloc, the timing of
these peaks in capacity use does not coincide in different regions. From this realization has sprung the idea that a long-
distance exchange of electric energy might be eminently desirable. For instance, East Germany, faced with rising demands
for electric power, would normally meet this demand by channel-
ing resources into investment in the energy industry, thereby
increasing her capacity to generate electricity in the peak demand hours of the day. From a bloc standpoint, however, this
investment may well be avoided in the short run. During these
very hours, Siberian generating stations are operating considerably below capacity and, if only electricity could be transported from Siberia to East Germany, could easily supply it to
the East German consumer without any need for additional investments anywhere in the Soviet bloc. This then was the idea
behind the call for the building of an electric energy grid,
connecting the networks of all countries "from the Elbe to the
Kamchatka peninsula" (separated from each other by about 150
degrees, involving a time differential of 10 hours). Present
plans call for a network of 60,000 megawatt capacity to be
ready in 1967 and to be the biggest in the world. Because of
tremendous technological problems, in particular the difficulties associated with large power losses during transport over
long distances, emphasis has so far been placed on power ex-

change within the European areas of the Soviet bloc. In 1959,
a grid went into operation between Czechoslovakia and Hungary,
in 1960 another one among Czechoslovakia, East Germany, and Poland. By 1962, the electricity networks of all four countries
were connected with each other, and in the same year a separate
link went into operation between Hungary and the Ukraine.[21]
All the aforementioned lines were of the 220 kV type. Plans
called for the 1963 opening of a 400 kV section connecting
Czechoslovakia, Rumania, and the Soviet Union.[22] Further in
the future, 1965 was to see the completion of a 380 kV transmission line between Czechoslovakia and the Soviet Union and
of 220 kV lines between Rumania and Bulgaria on the one hand
and Rumania and the Soviet Union on the other. Within the Soviet Union, in the meantime, lines are being erected between
the European and Asiatic areas, and Premier Khrushchev, in a
1962 speech, revealed plans for similar exchanges of energy between the Soviet Union and China (in the Amur and Sungari
River areas).

The administrative center of the energy exchange is a
dispatcher center at Prague (some sources mention another center at Mukachevo, U.S.S.R.). Operating under a Czech director,
it has directed CMEA electric energy exchange (among Czechoslovakia, East Germany, Hungary, Poland and the Ukraine) since
January, 1963. It was to add Rumania in the summer of 1963,
Bulgaria in early 1964, and White Russia later to its respon-
sibilities.

The Ferrous Metals Commission has recommended a number of
technological improvements in mining and metallurgy, as in the
rolling of steel profiles or the production of fire-resistant
materials by large presses. In early 1963, it initiated the
coordination of investment plans in this industry, which led
to the creation of "Intermetall," a special organization for
this purpose, in late 1964. Subsequently, the Commission has

sponsored standardization for steel products, such as lacquer-
ed fine sheets and tin plate, as well as for coke.

The Foreign Trade Commission is in general charged with
assisting in the preparation of (mostly bilateral) member
trade agreements, in particular with a view to realizing the
consequences of agreements on production specialization. However, it also advises on trade with the west, especially the
"anti-imperialist" areas. More specifically, the Commission
has been concerned with such items as these: the working out
of a "general trade contract" to serve as a legal basis for
all yearly and long-term intra-bloc trade agreements (with exact specifications about quantities, qualities, assortments,
delivery and payment conditions, and the conditions for assembly and servicing of machinery and equipment), creation of a
uniform methodology for long-term trade planning to 1980, including a commodity classification, simplification and standardization of commercial techniques, multilateral clearing,
and uniform principles of price determination.

The Machine-Building Commission has vigorously promoted
the introduction of new technological processes, automation,
mechanization, and standardization, and has been responsible
for the fact that research coordination and production specialization has been carried further in this than any other field.
It has closely cooperated with other Commissions so far as
their field of competence was involved, e.g., with the Agriculture and Chemicals Commissions in the case of specialization of agricultural and chemical machinery.

The Non-ferrous Metals Commission has investigated the
possibilities of increasing the supply, improving the quality
of, and decreasing the needs for such metals, promoted the production of rare and absolutely pure metals, and has arranged
the exchange of information on the melting and casting of aluminum and its alloys.

Finally, the Oil and Gas Commission has been primarily
concerned with the planning and construction of a pipe line,
discussed below, and the construction of chemical plants on
the basis of oil. It has engaged in large-scale geological
prospecting activity, discovering substantial resources in
Hungary and Poland. This concludes the summary discussion of
the work of the first Standing Commissions.

With the exception of Bulgaria, all member nations of
CMEA announced five year plans "attuned to" the plans of other nations by the middle of 1956. But the political turmoil
late that year in Hungary and Poland completely upset all
previous coordination plans. The Soviet, East German, and
Hungarian 1956-60 Five-Year-Plans were broken off, the Polish and Czech ones completely revised. Poland increased
output for consumption at the expense of investment. Prices
and deliveries in foreign trade within the bloc were changed,
e.g., Polish coal deliveries to East Germany were greatly reduced, the price of Polish coal considerably raised. Most
countries did not fulfill their 1956 plans. (Four of six blast
furnaces at Stalinstadt, East Germany's steel center, were
idle for some time because of lack of coal.) In addition,
East bloc critics held that the Berlin Plenum had taken no
cognizance of changes that had occurred in recent years and
that the protocol on the distribution of production of machines
had no scientifically founded basis for specialization decisions, anyway.

Many observers have characterized the Eighth Plenum
(in Warsaw, from June 18-22, 1957) as a turning point, where
stock was taken of the first faltering step towards production
coordination in the past and hopes were voiced for something
better in the future. As the official communiqué admitted,
members had changed their economic plans, and the Council had
to adjust accordingly its Berlin recommendations as to the vol-

ume of production, exports, and imports for the remaining 1957-
60 period. It was held to be more effective to eliminate many
of the details of the previous agreements (which promptly
caused complaints at the lower levels of government about "too
rough specifications as to production coordination") and to
concentrate on basic issues, e.g., the bottlenecks in raw material supplies, especially in coal, oil, oil-products, metallurgical coke, iron ore, and non-ferrous metals. These had
been existing for quite some time and were discussed at earlier meetings. East Germany had, since the last Plenum, and according to its recommendations, signed an agreement with Poland (on 4-17-1957). She promised therein to assist in the
development of Polish lignite deposits at Tarossow on the
Neisse River by sending technical documentations and 400 million rubles worth of mining equipment and consumer goods.
The equipment was to be produced with Polish deliveries of
sheet metal, pipes, castings, forms, and wrought ironware.
East German credits were to be repaid in coal from 1965 on,
when the new mines were scheduled to yield 35 million tons of
lignite annually. The Plenum now asked other countries to make
credits available to Poland for the same purpose. Czechoslovakia later did so. It also considered transportation problems,
and the members agreed on a treaty for a multilateral clearing organization.[23]

Viewing the future, the Eighth Plenum decided to work out
and coordinate long-range plans for important branches of the
economy until 1960 and later until 1975. Subsequently, from
September 27-29, 1957, the chairmen of the member countries'
Planning Commissions took up the details at a conference in
Prague. They decided to follow the same procedures for the coordination of the 15-year (1961-75) plans as they had in attuning the 5-year (1956-60) plans, with each country drawing up a
plan and submitting it to the Council rather than having one

central plan made by the Council. A unified plan for the
whole camp does not exist to this day (mid-1965).

Most Communist writers draw a line at this point in time,
admitting that not much had been really accomplished in the
way of production coordination when the year 1958 arrived.
Though there were dissenting voices, a conference of Soviet
bloc economists (at Liblice, Č.S.S.R., from December 12-14,
1957) clearly mirrored this kind of appraisal. The Czech
economist Kaigl, expressed the general dissatisfaction with
the state of affairs when he reported on the many differences
of opinion on pricing in socialist trade, and when he criticized plan coordination as an afterthought, following the
drafting in isolation of national development plans, multilateral clearing being hardly in existence, and economic considerations being generally put last after technical and political ones.

A study of the trade structure of the Communist countries,
as well as the observation of their persistent investment into
industries in which they apparently had a relative disadvantage also fail to confirm any accomplishments at this time.
This can be even shown for the field of machinery, where, according to official sources, the only significant production
coordination prior to 1958 has taken place. Siluyanov, who
complained about the persistence of the extremely wide nomenclature in machinery production and continued parallel production of machines and equipment, gives most of the following data which speak for themselves:[24] In 1957, the European
Communist countries produced over 70,000 cutting machine tools,
but less than 5 per cent (3,412) entered foreign trade at all,
and of these 3,060 were imported by the Soviet Union. The
same countries in the same year produced 24,000 units of forging and pressing equipment, less than 3 per cent (662) were
traded; they produced about 37,000 tractors, but only 5,380

were shipped abroad.

Many recent Communist accounts put the beginning of production coordination in 1958. Under the circumstances this is not surprising. Even if accomplishments up to then had been negligible, however, the idea of deeper international economic ties had firmly taken root.

This became particularly obvious at the Moscow Conference of Communist and Workers' Parties of socialist countries (November 14-16, 1957). It was primarily concerned with the question of economic competition between the socialist and capitalist world.[25] This was to secure at the same time peaceful coexistence and acceleration of the process of world-wide socialist revolution. The conference clearly saw two possibilities to achieve these goals: 1) the building of a heavy industrial base in each Communist country through large investments assured by central planning ("operation of the law of planned proportional development"), and 2) the deepening of a socialist division of labor without neglecting the first requirement above. The conference thusly laid down a principle which has shaped CMEA policy to the present. It involves the Communist conviction that "to strengthen the dictatorship of the proletariat," there must be in each country a quantitative increase and qualitative improvement in the industrial labor force. If this is done, while devoting a considerable share of the country's resources to the production of investment goods, the resultant increase in productivity will assure rapid increases in living standards and the eventual equalization among countries of levels of economic development. This process can be accelerated, if in addition (but never instead) countries specialize in accordance with comparative advantage in production or in order to reap economies of scale. In connection with these principles, a prophesy of Lenin is frequently cited.

> The different nations, after leaving the capitalist
> system, go through a phase in which the sovereignty of

the countries is consolidated, all peculiar national fea-
tures are fully developed. This is especially true for
economically weak countries. [This] process. . . coincides with the economic period in which the countries are
building a complex economy.

Later on, the individual countries approach each other more and more and the national boundaries begin to hin-
der a faster development of productive forces. That is,
in the course of development of the building of socialism, the frontiers among the individual countries in the
economic realm disappear.[26]

CMEA attempts at integration are thusly regarded as first
steps towards the withering of economic frontiers, but the complex economic development of each member country has at the
present first priority. In short, there is neither complete
national autarky, nor complete disregard of national frontiers
with resource allocation according to bloc-wide economic plans.

It is interesting to compare at this point the 1958 listing of CMEA's purposes with that of its founding days nine
years earlier. They were given as follows:[27]

1.   Coordination of national economic plans for five as
well as fifteen year periods. . . by specialization and
cooperation in production. . .,

2-4. cooperation to promote trade. . ., the development
of transport and transit facilities. . ., a clearing
system,

5.   development of economic and scientific-technical cooperation to standardize production, exchange technical
information, and carry out joint industrial construction
projects.

The first and dominant purpose was new. We shall now consider
how far this idea has been put into reality since.

3.   Coordinating Production and Investments:

1958-65, the "Decisive Step Forward"

During 1958, three important events took place. Two plenary sessions were preceded in May (20-23) by a meeting, again

in Moscow, of representatives of the Communist and Workers'
Parties of the member countries. They demanded that all future economic cooperation among socialist countries be based
"most solidly" on a socialist international division of labor.
Specifically, they ordered the Council to 1) step up the production of energy and raw materials, 2) deepen the specialization and cooperation in production, particularly in such
fields as machinery, chemicals, metallurgy, and 3) improve
the work of its organs. The latter provision might have been
concerned with price policies to be followed in trading. It
also involved the request to work out in detail the theoretical principles of the socialist international division of labor. The representatives demanded that the "relation of complex development of the national economy of the individual
countries with their international specialization"[28] be investigated. The conferees pointed out emphatically that a rational specialization of production among socialist states is
an essential prerequisite for the maximum utilization of the
advantages of the socialist world economic system. Apart
from these general directives, the Party Conference set specific guide lines for the next two Plenums.

The Ninth Plenum was held from June 26-30, 1958, in Bucharest. Dutifully it set out to realize in the "most determined
spirit" the international socialist division of labor. First
there was self-criticism: not enough attention had been paid
in the past to the problem of developing the important raw material sectors of the economies of the People's Democracies.
The raw material industries and power production remained behind the growing needs of the processing industries, especially machine building. As a result, joint construction of lead
and zinc mines in Bulgaria, coal and sulfur mines in Poland,
and of cellulose plants in Bulgaria and Rumania were to be undertaken.

While earlier doubts as to the capabilities of the partners had been decried as "unwarranted arrogance," it was now
admitted that countries which agreed to specialize found themselves unable to supply other countries counting on them.[18]
The Council made recommendations for specialization in the
production of industrial equipment for the chemicals and metallurgical industries, and for the development of standard factories for those industrial sectors in which more than one
country was to specialize. It asked member governments to begin bilateral negotiations about the most important exports
and imports from 1961-65.[29] Similar bilateral treaties had
been made ·after earlier Plenums for earlier periods. This
time, however, price formation rules were given by CMEA.

Finally, CMEA decided on the formation of three more
Standing Commissions, bringing the total number up to twelve.

The Construction Industry Commission has worked in three
areas, a) the organization and mechanization of the industry,
involving questions of pricing, of costs, of the industrialization of the building process, cooperative designing of projects, and the agreement, in 1960, on a standardized series of
construction machines (the types of excavators were reduced
from 27 to 8, turret cranes from 40 to 9) and specialization
in their production, b) the short and long run outlook as to
the supply of and demand for building materials. This led, in
1960, to joint efforts for establishing a building materials
industry in Albania, and, in 1962, to general investment coordination for 1963/64. It also resulted in efforts to produce new building materials on a chemical basis, e.g., plastics,
c) specific problems, such as international area planning (the
first project involved, in 1960, the Gorny-Slask region in Poland and Ostrava in Czechoslovakia, and led to agreement on
methodological rules for border region planning), agricultural
construction (buildings for cattle, pigs, and fowl with use of

local building materials, 1960, uniform norms for such buildings as to physical properties, fire protection, and use of
prefabricated reinforced concrete, 1961), residential construction (including questions of sanitation), 1961, construction of
oil refineries, 1963.

The Economic Problems Commission was staffed with academic economists and leading economic functionaries and planning
specialists. These were to develop the theoretical basis for
the international division of labor (and indices describing
its state and calculating its gain), which the Communists themselves admitted to be still very inadequate. A report from an
international seminar held late in 1958 in East Germany, e.g.,
stated "that the problem of the international division of labor is neither completely solved in the theory of political
economy nor in the theory and practice of foreign trade."[30]
Further, the Commission was to develop comparable indices for
production and the distribution of national income, indices of
production costs, and a methodology for comparing the economic
effectiveness of investments. In 1961, the Commission agreed
on such a system for a specific number of products.

It certainly speaks for an unbelievable underestimation
in the past of the theoretical problems involved, when such
questions were being taken up only in late 1960, six years after the first attempts were made "to lift economic cooperation
among the Communist countries onto a higher level."[31]

The Transportation Commission has coordinated long term
CMEA development plans in its sector. This involved (in 1959)
an analysis of transport needs until 1965 as to total volume
and direction, as well as (on the basis of long term development plans and trade agreements) to individual commodities and
types of carrier.[32] From a balancing of needs with supply, investment plans were coordinated for 1964/65. At the same time,
the Commission has proposed uniform comparable indices for the

planning, reporting, and analyzing of transportation.

All the major means of transport (of passengers as well as freight) have at some time been under investigation. In the case of ocean transport, this took the form via a Central Socialist Freight Bureau of coordinating export and import sea routes, of combining parallel lines, of introducing uniform freight rates, and agreeing on the mutual use of harbors. Further plans included standardization of ship types, common repair service, and the establishment of regular joint lines, often in cooperation with "anti-imperialist nations." East Germany, for instance, reported in 1964 to be operating joint lines to Cuba (partners Cuba, Č.S.S.R., Poland), Finland (since 1955), India, Kenia, the United Arab Republic (since 1958), the U.S.S.R. (since 1958), and West Africa (partner Poland). The Soviet Union, Poland and Czechoslovakia were operating a joint line to the Levant.

The Commission also decided originally to build up Szczecin and Rostock (besides Leningrad) as major ports, making unnecessary, for instance, the use of Hamburg by Czechoslovakia. This plan included the construction of a major north-south canal from the Elbe to Rostock. After Polish objections, however, only Szczecin was scheduled to become a "world harbor," with Rostock being expanded only for East German needs.[33]

A second major concern has been the railroads. Ever since 1959, the Commission has been working on the enlargement of railroad capacity, railroad electrification or the introduction of diesel locomotives, and the modernization and mechanization of constructing, maintaining, and utilizing railroads. The latter point involves, for instance, the use of automatic signalling equipment and mechanized construction and loading. The important directions (Soviet Union - Poland - East Germany) have received concentrated attention as to the construction of lines, faster border crossings, and mutual

use of freight cars. Eventually an international system of
railroads serviced by electro and diesel locomotives is to be
created, the first portion of which (Warsaw - Prague) is
scheduled for operation by 1965. Single frontier stations
with joint customs and passport control have already been put
into operation between Poland - Czechoslovakia, Czechoslovakia -
Hungary, Hungary - Rumania, and Rumania - Bulgaria. The Polish - East German border is to be next in line.

Much less attention has been paid to inland waterways,
air transport, and highways. In 1963, a nomenclature for high-
way construction and maintenance machinery was worked out (in
addition to technical norms for other machinery and carriers).
A long-run goal is the construction of an international network of standardized highways, including the appropriate system of service areas. In 1965, the Commission recommended the
production of only 25 types of standardized river craft, during 1966-70. It established two categories. One is to service the rivers Vistula, Oder, and Elbe, the canals in the
G.D.R., the Bydgoszcz system, and the Kaliningrad-Magdeburg
waterway. It is to consist of 12 types of vessels: 3 dry car-
go ships, four barges, four tugs, one tanker. The second category, with special design to sail very high up the river, is
to service the Danube.

At times, other specific problems are also discussed by
the Commission, as the avoidance of transportation through creation of productive capacities at the site of raw materials;
transportation via pipe line (1959); or the packaging of per-
ishable commodities (1961), to name just a few.

The third major occurrence in 1958 was the _Tenth Plenum_
from December 11-13, in Prague. It considered measures for
specialization and cooperation of production in the chemical
and ferrous-metals industries. So far as the latter is con-

cerned, it proposed specialization until 1965 in the production of iron and steel pipes and certain rolling mill products
(e.g., rolled sheets). This proposal took into account the
construction plans for new rolling mills so as to get the most
rational distribution of investments in this area and hence
the greatest usefulness in terms of low costs and high quality,
it was reported.

Similarly, a report by the Chemicals Commission was under
discussion. It was decided to set up basic chemicals production (sulfuric acid, chlorine, ammonia, plastics, synthetic
rubber, synthetic resins, synthetic fibers, and nitrogenous
and phosphorous fertilizers) everywhere, except in Albania.
Specialization and cooperation were agreed upon, in addition,
for special types of products until at least 1965. Synthetic
rubber, for example, was to be produced on the basis of natural gas and the gas which is a by-product of oil refining,
but different countries were to produce different qualities
(say, bytyl or nitryl rubber) depending on their resources, capacities, and labor force skills. Potassium salts were to be
produced only by the countries having the largest deposits,
and the production of varnishes, paints, washing materials,
and cellulose was divided. Research tasks were also allocated, e.g., on tire factories to the Soviet Union, on assembly
line installations to East Germany, on foam rubber to Poland.

Having the future development of the chemical industries
in mind, the members agreed on the construction of an oil
pipe line from the Soviet Union to various other Communist
countries. A first portion was to go from the Volga-Ural area
(Oktyabrski, Tuimasy, Kuibyshev) to Mosyr (via Sysran, Pensa,
Bryansk). There it was to split into a northern arm to Poland
and East Germany (via Pinsk and Brest) and a southern one to
Hungary and Czechoslovakia (via Brody, Lvov, Ushgorod). Completion of the 4,500 km underground line and its twenty pump-

ing stations was originally scheduled for after 1962. Each country was to build and own the portion going over its territory (Soviet Union: inception to Mosyr ≈ 1,600 km; Mosyr to Brest 457 km, Mosyr to Ushgorod: ≈ 962 km; Poland: 675 km; East Germany: 27 km; Czechoslovakia: 400 km; Hungary: 138 km). Giant petro-chemical centers were planned by Poland in Plock, by East Germany in Schwedt-on-the-Oder, by Czechoslovakia in Bratislava, and by Hungary in Szazhalombatta, south of Budapest. Even after completion of the line, however, oil deliveries through it were to be only 64 per cent of all deliveries from the Soviet Union. More oil was to be shipped to East Germany, for instance, via Soviet-built tankers and an oil harbor to be erected at Rostock (holding in fact 100,000 cubic meters on 10-1-1964).

A treaty between the five countries in accord with these decisions was signed on December 18 and 19, 1959, and construction was started immediately at the Czech-Soviet border. Specialists from the participating countries were trained at Ufa and Kuibyshev by the U.S.S.R., equipment was provided by all partners.[34] Completion of the line proceeded as planned. On February 3, 1962, the first Soviet oil entered Czechoslovakia, (reaching Bratislava on February 22). Eight months later, on September 17, 1962, Soviet oil entered Hungary; about a year after that, on November 7, 1963, oil arrived in Poland; and on December 18, 1963, it was being pumped into the East German section of the line. Therewith the construction of the line, named "Friendship," was completed.[35] (The East Germans anticipated and carried out an April 1, 1964, opening of the first experimental stage of the Schwedt refinery. Permanent operations began on July 1, 1964. It was planned to refine 1.2 million tons of crude oil by year's end. A treaty of April 14, 1964, provided in the meantime, for an extension of the line from Schwedt to Leuna, construction to be carried out by Polish

specialists. They began work in March, 1965, and were scheduled to complete it in two and one half years.) Within the
U.S.S.R., another 450 km extension had been built by 1965 from
Bryansk to Polozk, later to be extended by 550 km to the Lat-
vian harbor of Ventspils. Leading economic officials in the
bloc praised repeatedly the tremendous saving of costs made
possible by the pipeline project.[36]

As a further result of the Tenth Plenum, a Food and Light
Industries Commission constituted itself in April, 1959. It
has concentrated on the coordination to 1965 (and later to
1980) of research and production in the textile, shoe, leather, and food industries. Research efforts were coordinated
concerning cotton, wool, silk, knitwear, artificial fibers,
and food. Quality indices were established for rawhides, semi-
finished leather goods, shoes, cotton, and sugar. There were
discussions on the use of capacities, the reconstruction and
new construction of plants, the structure of raw materials
used, the exchange of samples and models, and the development
of the canning industry. In 1961, the Commission decided to
take measures for improving bloc fashion "aesthetically and
artfully."

The Eleventh Plenum in Tirana from May 13-16, 1959, put
special emphasis on 1961-65 production coordination plans.
CMEA approved specialization proposals for 245 machinery products. These involved equipment for mining (as multi-bucket
excavators), rolling and drawing mills, the oil industry, and
the chemicals industry; coal and rock loading machines; and
certain machine tools used in the production of ball-bearings
and roller-bearings. Of the latter the types produced were
reduced from 227 to 117, with 40 machine types assigned to
East Germany, 10 to Czechoslovakia, 12 to Poland, and 55 to
the Soviet Union.

The raw material and power problems were taken up again.

Measures were taken to increase coke production in order to
counter the persistent shortages of coke experienced in the
past years by the chemicals and ferrous metals industries. A
beginning was made to implement the high tension electricity
network idea of long standing discussed at the Seventh Plenum.

The Twelfth Plenum met in Sofia (December 10-14, 1959).
The members accepted a "Council Statute" and a "Convention on
Endowment with Legal Personality, Privileges, and Immunities"
of the Council. After ratification in the various countries,
these agreements went into effect on April 13, 1960.

Further specialization and cooperation decisions were
made, such as in oil extraction, the ferrous and non-ferrous
metals industries, for 141 units of equipment used in the chemicals industry (including types never produced before), and
for equipment of the sugar (32 items), meat (19 items), and
paper processing industries (14 items). All in all, 206 more
products of the machine building industries were assigned for
specialization. It was reported that now half of the most important groups and types of chemical industry equipment and 85
per cent of paper industry machines had been so assigned up
till 1965.

CMEA also dealt with questions of increasing iron and
steel output, of transportation of an ever growing volume of
trade, and of increasing agricultural output, especially of
wool, vegetable oil, fruits, and vegetables. It considered
cooperating in the areas of veterinary science and plant protection.

The bilateral treaties for the 1961-65 period which were
to embody the latest Council decisions were being signed at
about this time. Interestingly, an East German writer billed
the German-Russian treaty of November 21, 1959, as the "first
one" incorporating to a large degree the results of previous
long range coordination of production.[37] The Polish Foreign

Trade Minister said exactly the same thing about the Polish-
German treaty.[38]

This confirms once more what a hard road it is to travel
from national autarky to a true international division of labor on the grand scale envisioned by the CMEA members. The
longest part of the road still had to be traveled. By the end
of 1959, there was still a very wide range of products in the
machinery, light, and food industries untouched by agreements
on specialization. There was hardly any specialization in the
consumer goods sector. The only progress since 1958 was made
in the machinery and chemical industries. By early 1960, specialization had been decided for about 1,100 machinery items
and more than 500 products of the chemicals industry, covering
over 80 per cent of the member countries' chemical gross production. The parallel production of 31 machinery items had
been discontinued. East Germany was involved in the production
of 644 of the 1,100 items mentioned above.

The Thirteenth Plenum convened at Budapest from July 26-
30, 1960. The assembly decided to work out economic development plans for the 1965-80 period (as had been suggested by a
February, 1960, Conference of Communist Parties in Moscow).
It stressed the need for increased agricultural production in
the entire bloc and discussed the development for this purpose
of better agricultural chemicals and machinery.

A fourteenth Standing Commission for Peaceful Uses of
Atomic Energy (Moscow) was created. It constituted itself in
Moscow in October, 1960, and has since examined questions concerning nuclear instrument making and the production of iso-
topes and safety equipment. It set up working groups on reactors and the atomic power industry. The Soviet Union, in 1965,
supported a Hungarian proposal to build a large atomic power
station by the joint efforts of CMEA countries. As mentioned
above, the U.S.S.R. earlier has been collaborating in the

building of atomic power stations. Constructed were a 150,000
kw power station with a gas-cooled natural uranium and heavy-
water reactor in the Č.S.S.R. and a 70,000 kw power station
with an enriched uranium reactor and ordinary water as a mod-
erating and heat-transfer agent in East Germany.

New specialization decisions were made for equipment of
the energy industry (bringing the portion of production specialized to 85 per cent); the oil refining industry; the metallurgical industry; the building materials industry, especially for chemically produced building materials, such as
plastics; and of the dairy and cannery branches of the food
industry (number of equipment types reduced from 94 to 49 and
108 to 71, respectively).

Further, the need for a substantial improvement in the
quality of production in all CMEA countries was announced.

Later in the same year (November, 1960), eighty-one
Communist and Workers' Parties met at a Moscow Conference.
They reiterated their long-run goal of achieving the defeat
of capitalism "in the decisive sphere of human activity, the
sphere of material production." They continued to seek the
development of the socialist world economy via scientific-
technical cooperation and better coordination of long-term
economic plans incorporating the division of labor principles.

The Fourteenth Plenum met in Berlin from February 28 to
March 3, 1961. It pledged to "create the material-technical
basis for an abundance of products." Specifically, it dealt
with the chemical industry, transport, standardization, and
the question of increasing agricultural output. In this connection specialization decisions were made for agricultural
products, as well as for agricultural machinery and chemicals
used in agriculture. The Assembly also discussed theoretical
principles which could guide the international socialist division of labor until 1980.

The Fifteenth Plenum convened in Warsaw from December 12-
15, 1961. It was concerned partly with a general review of
CMEA's achievements, and noted past successes in developing
the bloc's raw material basis, in building the oil pipeline
and electric energy grid, in coordinating output plans to 1965
and main control figures even to 1980.

Members of this Plenum also signed a treaty concerning
the technical supervision and classification of ocean-going
vessels. At the same time, there was agreement to decrease
the types of merchant ships from 50 to 16 and of fishing vessels from 41 to 19 to pave the way for mass production and better capacity utilization. Transport questions via rail and inland waterways were also taken up.

The most important outcome of the fifteenth Plenum, however, was the approval of the draft of the "basic principles
of the international socialist division of labor." Herein it
completed the work of the previous plenum and fulfilled a di-
rective issued by the Moscow Parties' Conference of May,
1958.[39]

Another Conference of Communist and Workers' Parties of
CMEA nations convened in Moscow on June 6 and 7, 1962. With
the noticeable exception of Albania which sent no delegation
at all, all member countries were represented by the first secretaries of the parties' central committees and their government chiefs. The Conference was concerned with three issues:
1)   the historic task of the socialist world, i.e., "the creation of the material-technical basis of Communism." The
meeting expressed the hope that construction of socialism
could be completed in all socialist countries in such a way
that all could proceed to Communism at about the same time.
The socialist countries' rate of economic growth was pictured
as leading in the world. It was claimed that they now produced
37 per cent of world industrial production and would "soon"

overtake capitalism in the absolute level of production,

2)   the basic principles of the international socialist division of labor, as announced by the fifteenth Plenum. They
were approved, and their use for long range economic cooperation was urged,

3)   the necessity for an increase in the role, authority, and
responsibility of CMEA. In particular, the conferees seem to
have been concerned with "the still imperfect" production specialization in machinery and equipment, with the coordination
of the most important investments in the basic and manufactur-
ing industries to be begun in the near future,[40] and with a
then unspecified organizational change of CMEA.

The simultaneous meeting of the Sixteenth (Extraordinary)
Plenum in Moscow on June 7, 1962, immediately dealt with the
strengthening of CMEA's organizational structure. First, it
approved a change in the Statute, allowing non-European countries to become members. At the same time, Outer Mongolia was
admitted to membership. This undoubtedly was a gesture out-
lining the Soviet Union's sphere of influence as against
China. (Albania, China's new found ideological ally in Europe,
ignored this CMEA meeting.) Second, the Plenum voted the establishment of an Executive Committee, consisting of the deputies of CMEA chiefs of government. This, presumably, meant
the abolition of the old Deputies' Council. The new Committee
was given powers equal to the Plenum. It can make decisions
and recommendations between regular plenary sessions on all
questions of economic cooperation. Third, a Bureau for Comprehensive Questions of Economic Planning was formed. The
Deputy Chairmen of the member countries' Planning Commissions
were to work in it. Fourth, the plenum decided that plenary
recommendations as to production specialization must be followed by appropriate agreements or treaties within three
months. Fifth, three new Standing Commissions were created,

viz., for the Coordination of Scientific and Technical Research
(Moscow); for Standardization (Berlin); and for Statistics
(Moscow).

The Coordination of Scientific and Technical Research
Commission convened for its first meeting in July, 1962. By
late 1963, it agreed on a unified research plan for 1964/65.
The themes approved as part of this plan included a) production and use of plastics, b) the chemistry of artificial fertilizers, pest killers, animal feeding (including application),
c) scientific bases for automatic guidance technology to promote automation, d) the physics of solids and scientific
foundations of industrial electronics, e) industrial methods
of fiber production, f) improvement in the technology of steel
melting and measures against metal corrosion, g) organization
of development and construction of unique types of equipment
and apparatus for scientific research, h) protection of waters
and air space from pollution, i) photosynthesis, j) scientific
bases for guiding and organizing production and labor, k) complex mechanization of loading and storage work in industry and
transport. This plan was worked out by 500 scientists and
contained more than 1,100 individual tasks. In addition, the
Commission has been concerned with questions of the finance
and use of collective research results, patents, licensing,
and trade marks.

The Standardization Commission was created simultaneously
with a CMEA Institute for Standardization, but the latter did
not take up work until February, 1964, in Moscow. This was
the culmination of attempts, ever since 1956, to end the efforts by individual nations to create standardization within
their borders only. The lateness of this success (on at least
the organizational level) was explained by the need of overcoming ideological difficulties.

Some engineers and technicians were clinging, in
spite of the emerging new socialist conditions of production, still to habits and practices stemming from their
activity under capitalism. In the case of new construc-
tions, some of them tended not to use parts for machines
and factories which had already stood the test of time,
were being produced in current production, fulfilled all
requirements, and could be produced without difficulties
and reorganization in production. They changed measure-
ments in order to give to the construction in every respect their "personal touch."[41]

The resulting hodge-podge of products caused particular
difficulties in foreign trade.

The Marxist-Leninist parties, therefore, began to
attack the conceptions stemming from capitalism which
were the ideological roots for these problems and constituted a hindrance for the necessary tempo of deepening
the socialist international division of labor.[41]

In general, it has been the hope of CMEA planners to eliminate the great multitude of types produced of almost all products in all member countries, because they were being produced in too small quantities, given modern technical know-
how. Standardization was to be the basis for specialization,
optimum production series, and international exchange on a
large scale. By the end of 1964 (including the period prior
to the Commission's existence), CMEA had agreed in about 200
instances on the unification of national standards in machinery, metallurgy (including castings, weldings, iron ore, steel
types), the electro-technical (electronic tubes, transformers),
and paper industries. In 1965, it was to consider 400 themes,
including chemical and mechanical steel testing methods.

The Statistics Commission first convened in August, 1962.
It was primarily concerned with the creation of uniformity in
the member countries' statistics (e.g., with respect to statistical and plan indices, units of measurement, nomenclatures, and classifications) and with the improvement of the
quality of statistical methods and analyses.[42] For each indi-

vidual task the Central Statistical Administration of one particular country was to be in charge. Specifically, the following areas of statistics were to be dealt with in this way
in 1962: labor force data, data on the development and effectiveness of international specialization and cooperation in
industrial production, beginning with 17 indices for the machinery industry (East Germany in charge), data on social
consumption, sampling methods in national income accounting,
and input-output analysis. In 1963, this work was to be extended to questions of mechanization of statistical reporting,
data on education, culture, health and welfare, and on new
technology. The Commission also promised to accelerate work
on the comparability of indices needed for plan coordination.
In particular, and in addition to the above, work was to be
done to create uniform indices characterizing the level and
rate of growth of the economy; the material and cultural standard of life of the population (70 indices on education, health,
physical fitness, etc.), and natural population movement
(births, mortality, growth, marriages, causes of death); and
there was to be uniformity in census taking. East German
tasks now reportedly also included the creation of a uniform
product nomenclature for industry and agriculture, covering
1,800 products, and of comparable indices for size, growth,
and utilization of capacity in industry and construction as
a basis for investment planning. In 1964, work was being done
to unify transport and internal trade statistics and to pre-
pare for intensive 1965-67 work on statistical methods (material balancing, etc.).

The new CMEA Executive Committee held its first meeting
in Moscow on July 10-12, 1962. The deputy chiefs of government of all members but Albania participated. A work plan
was set up to include concrete measures for the coordination
of national economic plans, production specialization, and an

increase in foreign trade and scientific cooperation. The
Committee approved principles of international specialization
and cooperation in machine building and promised increased
specialization in this field.

The second meeting followed from September 25-28, 1962,
again in Moscow, and again ignored by Albania. It primarily
dealt with the coordination of long-term plans and specialization problems presented to it by the Standing Commissions,
eleven of which had met recently. Specifically, the coordinated control figures for the next five year period, including most important investments, were further elaborated. A
decision was made to increase and deepen the cooperation in
the foreign-exchange and financial sphere. Reports of the agriculture, machine building, and chemicals commission were
discussed. As a result, agreement was reached about covering
the demand for seed potatoes (previously supplied by Albania),
and about the production of new machines. Furthermore, decisions were made concerning an improvement in the ability to
let through international railroads and about increased utilization of CMEA's pool of freight cars. Finally, the statutes
of the three new standing commissions, established by the sixteenth plenum, were approved.

From December 14-20, 1962, the Seventeenth Plenum convened in Bucharest. It noted that Albania had now officially
confirmed its lack of interest in the organization which had
been obvious since late 1961. The Plenum then proceeded to
discuss the deepening and enlarging of plan coordination to
1965 (and beyond to 1980) in several major fields, together
with :
a)   the fastest possible development of the raw material,
fuel, and energy basis and its most economical use (1980 coal
output, for instance, was to be double that of 1960. The opening of the Prague electric energy dispatcher administration

was announced as imminent, and the accelerated completion of
the pipeline project was urged),

b)   an increase in steel production, especially of high quality and electro-steels,

c)   an increase in the output of plastics, synthetic rubber,
chemical fibers, and mineral fertilizers, and

d)   an increase in agricultural output. (The past record was
praised, in particular that of the last three years, which had
brought to CMEA 736,000 new tractors, a third increase in artificial fertilizer output, and an increase in the exports of
vegetables and grapes fourfold in Rumania, and sixfold in Bulgaria. The Plenum recommeded further specialization for artificial fertilizers, pest killers, seeds, and agricultural
machines, especially for melioration purposes.)

Finally, the Plenum established a new Standing Commission
for Foreign Exchange and Finance, which first convened from
February 11-12, 1963, and, in subsequent meetings, has dealt
primarily with multilateral clearing.

Concurrently with the Plenum, the Executive Committee
held its third meeting in Bucharest from December 16-20, 1962.
Its agenda consisted of four entries:

a)   measures to accelerate specialization, especially in machine building, in the period to 1965,

b)   drafting a treaty on the creation of a common CMEA pool
of 100,000 railroad freight cars (which went into effect on
July 1, 1964)[43] as well as coordinating the use of ocean
freighters,

c)   the introduction in CMEA trade of a system of multilateral clearing and the creation of a Bank of Socialist Countries.
(It was later reported by P.T. Nosko, head of the foreign-exchange department of the U.S.S.R. State Bank, that this new
Bank would handle the multilateral clearing operations in a
manner not yet decided and to be decided by the new Foreign Ex-

change and Finance Commission.[44] He conjectured that probably
a common currency would be used for such clearing, which would
be able to overcome the limits to trade imposed by bilateral-
ism. A second major purpose of the Bank was to be investment
plan coordination and the granting of credits for large joint
CMEA projects. These credits were to be given from deposits
and the Bank's own funds. The Bank would also have relations
with non-socialist countries.)

d)   discussion of current treaty prices in CMEA trade. It
was held that the principles of price determination agreed upon in June, 1958, had led to stable, mutually profitable
trade. However, thorough-going correction of these prices for
economic reasons was recommended on a large scale, using average 1957-61 world market prices as a basis.

The fourth meeting of the Executive Committee returned to
Moscow from February 15-21, 1963. It took up questions of cooperation among economic branches and organizational and legal
matters. In a meeting with Premier Khrushchev, the CMEA fuel
and energy balance to 1980 was discussed. It was urged to
unite the efforts of geological institutions so as to improve
their research into the interior of the earth and to establish
uniform rules for calculating the stock of natural resources.
Further discussion dealt with establishing uniform methods in
the member countries in planning measures against water pollution. Finally, 1963 specialization was considered.[45]

The fifth meeting in Moscow lasted from April 17-25, 1963.
It dealt with the development of the chemicals industry and
the specialization of cutting machine tools and packaging machinery. The supply of clover seed to 1970 was discussed.
Further debate was concerned with the coordination of statistics and of investments for 1964/65. The Committee agreed upon the order and dates for 1966-70 development plan coordination. Finally it drafted a multilateral clearing treaty and

a statute for the new bank.

Only vague reports about the sixth meeting (Warsaw, May 10-13, 1963) are available. They list as topics under discussion plan coordination, production specialization and cooperation, research coordination, agriculture, and foreign trade.

The seventh meeting of the Executive Committee was held in Moscow from July 3-5, 1963. It approved machinery specialization, involving complete technological sets for crude oil refining, electronics, the textile industry, construction and road building machinery, equipment for the cable industry, high voltage cables, and enclosed arc furnaces. Further discussion centered upon oil and gas prospecting in Europe and a Mongolian request for long-range geological cooperation. Bilateral negotiations on the latter point were urged.

Also in Moscow, and in the same month (July 24-26, 1963), the Eighteenth Plenum assembled. It recommended bilateral negotiations to take place between the various State Planning Commissions concerning cooperation to 1970. Such consultations subsequently (March, 1964) occurred, e.g., between East Germany and Bulgaria and East Germany and Czechoslovakia. A further concern was the establishment of two new Standing Commissions, for Geology (Ulan Bator) and the Radio-Technical and Electronics Industry (Budapest). At the same time, the old Food and Light Industries Commission, established at the tenth Plenum, was split in two, for Light Industry (Prague) and Food (Sofia).

The Geology Commission discussed the state of geological research in Outer Mongolia and the coordination of prospecting activities for the 1966-70 period. It also arranged the exchange of information on geophysical methods and considered the demand to 1970 of prospecting equipment, a nomenclature for which was worked out.

The Light Industry Commission has promoted cooperation in
the textile, clothing, woodworking, and printing industries.
It has also been concerned with mechanization and automation
in cotton spinning.

The newly created Food Commission held its first meeting
in October, 1963, deciding on the direction of technological
developments in milk processing. In late 1964, it sponsored
a conference of fishing experts at Klaipeda, Lithuania. It
discussed studies of fish stocks in tropical waters of the Atlantic and established fishing quotas and a 1965 program of
scientific research in the Atlantic and in the North, Baltic,
and Black Seas. Also discussed were methods of fish catching
without the use of nets, such as by electric current and light.
The Commission also worked on the design of food industry
plants and the mechanization of labor-intensive processes.

An eighth meeting of the Executive Committee followed
closely on the heels of the Plenum of July 26, 1963. A curt
statement simply announced that the Committee did what was necessary to realize the decisions of the July meeting of First
Party Secretaries and the eighteenth Plenum.

Information on the ninth meeting, however, is more plentiful. It occurred from October 15-22, 1963, in Moscow. The
Committee approved its 1964 work schedule concerning concrete
measures to coordinate the 1966-70 economic development plans.
It dealt with needed output increases of agricultural machinery, rolled steel and pipes, and electronics industry equipment. Finally, on the last day of the meeting, the member
countries signed an agreement (to go into effect on January 1,
1964, pending ratification[46]) on multilateral clearing in
transferable rubles and the founding of an International Bank
for Economic Cooperation, located in Moscow. This was the
bank under discussion at the third Executive Committee meeting in December, 1962. It was reported that the Bank's activ-

ity would be based on recognition of full equality and sovereignty of the CMEA members. Membership was open to other nations agreeing to the Statute. Each member has representatives on a Bank Council, its governing body. The Bank has an
initial capital endowment of 300 million rubles, paid by the
members in either transferable rubles, gold, or freely convertible currencies. The members' contribution is in proportion to their foreign trade volume, but each country has one
vote on the Council, independent of the capital contribution.
Council decisions must be unanimous.[47]

The functions of the Bank were given as operating multilateral clearing in transferable rubles (even with non-mem-
bers), keeping deposits in freely transferable rubles, gold,
and freely convertible currencies, carrying out normal international banking relations, and giving credit for CMEA investment projects. The transferable ruble was defined equal
to .987 412 g of gold and clearly labeled as not convertible
into gold.[48]

The Executive Committee came together for a tenth meeting in Bucharest from December 17-21, 1963. It approved,
first, production specialization for 35 complete technological sets and 6 types of technological equipment in the chemical industry. Secondly, recommendations for specialization
were made, involving measuring devices and equipment for oil
drilling and the food industry. Thirdly, agreement was reached on a concrete work plan for preparing the coordination of
principal national economic branches from 1966-70. Finally,
the committee studied and approved a statement on bloc natural
resource endowment and future geological work to be done. The
European members of CMEA signed the common freight car pool
treaty drafted a year earlier.

The Executive Committee convened in Moscow for its eleventh meeting from February 25-28, 1964. Agreement was reached

on the multilateral coordination of scientific-technical research in 1964/65. The need for uniform standards as a prerequisite for specialization was stressed again. The Committee
considered also questions of foreign trade, in particular participation at a U.N. conference for trade and development to
which CMEA had been invited. (Subsequently a CMEA delegation
went to the Geneva conference in March. Willy Hüttenrauch,
East German Deputy Minister for Foreign and Intra-German Trade,
was deputy delegation chairman.) The Committee also took no-
tice of a meeting among the chairmen of all Standing Commissions and the Secretariat department chiefs concerning 1964-70
coordination plans. (Such a 2 day conference had been reported earlier in February, 1964.)

The twelfth meeting of the Executive Committee occurred
in Moscow from April 21-24, 1964. It coincided with the 15th
anniversary of the first Plenum, and the official communications praised at length and in great detail the successes of
those past years. Beyond that a decision to increase agricultural output was announced. This included measures to improve
soil fertility by "chemifying" agriculture and to mechanize
agricultural production. This involved specifically increased
international cooperation in the production of mineral fertilizers, plant protectives, agricultural machinery, and (for
animal husbandry) of synthetic amino-acids and vitamins. In
another area, machinery specialization was approved for the
1964-70 period in the food, textile, pharmaceutical, electro-
technical, and shipbuilding industries. Finally, a special
request of Outer Mongolia was acted upon. Members were to
provide special aid for developing agricultural production
(e.g., via agricultural research institutes) and for intensifying geological prospecting activity there.

A thirteenth meeting of the Executive Committee was held
in Moscow from July 14-16, 1964. It reviewed past bilateral

consultations on economic cooperation and noted that preliminary decisions had now been made concerning the volume of production and exchange of the most important industrial products
during 1966-70. As usual, this concerned energy, fuels, other
raw materials, chemicals and machinery and had been done via
bilateral negotiations between planning agencies. New decisions were reached on cooperative expansion of coal mining capacities, the meeting of needs for transformer oils from 1966-
70, and an increased exchange of consumer goods.

A special event took place on September 17, 1964, at the
CMEA Secretariat in Moscow. An agreement was signed ending
the long-standing isolation of Yugoslavia from CMEA. In fact
she was admitted as an affiliate whereby CMEA seems to have
adopted a new policy of flexibility. Under the arrangement,
Yugoslavia will participate in some, but not all, organs of
CMEA, as if she were a member. In particular, she will join
the work of the Standing Commissions in the areas of coordination of scientific-technical research, chemicals, ferrous metals, foreign-exchange and finance, foreign trade, machine
building, and non-ferrous metals. She will also be observer
in other organs. This new arrangement is a major concession
to Yugoslavia, given CMEA's past insistence on full membership
(with the obligation to honor all decisions) or none at all.
This may well pave the way for a more flexible policy for members also, making it possible for some not to participate in
projects considered against their national interest without
the need to veto the entire project altogether.

The fourteenth meeting of the Executive Committee convened in Moscow from October 13-16, 1964. It concerned itself
with questions of transport, non-ferrous metallurgy, statistics, patents, and water economy.

The fifteenth meeting was held in Moscow from December
2-3, 1964. It considered problems of transportation, as well

as prices to be used in the long-term trade agreements about
to be concluded.

The Nineteenth Plenum met in Prague from January 28 to
February 2, 1965. Recommendations were adopted on the specialization of production of complete technological lines, units
and separate items of technological equipment for the chemical
industry, for catalytic reforming and hydro-filtering of diesel fuel, for timber machinery, textile equipment, and free-
play ball bearings.

It was noted that Rumania had joined the power grid, a
common fleet of 93,000 railway cars had been set up, and the
joint construction of the Kingisipp phosphorite ore mine and
ore-dressing plant had been completed (with the help of all
members but Rumania and Outer Mongolia).

A sixteenth session of the Executive Committee was held
in Prague from January 29 to February 2, 1965. It examined
the completion and prospects of the Friendship pipeline and
the possibilities of increasing the amount of drilling and
improving techniques and technology of drilling in oil and
gas-bearing layers at depths below 10,000 feet by 1970.

The Committee approved a system of statistical indices
showing the level and pace of development of the national
economies and also a single nomenclature for industrial and
agricultural production.

Production specialization for 1966-70 in the areas of
equipment for chemical, electro-technical, metalworking, and
light industries were approved.

The seventeenth meeting convened in Moscow from April
7-9, 1965. Considered were 1966-70 coordination of scientific-technical research, specialization in machinery, electro-
technical products, and electronics (a conference of experts
in this field to be held in late 1965), and cooperation in
the field of postal communications.

C. A SURVEY OF ALLEGED SPECIALIZATION DECISIONS

The author has collected the following allegations on actual assignments for specialization for individual countries.[49]

Albania

Basic Industries

Non-ferrous metals (e.g., chromium ore, iron-nickel ore)
Oil drilling and processing

Agriculture

Fruits and vegetables (incl. early potatoes)

Bulgaria

Basic Industries

Non-ferrous mining and metallurgy (e.g., sulfur, lead ore,
  zinc ore, copper ore, uranium ore)
Some chemical industry branches (unspecified)
Building materials (e.g., cement)

Metal-Working Industries (By 1964, 130 types of machines had
  been assigned to Bulgaria.)
Heavy machinery (e.g., oil drilling equipment, basic machine tools, such as simple lathes; Bulgaria used to produce 25, is to produce 13, of the 70 standard types of cutting machine tools selected by CMEA for specialization.)
General machinery, e.g.,
  industrial sewing machines
  other light and food industry machinery
  agricultural machinery, such as for vegetable and fruit
    harvesting, esp. vineyard tractors
  rubber-wheeled mowers
  hoisting equipment
  trailer combines, esp. "Dimitrovez 6" (for use in Bulgaria

as well as for export to the bloc and Near East). Bul-
garia <u>ceased</u> production of corn and sugar beet combines.
Vehicles: agreed <u>not</u> to produce large diesel locomotives,
    passenger automobiles, lorries
Shipbuilding (e.g., ships from 1,000-5,000 GRT, esp. 3,000
    GRT freighters, also specialized ships, as electro-ships)
Electro-technical (small in volume, to be based on inten-
    sive use of domestic non-ferrous metals) e.g.,
    electro-carts (mass produced since August, 1964, bloc mo-
        nopoly by 1980), electro-motors, transformers, automa-
        tic telephone equipment, storage batteries, lead acccu-
        mulators

Light Industries

Cellulose

Food/Drink/Tobacco Industries and Agriculture (labor intensive)
Fruits (incl. grapes), vegetables (esp. early ones, incl.
    potatoes), tobacco

Czechoslovakia

Basic Industries

Mining (e.g., soft coal, uranium ore)
Metallurgy (e.g., large long distance gas pipes)
Chemicals (e.g., benzol, xylene, naphthalene, "isopren"
    synthetic caoutchouc, vitamins A and E)

Metal-Working Industries

Heavy machinery, e.g.,
    equipment for cement factories with a furnace capacity up
        to 800 t per day
    equipment for rolling mills (chiefly heavy), such as
        coarse section iron rolling mill trains, very heavy rol-
        ling mill trains, wire rod mill trains, medium and fine
        sheet metal rolling mills

equipment for the coal industry, such as for chemical
soft coal refining, open cast lignite mining (as, for
instance, multi-bucket excavators, overburden trans-
porter bridges, stackers). CMEA reduced the types of
open pit mining equipment produced in the bloc from
63 to 34.

heavy equipment for forging and pressing

specialized machine tools, such as lathes, horizontal
drills, equipment for the production of ball bearings

equipment for sugar factories (CMEA reduced types in the
bloc from 32 to 17.)

blast furnaces

large marine diesels, 2,000 H.P. diesel motors (production
to be discontinued in the Soviet Union)

General machinery, e.g.,

equipment for the shoe and leather industry

equipment for the printing industry

equipment for the chemicals industry

potato combines

sugar beet combines

flax combines

wheeled tractors, up to 18 H.P. and above 30 H.P.

caterpillar tractors up to 45 H.P.

specialized means of transport

equipment for the textile industry, such as jet looms for
wool, synthetic fiber machines

dairy industry equipment

equipment for cattle-raising

Vehicles, e.g.,

rolling stock, in particular 1,200 and 1,650 H.P. steam
locomotives (to be discontinued), 2,500 kw electric
trains and locomotives, heavy long-distance diesel locomotives

automobiles, in particular 4 cylinder passenger cars
1000-2000 ccm), heavy trucks above 3.5 t (types "Tatra"
and "Skoda"), esp. 10 t, trucks with standard back,
buses 4 t (over 18 seats)

airplanes

Shipbuilding, e.g.,

river boats

Electro-technical, e.g.,

small hydraulic, specialized, and steam turbines below
100 MW, esp. 25 MW, mercury rectifiers, specialized generators (large), gas turbines, transistor radios, refrigerators (200 l), washing machines, medium sized
vacuum cleaners, mobile power stations, high pressure
aggregates

Fine mechanics/optics, e.g.,

stereo-cameras and projectors, industrial cameras

Light Industries

Cotton textiles

Food/Drink/Tobacco Industries and Agriculture

Sugar beets, hops

East Germany

Basic Industries

Mining, e.g.,

potassium salts (joint financing with C.S.S.R., only other producer in bloc: U.S.S.R.), uranium ore, lignite,
raw and processed

Metallurgy, e.g.,

Products of the second processing stage of steel mills,
such as sheet metal and drawing die mill products, all
cold-rolled, in particular: pipes (as small long distance gas pipes), complicated rolled profiles, highly

valuable special steels (as for chemicals industry
equipment), absolutely pure and special purpose metals,
as semi-conductors, conductors, non-ferrous metals, and
other elements for refining steel (as germanium, sili-
con, indium, titanium, zirconium.) The smelting of
iron ore is to be done in the Soviet Union, so that no
new blast furnaces are being built in the G.D.R.
zinc, nickel (to be biggest CMEA producer), magnesium
(after 1965 to be biggest CMEA producer)
Chemicals (highly processed, based on lignite and with passage of time increasingly on oil, since no expansion is
planned of lignite-based productions), e.g.,
calcined soda, plastics (especially with qualities and
characteristics such that they can replace steel),
synthetic fibers (especially pervinylchloride fibers,
polyamid-silk, polyester fibers, and fibers having
strong wool-like characteristics), synthetic rubber
(produced by butadien-sodium process), solvents, poly-
vinylchloride, artificial fertilizers, pharmaceutical
products, soaps and dyes, pest killers, films and photo-
chemicals

Metal-Working Industries (highly processed, of low material
intensity, highly labor and "intelligence" intensive,
i.e., of first-class technical level)
Heavy machinery, e.g.,
highly mechanized automatic precision machine tools. (The
G.D.R. is to produce 56 of 70 types of these machines
selected by CMEA for specialization. The Council abolished all but 212 standard types of cutting machine tools.
This decision was binding on all members, and 44 per cent
of the former G.D.R. production was discontinued.)
*duplicating milling machines, *honing machines, *thread
grinding machines, *gear hobbing machines, *pipe cut-

ters, *pipe thread cutters, ball and roller bearings
machine tools (G.D.R.: 39 of 108 types), lathes
equipment for cement factories with a furnace capacity of
1,000-2,000 t per day and more (G.D.R.: 80 per cent of
CMEA production)
equipment for (esp. light) rolling mills (G.D.R.: 15 per
cent of CMEA production), such as:
*continuous and semicontinuous wire rod mill trains,
*leaf-metal and tube rolling mill trains, fine section
iron rolling mill trains, drawing die mill trains
equipment for the lignite industry, such as
for open pit mining (G.D.R.: 95 per cent of CMEA production), as multi-bucket excavators, *briquette factories, for chemical lignite refining, overburden trans-
porter bridges, stackers, *conveyor bridges, *rotary
bucket excavators with a cutting power of 80 kg per cm.
light equipment for forging and pressing
(The Council abolished all but 144 standard types of
this equipment. This decision was binding on all members, and 52 per cent of the former G.D.R. production
was discontinued.)
equipment for sugar factories
large marine diesels, 4,000-5,000 H.P.
General machinery, e.g.,
equipment for the knitwear industry, equipment for the
chemicals industry, such as chemical fiber machines and
cellulose factories, equipment for fish processing,
equipment for lifting and transporting, equipment for
the paper and printing industry, wheeled tractors to 30
H.P., esp. 15 H.P., caterpillar tractors, 45-65 H.P.,
sugar beet combines, potato combines, grain combines,
textile machines, especially for cotton, meat industry
equipment, dairy industry equipment, equipment for cat-

tle and hog raising

Vehicles, e.g.,

rolling stock, in particular 900-1,800 H.P. steam locomotives (eventually to be discontinued), 900-1,800 H.P.
diesel locomotives, electro locomotives, *double-decker
passenger cars (with a "phenomenally low 202 kg weight
per seat."), *mechanically cooled refrigerator cars,
dining cars, sleeping cars

automobiles, in particular light to medium trucks up to
3.5 t (types "Robur" and "Barkas"), 2 cylinder passenger cars (up to 1,000 ccm), buses up to 18 seats

Shipbuilding, e.g.,

ocean freighters up to 15,000 GRT, especially of 3,000,
and 10,000 GRT; also specialized ships, as ships atomi-
cally powered (however, since 1962 decreased emphasis
on Rostock shipbuilding in favor of Gdansk), ocean passenger liners, river freight and passenger boats, fishing vessels

Electro-technical (especially for electronics and apparatus serving mechanization and automation), e.g.,

radio transmitters and receivers, measuring, guiding, and
regulating equipment for automation, transformers,
small hydraulic, specialized, and steam turbines, esp.
32 and 50 MW, large generators, railroad signalling
equipment, refrigerators, small and large vacuum cleaners, gas turbines, esp. 25 MW, high-pressure aggregates, equipment for peaceful uses of nuclear energy

Fine mechanics/optics (East Germany to be the main CMEA
producer), e.g.,

calculating machines, accounting machines, electric type-
writers, cameras for small to medium sized pictures,
incl. mirror reflex cameras, movie cameras, and projectors

Hungary

Basic Industries

Mining (e.g., bauxite)

Metallurgy (e.g., aluminum and aluminum products, to be
biggest CMEA producer)

Chemicals (e.g., automobile tires, pharmaceutical products,
as vitamin D3)

Metal-Working Industries

Heavy machinery, e.g.,

equipment for aluminum production, equipment for rolling
mills, such as wire rod mill trains, specialized machine tools, such as open front vertical drills, lathes,
and milling machines (Hungary is to produce 16 of the
70 types of cutting machine tools selected by CMEA for
specialization), diesel engines (excluding marine diesels)

General machinery, e.g.,

diesel tractors, caterpillar tractors, corn combines,
grain combines, meat industry equipment, equipment for
cattle and fowl raising

Vehicles, e.g.,

rolling stock, esp. sleeping cars (agreed not to produce:
freight cars), specialized diesel locomotives, such as
for the mining industry, and *motor trains

automobiles, esp. *buses above 4 t (over 18 seats) and
trucks, 4-7 t (agreed not to produce: passenger automobiles)

construction industry vehicles, 90 H.P. tractors

Electro-technical, e.g.,

generating sets, voltage decomposition machines, railroad signalling equipment, gas turbines up to 50 MW,
high-pressure aggregates, telephone and telegraph equip-

ment, textile testing and measuring instruments

Fine mechanics/optics, e.g.,

medical equipment

Food/Drink/Tobacco Industries and Agriculture, e.g.,

fruits and vegetables, incl. rice, early potatoes

Poland

Basic Industries

Mining, e.g.,

sulfur (joint financing with Č.S.S.R.), zinc (to be major
bloc producer), copper (after big deposit discovery at
Lubin, Poland is predicted to become biggest world producer, joint financing with Č.S.S.R.), soft coal and
coke (joint financing with Č.S.S.R.), lignite (joint
financing with G.D.R.)

Metallurgy, esp. products of the first processing stage of
steel mills

Chemicals (based on soft coal and with passage of time increasingly on oil) e.g.,

calcined soda, benzol, xylene, napthalene, synthetic rubber ("chloropren" caoutchouc), and pharmaceutical products, e.g., vitamins B_1, B_2, K_3 and calcium pantothen-
ate

Metal-Working Industries

Heavy machinery, e.g.,

equipment for the coal industry, Poland is to produce 5
(small) types of the 84 mining machines selected by CMEA
for specialization, such as for soft coal mining, for
chemical soft coal refining, for coking plants, coal
combines, for open pit lignite mining

rolling mill equipment (chiefly light, Poland is to produce 17 types of rolling machinery, such as fine section

iron mill trains, small rolling mill trains, 4,000-
5,000 H.P. ship diesel engines (production newly started with German, Czech, and Soviet help)

complete factories for light reinforced concrete

specialized machine tools, as complete wheel set machin-
ing lathes, horizontal presses up to 250 t, cold pressure automatics, horizontal face plate lathes, roller
grinding machines, toothed-wheel grinding machines for
ball bearings (Poland is to produce 35 of the 70 types
of cutting machine tools selected by CMEA for specialization.)

heavy forge-presses

blast furnaces

equipment for sugar factories

General machinery, (Poland is to produce 11 of 55 types of
general agricultural machinery selected by CMEA and 3 of
16 types of amelioration machinery), e.g.,

potato combines, one type of grain combines, flax combines, tractors (1 axle, for horticulture, and of medium size, Poland is to produce 4 of 10 types selected
by CMEA), equipment for hog and fowl raising

chemical industry machinery (Poland is to produce 26 of
151 types selected by CMEA)

paper industry installations (Poland is to produce 10 of
15 types selected by CMEA)

cables and ropes

textile machines, especially for wool

Vehicles, e.g.,

rolling stock, especially sleeping cars, passenger cars
for wide gauge, steam locomotives (eventually only in
Poland), some diesel and electro locomotives, tank cars,
self-unloading freight cars

automobiles, especially trucks up to 5 t and 10 t self-

    unloading trucks, busses of 4 t (newly started at Sanok
    after CMEA decision), passenger cars (over 2,000 ccm)
airplanes
Shipbuilding, e.g.,
    sea-going freight and passenger vessels, especially from
    1,000-5,000 GRT and 15,000-25,000 tdw and specialized
    ships
Electro-technical, e.g.,
    25, 50, 125, 200 MW condensing turbogenerators (latter
    with Soviet blueprints), 25 MW thermal turbogenerators,
    50 MW back-pressure turbogenerators, 220 kw transform-
    ers

Food/Drink/Tobacco Industries and Agriculture

    unspecified products

Rumania

Basic Industries

Mining, e.g., oil and gas
Metallurgy, e.g., medium-sized long-distance gas pipes
Chemicals (primarily based on oil), e.g.,
    oil and gas products, caustic and calcined soda, sulfur,
    soot

Metal-Working Industries

Heavy machinery, e.g.,
    equipment for cement factories with a furnace capacity
    of 400-450 t per day
    equipment for oil drilling, refining and prospecting
    basic types of machine tools, and some specialized ones,
    as knee and column-type milling machines, transverse
    planing machines, long planing machines with wide bench
    (Rumania is to produce 6 of the 70 types of cutting ma-
    chine tools selected by CMEA for specialization.)

General machinery, e.g.,

   corn combines, 37 H.P. wheeled tractors, machinery for
   vegetable and fruit harvesting

Vehicles, e.g.,

   rolling stock, especially 1,200 H.P. steam locomotives
   (to be discontinued later), 1,200 H.P. diesel locomotives, tank cars, freight cars, incl. self-unloading
   and 4 axle-types, also for lignite mining in Bulgaria,
   Czechoslovakia, and East Germany (CMEA recommended especially export of _regular_ freight cars to Hungary and
   Poland)

Shipbuilding, e.g.,

   tankers and ships from 1,000-5,000 GRT

Electro-technical, e.g.,

   electro-motors, switches, transformers

Light Industries, e.g.,

Cellulose and Paper (large-scale cooperative CMEA project
at Braila to produce eventually 200,000 t cellulose per
year from reeds. Production began in 1961 with 50,000 t.
Reportedly 4.4 t reeds produce 1 t artificial fiber cellulose, and 3.3 t reeds produce 1 t bleached paper cellulose.)

Agriculture, e.g.,

   fruits, vegetables, incl. early potatoes, wood

Soviet Union

Basic Industries

Mining, e.g.,

   potassium salts (joint financing with Poland; only other
   producer in bloc: East Germany), apatite ores and con-
   centrates, sulfur, raw phosphates (to be developed as
   joint CMEA project after 1963; _Neues Deutschland_ of

1-22-1964, p. 5, reported that "presently the super
phosphate factories of the Soviet Union are only utilized at 75 to 80 per cent of capacity, since there is
a lack of phosphate raw materials"), soft coal, oil and
gas, iron ore, copper ore, nickel ore (the latter three
being jointly financed with the C.S.S.R.)

Metallurgy, primarily products of the first processing
stage of steel mills, as crude iron and steel, but also
very large long distance gas pipes.

Chemicals (based on soft coal and oil), e.g.,
synthetic rubber, benzol, naphthalene, xylene, plastics

Metal-Working Industries

Heavy machinery (especially material intensive), e.g.,
equipment for oil drilling and refining
equipment for cement factories with a furnace capacity of
1,000-2,000 t per day and more
equipment for the coal industry, such as
for open cast mining (single-bucket excavators, shovel
excavators), coking plants, for chemical soft coal refining, coal combines, coal cutting machines
equipment for rolling mills, especially very heavy ones,
such as coarse section iron rolling mill trains, heavy
rolling mill trains
equipment for non-ferrous metallurgy
equipment for forging and pressing
specialized machine tools, such as for ball bearings, long
planing machines, turret head lathes
blast furnaces

General machinery, e.g.,
equipment for hog-raising, equipment for the printing industry, small mining machines, equipment for the textile
industry, especially synthetic fiber equipment, grain

combines, potato combines, corn combines, wheeled tractors above 30 H.P., and caterpillar tractors above 65
H.P.

Vehicles, e.g.,

rolling stock, in particular heavy 4,000 and more H.P.
diesel and electro locomotives, passenger automobiles,
heavy and specialized trucks, airplanes

Shipbuilding, e.g.,

sea-going vessels, all sizes, often specialized, such as
for fishing, tankers, and ships with atomic power

Electro-technical, e.g.,

*steam turbines above 100,000 kw, railroad signalling
equipment, large generators and electric power plants

Agriculture (esp. land intensive items), e.g.,

wheat, wool, cotton, wood, animal and vegetable fats

D.   SUMMARY

Since the founding of CMEA in 1949, a fundamental change
in economic thinking has occurred within the Communist bloc.
There are clear indications that, at least in theory, the earlier costly emphasis of each nation on producing everything
within the national boundaries, is now being rejected. This
becomes also obvious when studying the specialization decisions that have been made public. These decisions seem quite
reasonable and often appear to be based on the desire to reap
the benefits of either optimum plant sizes or a given area's
comparative advantage, arising from its technical know-how and
the supply of productive factors relative to demand. The former desire predominates. This is not to say, however, that
hoped for economies of scale or gains from specialization and
trade due to present comparative advantage are the sole criteria for international specialization of production or that

such specialization is necessarily very far-reaching. There
is also, at least at present, a basic commitment (strengthened by nationalism) to the full and balanced economic development of each individual nation, which sets definite limits
on how far specialization is carried. In short, the present
policy follows a middle road between autarky and complete one-
sided specialization, but is much closer to the former.[50]
Trends are as follows:

Energy production and mining are to be developed at a
rapid rate wherever there are worthwhile raw materials. Cost
of transporting the output is to be minimized by either locat-
ing energy and fuel intensive industries on the spot, or by
transporting only processed materials (e.g., coke rather than
raw coal, or electricity itself rather than coal to make electricity elsewhere), or by developing more effective means of
transportation (e.g., oil pipelines rather than ocean tankers
and railroad tank cars).

Coal, oil, and potassium salts are to be developed where
the largest deposits occur, hence soft coal in Czechoslovakia,
Poland, and the Soviet Union, crude oil in Rumania and the
Soviet Union, lignite in East Germany and Poland, potassium
salts in East Germany and the Soviet Union.

Metallurgical industries are to be developed, in line
with the above considerations, near the sources of energy,
fuels, and ores. Hence only a few countries will provide
crude metallurgical products; otherwise trade is to take place
primarily in semi-manufactured or manufactured goods, with individual countries specializing in particular types of ferrous or non-ferrous goods so as to take advantage of economies
of scale.

The production of iron and steel, for instance, usually
referred to as the first processing stage of steel mills (i.e.,
processing coal and iron ore into pig-iron and crude steel),

is to be concentrated in Poland and the Soviet Union. The
other CMEA countries, which do not have the necessary raw materials, are to abstain from expanding this part of their metallurgical industries. They join, however, in the second
processing stage of steel mills, such as the processing of
pig-iron and crude steel into various products, as sheets,
wire, and pipes, different products of this category being
assigned to different countries.

In the case of non-ferrous metals, Hungary is to become
the bloc's main supplier of aluminum, other non-ferrous metals are being developed wherever found, because the demand
is expected to exceed the supply for some time to come.

A chemical industry also is to be developed rapidly
everywhere on the basis of ubiquitous raw materials. This
would concern products as sulfuric acid, hydrochloric acid,
calcined soda, cellulose, ammonia, the most important artificial fertilizers, synthetics (fibers and rubber), and plastics. In addition, there is to be concentration of production where certain specific raw materials are found or labor
force skills are available: in Rumania based on oil, in the
Soviet Union based on soft coal and oil, in Poland based on
soft coal, and in East Germany based on lignite and skilled
labor. In addition, the raw material most easily transported, oil, is to be sent via pipeline to various CMEA countries
from the Soviet Union. The main emphasis in the 1960's will
be on the production of plastics. East Germany is to have a
prominent role, being the bloc's first exporter of chemicals
since the late 1950's.

Besides by the presence of specific raw materials, such
as coals or oil, specialization has also been urged on the
grounds of mass production economies. This is being carried
out for certain types of synthetic rubber, plastics, etc.,
and wherever expected internal demand is insufficient for op-

timum production capacity, as for some dyes, soaps, pharmaceutical products, and pest killers. In the middle of 1962, CMEA had decided on specialization for more than 2,000 chemical products to 1965.[51]

In the metal-working industries, countries with a weak raw material base (as East Germany) are to specialize in labor-intensive production,[52] while those with an adequate raw material supply take up also the production of heavy equipment (Czechoslovakia, Soviet Union). Labor force skills, existing industrial capacities, and demand conditions, however, are also taken into account. This seems to be the rationale behind the decision to let different countries produce the type of machinery needed for the same country's main branches of basic industry and agriculture. East Germany, for instance, is also to specialize in lignite mining equipment because she is the main lignite producer and presumably has existing capacities and skills in this area. Similarly, Hungary specializes in corn combines, since she is the largest CMEA corn producer outside the Soviet Union (and possibly has existing capacities and skills). The reader can easily find other examples in Section C above.

Furthermore, one can observe the following trend: The senior industrial countries are restricting their production of relatively simple industrial products in favor of such industrial newcomers as the Balkan countries. Bulgaria, for instance, imported freight cars, small electric motors, and most heavy chemicals in 1954, but was exporting them to the advanced countries in the area by 1959. From 1958 to late 1962, CMEA decided on specialization for more than 900 products. Included in this were 14 types of equipment for energy production, 26 for oil drilling, 8 for oil refining, and 53 for rolling mills, 180 types of chemical technological apparatus, over 200 machine tools, and about 50 types of agricultural equipment.[53]

In the light industries specialization by 1965 was practically non-existent. Authorities have stated that it should
be considerably less far-reaching in this area than in the basic and metal-working industries. If at all, it should concern mainly consumer durables (such as furniture and musical
instruments) and only exceptionally less durable items (such
as glass, ceramics, and wood products). Even then everybody
should produce all kinds of goods, but specialize in particular types of a given kind to reach optimum output series.[54]

In the food industries and in agriculture, specialization
seems to be a half-hearted affair also. At one time, three
major decisions were announced: 1) Hungary was to become a
major supplier of rice by 1963, 2) Albania, Hungary, and the
Balkan countries were to specialize in labor-intensive agricultural output, such as fruits, vegetables, and early potatoes,
3) the Soviet Union was to supply land-intensive products,
such as wheat or meat whenever a country's own production was
insufficient. However, the February, 1960, decision of the
First Party Secretaries made it abundantly clear that eventually each country was to supply its own needs. In addition,
the defection of Albania, and the Balkan countries' strong desire to play a different role than agricultural supplier undoubtedly served to undermine these decisions.

Finally, a word of caution. However reasonable the above
trends appear, one must not forget that these are just some of
the major decisions which might not even be realized. In the
case of finer specialization decisions, furthermore, CMEA members have encountered great theoretical difficulties. It is
easy enough to conclude that East Germany should specialize in
labor-intensive production. It is more difficult to carry out
such a decision in a significant way, and it is immensely more
difficult to decide whether East Germany or Czechoslovakia or

Poland should become the producer of automobile tires. Such problems and their tentative solution by the CMEA members are discussed in CHAPTER 4.

FOOTNOTES

[1]This fact is openly admitted today. See, for instance, Konrad Illgen, *Freundschaft in Aktion* (East Berlin: Dietz Verlag, 1961), p. 23.

[2]The gigantic metallurgical works in East Germany at Fürstenberg-on-the-Oder are examples. Both iron ore and coal had to be imported. The Hungarian steel mill Sztálinváros is another case in point. Both examples illustrate the absurdity of trying to be economically independent of all countries, capitalist and socialist alike.

[3]Joseph Stalin, *Ökonomische Probleme des Sozialismus in der U.d.S.S.R.* (East Berlin: Dietz Verlag, 1952), p. 31.

[4]For a frank Communist appraisal of this situation, see Werner Krause, *Das Entwicklungstempo der sozialistischen Länder im ökonomischen Wettbewerb der beiden Weltsysteme*, (East Berlin: Verlag Die Wirtschaft, 1960), especially p. 151.

[5]On July 11, 1947, the Soviet government announced the Molotov Plan, designed to stimulate the development of East European economies through trade, but it never was more than a propaganda device. In spite of it, some East European countries agreed to Marshall Plan participation, but withdrew when the CMEA project evolved.

[6]It was later argued that this late admission was due to the Soviet Union's desire for a peaceful settlement of the German question and that the U.S. insistence on bringing West Germany into the Marshall Plan eventually led the Soviet Union to consider also East Germany's integration into the bloc.

[7]It should be noted that Yugoslavia on the one hand and China and her satellites on the other have been looked upon by CMEA with suspicion for different reasons. Yugoslavia has continually been suspected of "right-wing revisionism" or "Trotskyite distortions;" China, however, of "left-wing sectarian dogmatism." In the words of M.A. Suslov (Secretary of the Central Committee of the Communist Party of the U.S.S.R.), "dogmatism is the most dangerous form of separation of theory from practice. . . The attempts to stay away from life behind

a bulwark of quotations signify the inability and unwilling-
ness to appraise a new historic situation, to apply and develop creatively the great principles of Marxism-Leninism under
new and changing conditions. This leads to the isolation of
Communists from the broad masses of workers and condemns them
to passive waiting or to radical, adventurous pseudo-revolu-
tionary actions. . . The dogmatist positions are expressed
most vividly by the leaders of the Albanian Party of Labor. . .
[They]. . . have proceeded to the direct attack on the Marxist-
Leninist unity of the Communist world movement. Their political course has an open anti-Soviet direction and a vicious,
slanderous character." (*ND*, 2-7-1962, p. 4).

     Subsequent statements by many Communist leaders have made
it absolutely clear that such criticism refers not only to the
Albanians, but also to "those who may be standing behind them."
See Walter Ulbricht in *ND*, 1-16-1963, p. 3. The Chinese and
Albanians on their part have made similar statements about the
Soviet Union. An Albanian statement, reprinted in the Chinese
press, attacks the Khrushchev group for pursuing "a policy of
big nation chauvinism. Its views are anti-Marxist. It en-
gages in treacherous activities and tries at all times and in
every way to strike at the parties that uphold the revolutionary Marxist-Leninist position with a view to forcing them away
from the correct road." See *The New York Times*, 1-27-1964,
p. 4. On more outspoken statements see the East German dis-
closure of Chinese demands that East Germany withdraw from
CMEA (*The New York Times*, 4-24-1964, p. 5) and Suslov's attack
on the "dangerous actions" of Peking's leadership (*The New
York Times*, 4-4-1964, p. 8).

[8]Frequent West German accounts, in particular, about complete
CMEA control over the national economies of the member countries and the binding character of its decisions must be rejected as totally unfounded. Typical examples (which could be
multiplied manifold) are Bruno Kiesewetter, *Das sowjetische
Vorbild in der Wirtschaftsentwicklung der Oststaaten* (West
Berlin: Dunker and Humblot, 1951), pp. 30-31, ("Integration
is being forced; for the plans worked out to the smallest detail by the Soviet technicians and engineers at the Moscow
Central Planning Agency cannot be changed by the ministries
of the eastern countries. The one-sided bias towards Soviet
interests goes even so far as to dissolve in the east bloc
nations the individual industrial ministries and to replace
them by departments of the Moscow Central Planning Agency."),
or Konstantin Pritzel, *"Die wirtschaftliche Integration der
sowjetischen Besatzungszone Deutschlands in den Ostblock und
ihre politischen Aspekte,"* BB (Bonn: BMfgF, 1962), pp. 145-6,
("In reality the recommendations of CMEA and its organs have
the character of binding directions to the member countries;

certainly this is true for the Soviet occupied zone of Germany and the Balkan satellites").

[9]Oftentimes national resistance has made decisions impossible or hard to carry out: The Czechs have protested the build-up of an automobile industry in Poland, their traditional export market. The East Germans refused to give up the production of heavy caterpillar tractors. Premier Khrushchev, at the June, 1960, Communist Party meetings at Bucharest, is known to have reprimanded the Balkan Communists for their persistent resistance to specialization decisons. See *The New York Times*, 1-19-1958; *"Der Aussenhandel der Sowjetischen Besatzungszone Deutschlands,"* Mat. (Bonn: BMfgF, 1952), p. 15; Karl C. Thalheim, *Die wirtschaftliche und soziale Entwicklung in Ostberlin und der sowjetischen Besatzungszone* (West Berlin: mimeographed), 10, 1958, p. 10.

At other times, countries have clearly acted contrary to CMEA decisions already made. To name just two, Poland sharply reduced coal deliveries to other Communist countries, notably East Germany, in 1956, while at the same time acting against CMEA decisions on machinery industry development and the volume and regional distribution of machinery exports. Rumania, in 1963, initiated an intensive drive for de-Russification (called Rumanification) which resulted, among other things, in the entry of western firms in Rumanian development schemes. In the Galati steel complex, western aid has replaced Soviet aid. More importantly, in the prototype CMEA venture at Braila (to produce cellulose from Danube delta reeds) the Czech, East German, and Polish collaborators have been replaced by Austrians, Italians, Swiss, and West Germans. At the same time, ignoring Hungary's agreed upon role in this field, Rumania was initiating an aluminum industry on the basis of local bauxite deposits. It also proposed that integration be postponed until all Communist countries (including, presumably, China) are CMEA members, and condemned strongly and persistently CMEA interference in her national economy. See especially the statement of April 22, 1964, by the Central Committee of the Rumanian Worker's Party. (As is well known, this independent course led the U.S. to drop export controls to Rumania, permitting the export of industrial installations, such as oil refinery equipment, steel mills and even nuclear reactors.) See Erich Klinkmüller and Maria Elisabeth Ruban, *op. cit.,* p. 85, and frequent reports in *The New York Times* between April, 1963 and July, 1964.

[10]The Secretary has been a Russian throughout, in 1958 and 1959 his assistants were a Pole and a Czech. The Secretariat organization chart was most recently reviewed by the Executive Committee. Apparently, there is at least one department with-

in the Secretariat corresponding to each Standing Commission
(discussed below). Employees must be nominated by the member
country and, in cases of important positions, be acceptable to
other members. The employees' functions are clearly outlined
in advance, and each member country is said to be entitled to
a certain number of positions in each department. Qualifica-
tions for employees, who enjoy diplomatic immunity, are listed
as "theoretical training, practical experience, organizational
skill, and fluency in Russian." Employment carries a 4 year
contract. Salaries are set in accordance with a similar position in the home country plus 25 per cent for those living
abroad. This, therefore, seems to apply to all but the Russians, since the Secretariat is located in Moscow. See *ND*,
5-3-1964, p. 6 and 5-29-1964, p. 7.

[11]More than 10,000 specialists were working in such commissions
in 1961. See *ND: Sonderausgabe* (for the Leipzig Spring Fair
1961), p. 4.

[12]*"Zehn Jahre Rat für gegenseitige Wirtschaftshilfe," Presse-
Informationen*, No. 41 (1724), April 10, 1959, pp. 2-5. This
source will hereafter be referred to as *PI*.

[13]*"Erfolgreiches Zusammenwirken-starke Wirtschaftskraft," PI*,
No. 44 (1727), April 17, 1959, pp. 3-6.

[14]East Germany's first long term trade agreements with Communist countries on a governmental level were signed as follows:
with Albania on 3-27-1951 (for 1951-55), with Bulgaria on
1-24-1958 (for 1958-60), with Czechoslovakia on 12-1-1951 (for
1951-55), with Hungary on 11-29-1951 (for 1951-55), with Poland on 11-10-1951 (for 1951-55), with Rumania on 1-23-1952
(for 1951-55), with the U.S.S.R. on 9-23-1951 (for 1951-55),
with China on 1-18-1960 (for 1960-62), with North Korea on
6-25-1952 (for 1952-53), and with Outer Mongolia on 11-6-1957
(for 1958-60).

[15]To quote figures, the East Germans report that from 1949 until the end of 1957, there were about 2,825 cases of technical-
scientific cooperation in favor of East Germany, while East
Germany cooperated with 3,650 requests of bloc countries to
provide such information. See Werner Krause, *op. cit.*, page
141. For a listing of areas of concern in this cooperation,
detailed by partner country, see *AH*, 8, 1961, p. 25.
    The Soviet Union, on the other hand, is reported to have
given about 29,000 complete technical documentations to bloc
countries between 1948 and 1960, having received more than
7,000 from them. See *AH*, 7, 1961, p. 16.
    In the area of personal exchange, 3,000 delegations of
experts (apparently consisting of about 3 or 4 persons each)

visited East Germany until the end of 1958 from CMEA countries
while 2,050 such delegations went the other way. See *Zehn
Jahre Rat für gegenseitige Wirtschaftshilfe*, (East Berlin:
Dietz Verlag, 1960), p. 55, and Werner Krause, *op. cit.*, page
144. The Soviet Union, until 1959, sent 2,000 and received
18,000 specialists. See *ND*, 2-9-1962, p. 5.

In 1957/58, 1,191 students from East Germany studied at
bloc colleges, in the previous academic year 1,070 foreigners
had studied at East German colleges. See *Statistische
Praxis*, 10, 1957, inside front cover. This source will hereafter be referred to as *SP*. One source (*AH*, 4, 1964, p. 31)
claims the existence of a Coordination of Technical Aid Commission, established in 1961 at Moscow. However, there is no
other corroboration on this point anywhere.

[16]The G.D.R., for example, delivered all requests until 1952,
but her policy changed after Poland began to compete with her
in the export markets for precision glass which Poland produced on the basis of German plans supplied earlier. It has
also been charged in the west that since the seventh Plenum
the recipients of documents have to pay for part of the research and development costs expended by the donor and that
prior to this time Poland and the Balkan countries had abused
the program without limit, going so far as to sell information
received from a CMEA member for western currencies in the
west. See Konstantin Pritzel, *op. cit.*, pp. 200-201. Eastern sources, on the other hand, claimed as late as 1962 that
document exchange was free of charge. They admitted, however,
another problem, viz., that this practice often leads to the
establishment of undesirable parallel capacities due to still
insufficient coordination with specialization decisions in
production. See *Wirtschaftswissenschaft*, 8, 1962, pp. 1215
and 1217. This source will hereafter be referred to as *WW*.

[17]It is interesting to note that a recent authoritative East
German study gives as a major reason for the original CMEA
concern with trade coordination only (besides the need to
first fully nationalize production and foreign trade in all
member countries) the absence of sufficient trust among the
socialist states and the absence of the correct attitude on
the part of the workers towards the principle of proletarian
internationalism. See Gertrud Gräbig, *Internationale Arbeitsteilung und Aussenhandel im sozialistischen Weltsystem* (East
Berlin: Verlag Die Wirtschaft, 1960), p. 35.

[18]Four hundred-forty-eight of these items affected production
in East Germany. Six years later, it was pointed out, however, that the 1956 decisions did "not represent any significant inroads into the production program of the individual

countries." See Ladislav Smid, *"Die sozialistische Zusammenarbeit im Maschinenbau,"* *Sozialistische Planwirtschaft*, 8/9, 1962, p. 10. It was also noted that East Germany did not follow 15 of the 448 decisions, because the other countries "were not able to cover the demand of the G.D.R. for these products." See Erwin Stobbe, *"Probleme der Perspektivplanung der internationalen sozialistischen Zusammenarbeit auf dem Gebiet des Maschinenbaus,"* in *Internationale sozialistische Arbeitsteilung und Perspektivplanung* (East Berlin: Verlag Die Wirtschaft, 1961), p. 107.

[19]Some sources also indicate for this period the creation of four other Commissions: Geology; Wood, Cellulose, and Paper, (Budapest); Forestry (Bucharest); and the Coordination of the Planning and Delivery of Complete Factories (Moscow). None of these Commissions, however, survived long by itself. The first two were dissolved after the eleventh Plenum. See *DW*, 12-23-1959, p. 5. Prior to that, the Wood, Cellulose, and Paper Commission met several times in Budapest. It discussed the 15-year outlook in the development of the wood industry, the wood using industries, the cellulose and paper industry, and of forestry with respect to output and technology. Included in its work were questions of increasing the productivity of forests, planting fast growing trees, fighting forest pests, mechanizing forestry work, finding wood substitutes, using wastes, and increasing plywood production. See *AH*, 23, 1957, p. 852 and 8, 1958, p. 306. This suggests that possibly the Forestry Commission became a part of the Wood, Cellulose, and Paper Commission and died with it. The Complete Factories Commission merged with the Foreign Trade Commission in late 1958. See Gertrud Gräbig, *op. cit.*, p. 30.

[20]P. Nikitin in *AH*, 16/17, 1957, p. 576.

[21]It was reported earlier that a billion kwh per year were to be supplied to Hungary by the Soviet Union after 1961, presumably for aluminum refining. See *AH*, 4/5, 1960, p. 4. The same source states that the unification of the electric energy systems made it possible to avoid the new construction of generating capacity of 500,000 kw in Eastern Europe.

[22]Rumania was to deliver 2 billion kwh per year to Czechoslovakia after the completion, with Czech help, of power stations with double that capacity in Rumania. See *AH*, 20, 1959, page 13.

[23]The text of this agreement, which was totally ineffective, is given in Laszlo Zsoldos, *The Economic Integration of Hungary into the Soviet Bloc: Foreign Trade Experience* (Columbus: The Ohio State University, 1963), Appendix II.

[24]See *AH*, 8, 1959, p. 9.   The Soviet import figure was given
by A. Ketkovich and J. Romanov in *AH*, 21, 1959, p. 7.

[25]Various socialist countries announced the goal of "catching
up with and surpassing" a particular capitalist country "in
the historically shortest span of time" in either per capita
or absolute production.   The Soviet Union, for instance, decided to "run against" the United States; Czechoslovakia and
Poland against France; East Germany against West Germany;
China against the United Kingdom; North Korea against Japan,
etc.   The dramatic changes in the last 40 years raised the
hopes of all to leave the now powerful pioneers of the industrial revolution behind, stranded and isolated in an alien
world.

[26]Quoted by G. Gräbig, *op. cit.*, p. 50.

[27]*AH*, 1, 1958, p. 7. "Specialization"is defined as agreements,
which are firmly incorporated in the national plans, on the
division of production and research. "Cooperation"is defined
as planned joint production of a particular product or complete factory so as to make use of the peculiar situation of
different countries as to the availability of materials and
capacity.

[28]See Willi Kunz and Rudolf Brauer, *"Internationale sozialistische Arbeitsteilung und Bildung von Wirtschaftskomplexen,"
Internationale sozialistische Arbeitsteilung und Perspektivplanung* (East Berlin: Verlag Die Wirtschaft, 1961), p. 23.

[29]East Germany signed treaties for this period as follows:
with Albania on 6-30-1959, with Bulgaria on 3-20-1959 and
4-11-1960, with the Č.S.S.R. on 6-1-1960, with Hungary on
4-8-1960, with Poland on 10-24-1958 and 2-29-1960, with Rumania (for 1959-1965) in March, 1959, with the U.S.S.R. on
11-21-1959, and with Outer Mongolia on 7-8-1960.

[30]See *AH*, 24, 1958, p. 851.   Two years later, at another such
seminar in Berlin, Nikolai Shinkov, Secretary of the Economic
Problems Commission, explained the insufficient division of
labor, as evidenced by low trade-output ratios, by the short
time elapsed since its inception, persistent autarkic tendencies, the significant economic differences in development
within the bloc, the lack of multilateral clearing, the un-
scientific methods of pricing, the unavailability and incom-
parability of indices of national income, investment effectiveness, labor productivity, costs, etc.   See *Internationale
sozialistische Arbeitsteilung und Perspektivplanung* (East Berlin: Verlag Die Wirtschaft, 1961) pp. 42-43.

[31]For a detailed discussion of some of these theoretical aspects see CHAPTER 4.

[32]The procedure followed was the reporting of transport needs to the Commission by the exporter. Legally, however, the importer decides on the question of transportation. Hence there have developed interesting discussions on how to achieve the most economical transportation while considering the wishes of all, exporting, importing, as well as transit countries.

[33]The official pronouncements, nevertheless, assure us that among socialist countries there exists no competition among the individual carriers, nor are there any objective conflicts of interest in the coordination of transportation. See *AH*, 15, 1959, p. 25.

[34]The Soviet Union was to fully equip the line to Mosyr and deliver pipes, machinery, and steel sheets to other countries involved in the project. The East Germans converted Soviet steel sheets into pipes (diameter 630 mm, length 30 m, weight over 10 tons) and built all (automated) pumping stations. Poland also provided pipes, Czechoslovakia armatures, and Hungary long distance communications equipment. Some pipes were also imported by the Soviet Union from Western Europe. This led, in early 1963, to a series of sharp diplomatic exchanges between West Germany and the Soviet Union, since the West German government enforced an embargo on the West German export of pipes and tried to pressure the British into following suit.

[35]By December 1, 1963, Czechoslovakia, Hungary, and Poland had received more than 6.5 million tons of oil via the pipeline. By May 11, 1965, Poland and East Germany had received 5 million tons. See *ND*, 12-8-1963, p. 3, and 5-13-1965, page 6.
    It should be pointed out, however, that at least one western source has told a rather different story. According to *The New York Times* of March 10, 1964, p. 51, construction of the pipeline project was "well behind schedule. . .caused, in part, by an acute shortage of line pipe. . . Only a small section of the . . . line has been laid in the Soviet Union. This runs for about 187 miles. Oil for Czechoslovakia and Hungary is hauled by rail from Kuibyshev to Rovno, where it is transferred to the pipeline. The branch pipeline to Poland, starting at Mozyr, is not yet in operation. The opening date is set to be in 1965." This story is at least partially corroborated by the official organ of the East German Communist Party, *Neues Deutschland* of September 12, 1964, p. 7: in clear contradiction to its own reports of December, 1963, it reported for September, 1964, the opening of the last

540 km of the pipeline from Michurinsk to Unecha. It also explained that the western part of the line had been built first, while oil was being transported on Soviet territory by rail to big reservoirs at Brody. The paper also reported that it had already become clear that in the near future the present pipeline would fail to cover the demand for oil by the four brother countries and that discussions were under way to lay a second line parallel to the first. This report was corroborated by the Press Department of the Soviet Embassy in London in *Soviet News,* No. 5032, of 9-14-1964, p. 124.

[36]K. Smirnov, Deputy Chairman of the State Production Committee for the U.S.S.R. Gas Industry, stressed the cheapness of transport via pipe line as against railroads. His colleagues in the partner countries agreed unanimously. Erich Apel, Chairman of the East German State Planning Commission, reported as typical that the production costs of ethylene, a base for plastics production, had just about halved. One ton of ethylene, for instance, can be produced from 2.25 tons of crude oil, but requires 7.4 tons of coke, or 25.5 tons of raw lignite, he reported. See *ND,* 12-8-1963, pp. 3 and 4. Meanwhile, gas pipe lines were also being constructed at various points in the bloc, as from Central Asia to the Urals (with an annual capacity of 21 billion cubic meters) and from Rumania to Hungary. The latter line of 365 km began to operate to Borsod in 1959, delivering 200 million cubic meters of methane gas annually to be used for dyes, artificial fertilizers, and other chemical productions. See *AH,* 21, 1961, p. 22 and *ND,* 3-22-1963, p. 7.

[37]F. Heiduschat, *"Zwei neue Handelsabkommen mit der Sowjetunion,"* *AH,* 23, 1959, p. 5.

[38]Interview with Witold Trampczynski in *AH,* 6, 1960, p. 15.

[39]For the complete text of this major pronouncement consult Appendix C.

[40]Walter Ulbricht, also in June, 1962, characterized the Moscow Conference as "the entrance of the socialist world system into a new phase of development." Utilizing the advantages of the system "requires especially," he said, "that big investments are being coordinated." See *ND,* 6-20-1962, p. 3. The same paper reported later as accomplished the coordination of investment plans for the years 1964 and 1965 (issue of 2-23-1963, p. 5), especially for ferrous metals (issue of 3-3-1963, p. 7) and the light and food industries (issue of 3-31-1963, p. 7). Altogether, CMEA members considered the investment coordination of 250,000 projects for 1964/65, empha-

sis being on optimum plant sizes. See *Polish Perspectives*, 2,
1964, pp. 56-57.

[41]See E. Beirau, *"Die Standardisierung - Schlüssel zu erfolg-
reicher sozialistischer internationaler Spezialisierung,"* *AH*,
2, 1963, p. 12.

[42]It is interesting to note in this connection that after a
prolonged debate in bloc statistical journals, "the class character of statistics" has now been established. "There is. . .
no statistics as such. Socialist statistics are basically
different from bourgeois statistics. Both have only some
methods in common. From which follows further that statistics
cannot be neutral toward the class ruling the state, but represent the interests of the ruling class: bourgeois statistics those of the minority of capitalist exploiters, socialist statistics those of the workers and peasants." See *SP*, 7,
1959, *Beilage*, pp. 6-7.

[43]Each member of the freight car pool contributes cars in accordance with the country's volume of international transports. Cars within the pool are used normally without rental
charge, except when a member uses on his territory more cars
of the pool than he contributed to it. In that case, a rental charge is paid to those members for whom the reverse is
true. The cars entering the pool must be modern, able to go
at least 100 km/hour. Two axle covered cars must load 20 t,
open ones 24 t, 4 axle covered cars must load 50 t, open ones
55 t. The agreement also specifies special conditions about
the construction of the cars (e.g., types of brakes), their
age, and their regular servicing. See *DW*, A, 25, 1964, page
23.

[44]*ND*, January 31, 1963, p. 7.

[45]*DW*, A, 36, 1964, p. 39, reported specialized production of
1,200 types of machines and 800 types of chemical products.

[46]The treaty has been in force since May 18, 1964. See *ND*,
5-20-1964, p. 5.

[47]This state of affairs was proudly contrasted with that in
western financial organizations. For instance, Willy Rumpf,
East German Minister of Finance and member of the Communist
Party's Central Committee, noted that "in the 'World Bank'
as well as in the 'International Monetary Fund' and in the
other capitalist finance organizations the U.S.A. is representing (through her capital contribution and the voting ma-
jority implied thereby) lastly the interests of the monopo-
lies, in order to secure the hegemony of the dollar on the

capitalist world market, to keep the currencies of other countries under control, and to carry through her neocolonialist
policy via 'development aid'." See *ND*, 10-31-1963, p. 7. On
the other hand, the Soviet Union with a contribution of 116
million rubles to the new Bank and Outer Mongolia with one of
only 3 million rubles, had equal voting power. See *ND*, 1-15-
1964, p. 7. The East German contribution was set at 55 million rubles, the Czech at 45, the Polish at 27, the Hungarian
at 21, the Bulgarian at 17, and the Rumanian at 16. See *The
New York Times*, 4-17-1965, p. 26. Only 20 per cent of the
contributions were to be paid in 1964.

[48]Reports stress that the Soviet Union has no advantages from
the fact that clearing accounts are in rubles, for "the sole
source of the transferable ruble for the Soviet Union, as also
for the other countries, can only be an export surplus." See
ND, 1-15-1964, p. 7. In an interview with Konstantin Nasarkin,
chairman of the Bank Council, in March, 1964, it was reported
that few credits had been needed by members since the beginning of the year. Seventy-five per cent of all clearing operations had been done with members' own funds. The maximum
interest on credit charged was 2 per cent involving seasonal
indebtedness above 3 per cent of a member's trade volume or
special credits extended. An excellent detailed statement of
the legal provisions can be found in *AH*, 4, 1964, *Beilage
"Recht im Aussenhandel."* A detailed Soviet discussion of the
Bank can be found in *The American Review of Soviet and Eastern
European Foreign Trade*, Jan./Feb., 1965, pp. 52 ff.
  More interestingly, Mr. Nasarkin predicted that after one
year the Council would discuss the possibility of forming part
of the capital in freely convertible foreign exchange or gold
and letting members exchange freely transferable rubles for
these. See *ND*, 3-18-1964, p. 7. According to a report in *The
New York Times* of 3-30-1964, p. 43, this is exactly what has
been demanded by Polish Deputy Premier Jarosiewicz. Specifically, the Poles have proposed that a country which for a
longer time possesses a surplus on its account could exchange
10 per cent of that surplus into gold and that a debtor country with negative balances for a longer period be required to
pay part of the debt in gold or convertible currencies. After a number of years and through a series of stages, attainment of 100 per cent convertibility was urged. The Poles
have also criticized the low interest rates levied on debtors
and the still lower ones received by creditors (0.25 to 1.5
per cent). Henryk Kotlicki, General Director of the Polish
Ministry of Finance, noted that even after more than a year
of Bank operations, member countries, "when concluding commercial agreements, continue to try to balance their accounts bilaterally." See Radio Free Europe, *Situation Report*, Poland,
5-3-1965, and 5-19-1965.

[49]Some of these products are said to be produced by several
CMEA members, others by a single country only. The latter has
been indicated by an asterisk. The absence of such an indication, however, does not necessarily imply production by more
than one country. Nor is this list to be regarded as an exhaustive one. Data for Albania, not now a member, relate to
the time before 1962; data for Outer Mongolia are not available.

[50]It should also be noted that former Premier Khrushchev had
been quite chagrined by the obstacles to specialization put
forth in the name of assuring a complex development of each
national economy. In November of 1962, he proposed the creation of a powerful international planning agency of CMEA countries. It was to have the task of setting up, on the basis of
scientific-technical priorities, a collective single development plan, treating the CMEA countries as a uniform economic
organism. He considered this the logical next step of the
common road to a united world economy. However, apart from an
enthusiastic endorsement by Walter Ulbricht and Bruno Leuschner of East Germany, nothing more has been heard of this. See
ND, 1-16-1963, p. 5, and 2-10-1963, p. 7. It is clear, nevertheless, that this is indeed the logical next step of development. Just as the national State Planning Commission would be
foolish to regard factors of production as immobile across
province boundaries or to insist that each province develop a
multi-branch structure of all industries, so the present im-
mobility of factors across national boundaries or the insistence to develop in complex fashion each national economy is
foolish from a bloc viewpoint. A supra-national planning
agency might well dispense with such obstacles. However, it
is equally clear that such visions are more likely to shatter
on the rock of nationalism even in a Communist world than they
are to be realized. National pride, as well as Communist
ideology, demand the creation of diversified national economies, and it has been extremely difficult to agree on not producing something. Besides this type of "bourgeois nationalism," the inability to compare costs has been a major road-
block. See Imre Vajda in Internationale sozialistische Arbeitsteilung und Perspektivplanung (East Berlin: Verlag Die
Wirtschaft, 1961), pp. 72-73.
     Very recently, the Soviet Union has made several attempts
to strengthen bilateral cooperation by establishing joint
councils, as with Czechoslovakia and Bulgaria. After failure
of the single CMEA plan, it is reported that hereby "cooperation. . . is rising to a qualitatively new and higher level."
See The New York Times, 1-10-1964, p. 59, and 2-21-1964, page
3.

[51]Nevertheless, complaints of insufficient specialization are

frequent. For instance, Bulgaria, Hungary, and Rumania are
said to all produce polyamide-fibers, -silk, and -cord. It
was suggested that they might do better if each one specialized in one of these, supplying the other two. See Peter Grabley, *"Spezielle Probleme der internationalen Spezialisierung
der Produktion der chemischen Industrie,"* in *Internationale
sozialistische Arbeitsteilung und Perspektivplanung* (East Berlin: Verlag Die Wirtschaft, 1961), p. 116.

[52]In the case of East Germany in light-weight machinery and
vehicles and electro-technical, optical, and fine mechanical
products. By the late 1950's, East Germany was also the bloc's
first exporter of products of the metal-working industries.

[53]See *AH*, 2, 1963, pp. 16 and 17.

[54]See the argument in APPENDIX C as well as Willi Kunz and
Rudolf Brauer, *op. cit.*, p. 27.

CHAPTER 4 INTERNATIONAL TRADE THEORY IN THE SOVIET BLOC

A study of the Communist literature on foreign trade since the end of World War II reveals an interesting metamorphosis. Until the early 1950's, theoretical articles dealing with foreign trade simply did not appear. In light of the autarkic tendencies in all of the Communist countries, as noted in CHAPTER 3, this is not really surprising. Foreign trade being nothing more than "an additional source of aid to the national economy," provided no particular challenge to theorists. Textbooks and articles limited themselves to propagandistic evaluations of socialist versus capitalist foreign trade.[1]

This changed suddenly after 1955. CMEA had entered its second phase of existence. It became fashionable to attack the wisdom of imitating the Soviet history of autarky and to contemplate a large-scale international division of labor within the Communist bloc. Since then, however, a second obstacle has seriously hampered the development of foreign trade theory in the bloc. This new obstacle is the unfortunate entanglement of all Communist theorists in their own ideology. The Marxian heritage is the direct cause for some uncomfortable questions. Should the "law of value" determine what is rational conduct of foreign trade? Or should it not be rather overridden by the "law of planned proportional development?" And if the former is allowed to play any part, how is one to find VALUE, that most elusive, enigmatic, and unfathomable thing which, it is claimed, only labor can create? There has not appeared a single article which is entirely free from the inner conflict of reconciling Marxist and "bourgeois" economic analysis. Ideology, like an evil spirt, casts a dark spell over all and everything and allows no fast solution to be found.

The immediate result of this is a certain ambiguity even

as to the goal of foreign trade. It is all right to point out
the advantages of following the law of value[2] and to contemplate the saving of "socially necessary labor": if it takes
700 hours of labor to produce watches that can be imported for
$50, while 500 hours of labor can produce sewing machines
yielding the same amount when exported, the possibility of saving 200 hours of labor is obvious (at least if we follow the
Marxian reasoning). A great number of Communist economists
have favorably considered this idea. It helps, of course, to
quote a relevant passage from the "Master," just to make sure
that no one suspects a dangerously independent thought. One
may also cite Ricardo, since Marx approved of things he said.
(Many of the patient explanations of Ricardo in the post-1955
Communist literature concentrated on absolute advantage, however, and once in a while the theory of comparative advantage
was "discovered" with great surprise.) What one may not do
without incurring the wrath of the Party and the label "bourgeois revisionist" is to go a step further and openly advocate
that the law of value alone be used in the name of efficiency
to determine exports and imports and the international division of labor. Yet, some have said so, others have implied
it. They had to be told of Ricardo's "class limitations" making it impossible for him to see "the true shameful and self-
ish reasons of trade under capitalism and the deepening of
disproportions by the law of value." They had to be reminded
that there is more to socialist trade than the saving of social labor: It is to develop the entire socialist world and
help conquer capitalism. It must ensure for each country its
own industrial base through relations of "equality, proletarian internationalism, and selfless help." It must lead to a
"uniform distribution of productive resources throughout the
socialist world" after the lesser developed nations have approached the level of the developed ones. This cannot be done

by following the law of value, but only by following that of
planned proportional development.[3]

Somewhat shaken, such Communist theorists then suggested
that, after all, direct economic gains (i.e., gains from trade
proper) do not matter so much because indirect economic gains
(as economies of scale) could be much more important. (Indeed, a high Polish government official told the author that
this would "certainly" be the case.) And they hastened to add
that non-economic objectives must, of course, never be forgotten.[4]

From all this a sort of triune goal has emerged as an acceptable description of what foreign trade is to accomplish:
1) create direct economic profitability (to be discussed in
this chapter), 2) create indirect economic profitability
(e.g., full employment, technological progress), and 3) gain
non-economic objectives (e.g., of political nature). None of
the three, it is held, can stand alone. That would be the
case if trade were regulated by the law of value. This regulating function must be denied to it. The primacy of the law
of planned proportional development must be enforced.

The longing for efficiency, however, is strong. Therefore, it is also held that one may "use the law of value to
better enforce the law of planned proportional development."
What is meant by this and how this present (1965) attitude
evolved, will be shown in this chapter.

A.   CRITERIA FOR MEASURING DIRECT ECONOMIC PROFITABILITY

1.   Simple Price Comparisons

The internal prices of all Communist countries are effec-
tively separated from external ones by the institution of the
foreign trade monopoly.[5] The reason usually given for this is
"to prevent the spontaneous influence of the law of value on
the economy and to ensure the economy's planned proportional

development." As a result, there are often highly irrational
internal price systems.[6] A comparison of these internal
prices with the external ones as a basis for conducting rational foreign trade must therefore be regarded as absurd.
But this was exactly what has been encouraged with the greatest vigor, in East Germany at least, from 1954 until the late
1950's (originally by Strobel).

As elaborated upon in APPENDIX B, in East Germany, the
state-owned foreign trade enterprises buy export commodities
from their producers at official internal prices (Betriebsabgabepreise).[7] After sale abroad, the central bank exchanges
the foreign-exchange receipts at the official exchange rate
for commercial transactions. The amount received in this way
is equal to the amount originally spent only by sheer coincidence. Quite likely, there is a positive or negative difference which in East Germany is called Preisausgleich (price
equalization payment, hereafter referred to as PAG). In the
case of imports, the case is similar. The foreign trade enterprises pay to the central bank the official DM equivalent of
the foreign exchange needed, but they subsequently sell the
imports at the official internal prices (Betriebsabgabepreise)
to the internal trading organizations. Again, they will end
up with more or less, and only by chance with the same amount,
of internal currency they started out with.

Unfortunately for the economist, the profitability of the
foreign trade enterprises (in the narrow sense of money intake
versus outgo) was equated originally with the direct economic
profitability of foreign trade, and the incentives of managers
have been tied to this former type of profitability. The PAG
was long considered in East Germany the perfect measure of the
gains from trade. For foreign trade as a whole, a net positive PAG was therefore "good," while a net negative one was
"bad." For an individual commodity, the same criterion was

used - though in the form of the PAG rate (PAG per DM 1,000 of
producer price) - and an increase in the positive or decrease
in the negative rate was regarded as the symbol of success
(which from the manager's personal standpoint it was!).

The absurdity of determining one's trade structure on the
basis of a comparison most of the elements of which (internal
prices, exchange rates) one can arbitrarily determine need not
be belabored. First of all, use of the PAG criterion might
interfere with already established policies, as Černiansky has
shown for Czechoslovakia.[8] Secondly, the PAG could be manipu-
lated to become any desired figure by changing internal prices
and exchange rates appropriately. There are many other factors that influence also the size of the over-all PAG, such as
changes in the trade balance or structure, and thereby contribute to the complete meaninglessness of the criterion for the
purpose it is intended to serve. Nevertheless, the PAG has
held almost the center of attention in the Communist foreign
trade literature for a decade. Even today it is still one of
several indexes "calculated for all commodities regularly, not
less than once a year, in virtually all the member-states of
Comecon."[9] The discussion about the PAG is summarized in the
remainder of this section.

The relation between the PAG and the state budget has
been regarded as significant. The over-all net PAG, (i.e., the
sum of all PAG's for all commodities entering foreign trade)
whether positive or negative, automatically becomes part of
the budget as revenue or expenditure, respectively. This will
be shown in detail in APPENDIX B. The East German planners,
e.g., have worried about the fact of a "subsidy" to foreign
trade in the form of a persistent net negative over-all PAG.
(It took many articles, however, to convince everyone that
only the net figure mattered.) The Second Five Year Plan's
directives demanded its abolition. In the course of these

considerations, the government thought of an ingeneous way of decreasing the "subsidy," viz, by changing the formula by which the PAG for export goods is calculated and refraining from collecting state profits on such goods. This can be illustrated as follows: Each commodity has two internal prices, the official producer price Bi *(Betriebsabgabepreis* expressed in internal currency) and the official industry price Ii *(Industrieabgabepreis* expressed in internal currency). The latter is equal to the former plus state profits P *(Produktionsabgabe* or *staatliches Reineinkommen)*. While the producer receives Bi, the commodity is sold at Ii. Up to 1956, state profits P had to be paid for imports as well as exports, since then for imports only. Until 1956, the PAG for an export commodity was equal to the DM equivalent of the foreign-exchange receipts, E, minus Ii, since then to E minus Bi. For imports, the PAG always was Bi minus the DM equivalent of foreign exchange expended, E'. Assuming arbitrary figures for Bi, P, Ii, E, and E', the old and new systems, in their effect on the size of the PAG and the state budget (PAG plus P), can be compared as follows (in DM).

Assumed Data

	Export commodity	Import commodity	net
Producer price, Bi	100	100	
State profit, P	50	50	
Industry price, Ii	150	150	
Foreign-exchange equivalent, E or E'	400	500	

Calculated Data: Old System

PAG	250	-400	-150
P	50	50	100
Budget effect	300	-350	- 50

Calculated Data: New System

	Export commodity	Import commodity	net
PAG	300	-400	-100
P	not collected	50	50
Budget effect	300	-350	- 50

It becomes obvious immediately that the budget was affected in no way whatsoever by introducing the new system. In the
new system it gained as a positive PAG what it lost as state
profit, and the "decreasing of the subsidy to foreign trade"
was nothing but a piece of arithmetic.

This has irked to no end the steadfast believers in "rational trade via the PAG." It has especially irked Wilfried
Schöne, the most steadfast of them all.[10] Fully aware of all
the criticisms made of the PAG, he held a comparison of G.D.R.
prices with their foreign-exchange equivalent to be superior
to any method of determining trade profitability and international specialization. He argued a country is gaining from
trade, if only imports evaluated at internal prices equal or
exceed exports likewise evaluated, trade being balanced at external prices.

Schöne approved of the old system of determining the PAG,
and vigorously attacked the new one. He argued that state
profits should be paid for exports, since they are part of
production value (signifying "East Germany's high expenditures
for cultural, scientific, social, and educational purposes").
He felt that this would be worth the trouble, even if it meant
a circuitous routing of funds. A negative PAG should not ar-
tificially be abolished, for it is the most important economic lever needed to increase productivity. He equally vigorously fought those who wanted to distort the "pure PAG figures"
even more. For instance, some suggested to use a figure below
the producer price, B_i, to determine the PAG in those cases

where a low cost firm is making "excess" profits at the official producer price.[11]   Others felt the payment of state profits to be equally absurd for imports as exports.[12]

The first faint rumblings of discontent with the whole system could be heard by 1957. Krätzschmar noted a strange effect in using the PAG rate in determing and comparing different commodities' export profitabilities: an increase of the internal price, completely made good by a corresponding increase of the foreign price, worsened nevertheless the PAG rate substantially.[13] Many East German economists have since broken outright with the concept. But some were still clinging to it by 1961 as a useful criterion for judging the direction the international division of labor should take.

Some recent reports even indicate a new sophistication to the PAG system (officially not confirmed). According to these, the East German government instituted a double PAG system on January 1, 1959. One of the two PAG's is identical with the one described above. A second PAG, however, which is paid into or out of the central bank, is added to eliminate distortions due to "unreal" exchange rates. Assuming generally overvalued rates of DM for foreign currencies, exporters get and importers pay too little as they exchange foreign currencies at the central bank. Hence the second PAG is defined as "the DM equivalent calculated by a purchasing power rate minus the equivalent at the official rate" in the case of exports, and vice versa for imports. This may be illustrated as follows:

Suppose that the producer price, B_i, of an export commodity is DM 100, the world market price being \$30. The official rate of exchange being 2.2 DM/\$, the old PAG would be DM 66 minus DM 100, or minus DM 34. Exports are "unprofitable," DM 34 having to be paid out of the state budget. The new PAG, however, would be (assuming a purchasing power parity rate of 4.2 DM/$) DM 126 (the amount the exporter "should have gotten") minus DM 66 (what he did get), i.e., DM 60, which the central bank must pay. Now the total PAG becomes minus DM 34 plus DM 60, or DM 26. Export is profitable, after all.

The fact that this sort of manipulation can be made under-lines the worthlessness of the PAG concept. The government, by simple decree, could change all variables used for decision making. Hence it could make any pattern of specialization and trade appear reasonable.

2. Indicators of Profitability

Those who did not share the widespread enthusiasm for the PAG began a search of their own for a more meaningful crite-rion of trade profitability. The first articles on this sub-ject appeared in Hungary and Czechoslovakia in 1954, in Poland in 1955, in Bulgaria, Rumania, and East Germany during the following two years, and in the Soviet Union not until 1958. These articles reveal that there are five basic types of "in-dicators" that are being suggested for use in deciding ration-ally on the regional and commodity structure of international trade and the international division of labor. These will be considered in the following pages.

It should also be noted that the proposals have not re-mained just that. In Hungary, for example, a joint executive order by the Ministry for Foreign Trade and the production ministries (of March 10, 1959) and a previous one by the Fi-nance Ministry and the Ministry for Foreign Trade (of May 3, 1958) had demanded that at least 70 per cent of the export vol-ume be investigated by such indicators, the exact products to be selected by a central committee.[14] The East German State Planning Commission ruled on January 31, 1958, that it would use such indicators in future planning, but, it was added, characteristically, that such data are only a guide for the

enforcing of the law of planned proportional development.[15]
The Central Committee of the East German Communist Party has
repeatedly urged to put the foreign trade profitability question into the center of attention and start a systematic indicator analysis to improve the trade structure. The East German Ministry for Foreign and Intra-German Trade issued an executive order in early 1959 to calculate and utilize trade
profitability indicators[15] (later reported to have been actually calculated for about 75 per cent of exports). Finally,
the above-mentioned conference report by Georgiev noted the
general use by 1964 by all CMEA countries of the indicators
discussed below.

a.   The Foreign Exchange Indicator

After the discussion of the PAG, this indicator, usually
denoted by the symbol De in the East German literature, is
disappointing. One has to look hard for any improvement over
the PAG, if there is any at all. It will be recalled that the
PAG constituted a comparison of the internal producer price
and the foreign exchange paid or received, translated at the
official exchange rate. Hence the PAG profitability criterion
can be expressed as in formulas 1a) and 1b):

1a)   PAG for exports = $(xPw \cdot R) - Bi$

1b)   PAG for imports = $Bi - (mPw \cdot R)$, where

xPw   is the world market price for exports f.o.b. border ex-
      porting country in terms of foreign currency

 R   is the official exchange rate for commercial transactions
      in DM (etc.) per unit of foreign currency

 Bi   is the official internal producer price (Betriebsabgabe-
      preis) in domestic currency

mPw   is the world market price for imports c.i.f. border im-
      porting country in terms of foreign currency.

The foreign-exchange coefficient De differs from the PAG
only by 1) considering costs beyond the point of emergence of
the finished physical commodity, and 2) being expressed as a

ratio rather than a difference. This supposedly makes it better than the PAG; and it shows profitability "from the standpoint of the internal social labor effort," in spite of the
continued use of irrational internal prices and possibly arbitrary exchange rates.

One finds a number of variations of this coefficient.
Using the following symbols in addition to the ones above,
formulas 2a) through 2h) express these variations.

Ai   are additional internal costs, such as for administration,
     storage, selling, packaging, transportation, insurance,
     etc.

Aw   are additional world market costs, i.e., the same type of
     expenditure as under Ai, but incurred in foreign exchange
     beyond the border.

Ki   are the actual internal producer costs (Selbstkosten),
     i.e., the sum of wages, material costs and depreciation
     allowances, which together with a producer profit or loss
     equals Bi

Ii   is the official internal industry price (Industrieabgabe-
     preis) which is equal to Bi plus state profits or turn-
     over tax P (Produktionsabgabe)[16]

Formulas 2a) through 2f) have been suggested for exports,
2g) and 2h) for imports.

$$2a) \quad De = \frac{xPw}{Ki + Ai} \qquad\qquad 2b) \quad De = \frac{xPw}{Ki}$$

$$2c) \quad De = \frac{Ki + Ai}{xPw - Aw} \qquad\qquad 2d) \quad De = \frac{xPw \cdot R}{Bi + Ai}$$

$$2e) \quad De = \frac{xPw \cdot R}{Ii + Ai} \qquad\qquad 2f) \quad De = \frac{xPw \cdot R}{Ki + Ai}$$

$$2g) \quad De = \frac{Bi}{(mPw \cdot R) + Ai} \qquad\qquad 2h) \quad De = \frac{Ii}{(mPw \cdot R) + Ai}$$

Some writers proposed some further refinements, such as the inclusion in Ii of theoretical state profits when means of production are exported (for them state profits are usually zero,
hence Ii = Bi) and the evaluation of the material component in
Ki, Bi, and Ii not at undervalued internal prices, but at
world market price times exchange rate. Even then, however,

East German theoreticians are worried about the comparability of numerator and denominator, because G.D.R. costs, as they put it, include costs of the social and cultural care of workers and non-exploitative wages, and they exclude calculated risks, while this is not so with world market prices.

The calculation of weighted average De figures for larger groups, as all the exports of one industry or to one area, has also been suggested. If n is designated as the percentage of total exports of an industry (or to a particular area) which the individual export commodity represents, this could be expressed in the following form:

Formula 2i) Average De for industry or area = $\dfrac{\Sigma n \cdot De}{\Sigma n}$

As was said above, the similarity between PAG and De is rather pronounced. What was criticized in the former still holds for the latter. The juxtaposition of arbitrarily determined and irrational internal prices with external prices translated (in some of the formulas at least) via equally arbitrary exchange rates can hardly be regarded as a satisfactory way of making trade more rational. Some East Germans have expressed this view also. Nevertheless, the East German State Planning Commission has used De since early 1958, and, by the middle of 1960, De had been calculated for half of the G.D.R.'s export volume.[17] In Hungary, De has also been used for agricultural exports (in addition to such data as world market receipts per acre.)[14]

b.   The Material Indicator

The calculation and use of this indicator has only been reported for East Germany. It reflects the East German desires, all of which are inter-related, of holding raw material imports to a minimum, increasing labor-intensive exports, and accumulating at least a small foreign-exchange reserve. The material indicator, usually denoted Dm, shows considerable im-

provement over the ones discussed above. It avoids completely
the use of the East German price system. The literature shows
two variants for exports, but just one formula for imports.
These are given below as Formulas 3a) and 3b) on the one
hand, and 3c) on the other. In addition to symbols used earlier, we have

mw   world market price of all (domestic as well as imported)
      raw materials, semi-finished, and finished goods enter-
      ing the product

Mw   world market price of imported raw materials, semi-finish-
      ed, and finished goods entering the product

$$3a) \quad Dm = \frac{xPw - Aw}{mw} \qquad\qquad 3b) \quad Dm = \frac{xPw - Aw}{Mw}$$

$$3c) \quad Dm = \frac{mPw}{mw}$$

The export indicators measure the net foreign-exchange
gain, taking account either only of previous foreign exchange
spent on material imports 3b) or also of the potential foreign exchange lost by not exporting domestic materials 3a).
An export in cases where 3a) is less than unity is obviously
absurd. The import coefficient 3c) is to show whether it
might not be preferable to import material and produce at home
rather than import the finished product. This might be the
case when 3c) is very much greater than unity.

As in the case of De, the calculation of averages has
been suggested, such as

$$3d) \quad \text{Average Dm for industry or area} = \frac{\Sigma n \cdot Dm}{\Sigma n}$$

Specific difficulties have arisen with this indicator
for two reasons. First, the question of what is meant by
"world market price" has no simple answer. This problem will
be taken up below (and is, of course, equally important for
De). Second, it is by no means clear whether mw or Mw should
be deducted as they enter the last production stage or rather,

from a more global point of view, encompassing all production
stages. If one takes the former and easier route, the result
may not be very meaningful. An actual case has been reported
of a heavy machinery product where the deduction of material
entering the last stage of production resulted in a Dm of
1.33. Then the previous stage was analyzed (electrical equipment for the heavy machinery product). More than two thirds
of its costs were wages. Deducting thereupon, material from
the standpoint of the last two production stages, Dm became
1.92.[18]

It is reported that this indicator has been actually used
by the East German State Planning Commission since early 1958,
at least for exports, and that by the middle of 1960 such indicators existed for half the export volume. Some governmental agencies were using the Dm figure already in 1957.[19]

c.   The Labor Indicators

The so-called global and last stage labor indicators of
trade profitability, which are the subject of this section,
have received the greatest attention throughout the Communist
bloc and are known to have been used intensively by CMEA.[20]
They were developed by the Czech economist Viliam Černiansky.
As the admirers of the PAG and the De coefficient, Černiansky
and those who followed his lead wanted to have a measure of
the gains from trade or "the saving of socially necessary labor" in order to create a reasonable pattern of trade. Since
labor hours of exports and imports could not be compared directly, it had to be done via the measuring rod of money.
Černiansky and his followers, however, rejected the use of internal prices as they were. They proceeded to "purify" them
from the distortions of a governmentally fixed price structure. By excluding from the prices those parts that did not
represent "true production value" a quantum was to be found
that "truly expressed social labor."

In presenting these coefficients the following symbols will be used in addition to those employed earlier:

mi   internal price of all (domestic as well as imported) raw materials, semi-finished, and finished goods entering the product (usually deducted in East Germany, Hungary and Poland)

Mi   internal price of imported raw materials, semi-finished, and finished goods entering the product (usually deducted in Bulgaria and Czechoslovakia)

Si   state profits and net taxes (taxes minus subsidies) from all production stages

si   as Si, but for last production stage only

Ni   internal price of by-products (*Nebenprodukte*)

All labor indicators have been developed for exports only. The so-called global indicator is given as Formula 4a) below.

$$4a) \quad \text{global labor indicator} = \frac{Ki - Si - Mi + Ai}{xPw - Mw - Aw}$$

This ratio shows that x units of domestic currency have produced y units of foreign exchange. In contrast to a formula, as 2c) above, however, the x units of domestic currency are believed to truly represent nothing but domestic labor applied directly (wages) or indirectly (raw materials, depreciation). The ratio constitutes a real exchange rate for a given export transaction, and those goods with the most favorable rates of this kind are claimed to be preferable in export to the ones with less favorable rates.

Though one might argue that the "purified" numerator of the above formula still represents arbitrary internal prices, Communist theorists do not agree. The formula has been used very widely in Czechoslovakia. The foreign trade enterprises, under the guidance of the Ministry of Foreign Trade, have calculated this indicator for 80 per cent of exports. In cases where indicators for individual commodities differ widely from the average, a special committee is formed (consisting of representatives of the Ministry of Foreign Trade, the production ministries involved, the foreign trade enterprises, and the producing firms) to investigate more fully and make then recommendations to the State Planning Commission.[21] In Hungary the Foreign Trade Ministry and the foreign trade enterprises use this formula for analyses from the standpoint of the economy as a whole, but a variation of the formula for industry-by-industry studies. (The variation concerns the definition of imports, all material purchases from other domestic industries as well as from abroad being regarded as "imports" of the particular industry.)[14] In East Germany, in addition to all the others, this formula has also been used since early 1958. It has, furthermore, been used in Bulgaria, China, Poland, Rumania, the Soviet Union, and Yugoslavia.[22]

A variation of the global (all labor) indicator is the last-stage (live labor) indicator of which the author found eight variations. These are given below as formulas 4b) through 4i) and designated, as customary in the East German literature, by the symbol Da.

4b) $Da = \dfrac{Ki - mi + Ai}{xPw - mw - Aw}$ 4c) $Da = \dfrac{xPw - mw - Aw}{Bi - mi + Ai}$

4d) $Da = \dfrac{xPw - mw - Aw}{Ii - mi + Ai}$ 4e) $Da = \dfrac{(xPw - mw - Aw) \cdot R}{Ki - mi + Ai}$

4f) $Da = \dfrac{(xPw - mw - Aw) \cdot R}{Bi - mi + Ai}$ 4g) $Da = \dfrac{(xPw - mw - Aw) \cdot R}{Ii - mi + Ai}$

4h) $Da = \dfrac{xPw - mw}{Bi + Ai}$ 4i) $Da = \dfrac{Bi - si - mi - Ni + Ai}{xPw - mw - Aw}$

These ratios are to show how many units of domestic currency, representing in this case "live" labor only, fetch how many units of foreign exchange, similarly representing "live" labor. The ratios are a world market price of the last stage labor cost. (It is, of course, of no significance that numerator and denominator are sometimes interchanged.) For a more general view, again, averages can be constructed, such as

4j) Average Da for industry or area $= \dfrac{\Sigma n \cdot Da}{\Sigma n}$

The formula originally advanced by Černianský is 4b)
above. It has been the target of an enormous barrage of criticism, even apart from the one, inspired by ideology, that one
must not worry about the law of value. Some critics do not
like the formula as such, others like it, but are doubtful
that the practical difficulties of calculation can be overcome
in a satisfactory manner. Among the criticisms of substance
are the following:

1)   It is feared that use of this formula would encourage material intensive exports which is just what one may want to
avoid.

2)   One may overlook an even more profitable export at an
earlier stage of production.

3)   One should not exclude state profits, because they are
part of value. Especially the Russians and Chinese have
brought forth this objection. They hold that the numerator
and denominator would not be comparable otherwise and that
likewise the indicators for different commodities would not be
comparable within a country or internationally. (As reasons
are given longish Marxist argumentations, such as differences
among commodities as to the relation producer costs Ki and
"true value," because the size of accumulation depends on the
share of wages within costs, and differences in wage policies
among countries with wages following a productivity increase
not everywhere to the same degree.) The use of Ii instead of
Ki in some of the formulas, of course, meets this objection.

4)   The indicator loses any meaning in cases where by-products are of importance. This is especially true for chemicals where there is a wide choice of production functions, and
previous by-products can be used later on or can be sold,
sometimes for more than the main product. The Hungarians have
met this criticism by using formula 4i) above.

5)   The exclusion of imported as well as domestic materials

from the formulas is absurd, because it matters very much to what degree imports are necessary and what the country's raw material endowment is. How can one possibly, the Chinese have asked, determine the international division of labor by a labor coefficient only? Why does Rumania export oil? Is it only because Rumanian live labor is best at getting oil, or have, by chance, natural resources something to do with it, too?

6)   In spite of all the talk to the contrary, internal prices are still used in these formulas and they are not "values."

Those, on the other hand, who approve of the formula, but are concerned about practical difficulties, have this to say:

1)   It is very difficult to decide for all the products and materials under investigation what the world market price is. Some suggest to use an average price from the capitalist world market over some past period, usually the previous year, others would want to use prices actually paid or received by the particular country (though it is hard to see how this could be done in evaluating domestic materials that could have been exported potentially), while a third group advocates the use of typical rather than average prices, i.e., prices paid or received for the largest part of the import or export volume, respectively, if they can be expected to remain at that level. Additional trouble arises from the question whether and how capitalist world market prices are to be "purified from monopolistic, speculative, and cyclical fluctuations." Some items, furthermore, do not have world market prices. This particular problem has apparently been solved in East Germany by calculating an indicator that stands somewhere in-between the global 4a) above and the last stage indicator (4b-i). Materials without world market price are themselves broken up into wages and material costs and the elements then treated as belonging to the last production stage of the good. This in ef-

fect means that such materials are not deducted from total
costs.

In the G.D.R., the foreign trade enterprises are given
special coefficients for four categories of goods (raw materials, semi-finished goods, finished goods, and auxiliary materials, such as grease and electricity) with which to estimate world market prices.[23] In Hungary, on the other hand,
the Ministry of Foreign Trade has published a detailed foreign-exchange price list for all materials. The use of this
list is obligatory. If any items are not found in it, the
price is to be established from the average net export or import price on the capitalist world market or in some other
way, but it has to be approved by the Ministry and is obligatory thereafter.[14]

2) It is very difficult to gather correct cost data for thousands of goods and to split them into wages, domestic material
costs, and imported material costs. In addition, costs differ
widely among plants, some materials include state profits and
taxes from earlier production stages, while others do not, and
nobody is certain what to do about it.

Finally, as was mentioned earlier, the question arises
whether costs should be split in this way from the standpoint
of the last production stage or the entire production process.
If one does the former, one can get practically any result depending on the number of production stages. (In the case of
the machinery product mentioned earlier, Da was .36 making the
split from the last stage only, it became .52 by including the
previous stage.) Hence many would like to look at the whole
production process or at least split all semi-finished and
finished goods entering the last stage into wages and material
costs. In East Germany, the Department for Balancing and Distribution of the Means of Production at the State Planning
Commission has begun to determine the basic material content

of different products from the standpoint of the whole economy.[24] On the basis of such a list, which is re-examined and
expanded every year, the foreign trade enterprises are to determine the internal and foreign-exchange value of the material contained in the commodity. Deducting this from total
cost, an estimate of wages remains. The great advantage of
this procedure is believed to be the neglect of the particular
situation of a particular plant and the comparability of all
coefficients calculated once the same method is used everywhere.[25]

In general, one can state that these indicators still are
regarded with suspicion. In Hungary, for instance, independent estimates of producer costs, Ki, varied ±15 per cent of
"actual costs," estimates of world market prices ±8 per cent,
and the resultant coefficients were regarded as having a ±25
per cent margin of error for machinery products, ±20 per cent
for textiles.[14]

In spite of all, however, also the Da indicator is widely
used, particularly in the European Communist countries and, as
will be shown shortly, within CMEA.

d.   The Social Cost Indicator

The Chinese also proceeded to search for a formula serving as a basis for specialization decisions. They proposed to
save "true social costs," taking also account of a country's
capital and natural resource endowment. In good Marxist fashion, the value of a commodity was described as c + v + s,
where c is the constant capital of production, v is variable
capital, and s is surplus value. If we define r as the average rate of accumulation for the year, i.e., s divided by
v + s, a commodity's value can obviously also be written as
$c + v + \frac{v \cdot r}{1 - r}$. This value, they argued, is not expressed by
internal prices, but can be calculated from v and r which are
believed to express society's labor correctly. For the mate-

rial component, c, they propose not to use internal prices,
but "value" which can be derived by going back a few stages in
the production process. An example of how the "value" of a
certain type of glass might be calculated in China as a preliminary to deciding on its export profitability has been published and with slight variation in the order of presentation,
can be paraphrased as follows. Two obvious misprints in the
article have been corrected by the author:[26]

How to find the "value" of 1 unit of glass, producer price,
Bi = 1,377 yuan:

> The average rate of accumulation for the given year was
> r = .209 (20.9 per cent). The producer cost, Ki, could be
> broken down as follows:

c { raw materials	311 yuan
{ auxiliary materials	400 "
{ electricity	240 "
v wages	65 "
total	1,016 yuan

> Hence society's surplus value was
>
> $$s = \frac{v \cdot r}{1-r} = \frac{65 \cdot .209}{1-.209} = 17.2 \text{ yuan}$$

> The values for v and s, but not for c, were considered re-
> liable. The "value" of c had to be found by "purifying"
> the price of c.
>
> 1) Investigation showed that the biggest part of <u>auxil-
>   iary materials</u>, namely 290 yuan, were wooden <u>boards</u>.
> Their producer cost Ki per unit broke down as follows:

c { raw materials	8,713 yuan
{ electricity	368 "
v wages	370 "
total	9,451 yuan

> Hence surplus value in this case was
>
> $$s = \frac{370 \cdot .209}{1-.209} = 97.8 \text{ yuan}$$

> Not wanting to go further back in the production process,
> the value of one unit of wooden boards was determined as
> c + v + s = 9,548.8 yuan. For the production of one unit
> of glass only .02517 units of wooden boards were needed,
> however, i.e., a value of 240.3 yuan. Since the price of
> this amount was 290 yuan, the 400 yuan auxiliary material
> figure for glass could be corrected by deducting the
> "false price" of 290 yuan and adding the "true value" of

240.3.   Then the auxiliary material figure became 350.3
yuan.
2) Foregoing further adjustments for other auxiliary ma-
    terials, the authors then proceeded with raw mater-
ials. The biggest part therein, 278 yuan, was sodium hydroxide. Again its cost per unit was broken down:

c	raw materials	5,725 yuan	
	auxiliary materials	4,399	"
	electricity	2,308	"
v	wages	1,353	"
	total	13,785 yuan	

From this followed a surplus value of s = 357.5 yuan

In this case it was deemed desirable to go somewhat further back to the prior stage of production to correct
the components of c before establishing the value of one
unit of sodium hydroxide.
   a) It turned out that the biggest part of auxiliary ma-
       terials for sodium hydroxide production was hemp
sack worth 2,112 yuan. The unit production costs were

c	raw materials	79.5 yuan	
	auxiliary materials	2.6	"
	electricity	13.2	"
v	wages	7.9	"
	total	103.2 yuan	

Surplus value, therefore, was s = 2.1 yuan.

Breaking off this line of inquiry at this point, the
value per unit of hemp sack was established as c + v +
s = 105.3 yuan. Per unit of sodium hydroxide, 12.5
units of hemp sack were needed, i.e., a value of
1,316.3 yuan. Now the 4,399 yuan auxiliary material
figure under sodium hydroxide was corrected by deducting a "false price" of 2,112 yuan and adding the "true
value" of 1,316.3, which gave 3,603.3 yuan as the "true
value" of auxiliary materials for sodium hydroxide production (neglecting other auxiliary materials besides
hemp sacks).
   b) The biggest part of raw materials for sodium hydrox-
       ide, on the other hand, were 4,942 yuan worth of
salt. Production costs per unit of salt were

c	electricity	357 yuan	
v	wages	329	"
	total	686 yuan	

Hence a surplus value s = 86.9 yuan

Breaking off again the line of inquiry at this point,
the value per unit of salt was found as c + v + s =

772.9 yuan. Per unit of sodium hydroxide, 1.9 units of
salt were needed, that is a value of 1,468.5 yuan. Now
also the 5,725 yuan raw materials figure under sodium
hydroxide was corrected by deducting the "meaningless
price" of 4,942 yuan and adding the "true value" of
1,468.5 yuan, which gave 2,251.5 yuan.

Foregoing corrections of other raw materials as well as for
electricity, the "true value" per unit of sodium hydroxide
turned out to be

raw materials (corrected for salt)	2,251.5 yuan
auxiliary materials (corrected for hemp sacks)	3,603.3 "
electricity	2,308.0 "
wages	1,353.0 "
surplus value	357.5 "
total	9,873.3 yuan

For one unit of glass only .01037 units of sodium hydroxide were needed, that was a value of 102.4 yuan. Now the
311 yuan raw material figure under glass could finally be
corrected by deducting the "wrong" sodium hydroxide price
of 278 yuan and adding the "true value" of 102.4 yuan.
This gave a corrected raw material figure of 135.4 yuan.
Foregoing possible adjustments for other glass raw materials as well as electricity, the "true value" per unit of
glass was calculated as follows:

raw materials (corrected for sodium hydroxide)	135.4 yuan
auxiliary materials (corrected for wooden boards)	350.3 "
electricity	240.0 "
wages	65.0 "
surplus value	17.2 "
total	807.9 yuan

It will be noted that this value figure is very different
from the producer price per unit of glass given in the beginning, 1,377 yuan.

Having established this unique way of finding "value" for
all commodities, the Chinese economists proposed to use and
actually are using the following formula for export profitability:

Formula 5) Export profitability indicator,

$$Pe = \frac{c + v + \dfrac{v \cdot r}{1-r} + Ai}{(xPw - Aw) \cdot R}$$

For the above example this formula gave the following result:

$$Pe = \frac{807.9 + 272}{671} = 1.61$$

This was interpreted to mean that for 1.61 yuan of internal value only 1 yuan worth of foreign value could be gotten. Export of the item was, therefore, deemed unprofitable.

e.   The Investment Indicator

The indices of foreign trade profitability, as discussed above, are primarily directed towards determining the most profitable use of existing production capacity. It was felt, however, that different indices were needed for deciding on the location of additions to productive capacity. CMEA countries have, therefore, begun to calculate indices of the foreign-exchange profitability of investments.[27] Index (6a), for instance, is being used in the Soviet Union. It compares the annual additional gross foreign-exchange earnings from additional production and export with the investment costs necessary to bring forth such new production. Indices (6b)-(6d) are used in Poland. (6b) is equivalent to the Soviet index except for substitution of a net foreign-exchange figure, (6c) further introduces consideration of the time over which investments can be used, and (6d) combines (6c) with a type of the well known labor index in order to consider current operating costs also. Index (6e) is used in Hungary (developed by M. Turanszki), where it is assumed that each investment must amortize itself within five years. It is systematically applied within Hungary (within the light industry it is calculated for all investment projects exceeding 2 million forints, for example). A variant, such as (6f), is also in use. In Czechoslovakia formula (6g) is in use, as discussed in section C below.

6a) $\dfrac{xPw}{I}$ 6b) $\dfrac{I}{xPw - Mw}$ 6c) $\dfrac{I}{(xPw - Mw)m}$

6d) $\dfrac{Ki - Mi}{xPw - Mw} + \dfrac{I}{(xPw - Mw)m}$ 6e) $\dfrac{xPw}{Ki + \dfrac{I}{5}}$

6f) $\dfrac{xPw - mw'}{Ki - mi' + \dfrac{I}{5}}$

Symbols:

I   investment costs for additional production for export (machinery, equipment, materials)

m   number of years for which investment can be used (The Polish State Planning Commission set $\dfrac{1}{m}$ = .15, i.e., it insists that the investment be amortized in about seven years)

mw'   world market price of imported materials and of domestic materials which could be exported

mi'   internal price of imported materials and of domestic materials which could be exported.

All other symbols have their usual meaning, but refer to the extra production made possible by I.

B.   FOREIGN TRADE PRICING

In the above discussion reference was frequently made to "world market prices." Just as the Communists had to decide how to adjust internal prices to better reflect costs, they have engaged in a heated debate over the kind of prices that should be used in foreign trade among the Communist nations. There are two opposing groups arguing about this question. One group proposes to use some average of internal prices of socialist countries. They feel these would reflect "true values," and it would become possible thereby "to let all socialist countries reap the fruits of production specialization via a continuous fall of foreign trade prices as productivity increases and costs and values fall."[28] Recent reports indicate that CMEA's Commission for Economic Problems is investigating

the creation of such a price basis for socialist world trade
via the improvement of internal price systems.

Another group believes that there can be no other criterion for socialist foreign trade than the (capitalist) world
market price since it is closest to value and "alone can assure equivalent exchange." Furthermore, this group holds,
trade among socialist countries would be seriously disrupted
if any other price basis existed, for socialist countries
would be tempted to trade with the capitalists each time import prices are lower or export prices higher in the capitalist market. Proponents of this view have accused the former
group of muddled thinking because they fail to see the absurdity of averaging arbitrary national prices via arbitrary
exchange rates. The adherents of the former view take refuge
under the cover of ideology: Must not the socialist countries
free themselves from capitalism? How then can they use the
prices of monopoly capital? Are not the followers of the
world market price idea underestimating the scientific pricing practices of the socialist nations on the basis of the
value created by socially necessary labor? Does not the use
of capitalist world market prices perpetuate exploitation of
the underdeveloped countries by those already highly industrialized?

In fact western world market prices are being used. The
actual history seems to be the following.[29] Originally average capitalist world market prices of 1950 were used as a
basis for negotiation among socialist states. Adjustments
were made if necessary. It was generally agreed that the
world market prices had to be "purified from monopolistic,
speculative, and cyclical influences" - which, the opponents
of the world market price view gleefully point out, is an
impossible undertaking. Nevertheless, somehow it has been and
is being done.

Since 1957, a CMEA price clause became valid for all socialist countries. Prices were expressed in rubles on the
basis of average world market prices of the previous year on
the principal market. There is some question about what this
means. Most writers understand by it the price which the
principal producer (provided he is also the principal exporter) is charging to the principal buyer. At least this is supposed to be that way for finished goods. For raw materials,
prices on intermediary markets, such as commodity exchanges,
are also held to be admissible (freed from speculation, of
course).

There still remain a lot of problems, however. Some suggest to use the main market in Europe. Others are troubled
about price differentiation by the main producer and exporter.
Another difficult question is the handling of transport costs.
Černianský used the example of Czech coke exports to Hungary:
The world market price was $24 per ton f.o.b. Hamburg, trans-
port costs from either Hungary or Czechoslovakia to Hamburg
per ton were $4 or $3, respectively. Selling at Hamburg,
Czechoslovakia could net $21 per ton; buying at Hamburg, Hung-
ary had to pay $28. Černianský and many others would propose
that the difference be split and trade in this case take
place at $24.50 per ton. Others could not quite see the logic
of this and pointed out weird consequences with the help of
this example, as the fact that the exporter is the better off
the farther the importer is away from the principal market.
A proposal was made in this connection to create an international freight equalization pool which is something like a
basing point system. In fact seller and buyer do share equally the difference between transport costs incorporated in the
world market delivered price and the actual transport cost.

The evidence suggests that world market prices are actually being set at three levels. First, there are long term

bilateral contracts which usually specify yearly minimum physical deliveries and values for key positions. If values are
not given, clauses are attached as to the required use of
world market prices. Second, there are yearly negotiations
for other important goods. Third, the foreign trade enterprises take care of the rest. In accordance with the CMEA decision from the Ninth Plenum, each socialist trade agreement
defines the principal market, determines which documents are
admissible to determine the price, and how required adjustments are to be made. Therefore, prices are held to be easily and objectively determinable. The seller is to document
prices, but the buyer may present counter-documentation.
Then prices might have to be adjusted, but once they are
agreed upon, further documents, even if they prove the objective wrongness of the price, are ignored. Apparently, the
documentation process takes a long time, and frequently agreements are signed with only quantity decisions made and "provisional" prices. Some have proposed the establishment of a
price court to quickly make a decision when the negotiators
cannot agree on a price, because according to the civil law
in all socialist countries a contract with provisional prices
is no contract and cannot be enforced. ·Since 1960, and at
present (1965), the same procedure is in use, but prices are
kept stable for several years.[30]

However, there is still much pressure for the creation
of an "own" socialist world market price in the future. The
reason given is the impossibility of getting rid of all capitalist speculative influences, the danger of unwillingly importing capitalist crises with a lag, as well as imitating the
capitalist exchange of non-equivalents. Such socialist prices
are proposed to be the result of a multilateral agreement, express average socially necessary labor in the camp, and decrease over time because of the law of increasing productiv-

ity. Their introduction is urged step by step, first for
goods which have already their principal market in the socialist world, then for goods most important in the international
specialization scheme (raw materials, chemicals, machinery)
and for goods which are new and have no capitalist price. For
all other goods, capitalist prices are urged to be continued
in use, but held constant for 10 year periods. Only after socialist countries have fulfilled their main task of surpassing
capitalism, would the use of capitalist prices (now still reflecting superior capitalist productivity) be entirely abandoned.

C.   THEORY AND CMEA DECISIONS

The extent to which the above theoretical tools have been
put to actual use within the CMEA commissions has become known
through a recent article.[31] According to its authors, who are
among the leading theoreticians in East Germany and Czechoslovakia, CMEA has definitely rejected the PAG. Since internal
prices do not reflect relative real costs, the calculation of
indicators has been approved, but general reforms in the internal price systems to make prices reflect values are being
urged as the better ultimate solution and are in fact under
way. Apparently, a formula, as 4e) above is being used. Such
indicator is being calculated in two versions, in order to reflect present as well as expected conditions: 1) actual
costs and world market prices are used, and 2) expected costs
and world market prices are used, the latter being, for instance, an agreed upon future price or a forecast. The authors also give one (fictitious) example which is said to be
typical of the procedure used.

Suppose the following labor indicators have been calculated by the trade organs in the countries named for a given
commodity:

East Germany: 30 (i.e., per 100 DM spent on labor internally, there are net foreign-exchange receipts, translated at the official exchange rate, of 30 DM)

Poland   40 (i.e., similarly, for 100 zlotys spent internally on labor, foreign exchange worth 40 zlotys is earned)

Czechoslovakia: 33

Hungary: 50

Then the decision will not be that Hungary should specialize in the production of the item in question. Just as internal prices were held to be not comparable, these indicators are not comparable with each other. They are, however, comparable with other indicators in the same country, in particular with the country's average indicator. Suppose that the relation to the national averages are as follows:

Country	Labor Indicator good x national average		Difference in per cent
East Germany	30	28	+7.1
Poland	40	60	-33.3
Czechoslovakia	33	40	-17.5
Hungary	50	95	-47.4

Then East Germany should specialize in good x, since she has a comparative advantage. As usual, we are assured that the actual specialization decision, however, is not made on this basis alone. Other questions are also considered, such as whether new investments would be required, while somewhere else only modernization of existing capacities would be needed, what will happen to the balance of payments, will such a decision interfere with the country's economic development. CMEA is said to make special efforts to help her poorer members develop, and this might well entail the neglect of short-run comparative cost considerations. A more recent article expands on this issue.[32] The authors reaffirm the need for some kind of value criteria, since natural indices are often contradictory and hence useless (e.g., steel production per worker in East Germany exceeds that in Poland, but the relation is inverted if expressed per square meter of furnace surface). It is reaffirmed that CMEA's Economic Problems Commission is working with live labor indicators, such as 4b) above, but it is criticized that only current operating costs are being considered in such a case. The Commission is said to take into account, therefore, also investment outlays by either separately looking at results from the well known recoupment formula or by combining it with the live labor indicator.

The former would take the form of comparing the times T required for amortization of additional investments where there is conflict between larger additional investment I_2 (and small annual operating costs Ki_2) and smaller additional investment I_1 (and large annual operating costs Ki_1), where the subscripts refer, as is usual, to variants of a given investment project within a country.

$$6g) \quad T = \frac{I_2 - I_1}{Ki_1 - Ki_2}$$

Assuming comparability of operating and investment figures, investment would occur in the country that can amortize faster.

The latter method has been illustrated by a formula corresponding very closely to 2c) above, but differing via incorporation of actual investment outlays. In fact it is just another version of the investment indicators discussed above:

$$6h) \quad \text{Export profitability} = \frac{xPw - Aw}{Ki + Ai + N \cdot I},$$ where N is to

be a "normative coefficient of the profitability of investment" which must be "uniform for all countries."

Clearly, this is nothing else but the addition of an interest charge on capital invested to all other costs.[33] A truly non-

Marxian achievement and remarkable step toward rationality!
At the same time, however, a reactionary remark by the authors
must also be reported. After presenting formula 6h) together
with a hypothetical example of its use very much like on page
187 above, they reach the opposite conclusion from Brauer and
Černiansky̌: one can tell nothing about specialization from
the percentage figure in the last column, for a country, though
relatively best at producing a good, might still not have the
lowest absolute costs. Ricardo, it seems, has again been forgotten.

In short, as was pointed out before, the law of value is
a guide, but not always and even then only one of many. Somewhere there are certain to be compromises between a wider international division of labor and the maximum development of
national economies.

D.   AN EVALUATION

From the standpoint of the Communists themselves, some
of the most recent theoretical developments, just as the practical actions discussed in CHAPTER 3, are an encouraging step
in the right direction. They are encouraging because it has
been realized that existing internal prices cannot furnish an
adequate guide to rational foreign trade decisions.

No less a luminary than Walter Ulbricht noted at the
Sixth Party Congress of the Socialist Unity Party:

> The fact that prices frequently reflect value in
> distorted fashion, and we are, therefore, incapable of
> telling what at present the production of a commodity
> actually costs, hampers the leaders and employees of
> firms in their struggle for strict frugality and causes
> us daily great economic losses.[34]

The latest developments are encouraging also because the calculation of indicators, as described above, whatever their im-
perfections, betrays an understanding of the fact that one
must overcome the divorce of domestic price structures from

real costs.

Of course, the indicators are not perfect. Many of them
implicitly assume labor as the only scarce factor of production, or at least that other factors are completely immobile.
This must introduce a costly bias into decisions. Suppose
there are two goods, a and b, with all the elements entering
the labor indicator formula being the same for both. Then the
indicators would be alike, and the planners might decide that
either a or b should be exported. Yet, if the marginal capital
to output ratio is higher in a than b, b should be exported
rather than a, because in the long run the same amount of labor, but less capital, would be needed for the same increase
in output. The CMEA nations, from their own standpoint (which
is to increase output as fast as possible to overtake capitalism), should not ignore the fact that two productive processes
with equal returns to domestic labor costs, but different
amounts of capital involved, are not equally economical. The
recent developments of investment profitability indicators is
a recognition of this fact, even if it is not a solution of
the problem. That problem is directly being tackled (though
again quite imperfectly) in the reforms of internal price systems, as they are currently being undertaken in the bloc countries.

In East Germany, according to a decision of the Presidium
of the Council of Ministers on December 19, 1962, a reform of
industrial prices was initiated on April 1, 1964, a second
phase went into effect on January 1, 1965, and the reform is
to be concluded in 1966. These prices are based on expected
1967 prime costs of production, are to eliminate subsidies to
a large extent, and are to overcome substantially the differential treatment of producer goods and consumer goods in pricing.
At the same time, a revaluation of the entire capital stock at
current reproduction costs went into effect on January 1, 1964,

with new and realistic depreciation allowances being put into
use simultaneously with the various phases of the price reform.[35] But there is still a long way to be travelled towards
a rational price system.

FOOTNOTES

[1]This evaluation boiled down to the statement that socialist
foreign trade, being based on people's property and the foreign trade monopoly, serves the exchange of equivalents, but
capitalist foreign trade is a way of ridding the economy of
overproduction and spreading exploitation. See, for instance,
the official Soviet textbook on economics in its German translation, Akademie der Wissenschaften der U.d.S.S.R., Institut
für Ökonomie, *Politische Ökonomie*, (East Berlin: Dietz Verlag, 1955), pp. 584-86 and 693-97. The whole book devoted
eight of 708 pages of text to foreign trade. The third, revised and enlarged edition of 1961 does not do much better.
The relevant ratio now is 28 to 812 pages. Other literature
on the subject, however, now is plentiful, indeed.

[2]By this is meant, in the foreign trade context, the classical principle of comparative advantage, according to which
growth is promoted by specialization, and the pattern of
specialization, in turn, is determined from a comparison of
the opportunity cost of producing a given commodity with the
price at which the commodity can be imported or exported.
(Opportunity cost is the value of the factors used to produce the commodity in their best alternative employment.)
The reader may wish to refer to a recent discussion of the
subject, as in Hollis B. Chenery, "Comparative Advantage and
Development Policy," *The American Economic Review*, March,
1961, pp. 18-51.

[3]This argument is, of course, not new. It has its equivalent
in the western literature in such criticisms of comparative
cost as the "theory of balanced growth," which rejects that
of comparative costs as too static. A summary statement of
the present Communist attitude can be found in Rudolf Brauer,
*Probleme der Ermittlung des ökonomischen Nutzens der soziali-
stischen internationalen Arbeitsteilung und des Aussenhandels
sozialistischer Staaten* (East Berlin: Verlag Die Wirtschaft,
1962), esp. pp. 29-39. He claims that the last remnants of a
scientific approach have disappeared from bourgeois foreign
trade theory with elimination of the classical labor theory of
value. It has sunken to the level of pure apologetics, hiding
and justifying the exploitation of the underdeveloped coun-

tries. He argues that the positive kernel of the Ricardian
system, however, lives on in the political economy of Marxism.

[4]This again, is a familiar tune in the western literature.
For a discussion of such and other modifications of comparative cost theory see H.B. Chenery, *op. cit.*

[5]See also pp. 51-54 and 369-71.

[6]By this the author does not mean arbitrariness from the
standpoint of the market economy. If the prices reflected
somehow costs and the preferences of the planners and were
internally consistent, they would still be arbitrary in the
sense that they are not market prices and would not reflect
consumer preferences, but they would be rational in the sense
that they could be used to enforce the decisions of the planners. But not even that is the case. On this point see also Wolfgang F. Stolper, *"Die Berechnung des mitteldeutschen
Sozialprodukts und die internationale Integration des Sowjet-
blocks," Konjunkturpolitik,* 5, 1960, p. 283.

[7]This is to continue through 1965, but thereafter *Industrieab-
gabepreise,* as changed by the price reform, are to be used between producers and the foreign trade organs. See *AH,* 1,
1964, p. 2.

[8]A high internal price for barley had been set to avoid usage
as feed and to encourage export for brewing. The PAG criterion would make export appear unwise. Similarly, extremely
high internal prices for non-ferrous metals were to discourage their use and decrease import needs, yet the PAG would encourage imports. Finally, low internal lignite prices were
to be a lever for making lignite a substitute for other fuels
domestically. No exports were desired, but again the PAG
figures would encourage them. See *AH,* 7, 1957, pp. 251-52.

[9]See the report of E. Georgiev on a conference of economists
held in late January and early February, 1964, at Sofia.
This conference was organized by the Bulgarian Foreign Trade
Research Institute and was the follow-up to an earlier one
on foreign trade theory held at Prague in November, 1957.
Vneshnyaya torgovlya, 7, 1964.

[10]Wilfried Schöne, *"Der Aussenhandel muss die Produktionsabgabe realisieren," AH,* 6, 1957, pp. 210/1, and *idem, "Sub-
vention, Preisausgleich, und Produktionsabgabe im Aussenhandel," AH,* 1, 1957, pp. 18-19.

[11]Such excess profits have to be handed over to the government *(Egalisierungsdifferenz)* and are channeled to high-cost,

excess loss firms. The suggestion mentioned was made by the
firm C.G. Hänsch, *"Egalisierungsdifferenz bei Exportpreisen,"*
AH, 8, 1957, p. 295. It was turned down on the grounds that
the *Egalisierungsdifferenz* was part of value to be realized in
foreign trade, since not the effort of the single producer but
the social average determined what value was. See Wilfried
Schöne, *"Zur Egalisierungsdifferenz und den Problemen der Pro-*
duktionsabgabe beim Import," *AH,* 8, 1957, pp. 295-96.

[12]Wolfgang Koch, *"Preisausgleich und Produktionsabgabe im Aus-*
senhandel," *AH,* 8, 1957, pp. 294-5. Using the example in the
text, it can easily be shown that non-collection of state
profits from imports as well as exports would again leave the
budget unaffected: the negative PAG would become -350, the
net PAG remain -50. Schöne in a rebuttal stressed again the
control function of a double flow of funds as well as the necessity of treating exports and imports alike to "make the
PAG's comparable." See his article given in footnote 11.

[13]Alfred Krätzschmar, *"Die Problematik des Preisausgleichs-*
Satzes bei der Kontrolle der Preise," *AH,* 8, 1957, pp. 293-94.
Suppose the internal price of an export good rises from DM
1,000 to DM 1,200, the foreign-exchange equivalent from DM
1,200 to DM 1,400. Then the absolute PAG in both cases is
+DM 200, but the PAG rate generally used (PAG per DM 1,000
producer price) has fallen from +DM 200 to +DM 167.

[14]*AH,* 12, 1960, pp. 20-23.

[15]*AH,* 2, 1958, p. 61; 4/5, 1958, p. 150; 23, 1958, pp. 807-8;
2, 1960, pp. 7-9; 12, 1960, p. 18.

[16]A description of the relationship of the various inland
prices to each other is found in Ernst Skrbek [sic], *"Die*
Preisbildung im Inland," *AH,* 13, 1957, p. 473.

[17]Surprisingly, the State Planning Commission found out in
1960, however, that De does not show the profitability of
trade for exactly the above mentioned reasons. Yet it has
used formula 2a) in preference to any other since 6-19-1962.
See *AH,* 2, 1960, pp. 7-9 and 19, 1962, pp. 28-29.

[18]*AH,* 24, 1958, pp. 844-45.

[19]*AH,* 24, 1957, pp. 872-73; 3, 1959, p. 24; 12, 1960, pages
20-23.

[20]Rudolf Brauer, *op. cit.,* pp. 95 and 99.

²¹*AH*, 7, 1957, pp. 251-52; 15, 1957, pp. 540-41; 24, 1958, pp. 844-45.

²²*AH*, 24, 1957, pp. 868-69; 24, 1958, pp. 844-45.

²³Heinz-Rudolf Zopf, *Die speziellen Kennziffern zur Charakterisierung der Rentabilität des Exports von Förderanlagen und ihre Bedeutung als Anhaltspunkt für die internationale sozialistische Arbeitsteilung* (East Berlin: Hochschule für Ökonomie, Diplomarbeit, 1959).

²⁴*AH*, 2, 1959, pp. 23-24.

²⁵It might be interesting to give here the raw material breakdown under this scheme of one particular commodity, an East German motor scooter (Moped SR 2, without lights and tires): "1) rolled steel; a) first processing stage of which drawn sheets, b) second processing stage of which cold rolled hoop iron, pure bar iron, alloyed bar iron, welded pipes, seamless pipes; 2) copper and copper alloys of which brass, 3) rolled aluminum, 4) gray cast iron, 5) other cast iron, 6) steel forgings, 7) varnishes and paints." As is obvious, also these items could be broken further into wage and material costs, and it is perfectly arbitrary where to stop this endless process. *Ibid.*

²⁶See Ssü Shön-Djün, Schan Shu-Ssu, *"Die Rentabilität des Aussenhandels (II),"* *AH*, 14, 1959, pp. 15-17.

²⁷See E. Faude, *"Kennziffern zur Untersuchung der Devisenrentabilität von Investitionen,"* *AH*, 1, 1963, pp. 26-29, and the excellent list of other bloc literature cited there. See also *WW*, 6, 1962, pp. 906-14.

²⁸Members of this group are Bulgarian (Tosheff), German (Gräbig), Hungarian (Vajda), and Russian (Ostravityanov).

²⁹According to Gertrud Gräbig, *Internationale Arbeitsteilung und Aussenhandel im sozialistischen Weltsystem* (East Berlin: Verlag Die Wirtschaft, 1960), esp. pp. 84-98.

³⁰In 1964, e.g., trade occurred on the basis of average world prices of 1957-1958. See *The New York Times*, 1-21-1964, page 8. The same source also states that nothing has come of the contemplated base change promised at the third meeting of the Executive Committee. These changes were to account for the long term trend of falling raw material and rising industrial prices, thusly principally favoring East Germany and Czechoslovakia. Reportedly, the raw material exporting member countries succeeded in postponing any action on the issue before

1965. According to *The New York Times* of 3-30-1964, p. 43, the Polish Deputy Premier Piotr Jarosiewics predicted a shift to average 1960-1964 world prices.

[31]Rudolf Brauer and Viliam Černiansky, *"Die Bedeutung der Kennziffern der Rentabilität des Aussenhandels für die sozialistische internationale Arbeitsteilung,"* WW, 7, 1960, pages 977-90.

[32]W. Schastitko and W. Terechow, *"Die internationale sozialistische Arbeitsteilung und die Kriterien ihres Nutzeffekts,"* WW, 1, 1964, pp. 144-151.

[33]Note that such a charge on fixed capital and inventories has been officially introduced in Hungary at the rate of 5 per cent on the average since January 1, 1964. A 6 per cent charge exists in Yugoslavia. The East Germans are "experimenting" with a similar charge. See DW, A, 3, 1964, p. 5, A, 38, 1964, p. 29, and WW, 7, 1964, pp. 1175 ff.

[34]Walter Ulbricht, *Das Programm des Sozialismus und die geschichtliche Aufgabe der SED* (East Berlin: Dietz Verlag, 1963), p. 92.

[35]See DW, A, 1964, issues 7, p. 8; 8, p. 3; 9, p. 3; 10, p. 6; 12, p. 17; and A, 1965, 1, p. 12. These new prices are said to be close to the socially necessary labor effort and are scheduled to be used in such formulas as 2c) above (in place of Ki). See also AH, 4, 1964, p. 19. The price revisions in East Germany are part of the New Economic System of Planning and Administration, which is defined as the "organic connection of the scientifically based management of the economy and the scientifically founded long run central state planning with the comprehensive application of material incentives in the form of a well integrated system of economic levers." This means that prices and wages are to be set such as to interest firms and workers to decrease costs, increase productivity, improve quality, and promote technological progress. See *Handbuch der D.D.R.* (East Berlin: Staatsverlag der D.D.R., 1964) pp. 375-90.

   For remarks on the recent price revisions in the Soviet Union the reader is referred to Morris Bornstein, "The Soviet Price Reform Discussion," *The Quarterly Journal of Economics*, February, 1964, and *idem*, "The 1963 Soviet Industrial Price Revision," *Soviet Studies*, July, 1963.

CHAPTER 5 — MEASURING EAST GERMAN ECONOMIC INTEGRATION

An attempt will be made in this chapter to test whether there have been any visible and significant changes in the East German economy as a result of her membership in CMEA, the impact of Soviet reparations policy having already been discussed in CHAPTER 1. It is certainly not obvious which should be the criteria for measuring the degree of economic integration of one area with another. The term "integration" itself, though widely used in the economic literature in both west and east, has rarely been defined. Writers usually seem to mean by it some sort of cohesion and solidarity across national boundaries.[1] The classical economists might have tested integration via the criterion of the perfect market. They might have defined perfect integration as the state of affairs where, taking account of transport costs, quality differences, etc., prices of goods and factors of production would be the same everywhere. This would require, of course, the free movement across national boundaries of goods and, unless certain definite conditions are met, also of factors of production. Otherwise an international relocation of industry, which is a condition for gains in productivity through international integration, would be narrowly restricted.

In fact, we know that international labor migration has certainly ceased as a factor of integration in most parts of the world and offers no prospect of playing any important role in the near future. Only one example of such movements within the bloc has become known to this author, viz., of Bulgarian labor to the Soviet Union, but such movements have very limited impact.[2] The reallocation of the labor force within a given country in the direction of the industries this country is to develop with priority because of international specialization agreements is, however, also indicative of integration. This will be discussed in Section A below with respect to East

Germany.

As will be shown in CHAPTER 6, the international movement
of capital is also of limited importance within the Communist
bloc. But, again, the reallocation of investments within a
given country, in accordance with CMEA agreements, is a step
towards integration. This will be discussed in Section B below with respect to East Germany.

In addition, one can test whether such conscious realло-
cation of the factors of production within a country, in accordance with international agreements, has had any noticeable
effect on the economic structure, as measured by the output
shares of various industries. This question will be taken up
in Section C below, also for the East German case.

Finally, changes in the commodity structure of trade,
with the rest of the world as a whole, with the bloc in particular, and with individual bloc countries, should be expected
as a consequence of an international division of labor in the
bloc. One would also expect that international specialization
and exchange lead to changes in the importance of foreign
trade for a country in the sense that its dependence on other
nations is increased. A greater share of its (more specialized) production will be exported, and imports will provide a
greater share of the available goods in which its trading
partners specialize. These questions are discussed in Section
D below.

A.   THE DISTRIBUTION OF THE LABOR FORCE

Table 5 presents data on the distribution of East Germany's industrial labor force. Though with possible productivity changes this need not necessarily be so, it can be seen
that East Germany's labor force has been reallocated in a
fashion one would expect given the combined effects of reparations policy, Germany's division, Communist ideology, and

Table 5. Distribution of East Germany's labor force,
by industries, in per cent of total industrial
employment, 1936 and selected postwar years[a]

Industry	1936	1950	1952	1954
Basic Industries[bc]	20.3	24.8	24.7	25.2
Energy	2.3	2.2	2.2	2.3
Mining[b]	4.9	7.4	7.2	7.8
Metallurgy	1.9	3.0	3.5	3.0
Chemicals	5.9	8.7	8.4	8.8
Building Materials[c]	5.3	3.5	3.2	3.2
Metal-working Industries	30.2	33.3	34.8	35.4
Heavy Machinery	2.8			
General Machinery	7.2			
Vehicles	3.1	23.7	24.5	24.5
Ship Building	.5			
Castings, Forgings	2.3			
Metalwares	7.8			
Electro-technical	4.7	6.4	7.1	7.6
Fine Mechanics/Optics	1.8	3.2	3.2	3.3
Light Industries[c]	40.8	34.3	32.1	31.2
Woodworking & Cultural	5.9	6.4	5.6	5.3
Textiles	18.2	14.4	13.6	13.4
Clothing	3.6	6.1	6.1	3.8
Leather/Shoes/Furs	2.6			2.5
Cellulose/Paper	1.7	2.5	2.3	2.1
Printing	5.2	2.3	2.0	1.7
Glass/Ceramics[c]	3.6	2.6	2.5	2.4
Food/Drink/Tobacco	8.4	7.5	8.5	8.2
All Industries	100.0	100.0	100.0	100.0

Sources:

1936 data calculated from absolute data on employment
given in *Statistisches Handbuch von Deutschland 1928-
1944* (München: Franz Ehrenwirth-Verlag, 1949), pp. 270-272,
assigning one third of Berlin employment in each industry to
East Berlin, and defining industries according to the postwar
East German classification. For all other years from *SJDDR*
1955, pp. 125-31, *1958*, pp. 278-81, *1959*, pp. 297-99, *1960/1*,
pp. 263-65, *1962*, pp. 243-45, *1963*, pp. 73-75, *1964*, pp. 93-95.

Table 5   continued

1956	1957	1958	1959	1960	1961	1962	1963
25.2	25.2	25.2	25.8	25.9	25.9	26.1	26.2
2.3	2.3	2.2	2.2	2.3	2.4	2.4	2.4
7.7	7.7	7.6	7.5	6.9	6.8	6.9	6.9
3.1	3.1	3.2	3.1	3.7	3.9	3.9	3.8
8.9	8.9	8.9	9.6	9.7	9.6	9.7	9.8
3.2	3.3	3.3	3.4	3.4	3.3	3.2	3.2
35.8	36.5	36.7	36.4	36.4	37.0	37.3	38.1
6.3	6.5	6.4	6.3	6.3	6.3	6.3	6.4
6.1	6.1	6.1	6.2	6.4	7.1	7.1	7.2
6.7	6.9	7.0	6.7	6.6	6.5	6.4	6.7
1.5	1.5	1.5	1.4	1.4	1.3	1.3	1.4
1.8	1.8	1.7	1.7	1.7	1.7	1.7	1.6
3.0	3.0	3.1	3.2	3.1	3.1	3.2	3.2
7.0	7.2	7.4	7.5	7.6	7.7	8.0	8.1
3.4	3.4	3.4	3.4	3.4	3.4	3.4	3.4
31.7	31.0	30.7	30.3	30.1	29.5	29.2	28.3
5.5	5.3	5.3	5.5	5.5	5.5	5.4	5.3
13.3	12.9	12.6	12.0	11.9	11.5	11.2	10.9
4.0	4.2	4.3	4.3	4.2	4.2	4.2	3.9
2.5	2.4	2.5	2.5	2.5	2.4	2.4	2.4
2.2	2.2	2.2	2.3	2.2	2.2	2.2	2.2
1.6	1.5	1.5	1.4	1.4	1.3	1.3	1.3
2.6	2.4	2.4	2.4	2.4	2.3	2.3	2.4
7.3	7.2	7.3	7.5	7.6	7.6	7.4	7.4
100.0	100.0	100.0	100.0	100.0	100.0	100.0	100.0

Notes:

[a]Detail may not add to respective totals due to rounding. The basic data refer to yearly averages of all industrial workers and employees, including home workers (except for 1950-54), apprentices (only for 1956-58 and probably 1936), those working part-time or absent from work due to vacation or sickness, and covering socialized as well as private industry. Employment in private industry decreased from 24.3 per cent of total employment in 1950 to 4.3 per cent in 1963. Since pri-

involvement in CMEA. Compared to prewar days, employment in
the basic and metal-working industries has relatively increased, while that in the light and food industries has declined.

In particular, employment in mining, metallurgy, chemicals, heavy machinery, vehicles, shipbuilding, electro-technical, and fine mechanical/optical production has been expanded relatively compared to the prewar era. The building material industry, castings and forgings, metalwares, textiles,
printing, and glass/ceramics on the other hand, have been relatively decreased in importance. Only very few industries,
such as energy, general machinery, and some of the light industries, have maintained their relative positions in terms of
employment.

Unfortunately, it was not possible to find employment
data for the area of East Germany for 1944. It is conceivable, therefore, that most of these changes actually occurred
between 1936 and the end of the war. It will be noted that
there was hardly any significant change between 1950 and 1963.
Slightly increasing shares can be found in the metallurgical,

---

vate industry was during the whole period strictly governmentally directed, however, its inclusion in our data for our purposes seems justified.

[b]Postwar official data exclude employment in uranium mining
(which did not exist prewar). This must be so, since *SJDDR
1959*, p. 297, gives 1959 employment in ore mining, excluding
iron ore mining, as 21,583. But 1959 uranium mining employment is known as 57,493 (*ND* of 3-10-60 implied this number by
giving the number of improvements suggested in uranium mining
in 1959, which number was given absolutely as well as per
worker). Hence, the share of mining and basic industries in
employment should probably be about 2 percentage points higher for the late 1950's and even more so for earlier years.

[c]The official data for 1950-54 include glass/ceramics employment under building materials. The author separated the two
industries by assuming employment for 1950-54 to have been
distributed between the two as from 1955-59.

chemicals, general machinery, and electro-technical industries, a clearly falling one in textiles. Only the 1936-1950 or 1936-1963 differences, however, are striking. CMEA decisions, in view of the discussion in CHAPTER 3, could not possibly have had any visible effects until 1958 at the earliest. The changes observed between 1958 and 1963, though small, are in the expected direction of slowing down in East Germany the development of (certain branches of) mining, heavy machinery, and vehicles, while expanding chemicals, general machinery, and electro-technical production. But the evidence in Table 5 by itself is certainly not conclusive, nor are those changes significant.

More detailed data (breaking each industry into about five subgroups) are available since 1959 in the sources listed for Table 5. A study of employment within any one industry shows remarkable stability from 1959 to 1963 of absolute employment levels as well as relative shares of the subgroups in each industry. In fact, among the published data for 68 subgroups, there were only eight cases in which relative shares changed by more than 2.5 percentage points over the period: employment in lignite mines, lignite coking and briquetting plants changed from 52.6 per cent of total mining employment in 1959 to 58.0 per cent in 1963. The corresponding figure for non-ferrous metals mines changed from 10.4 to 1.0. Employment with blast furnaces, steel mills, and hot-rolling mills changed from 78.1 per cent of total employment in metallurgy to 66.1 per cent, but the absolute level of employment increased slightly. In the general machinery industry, employment in the production of machinery for the metalworking industries held 0.2 per cent in 1959, but 3.3 per cent in 1963. Within the vehicles industry, employment in the production and repair of trucks held 18.9 per cent of that industry's total in 1959, but 22.9 per cent in 1963. Within ship-

building, employment in the construction and repair of ocean
and coastal ships declined from 63.0 per cent to 58.9 per
cent, that for fishing vessels from 20.5 per cent to 17.7 per
cent. Finally, employment in the production of electro-ma-
chines, transformers, and switch elements dropped from 23.6
per cent of electro-technical employment to 18.0 per cent.
However, in the latter case the absolute volume of employment
rose slightly. Obviously, all this could be interpreted as
corresponding to CMEA decisions previously discussed (and
there is no evidence contradicting any such decisions), but
one can certainly not conclude from this anything about a significant CMEA influence.

B.   THE DISTRIBUTION OF INVESTMENTS

Among the data most difficult to collect for the East
German economy are those on investment. The author has never
found any reliable information on inventory investment and
residential construction activity. This, however, is not serious in the context of this topic. When assessing the impact of policies designed to integrate East Germany into the
Communist orbit, one is naturally most interested in the distribution of another type of investment, viz, plant and equipment. Data on this type of investment, including depreciation,
have been occasionally published, and innumerable publications
contain indexes referring thereto. Unfortunately, the industry breakdown of such data is usually missing or very imperfect, and the data are often useless for a number of other
reasons. Besides the obvious one that indexes are not very
helpful when there is no knowledge about even a single absolute magnitude, only two reasons shall be given here:
1)   sources usually fail to state whether the data refer to
actual or plan figures. Sometimes, this author suspects, a
given set of indexes is based on a series of absolute numbers

which is a mixture of both.

2)   sources usually fail to state whether the data refer to
total actual gross investment in plant and equipment in the
economy or to investment undertaken by one or more subgroups
in the economy. Such subgroups are a) centrally administered
nationalized plants, b) locally administered nationalized
plants, c) cooperative enterprises, d) mixed state and private enterprises, and e) private enterprises. To complicate
matters further, some sources list investments of the nationalized sector, if financed from the government budget, but exclude investments of the same sector from the plants' own
funds and from credits received by them through the banking
system. Most sources fail to mention altogether the scope of
their coverage.

Several attempts at estimating East German investments
in plant and equipment at current as well as constant prices
have been made. Excerpts from one of these, which only covers
major industry groups, are reproduced in Table 6.

As can be seen from Table 6, investment in plant and
equipment in the basic industries was since 1950 relatively
more important than in 1936 and the wartime economy of 1944.
Investment in the metal-working industries was relatively lower in 1955 than in 1936 and 1944, though it had reached the
1944 level in 1951 and declined since. Investment in the
light industries in 1955 held a position of lesser importance
than in 1936, but was still above its 1944 share, though it
had been even below that position in 1952. The uprising of
1953 and the "New Course" of Economic Policy after Stalin's
death might conceivably account for the change in the relative
shares of the metal-working and light industries in investment
during the later years covered in the table. It will be noted
that also the food industries' share has declined until 1952
and risen since.

Table 6. Distribution of East Germany's gross
investment in industrial plant and equipment,[a]
by industry groups, in per cent of total,
in real terms, 1936, 1944-55

		Industry			
Year	Basic	Metal-working	Light	Food/Drink/Tobacco	Total
1936	47.9	23.1	19.4	9.6	100.0
1944	52.5	32.8	9.8	4.9	100.0
1945[b]	43.9	19.1	22.9	14.0	100.0
1946	44.1	17.6	24.3	14.0	100.0
1947	46.2	19.2	21.5	13.1	100.0
1948	42.0	23.2	20.1	14.7	100.0
1949	46.9	22.8	16.8	13.5	100.0
1950	56.7	21.8	11.1	10.5	100.0
1951	57.8	31.4	5.1	5.7	100.0
1952	60.5	29.6	5.0	4.9	100.0
1953	58.0	24.5	11.5	5.9	100.0
1954	60.7	15.6	12.8	11.0	100.0
1955	59.8	16.3	14.4	9.4	100.0

Source:

   Calculated from absolute data in constant 1950 East Ger-
   man prices, as published by Helmut Korpky, *"Die Brutto-
Anlage-Investitionen der mitteldeutschen Industrie 1924-1955,"*
VzW, 4, 1957, p. 399. The same source lists data in current
prices, which would show almost the identical distribution.
Detail may not add to total due to rounding.

Notes:

   [a]The very small investment by artisans given separately
   has been evenly split by the author and allocated to the
light and food industries.
   [b]May to December.

It is, of course, difficult to interpret any such data.
It was pointed out above in the discussion of employment data
that the distribution of the labor force could be consistent
with any given objective as to the distribution of output, depending on productivity. There is a similar situation in the
case of investments. If the marginal capital-output ratio in
the basic industries were higher than in the light industries,
and in the light industries higher than in the metal-working
industries, for example, a distribution of investments mostly
into basic industries, then into light industries and least of
all into metal-working industries could still be consistent
with the announced objective of increasing the output of the
metal-working industries most of all, and of the light industries least of all.

In fact it is probably true that this ratio is highest
for the basic and lowest for the consumer goods industries.[3]
Given the East German objectives of increasing the output of
the basic and metal-working industries fastest, one would expect a distribution of investments as shown in Table 6, at
least since 1948. The somewhat greater emphasis on the consumer goods industries after 1953 was probably temporary and
an outcome of the "New Course" and the 1953 uprisings.[4] Unfortunately, data for the years after 1955, most interesting
in connection with the influence of CMEA, have not been published by this source.

On the basis of other sources, estimates for the distribution of investments in plant and equipment by individual
industries have, however, recently been made by other scholars.[5] They cover the years 1950 through 1957 and, as was the
case in Table 6, investments made by all units given above
under (a) to (e). The estimates were made in current East
German prices and are given in Table 7.

According to these estimates, investments in the basic

Table 7.   Distribution of East Germany's gross
investment in industrial plant and equipment,
by industries, in per cent of total, at
current East German prices, 1950-57[a]

Industry	1950	1951	1952	1953
Basic Industries	40.3	46.7	49.1	57.3
Electricity	6.0	9.9	8.0	10.9
Mining	6.0	6.4	11.0	10.4
Metallurgy	14.7	16.4	14.9	19.8
Chemicals	8.9	9.2	10.8	12.2
Building Materials	4.7	4.8	4.4	4.0
Metal-working Industries	48.5	43.1	40.9	34.8
Electro-technical	8.5	8.7	8.2	9.4
Fine mechanics/optics	4.8	4.8	4.4	4.6
All others	35.2	29.6	28.3	20.8
Light Industries	5.6	5.3	5.5	4.6
Food/Drink/Tobacco Ind.	5.3	4.9	4.6	4.3
All Industries	100.0	100.0	100.0	100.0

Source:

   Calculated from data given in Table IV of source cited
   in footnote 3 above.

   [a]Detail may not add to totals due to rounding.

industries increased from 40.3 per cent of total industrial
investment in 1950 to 61.9 per cent in 1954, and then declined
to 52.0 per cent in 1957. These estimates for the years 1950-
1952 are significantly below those presented in Table 6, even
if the data in that Table were expressed in current prices.

   Investments in electricity were found to have risen from 6
per cent of total investments in industry in 1950 to 20 per
cent in 1955, then fallen drastically to 4.5 per cent in 1957.
The weighted average for the years 1951-55, according to this
estimate was 12.8 per cent. According to a member of the East

Table 7   continued

1954	1955	1956	1957
61.9	61.6	57.8	52.0
15.4	20.0	7.3	4.5
11.9	11.0	13.9	15.9
19.0	16.9	19.7	14.1
11.9	8.9	10.8	11.7
3.7	4.8	6.1	5.8
29.0	29.4	31.8	37.8
9.1	9.9	11.1	10.2
4.5	4.9	4.0	4.2
15.4	14.6	16.7	23.6
4.4	4.8	5.1	5.0
4.4	4.4	5.2	5.0
100.0	100.0	100.0	100.0

German State Planning Commission, however, the true figure was
10.9 per cent for the 1951-55 average.[6] The 1956-60 Plan envisaged even a higher average of 17 per cent of industrial investments going into electricity production. This seems indeed to have occurred. A most recent study by the West Berlin
Deutsches Institut für Wirtschaftsforschung[7] shows that from
1956-60 gross fixed investment in energy (probably electricity
plus gas), at current East German prices, fluctuated between
18.0 and 19.1 per cent of total investment (categories a - e,
above) in industry. Industry in that study, however, includes
construction. The corresponding percentages were 19.9, 19.4,
and 21.2 for 1961-63.

According to Stolper, investments in mining rose from 6
per cent of industrial investments in 1950 to 15.9 per cent in

1957, those in metallurgy were 14.7 per cent in 1950, 14.1 per
cent in 1957, and fluctuated up to 19.8 per cent in the inter-
vening years. His estimates give a 1951-55 weighted average
of 10.1 per cent for mining, 17.4 per cent for metallurgy, and
of 13.7 per cent for both combined, while the State Planning
Commission claims a combined percentage of 18.0 for these
years, planning on an average of 10 per cent for 1956-60 and
higher thereafter. 1965 reports claim that "in the last years,"
i.e., presumably since 1960, forty per cent of industrial investments went actually into energy and fuels.[8] The *DIW* study
seems to corroborate the official pronouncements. It gives
mining investment as 26.5 per cent of total industrial plus
construction investment in 1955, as 24.2 per cent in 1963.
The percentage never went above 26.5 and never below 22.4 (in
1960). Metallurgy investment is given as 8.9 per cent in
1955 and 9.2 per cent in 1963, the high for the period. The
lowest share was in 1960 (8.1).

Stolper's estimates for the chemical industry are rising
from 8.9 per cent of total industrial investment in 1950 to
12.2 per cent in 1953, then fluctuate between 8.9 and 11.9
per cent until 1957. The 1951-55 weighted average is estimated at 10.6 per cent, but reported as 13 per cent by the
State Planning Commission. According to the latter, the percentage was to be 14.3 for 1956-60 and higher thereafter, as
one would expect, given CMEA objectives for East Germany.
As one would expect also, the same source indicates that almost all chemical investments up to 1957 went into basic chemicals production, since then into synthetic fibers and plastics, especially at the petro-chemical center at Schwedt.
In 1958, the chemicals industry actually received 13 per cent
of industrial investments, in 1963 it received 18.9 per cent.
For the balance of the 1960's chemical industry investments
are scheduled to be bigger than for any other industry, reach-

ing in fact a volume greater than 200 per cent of all chemical
investments from 1951-63.[9] These official data, however, are
contradicted by the *DIW* study, showing chemicals investments
taking 12.5 per cent of the total for industry and construction in 1955, rising to 19.5 per cent in 1960, and falling to
13 per cent in 1963.

Investments in the building material industry are estimated by Stolper as fluctuating between 3.7 and 6.1 per cent
of total industrial investment from 1950-57, the 1951-57
weighted average being 4.8 per cent. The State Planning Commission planned, however, for a 1951-60 average of 8.3 per
cent. The *DIW* study estimates the share of building materials
and construction industry investments as rising from 5.8 per
cent of industry plus construction investments in 1955 to 9.6
per cent in 1963.

Stolper's estimates for the metal-working industries fall
from 48.5 per cent of all industrial investments in 1950 to
29 per cent in 1954, then rise to 37.8 per cent in 1957. A
look at Table 6 shows immediately that his estimates are completely at variance with estimates given there by being considerably higher for all years. (This again holds true also
when changing Table 6 to current prices.) The 1951-55 weighted average in the Korpky estimate (Table 6) is 23.9 per cent,
the 1951-57 weighted average of Stolper 35.3 per cent, while
the State Planning Commission in the middle of 1959 forecast
a 1951-60 average of 15.2 per cent. This suggests that the
Korpky estimate is more trustworthy. This author ventures to
guess that Stolper's estimates of investments in all the
metal-using industries (except electro-technical and fine
mechanical/optical production), given as falling from 35.2 per
cent in 1950 to 14.6 per cent in 1955, then rising to 23.4 per
cent in 1957, are too high for all years, while those for the
electro-technical industry (rising from 8.5 per cent in 1950

to 10.2 per cent in 1957) and fine mechanics/optics (fluctuating between 4 per cent and 4.8 per cent from 1950 to 1957) are
probably correct. According to the East German Planning Commission, investments in the metal-using industries until 1953
were almost entirely in heavy machinery, since 1952 shipbuilding was stressed, and by 1959 electro-technical production.
This again would be in line with the CMEA developments discussed in CHAPTER 3.

Stolper's estimates for the light industries range from
5.6 per cent of total industrial investment in 1950 to 4.4 per
cent in 1954 and 5 per cent by 1957, while food industries investments are estimated at almost the same relative share as
those in the light industry for every year. This again con-
tradicts Table 6, where the estimated shares are higher. In
fact they probably were higher. The State Planning Commission
estimated in 1959 a share of 34.9 per cent of investments in
the consumer goods industries for the 1951-60 period. The actual share from 1952-58 was 29.4 per cent, the plan for 1959-
65 was 26.9 per cent.[10] The Sixth Party Congress of East Germany's Communist Party has determined for the late 1960's the
foremost development of the following industries: chemicals,
metallurgy (2nd processing stage), electro-technical, energy,
and machine building.[9] This clearly is in line with CMEA decisions and is corroborated by the trends in investment insofar as they can be observed from the aforementioned data.

C.   THE STRUCTURE OF OUTPUT

A study of the structure of the East Germany economy insofar as reliable data are available (from 1955-59) reveals no
drastic changes.[11] The importance of industry slightly increased from 52.2 per cent of real GNP in 1955 to 53.7 per
cent in 1959, that of agriculture/forestry on the other hand,
declined somewhat from 14.3 to 12.4 per cent. Similar neglig-

ible declines were registered for the relative share of trade
(11.0 to 9.2 per cent) and services (10.1 - 9.4 per cent), a
similar negligible increase for transport and communications
(7.8 - 8.3 per cent). Most noticeable was the gradual rise in
the share of the construction industry from 4.5 to 7.0 per
cent.

    Of much greater interest, however, would be changes with-
in the industrial sector. The basic industries have somewhat
declined in relative importance compared to their 1955 position (from 35.2 per cent of GNP created in industry in 1955 to
34.0 per cent in 1959). It is questionable, however, whether
such a small change is significant.[12] It may be much more significant, however, that the basic industries have ceased to
expand relatively. This probably shows the abandonment of the
autarkic policy pursued until the middle 1950's. Before CMEA
evolved into an instrument of international division of labor,
the East Germans had given high priority to the development of
their metallurgical industry, for instance. The great projects
concerned with the increased production in the metallurgical
and mining industries became symbols of the First as well as
the Second Five Year Plans. During the First Five Year Plan
(1951-55), all efforts centered around the new steel mill being
built at Fürstenberg-on-the-Oder *(Eisenhüttenkombinat J.W.
Stalin)*, which was to import ore from Krivoi Rog (U.S.S.R.)
and coal from Silesia (Poland), as well as the *Lauchhammerwerk*, which was to transform East German lignite into a high-
temperature coke that could replace soft coal.[13] The equivalent to the *Lauchhammerwerk* for the Second Five Year Plan was
the *Schwarze Pumpe* project in Hoyerswerda, Niederlausitz. As
was shown in CHAPTER 3, there are indications that ineffici-
encies are being recognized and remedied. The discontinuation
of expanding the relative position of a basic industry that
has to rely completely on imports of the most important raw

materials signifies this.

The relative importance of the chemical industry has not changed between 1955 and 1959. It is certainly too early to expect any visible impact of the CMEA specialization decisions in this industry at this date.

The metal-working industries' share of total industrial output has continued to increase after 1955 from 32.1 per cent in 1955 to 35.9 per cent in 1959. Though the increase was not of overwhelming magnitude, it might very well reflect the impact of the earliest CMEA specialization decisions which were concerned with machinery rather than chemical production.[14] Here again, however, one must wait for more time to elapse and more detailed data to become available to be certain of any trend. In particular, the present data do not permit to test whether the original East German preoccupation with the production of very heavy machinery has been given up, though there are frequent official statements to this effect.

The light and food industries have, on the whole by 1959 maintained their 1955 relative positions. There has been only a very slight decline in their relative share in industrial output from 21.9 to 20.7 per cent and 10.9 to 9.4 per cent, respectively.[15]

Data for 1960-64 are only available from the official East German statistics and are by no means reliable for methodological reasons, as has been abundantly shown by Professor Stolper. According to such East German claims, total industrial production, always compared to the previous year, grew by 8.2, 5.9, 6.2, 4.3, and 5.6 per cent, respectively, for 1960-63 and the first half of 1964.[16] Substantially higher rates of growth (3 or more per cent higher) occurred in 1960 in general machinery, shipbuilding, electro-technical output, in 1961 in general machinery, metal goods, clothing, in 1962 in heavy and general machinery, electro-technical goods, fine

mechanical-optical output, in 1963 in vehicles, shipbuilding,
metalgoods, fine mechanical-optical output, and in the first
half of 1964 in energy, building materials, shipbuilding,
electro-technical output, and glass-ceramics.

Comparing the 1959 data with those for 1944, the following
can be said: The basic industries were more important in 1959
(34.0 per cent vs. 23.5 per cent of industrial output) which
certainly reflects the division of Germany and the original
East German attempts to heal the wounds of partition by a policy of autarky. The metal-working industries were less important than in 1944 (35.9 per cent vs. 46.5 per cent) but there
was a clear trend of their share approaching the extraordin-
arily high share of war-time 1944. This reflects both the
original emphasis of the reparations policy and the continued
importance attached to these industries by CMEA. The consumer
goods industries, finally, held in 1959 a similar depressed
position as in 1944 (30.1 per cent vs. 30.0 per cent); then
because of war, now because of the Communist policy inspired
by ideology.

D.   THE STRUCTURE AND IMPORTANCE OF FOREIGN TRADE

1.   The Trade Structure with the Rest of the World as a Whole

An important question still has to be answered. Whatever
changes one may find in the distribution of the labor force,
of investments, and of output, these must not necessarily be
part of a scheme of international integration, but could be a
purely internal affair. For this reason let us now turn to
the commodity structure of East Germany's foreign trade, as
shown in Tables 8 and 9.

a.   Exports

Of East Germany's exports in 1936, 85.7 per cent were
industrial, the rest were agricultural and forestry products,

Table 8.   Percentage distribution of East Germany's
commercial commodity exports to all areas,
by sectors, 1936, and selected postwar years[e]

Sector	1936	1947[a]	1948[a]	1949[a]
All Industries	85.7	94.9	99.3	
Agriculture and Forestry[c]	14.3	5.1	.7	
Basic Industries	17.7	43.4	55.4	
Energy	.3			.6
Mining[d]	2.8	30.7	26.8	
Metallurgy	3.2	5.9	15.3	
Chemicals	11.0	6.8	13.3	14.6
Building Materials[b]	.3			2.1
Metal-working Industries[c]	34.2	4.2	13.0	18.7
Heavy Machinery	6.9			3.0
General Machinery	10.6			4.4
Vehicles	2.4			5.4
Ships	-	2.4	7.3	-
Castings and Forgings	.1			.0
Metalwares	5.9			.0
Electro-technical	5.1	.3	1.9	2.1
Fine Mechanics/Optics	3.3	1.5	3.8	3.8
Light Industries	28.6	50.4	24.6	
Woodworking and Cultural	2.7	4.1	12.5	12.5
Textiles	14.3	40.8	8.4	16.5
Clothing	1.7			
Leather/Shoes/Furs	1.2			.4
Cellulose/Paper	2.2	.3	1.7	.4
Printing	1.9			.4
Glass/Ceramics[b]	3.9			
Waste Materials	.8			
Food/Drink/Tobacco Industries	5.1	2.0	6.3	
Vegetable Products	11.5	4.5	.6	4.1
Animal Products (incl. fish)				
Forestry Products	2.8	.6	.1	
All Sectors	100.0	100.0	100.0	100.0

Table 8   continued

1950	1951	1952	1953	1954	1955	1956
96.1	97.3	98.4	98.9	99.2	99.2	
3.8	2.6	1.6	1.0	.8	.8	
39.4	30.6	30.0	24.3	30.1	31.9	
.4	.7	.4	.3	.3	.2	
13.6	9.2	9.3	7.5	13.7	14.0	
.3	.2	.1	.2	.3	.3	
21.9	18.0	17.7	14.5	14.5	15.9	16.7
3.2	2.4	2.5	1.8	1.4	1.5	
31.9	47.5	49.8	62.7	57.4	56.3	53.8
5.1	9.1	10.0	20.0	16.6	14.2	
11.1	14.2	16.7	18.6	12.7	11.7	10.8
2.6	3.2	2.7	3.3	8.0	9.0	
.0	.1	.1	.5	4.5	6.8	
.0	.0	.0	.0	.0	.0	
1.2	.9	1.2	1.0	.9	1.0	1.0
5.1	13.1	11.8	12.6	9.2	7.4	6.9
6.5	7.0	7.3	6.6	5.5	6.3	6.5
19.3	15.5	12.8	10.2	9.1	9.7	11.7
6.6	5.2	2.7	1.8	1.6	1.5	
6.5	4.5	5.0	4.1	3.8	4.3	4.3
.3	-	.0	.0	.0	.1	
.0	.2	.2	.2	.3	.4	
1.9	1.8	1.1	1.1	.9	.9	
.2	1.4	1.2	1.1	1.0	1.1	
3.2	2.4	2.5	1.8	1.4	1.5	
.5	-	-	.0	.0	.0	
5.5	3.7	5.8	1.7	2.6	1.3	⎫
1.9	1.9	.7	.3	.6	.6	⎬ 2.2
.0	.0	.0	.0	.0	.0	⎭
2.0	.8	1.0	.7	.2	.2	
100.0	100.0	100.0	100.0	100.0	100.0	100.0

Table 8 continued

Sector	1957	1958	1959	1960*
All Industries				
Agriculture and Forestry[c]				
Basic Industries		31.0	31.0	
Energy				
Mining[d]				
Metallurgy				
Chemicals	15.6	14.7	14.8	12.3
Building Materials[b]				
Metal-working Industries[c]	48.2	51.3	51.2	51.7
Heavy Machinery	11.2	11.8		10.6
General Machinery	10.2	11.4	11.5	11.1
Vehicles	8.0	7.9	8.2	8.2
Ships	4.9	5.5	6.1	6.8
Castings and Forgings	.0			
Metalwares	1.1			
Electro-technical	6.6	7.4		
Fine Mechanics/Optics	6.2	7.1		
Light Industries		13.0	13.3	
Woodworking and Cultural				
Textiles		5.6		
Clothing				
Leather/Shoes/Furs				
Cellulose/Paper				
Printing				
Glass/Ceramics[b]				
Waste Materials				
Food/Drink/Tobacco Industries				
Vegetable Products	1.9	4.7	4.5	
Animal Products (incl. fish)				
Forestry Products				
All Sectors	100.0	100.0	100.0	100.0

*The percentage for chemicals was ≈15, and 13.5, for metal-working industries ≈50 and 51.3 for 1962 and 1963, respectively. 1963 textile plus clothing exports had a share of 8.8 per cent, 1963 glass-ceramics exports one of 1.1 per cent.

Table 8   continued

Sources:

This Table has been calculated from data in current
prices (until 1949:RM, thereafter in rubles) which
have been derived as follows: 1936 exports to territories
then not German have previously been estimated at RM 1,227.5
million (See *Supplement*, Chap. I). *Statistisches Handbuch von
Deutschland 1928-1944* (München: Franz Ehrenwirth-Verlag,
1949), pp. 276-78, contains a similar total of RM 1,132.376
million, broken down by industries.   The author assumed the
difference of RM 95.124 million to have been exports of agriculture and forestry and of this 58.6 per cent agricultural
exports (as 1950-55 average).   The industrial export breakdown as given in this source was used, always assigning one
third of Berlin exports to East Berlin.   To these data were
added exports to territories German in 1936, previously estimated at RM 4,300 million (*Supplement*, Chap. I). According to
Bruno Gleitze, *Ostdeutsche Wirtschaft*, pp. 6-7, RM 838 million
of these were products of the food/drink/tobacco industry and
agriculture (food sector), i.e., 19.5 per cent of total exports to German territories, while the percentage was only
6.6 per cent in exports to non-Germany.   The author assigned
30.9 per cent of this amount to the food/drink/tobacco industry and the rest to agriculture, since this was the relation
of the corresponding exports to non-German territories.   The
remaining exports of the other industries and of forestry to
German territories, totalling RM 3,462 million, have been
divided as the corresponding exports to non-German territories, after one adjustment, viz., the separate estimate of
energy exports as the 1950-55 average.   Though, as was just
shown, the commodity composition in general (as between food
and industrial sector) differed significantly for exports to
German and non-German areas, there was no particular reason
to believe that the composition within industrial exports was
so differing, except for energy exports which were certainly
more significant for German than non-German areas of export.
(According to *DIW Wochenbericht*, 4-17-1953, p. 63, and *SBZ
Archiv* Nr. 11, 1954, p. 170, East German trade 1936 with
abroad was structurally like trade of the rest of Germany with
abroad.)   The exports to non-German and German areas were
then added for each industry and the percentage distribution
of the over-all total of RM 5, 527.5 million exports was calculated as it appears in the Table.   All industries were defined
in the postwar East German sense.

The postwar data have been derived from the following
sources: *Jahrbuch der D.D.R. 1960*, pp. 236-38, *Handbuch der
D.D.R.* (1964), pp. 548-49, *SJDDR 1955*, pp. 243-245, *1959*, page
573, *AH*, 14, 1957, p. 499; 4/5, 1958, p. 145; 12, 1958, page

Table 8 continued

430; 4/5, 1959, pp. 10-18; 16/17, 1959, p. 28; 18, 1960, page
1; 9, 1963, p. 4, *VS*, 1, 1957, p. 3; 1, 1958, p. 6; 4, 1958,
pp. 126-28; 3/4, 1959, p. 123, *SP*, 3/49, p. 41; 2, 1951, page
27; 5, 1957, p. 87; 9, 1961, p. 231; 10, 1961, pp. 262-64, *ND*,
2-14-57, p. 3; 2-3-59, p. 4; 1-21-60, p. 3, *Der Morgen*,
2-16-57, *PI*, 12 (1695), 1-28-59, p. 4, *Sonderausgabe*, 5-6-65,
p. 13, 61, 6-9-65, p. II, Karl C. Thalheim, Peter D. Propp, *Die
Entwicklungsziele für die gewerbliche Wirtschaft der SBZ in
der zweiten Fünfjahrplan-Periode* (Bonn: BMfgF, 1957), pp.
53-54, *DW*, 6-21-1956; 41, 1964, p. 5, *Berliner Zeitung*,
6-19-56, and *"Der Aussenhandel der sowjetischen Besatzungszone Deutschlands."* Mat. (Bonn: BMfgF), Anlagen 1 and 3.

Notes:

[a]1947 to 1949 data should be regarded as rough approxi-
mations.

[b]The sources contained exports of building materials and
glass/ceramics combined for 1950-54. They were split by
assuming the same relationship between the two categories of
exports as in 1955.

[c]The sources gave 1955 exports of metal-working industries excluding as well as including complete factories,
but for 1957, 1958, and 1960 only excluding, though the amount
of complete factory export was given. The author has divided
this latter total among the various industries as it was divided in 1955.

The 1951 and 1955 statistics contain a small amount of
unallocated metal-working industry export. It was allocated
among the metal-working industries according to the importance
of their allocated exports. A similar adjustment was made in
agriculture and forestry for 1953 and 1954 with exports; and
for 1950, 1951, 1954, 1955 with metal-working imports.

[d]The author's uranium estimates are included.

[e]Dash (-) means "amount zero."
Blank space means "no information."
.0 means amount was less than one twentieth of one per
cent
Detail may not add to total due to rounding.

mostly agricultural goods sent to other German areas. The basic industries supplied 17.7 per cent, the metal-working industries 34.2 per cent, and the light industries 28.6 per cent
of total exports. Textiles, chemicals, and general machinery
were the three principal export branches, providing together
more than a third of the total. Another quarter came from
heavy machinery, metalwares, electro-technical and food industries. All other industries contributed less than 4 per cent
to the export total.

During the postwar period, the neglect of agricultural
production in East Germany, as well as the decline in trade
with the other German areas, are reflected in a drop of agricultural exports to practically zero.

The share of the basic industries in exports, just as in
production, at first increased significantly in relative importance compared to prewar days. Then it declined to 1953,
rose in 1954 and held steady since at a level considerably
above 1936. The original increase and subsequent decline was
largely due to the behavior of the mining (potassium salts,
uranium ore), and chemical industries. It will be noted immediately that it was the Soviet Union which encouraged the
production and export of these goods, at first via and in addition to her reparations policy and later in the CMEA framework. There is certainly no evidence that the more recent
CMEA plans concerning the increased importance of East German
chemicals have had any significant impact.

Exports of the metal-working industries immediately after
the war were less important than in 1936, but their shares
rose substantially between 1947 and the early 1950's. This is
easily explained by the fact that large non-commercial exports
of these goods went to the Soviet Union as reparations. As
the burden of reparations declined, commercial exports of this
group of industries increased rapidly in absolute as well as

relative terms, just as did production. The relative decline
in 1954 and 1955 has been officially explained by stepped up
investments at home, that in 1956 and 1957 by adjustments to
the new CMEA specialization decisions.[17] Thereafter, the
relative share of these industries was to increase steadily,
plans calling for an all-time high of 67.3 per cent in 1960.
Realized data for the industries, however, show no such rise,
though they were still in 1963 much more important providers
of exports than in 1936. 1965 plans are again calling for a
rise in the export share of metal-working industries to 59.1
per cent. The export of complete factories, in particular,
is to be emphasized. More than 100 chemical factories alone
are to be exported to the U.S.S.R. from 1966-70. From 1955-
64, East Germany exported to many countries over 800 complete
factories, including 12 sugar factories, 103 cement factories,
131 power plants, 57 textile plants, 76 building materials
factories, and 25 food processing plants.[18]

Light industry exports were of enormous significance in
the early postwar years, but, since 1948, much less important
than before the war, contributing 13.3 per cent of the total
in 1959, compared to 28.6 per cent in 1936. The original rise
of such exports in 1947 certainly was due to the fact that not
much was left to export commercially except potassium salts
and textiles, reparations taking the rest. The decline in
textile exports is, therefore, particularly noticeable for the
following years, though there seems to have been some revival
in the early 1960's.

A somewhat different look at the structure of East German
exports is afforded by another recent source.[19] These data
are, however, based on a different classification than the
East German one used above, and this classification should not
be considered a condensed version of the East German industry
classification used throughout this study.[20] The classifica-

tion underlying the following comments is that of the Soviet
Union foreign trade statistics, also adopted by CMEA as the
standard classification among the members and henceforth referred to as "CMEA classification".[21] The category "machinery
and equipment" is identical with the Soviet commodity class 1,
"raw materials and fuels" with classes 2 through 5, "food,
drink, and tobacco and their raw materials" with classes 6
through 8, and "industrial consumer goods" with class 9.[22]

The "machinery and equipment" category contains many commodities listed under metal-working industries in the East
German industry classification, but not all. While typewrit-
ers, for example, are included, some fine mechanical goods
(clocks) belong to the industrial consumer goods class. "Raw
materials and fuels" contain most goods of the East German
basic industries, but also castings, raw wood and processed
wood, cellulose and paper (even stationery), glass, textile
raw materials, furs, seeds, and raw tobacco. "Food, drink,
and tobacco and their raw materials" includes the East German
industry of the same name (tobacco referring to processed tobacco), and most agricultural goods; while "industrial consumer goods" include everything else, including some products
of the chemical industry (drugs, movies), but excluding some
consumer durables, grouped in above-named categories. It is
easiest to consult the Soviet commodity classification in each
instance if exact information is desired.

According to this classification, East German exports of
machinery and equipment increased from 28 per cent of total
exports in 1950 to 55.7 per cent in 1955 and were between 47.3
and 48.4 per cent from 1958 to 1962. The corresponding data
for raw materials and fuels were 52.7 per cent in 1950, but
between 31.8 and 35.4 per cent from 1955 to 1962. The exports
of food, drink, tobacco and their raw materials were 6.8 per
cent of the total in 1950, 1.8 per cent in 1955, and between

2.4 and 3.5 per cent from 1958-62. Finally, exports of industrial consumer goods, while providing 12.5 per cent of the
total in 1950 and 10.7 per cent in 1955, increased their share
steadily to 17.7 by 1962. Except for the latter fact, therefore, this information adds little to the discussion above. A
significant CMEA impact towards change is not noticeable.

b.   Imports

In 1936, more of East Germany's imports were industrial
than of her exports. Forty-eight per cent of imports were
products of the basic industries, notably coal and steel from
other German areas, 19.3 per cent were products of the metal-
working industries, and 11.6 per cent each of the light and
food industries, with a large percentage of textile raw materials.

In the postwar era, agricultural imports have risen substantially in relative importance, which reflects the East
German neglect of production in agriculture. Unfortunately,
data beyond 1955 are rare, but those that are available do not
tell much of integration into the bloc. 1959 basic industry
imports were slightly lower than before the war, relatively.
Their share had been declining during the autarkic efforts of
the early 1950's (the high 1947 figure simply reflected the
fact that not much was imported beyond coal and steel), and
has been rising since 1954. Data are too scarce to judge
whether the rise in the share of metallurgical imports from
1952-58 and the rise of chemical imports between 1953 and
1960 reflect the effects of an international division of labor.[23]

The emphatic development of the metal-working industries
is clearly reflected in a fallen share in these imports by
1955 compared to the prewar era. The rise of this share since
1955, however, might well reflect the division of production
among different CMEA nations.

On the other hand, the neglect of the light industry in
East Germany, during the 1950's, was clearly mirrored in a
greater share of the light industry imports than before the
war.

According to the CMEA classification, the East German import structure shows[19] the following development. In 1950,
5.5 per cent of imports were machinery and equipment, by 1955
only 3.4 per cent, but 9.5, 12.3, 13.2, and 12.5 per cent in
1958 and 1960-62, respectively. Raw material and fuel imports
held a 56.7 per cent share of all imports in 1950, with little
variation thereafter (59.5 and 57.5 per cent in 1961-62).
Food, drink, tobacco and their raw material imports provided
34.1 per cent of the total in 1950. The percentage fell
steadily to 21.7 in 1961, but rose to 25.5 in 1962. Finally,
industrial consumer goods imports held a 3.7 per cent share
in 1950, rising to 7.8 per cent in 1958 and falling to 4.5 per
cent by 1962. Again the earlier discussion is corroborated.
Only the development of machinery and equipment imports might
be interpreted as due to CMEA influence.

2.   The Trade Structure with the Communist Bloc

It is of special interest to note the difference in the
commodity structure between East Germany's trade with east and
west insofar as data are available. These are suggested by
Tables 10 and 11 below, and can be seen directly by comparing
Tables 8 and 9 with Tables 12 and 13.

As shown in Table 10, the bloc countries received from
1950-55 a lower proportion of basic industry exports than of
all exports to the bloc (the 1954 rise in their share of mining export is due to the inception of commercial export of
uranium), hence basic industry export in Table 12 appears of
less importance than in Table 8. As one might expect from
CMEA policy, the relative importance of mining and metallurgy

Table 9. Percentage distribution of East Germany's
commodity imports from all areas, by sectors,
1936, and selected postwar years

Sector	1936	1947	1948	1949
All Industries	90.5	92.2	75.1	
Agriculture and Forestry	9.5	7.8	24.9	
Basic Industries[a]	48.0	76.0	62.2	
Energy	.3	-	-	
Mining	16.4	23.7	22.0	27.6
Metallurgy	14.6	46.7	34.9	26.2
Chemicals	15.8	5.6	5.3	8.1
Building Materials[a]	.9	-	-	
Metal-working Industries[b]	19.3	3.6	1.9	
Heavy Machinery	1.6	} 3.2	} .5	
General Machinery	1.4			
Vehicles	1.9			
Ships	.1			
Castings/Forgings	2.9			
Metalwares	5.7			
Electro-technical	3.7	.0	.2	
Fine Mechanics/Optics	2.0	.4	1.2	
Light Industries[a]	11.6	4.2	4.3	
Woodworking and Cultural	1.7			
Textiles	7.9	1.5	.5	
Clothing	.0			
Leather/Shoes/Furs	.5			
Cellulose/Paper	1.2	1.4	2.3	
Printing	.1			
Waste Materials	.1			
Food/Drink/Tobacco Ind.	11.6	9.4	6.7	
Vegetable Products	5.8	} 5.5	} 22.2	
Animal Products (incl.fish)	2.3			
Forestry Products	1.4	2.3	2.7	
All Sectors	100.0	100.0	100.0	100.0

Table 9 continued

1950	1951	1952	1953	1954	1955	1956
86.8	83.9	80.5	78.4	79.5	78.2	
13.2	16.1	19.5	21.6	20.5	21.9	
44.6	41.3	38.2	36.9	37.8	38.6	
.2	.6	.2	.4	.7	.4	
18.3	17.9	17.6	16.9	17.0	16.8	
16.9	14.2	12.8	13.6	13.7	14.5	
8.6	7.9	7.3	5.6	6.0	6.4	
.8	.7	.4	.4	.3	.3	
8.2	5.2	5.6	5.2	4.8	4.7	
.8	1.8	1.2	1.5	1.0	1.0	
.4	.8	1.0	.7	.7	.7	
2.2	.3	1.2	.9	1.2	1.3	
.0	.0	-	.0	.0	.0	
.6	.3	.2	.5	.5	.1	
2.0	1.0	1.4	1.2	.9	.9	
1.9	.7	.4	.2	.2	.3	
.4	.4	.3	.2	.3	.3	
11.7	15.5	19.2	15.5	18.1	19.0	18.8
.4	.7	1.1	1.0	1.6	2.1	
8.4	12.8	15.4	12.6	13.6	14.0	
-	-	-	.0	.7	.6	
2.0	.1	1.1	.8	.8	.7	
.4	1.2	.6	.5	.5	.7	
.1	.2	.5	.3	.5	.5	
.4	.4	.4	.3	.4	.4	
22.3	21.9	17.5	20.8	18.8	15.9	
12.0	14.9	17.9	19.7	18.6	19.8	38.0
1.1	1.0	1.4	1.7	1.8	1.4	
.1	.2	.1	.2	.1	.7	
100.0	100.0	100.0	100.0	100.0	100.0	100.0

Table 9   continued

Sector	1958	1959	1960	1961
All Industries				
Agriculture and Forestry				
Basic Industries[a]	42.0	41.0		40.0
Energy	-			
Mining	16.0			
Metallurgy	20.0			
Chemicals	6.0		7.7	3.9
Building Materials[a]	-			
Metal-working Industries[b]	12.0	13.0	12.0	15.6
Heavy Machinery				
General Machinery				
Vehicles				
Ships				
Castings/Forgings				
Metalwares				
Electro-technical				
Fine Mechanics/Optics				
Light Industries[a]	16.0	15.0		4.5
Woodworking and Cultural				
Textiles	10.0			
Clothing				
Leather/Shoes/Furs				
Cellulose/Paper				
Printing				
Waste Materials				
Food/Drink/Tobacco Ind.				
Vegetable Products	30.0	31.0		39.9
Animal Products (incl.fish)				
Forestry Products				
All Sectors	100.0	100.0	100.0	100.0

The 1957 share of metal-working industries was 6.8

exports by 1963, compared to 1955, was slightly reduced, but so was the share of chemicals exports, which one would not expect.

The special interest of the bloc in East Germany as a supplier of machinery is seen by the fact that the bloc received a much larger proportion of metal-working industry exports than of all exports to the bloc (Table 10). This was true for every year from 1950-55 and again for 1960, and almost for every individual industry in this group. Hence metal-working exports in Table 12 appear much more important than in Table 8. The limited interest of the Communist countries in the products of the light and food industries and agriculture and forestry is reflected in the low exports of these products to the east.

On the import side, until 1952, the bloc delivered a larger proportion of agricultural and forestry products than was the case for all products (Table 11). For most years it also de-

---

Sources:

   Postwar data as Table 8 and *AH*, 12, 1964, p. 23. 1936 import data from *Supplement*, Chap. I. According to sources given, RM 605 million of imports from German areas were of the food sector. It was assumed that mining and metallurgy imports from 1936 German areas held the same percentage of total imports as 1950 mining and metallurgy imports from all areas. Other 1936 imports from German areas were assumed distributed as 1950 imports of such other goods from West Germany. 1936 imports from non-German areas were assumed to have been distributed as all-German imports from those areas. See *SHD*, pp. 396, 398, and 400.

Notes:

   [a]In this Table glass and ceramics imports are included under building materials, since it was not possible to separate the two. Due to the extremely small importance of these imports, however, the comparability with the export table should not be affected appreciably.

   [b]See note (c) to Table 8.

Table 10. Percentage of East German commodity
exports going to the Communist bloc,
by sectors, selected years

Sector	1950	1951	1952
All Industries	69.0	79.3	75.8
Agriculture and Forestry	48.5	63.0	33.9
Basic Industries	66.6	67.9	62.8
Energy	56.2	44.4	72.2
Mining	68.5	52.1	30.1
Metallurgy	45.5	76.7	96.2
Chemicals	68.4	79.9	80.2
Building Materials	49.7	44.8	58.7
Metal-working Industries[a]	81.1	91.1	90.4
Heavy Machinery	95.3	98.8	98.4
General Machinery	76.0	87.9	91.7
Vehicles	87.6	87.6	80.3
Ships	-	100.0	100.0
Castings/Forgings	87.5	-	33.3
Metalwares	57.9	53.3	56.0
Electro-technical	92.3	97.9	98.6
Fine Mechanics/Optics	71.4	81.0	72.1
Light Industries	59.4	69.8	65.5
Woodworking/Cultural	78.1	79.8	63.9
Textiles	40.9	64.5	65.7
Clothing	60.5	-	87.5
Leather/Shoes/Furs	-	72.6	55.4
Cellulose/Paper	51.3	40.3	56.6
Printing	21.9	88.0	77.2
Glass/Ceramics	59.5	69.8	65.6
Waste Materials	97.8	-	-
Food/Drink/Tobacco Industries	49.5	63.6	39.6
Vegetable Products	13.8	66.2	32.7
Animal Products (incl.fish)	100.0	50.0	66.7
Forestry Products	81.4	55.3	33.9
All Sectors	68.2[b]	78.9	75.1

Table 10 continued

1953	1954	1955	1960
79.2	80.6	75.7	
43.4	5.0	36.7	
60.3	70.1	63.6	
83.5	68.0	85.3	
33.5	70.7	64.0	
86.2	53.8	58.6	
73.9	72.8	65.8	
55.6	38.8	34.6	
93.1	93.3	89.4	89.4
99.3	98.6	93.7	89.2
94.7	93.3	88.8	87.3
74.2	88.9	89.9	93.7
100.0	100.0	99.5	98.2
-	-	-	
52.9	58.4	43.8	
99.2	97.7	93.5	
73.2	77.2	71.3	
49.4	48.4	41.6	
37.0	41.4	35.6	
48.0	44.2	35.2	
70.0	78.3	84.6	
42.6	63.3	50.3	
44.8	42.1	34.0	
79.1	76.8	74.6	
49.4	48.5	41.6	
14.3	25.0	25.0	
19.2	35.7	29.4	
16.1	2.6	25.7	
100.0	100.0	80.0	
57.4	5.9	67.6	
78.8	80.0	75.3	75.7

Table 11. Percentage of East German commodity
imports coming from the Communist bloc,
by sectors, selected years

Sector	1950	1951
All Industries	73.9	71.1
Agriculture and Forestry	88.9	83.2
Basic Industries[a]	71.6	76.4
Energy	72.4	15.7
Mining	94.9	94.2
Metallurgy	66.7	75.2
Chemicals	32.5	43.6
Building Materials[a]	64.5	62.0
Metal-working Industries	44.7	43.0
Heavy Machinery	41.6	56.4
General Machinery	23.8	21.2
Vehicles	80.1	79.1
Ships	-	-
Castings/Forgings	.0	54.8
Metalwares	26.5	59.3
Electro-technical	51.0	1.2
Fine Mechanics/Optics	5.5	23.9
Light Industries[b]	77.7	82.3
Woodworking/Cultural	10.1	57.5
Textiles	84.6	94.5
Clothing	-	-
Leather/Shoes/Furs	97.6	44.0
Cellulose/Paper	1.2	13.9
Printing	-	2.0
Waste Materials	-	5.8
Food/Drink/Tobacco Industries	87.1	59.8
Vegetable Products	89.1	88.0
Animal Products (incl.fish)	93.4	24.4
Forestry Products	23.5	19.0
All Sectors	75.9[c]	73.0

Table 11 continued

1952	1953	1954	1955
74.5	76.8	74.8	71.2
77.4	74.6	69.8	68.7
78.5	79.9	79.8	78.4
48.1	28.6	13.0	22.0
95.9	95.7	95.0	93.4
73.2	75.2	77.9	74.5
47.4	48.6	49.9	52.4
59.1	61.5	67.1	68.9
57.4	58.4	52.6	39.5
59.8	71.5	57.1	20.0
70.0	56.8	52.7	22.9
95.1	91.4	91.1	86.6
-	-	-	-
55.6	34.8	13.4	12.5
33.9	42.8	39.2	27.8
17.7	23.0	27.0	14.8
19.1	18.6	11.0	14.6
77.0	75.1	73.5	72.6
34.5	40.3	50.4	43.8
86.8	84.3	82.5	83.1
-	100.0	98.4	97.0
59.8	53.1	45.7	48.6
42.6	26.9	62.2	10.3
12.3	19.8	36.9	38.9
5.4	2.3	-	3.4
68.5	77.1	71.7	61.1
80.6	77.6	71.4	71.2
42.1	43.8	58.2	45.9
25.6	33.8	7.8	44.5
75.1	76.3	73.8	70.6

Table 12. Percentage distribution of East Germany's
commercial commodity exports to the Communist bloc,
by sectors, selected years

Sector	1950	1951	1952
Industry	97.3	97.9	99.2
Agriculture and Forestry	2.7	2.1	.7
Basic Industries	38.5	26.4	25.1
Energy	.4	.4	.4
Mining	13.7	6.1	3.7
Metallurgy	.2	.2	.1
Chemical	22.0	18.3	18.9
Building Materials	2.3	1.4	2.0
Metal-working Industries[a]	37.9	54.8	60.0
Heavy Machinery	7.2	11.4	13.1
General Machinery	12.4	15.8	20.4
Vehicles	3.4	3.6	2.9
Ships	-	.1	.1
Castings/Forgings	.0	-	.0
Metalwares	1.1	.6	.9
Electro-technical	7.0	16.2	15.5
Fine Mechanics/Optics	6.8	7.2	7.0
Light Industries	16.9	13.7	11.1
Woodworking/Cultural	7.6	5.2	2.3
Textiles	3.9	3.7	4.4
Clothing	.2	-	.0
Leather/Shoes/Furs	-	.2	.1
Cellulose/Paper	1.5	.9	.8
Printing	.0	1.5	1.3
Glass/Ceramics	2.8	2.2	2.2
Waste Materials	.8	-	-
Food/Drink/Tobacco Industries	4.0	3.0	3.0
Vegetable Products	.4	1.6	.3
Animal Products (incl.fish)	.0	.0	.0
Forestry Products	2.3	.5	.4
All Sectors	100.0	100.0	100.0

Table 12 continued

1953	1954	1955	1960	1963[b]
99.4	100.0	99.6		
.6	.0	.4		
18.6	26.4	27.0		
.3	.2	.3		
3.2	12.1	11.9		} 10.8
.3	.2	.3		
13.6	13.2	13.9		10.7
1.3	.7	.7		
74.0	66.9	66.8	61.1	
25.2	20.4	17.6	12.5	
22.4	14.8	13.8	12.8	
3.1	8.9	10.7	10.2	
.7	5.6	9.0	8.8	
.0	-	-		
.7	.7	.5		
15.8	11.2	9.2		
6.1	5.3	6.0		
6.4	5.5	5.3		
.8	.8	.7		
2.5	2.1	2.0		
.0	.0	.1		
.1	.3	.2		
.6	.5	.4		
1.1	.9	1.1		
1.1	.8	.8		
.0	.0	.0		
.4	1.2	.5		.7
.1	.0	.2		
.0	.0	.0		
.5	.0	.2		
100.0	100.0	100.0	100.0	100.0

Table 13.   Percentage distribution of East Germany's
        commodity imports from the Communist bloc,
              by sectors, selected years

Sector	1950	1951
All Industries	84.5	81.7
Agriculture and Forestry	15.5	18.3
Basic Industries	42.1	43.2
Energy	.1	.1
Mining	22.8	23.1
Metallurgy	14.8	14.6
Chemicals	3.7	4.7
Building Materials	.6	.6
Metal-working Industries	4.8	3.1
Heavy Machinery	.4	1.4
General Machinery	.1	.2
Vehicles	2.3	.3
Ships	-	-
Castings/Forgings	.0	.2
Metalwares	.7	.8
Electro-technical	1.2	.0
Fine Mechanics/Optics	.0	.1
Light Industries	12.0	17.4
Woodworking/Cultural	.0	.6
Textiles	9.4	16.5
Clothing	-	-
Leather/Shoes/Furs	2.5	.1
Cellulose/Paper	.0	.2
Printing	-	.0
Waste Materials	-	.0
Food/Drink/Tobacco Industries	25.6	18.0
Vegetable Products	14.1	17.9
Animal Products (incl. fish)	1.4	.3
Forestry Products	.0	.0
All Sectors	100.0	100.0

Source:

        As Table 9.

Table 13 continued

1952	1953	1954	1955
80.0	78.9	80.5	78.7
20.1	21.1	19.4	21.3
40.0	38.6	40.8	42.8
.1	.1	.1	.1
22.5	21.2	21.9	22.3
12.5	13.4	14.4	15.3
4.6	3.6	4.1	4.8
.3	.3	.3	.3
4.3	4.0	3.4	2.6
.9	1.4	.8	.3
.9	.5	.5	.2
1.5	1.1	1.5	1.6
-	-	-	-
.1	.2	.1	.0
.6	.7	.5	.4
.1	.1	.1	.1
.1	.1	.0	.1
19.7	15.3	18.0	19.5
.5	.5	1.1	1.3
17.8	13.9	15.2	16.4
-	.0	1.0	.9
.9	.5	.5	.5
.4	.2	.0	.1
.1	.1	.2	.3
.0	.0	-	.0
16.0	21.0	18.3	13.8
19.2	20.1	18.0	20.0
.8	1.0	1.4	.9
.0	.1	.0	.4
100.0	100.0	100.0	100.0

livered a larger proportion of <u>basic industry</u> products (coal, coke, ores, metals) and of <u>light industry</u> goods (textile raw materials). <u>Metal-working industry</u> products, except vehicles, have predominantly come from the west. The most interesting test as to changes CMEA has brought about in all this since the late 1950's can, unfortunately, not be made for lack of data for the period after 1955.

Sources: Table 10

     As for Table 8

Notes:
[a]1957 datum: 87.8 per cent

[b]differs from percentage that might be calculated from Table 3, cols. 2 and 3, because of author's correction of 1950 trade figure with West Germany. See *Supplement*, Chap. I.

Sources: Table 11

     As for Table 9

Notes:
[a]includes glass/ceramics

[b]excludes glass/ceramics

[c]differs from percentage that might be calculated from Table 4, cols. 2 and 3, because of author's correction of 1950 trade figure with West Germany. See *Supplement*, cha. I.

Sources: Table 12

     As in Table 8 and *AH*, 4, 1965, p. 17. It was assumed in addition that of total glass and ceramics exports the same proportion went to the bloc each year as in the case of all light industry exports, excluding this category. Hence exports of building materials to the bloc followed as a residual from the known bloc exports of building materials and glass/ceramics combined.

Notes:
[a]1957 datum: 56.3 per cent

[b]CMEA members only

3. The Trade Structure with Individual
Communist Countries

More is known, however, about the commodity structure of
trade with individual Communist countries. Such data are
given below in Tables 14 through 21 for the various member
nations of CMEA (including Albania).[24]

These Tables are based on the CMEA classification discussed above. All of them were given in percentage form in
the original sources. This author does not know whether these
percentages have been calculated from East German data (as
shown in CHAPTER 2 and earlier in this CHAPTER) or foreign
data (see *Supplement,* Chap. IV). Hence it is not necessarily
legitimate to use absolute trade data, given in CHAPTER 2,
apply these percentages to them, and arrive at absolute magnitudes. Nevertheless, rough insights could be gained from
such a procedure.

Some tables also contain a somewhat doubtful comparison
with 1936. This refers to trade of all Germany with the country in question in its 1936 boundaries, but the commodity
classification is CMEA's.[25] As can be seen from the 1936
totals, these data are minimum figures only.

From the information presented in Tables 14-21 a number
of observations can be made. The 1936 trade structure with
the later CMEA countries clearly reflected the differences
in economic development between Germany and Eastern Europe.
While Germany's exports predominantly consisted of machinery and "raw materials" (such as chemicals), her imports from
the area consisted of agricultural and food products and other "raw materials" (such as tobacco, textile raw materials).
There were hardly any machinery imports from Eastern Europe.
In the postwar era this has changed. East Germany's exports
were still largely of the same categories, but she has been
importing rising proportions of machinery after the middle

Table 14.   Commodity composition of East German
trade with Albania, in per cent of total
exports and imports[a]

		Categories			
Year	M	R	F	C	Total
		East German Exports			
1951	57.0	> 9.2			100.0
1952	37.0	>34.2			100.0
1953	71.4	>13.9			100.0
1954	67.0	>13.0			100.0
1955	52.7	>13.3			100.0
1956	71.9	>12.8			100.0
		East German Imports			
1952		>11.0	22.4		100.0
1953		>63.5	18.2		100.0
1954		>27.5	36.8		100.0
1955		>64.6	28.6		100.0
1956		>36.7	60.1		100.0

Source:

   AH, 2, 1958, p. 53

Note:

   [a]Category M = Machinery and Equipment
             R = Raw Materials and Fuels
             F = Food, Drink, Tobacco
             C = Industrial Consumer Goods
   Blank spaces in the Table mean "no data available."
   Detail may not add to 100 per cent due to rounding.

Table 15. Commodity composition of East German
trade with Bulgaria, in per cent of total
exports and imports[a]

		Categories			
Year	M	R	F	C	Total
East German Exports					
1936[b]	29.0	15.1	-	-	44.1
1950	53.1	46.5	-	.4	100.0
1951	73.3	24.2	1.5	1.0	100.0
1952	66.8	31.2	.3	1.7	100.0
1953	70.5	24.0	.2	5.3	100.0
1954	70.0	23.8	.4	5.8	100.0
1955	63.8	23.4	.7	12.1	100.0
1958	54.0				100.0
East German Imports					
1936[b]	-	34.7	49.3	-	84.0
1950	-	32.2	64.7	3.1	100.0
1951	-	38.7	60.1	1.2	100.0
1952	-	43.1	53.5	3.4	100.0
1953	-	27.2	64.9	7.9	100.0
1954	.1	31.4	43.8	24.7	100.0
1955	.1	25.5	48.0	26.4	100.0
1960	3.1				100.0
1961	12.7				100.0

Sources:

        AH, 19, 1956, pp. 667-68; 23, 1957, pp. 833-34; 2,
        1959, p. 33; 10, 1962, p. 30, *PI*, Nr. 41 (1577),
4-11-1958, p. 7.

Notes:

        [a] see note to Table 14

        [b] minimum data referring to trade of all Germany

Table 16.   Commodity composition of East German
trade with Czechoslovakia, in per cent of total
exports and imports[a]

Year	M	R	F	C	Total
		Categories			
		East German Exports			
1936[b]	23.9	40.7	2.2	8.9	75.7
1950	38.0				100.0
1951		46.0		4.4	100.0
1955	34.3	42.2	4.0	19.5	100.0
1956	40.0			8.0	100.0
1957	49.0	34.0	5.0	12.0	100.0
1958	53.6	34.2	3.7	8.5	100.0
1960	51.0	33.1	.6	15.3	100.0
1961-65 Plan	60.0	30.0	10.0		100.0
		East German Imports			
1936[b]	-	56.3	-	14.3	70.6
1950	5.2				100.0
1951		83.9		4.2	100.0
1955	6.9	51.1	42.0		100.0
1956	16.0			19.0	100.0
1957	22.0	45.7	8.5	23.8	100.0
1958	33.3	38.3	7.8	20.6	100.0
1960	38.2	38.1	.7	23.0	100.0
1961-65 Plan	>40.0				100.0

Sources:

   JDDR 1961, p. 258, *VS*, 3/4, 1959, p. 121, *Neue Zeit*,
   9-5-1958, *Berliner Zeitung*, 9-3-1958, *PI*, Nr. 28
(1564), 3-7-1958, p. 4; 98 (1634), 8-29-1958, p. 5; 50 (1876),
5-2-1960, p. 5; 68 (1894), 6-15-1960, p. 6, *DW*, 3-10-1960, *AH*,
17/18, 1956, p. 603; 2, 1958, p. 41; 4/5, 1959, p. 19; 18,
1959, p. 9; 4/5, 1961, p. 4.

Notes:

   [a]see note to Table 14
   [b]see note to Table 15

Table 17. Commodity composition of East German
trade with Hungary, in per cent of total
exports and imports[a]

Year	M	R	F	C	Total
		Categories			
		East German Exports			
1936[b]	24.8	22.3	-	17.3	64.4
1951	60.0	35.0	2.0	3.0	100.0
1955	43.2	42.8		14.0	100.0
1956	>39.0				100.0
1957	<39.0			>13.0	100.0
1958	42.0	40.3	1.3	16.4	100.0
1961	50.3	36.8	.5	12.4	100.0
1965 Plan	53.0	30.0	1.0	16.0	100.0
		East German Imports			
1936[b]	-	22.8	43.5	4.1	70.4
1951	5.0	6.0	89.0	-	100.0
1952			75.0		100.0
1953	23.8	12.4	61.2	2.6	100.0
1955	11.0	15.8		73.2	100.0
1957	22.8	23.8	51.9	1.5	100.0
1958	17.9	25.8	53.9	2.4	100.0
1961	26.5	21.2	33.2	19.1	100.0
1965 Plan	39.0	12.0	41.0	8.0	100.0

Sources:

VS, 3/4, 1959, p. 122, AH, 4/5, 1958, pp. 130-31; 9,
1958, p. 325; 10, 1959, p. 7; 16/17, 1962, p. 23;
4, 1965, p. 26.

Notes:

[a] see note to Table 14

[b] see note to Table 15

Table 18.   Commodity composition of East German
trade with Outer Mongolia, in per cent of total
exports and imports[a]

Year	M	Categories R	F	C	Total
		East German Exports			
1959	≈25	-	-	≈75	100.0
		East German Imports			
1959	-	100.0		-	100.0

Source:

    AH, 4/5, 1960, p. 20

Note:

    [a]see note to Table 14

Table 19. Commodity composition of East German
trade with Poland, in per cent of total
exports and imports[a]

Year	M	R	F	C	Total
		Categories			
		East German Exports			
1936[b]	33.2	11.7	-	6.0	50.9
1949		70.0			100.0
1950	33.3				100.0
1953	66.7				100.0
1955	56.7	35.3	8.0		100.0
1956	66.7				100.0
1957	33.3				100.0
1958	38.6	37.8	23.5		100.0
1960	47.7	32.2	6.4	13.7	100.0
1961	44.5[c]	37.9	1.9	15.7	100.0
		East German Imports			
1936[b]	-	39.4	13.0	-	52.4
1949		77.0	19.0		100.0
1950	5.9				100.0
1955	.4	83.4	16.2		100.0
1957	2.1				100.0
1958	6.9	89.0	4.1		100.0
1960	13.6	81.0	4.1	1.3	100.0
1961	10.1	81.0	4.3	4.6	100.0
1963	≈20.0				100.0

Sources:

*"Der Aussenhandel der sowjetischen Besatzungszone
Deutschlands,"* Mat. (Bonn: BMfgF), pp. 32-33; DW,
11-25-1954 and 3-10-1960, VS, 3/4, 1959, p. 122, ND, 6-27-1957,
AH, 4/5, 1958, p. 127, *"Aussenhandel Volksrepublik Polen-
Deutsche Demokratische Republik,"* AH Sonderbeilage (Leipzig
Spring Fair, 1959), p. 10; 21, 1962, p. 21; 7, 1964, p. 36,
PI, Nr. 108, (1791), 9-21-1959, p. 6.

Notes:

[a] see note to Table 14

[b] see note to Table 15

[c] in 1964, "about 60 per cent" for the East German industry machine building, see ND, 6-16-1965, p. 7.

Table 20.   Commodity composition of East German
trade with Rumania, in per cent of total
exports and imports[a]

Year	M	R	F	C	Total
		Categories			
		East German Exports			
1936[b]	25.4	31.9	-	15.1	72.4
1950	63.6				100.0
1954	77.0	17.0	1.0	5.0	100.0
1957	48.0	18.0	-	34.0	100.0
1958	46.0	24.0		30.0	100.0
		East German Imports			
1936[b]	-	70.6	11.4	-	82.0
1950	-	53.3	46.7	-	100.0
1954	3.0	50.0	44.0	3.0	100.0
1957	20.0	29.0	47.0	4.0	100.0
1958	36.0				100.0
1960	41.6	27.4			100.0

Sources:

AH, 2, 1958, p. 47; 4/5, 1958, p. 129; 20, 1959,
p. 15; 16/17, 1962, pp. 20-23; ND, (Leipzig Spring
Fair, 1961 edition), p. 4.

Notes:

[a] see note to Table 14

[b] see note to Table 15

Table 21. Commodity composition of East German
trade with the Soviet Union, in per cent of
total exports and imports[a]

Categories

Year	M	R	F	C	Total
			East German Exports		
1936[b]	70.3	19.0	-	4.2	93.5
1950	28.2	61.7	7.2	2.9	100.0
1951	50.0				100.0
1953	67.7	26.8	2.6	2.9	100.0
1955	77.5	20.2		2.3	100.0
1956	76.2	20.1	.7	3.0	100.0
1957	54.5				100.0
1958	56.4	31.7	-	11.9	100.0
1959	58.7	28.1	-	13.2	100.0
1960	62.3	26.3	-	11.4	100.0
1961	56.8	27.9	.2	15.1	100.0
1965 Plan	64.5	23.8	-	11.7	100.0
			East German Imports		
1936[b]	-	76.2	-	2.5	78.7
1950	4.0	60.8	35.0	.2	100.0
1953	2.5	58.0	39.0	.5	100.0
1955	1.2	73.8		25.0	100.0
1956	1.6	70.8	26.0	1.6	100.0
1958	3.5	70.7	25.3	.5	100.0
1959	4.0	65.1	29.9	1.0	100.0
1960	3.4	70.5	25.7	.4	100.0
1961	5.5	71.9	21.8	.8	100.0
1965 Plan	3.6	84.4	12.0	-	100.0

Sources:

Neue Zeit, 2-12-1957, 5-17-1960, *AH*, 1954, p. 973;
10, 1957, pp. 349-50; 10, 1958, pp. 348-49, 4/5,
1959, p. 17, *VS*, 3/4, 1959, p. 120, *PI*, Nr. 54 (1880), 5-11-
1960, p. 2, *ND*, 8-11-1962, p. 5, *JDDR 1961*, p. 258.

Notes:

[a]see note to Table 14
[b]see note to Table 15

1950's, in particular from Bulgaria, Czechoslovakia, Hungary, Poland, and Rumania, but not from the U.S.S.R. In some instances, the imports of industrial consumer goods have also been rising relatively, while the relative importance of raw materials and food imports has been declining. East German machinery exports have since the late 1950's only increased relatively with Czechoslovakia, Hungary, and possibly Poland.

4.   The Importance of Foreign Trade

One final question shall be taken up. Is East Germany getting more dependent on the other bloc nations than she was a few years ago? It would be of great interest if one could express, for instance, the value of exports as a percentage of GNP. This is not an easy undertaking, however. It would make absolutely no sense to express, e.g., the DM equivalent of the ruble foreign trade data as a percentage of official East German GNP data (defined in a sense completely at odds with the western definition and available in various varieties, such as at internal factory prices, internal market prices, constant plan prices). Such comparisons are, nevertheless, being made by East German writers (which is at least understandable) as well as by western writers (which is not).[26]

This author sees two possibilities for measuring trade dependence. A somewhat impressionistic answer to the question is given via a list of export and import ratios for individual commodities, calculated from officially published data in physical units. Such a list is presented in Tables 22 and 23.

Export ratios are defined as export divided by production, import ratios as imports divided by the sum of production plus imports. An increase in such ratios would, presumably, denote greater dependence on foreign trade partners than before. Since the goods selected represent the most important ones traded in each industry, a rise in most ratios could be regarded as an indication that the particular ratio for the whole

Table 22. East German export ratios (exports
divided by production) for selected
commodities, in per cent, selected years

Commodity	1950	1955	1959	1962	1963
Energy					
Electricity	.7	.8	1.0	.3	.2
Gas	.0	.2	.2	.2	.2
Mining Products					
Lignite Briquettes	3.8	10.2	11.7	11.1	11.6
Potassium Salts	68.6	64.5	63.3	65.5	62.9
Soft Coal	-	.7	.3	.0	.0
Lignite low temperature coke	3.1	.7	.6	.6	.7
Lignite high temperature coke	-	-	5.1	7.1	6.8
Chemicals					
Sulfur	40.0	31.5	13.5	34.6	17.2
Sodium Sulfate	-	61.4	57.0	63.6	66.4
Calcined Soda	-	17.1	18.4	25.9	25.9
Carbon disulphide	-	3.8	8.9	5.1	5.5
Sulfuric acid	-	6.6	2.4	4.2	.1
Ammonia	.	1.1	.4	1.1	.2
Caustic Soda	-	3.1	7.5	8.9	5.0
Potassium Carbonate	58.3	61.6	59.9	58.0	58.1
Potassium Hydroxide	8.4	24.5	20.7	17.2	19.4
Calcium Carbide	2.3	4.2	-	-	-
Magnesium Sulfate	-	22.8	20.7	26.3	40.2
Nitrogen Fertilizer	15.0	28.4	31.1	29.9	27.3
Acetic Acid	-	16.4	23.1	27.1	26.3
Solvents	-	22.1	16.4	14.3	17.2
Plasticizers	-	28.0	19.0	14.4	7.9
Raw Film	-	3.9	2.9	2.4	1.2
Black/white Film	-	64.9	76.5	76.4	77.7
Color Film	-	86.9	83.9	86.0	86.1
Photographic Paper	.	21.6	25.4	22.8	22.2
Soap	-	7.7	16.8	16.9	21.9
Paints	12.5	4.6	5.2	8.1	9.2
Polyvinylchloride	20.6	28.3	23.7	29.9	32.7
Polystyrol	15.0	9.1	17.0	14.4	16.9
Synthetic Rubber	46.5	53.6	54.3	51.0	46.1
Auto Tires	-	.8	6.3	2.8	6.6
Bicycle Tires	-	22.5	14.8	25.8	35.4
Bicycle Tubes	-	8.8	15.5	24.5	33.2
Diesel Fuel	41.4	38.8	35.1	23.7	24.8

Commodity	1950	1955	1959	1962	1963
Gasoline	13.3	20.5	.	30.6	31.8
Penicillin	-	30.0	18.9	8.5	.4

Building Materials

Cement	13.5	23.0	4.6	3.3	8.1
Plaster of Paris	13.3	14.5	15.8	15.7	17.3
Bricks	-	.0	1.1	.	.
Roofing Tiles	.	1.1	.6	.4	.3

Heavy Machinery

Marine Diesel and Gas Motors	-	38.0	26.0*	71.6*	67.5*
Stationary Diesel and Gas Motors	-	28.2	29.8*	30.5*	25.2*
Gasoline Motors	-	.9	.3	2.3	.8
Horizontal Face Plate Lathes	-	84.0	78.9	73.8	84.8
Turret Lathes	-	10.9	27.9	30.4	51.1
Automatic Lathes	-	38.1	21.3	31.0	35.8
Other Lathes	-	15.5	20.1	25.2	29.1
Milling Machines	-	53.7	38.9	42.5	49.2
Jig Drills	-	98.4	79.2	82.0	70.3
Precision Drills	-	16.0	101.6	76.0	32.2
Single Spindle Drills					
up to 20 mm diameter	-	6.6	4.2	6.3	4.3
above 20 mm diameter	-	8.9	13.7	22.3	18.3
Radial Drills					
up to 40 mm diameter	-	31.0	56.0	50.0	37.3
above 40 mm diameter	-	53.8	30.3	43.6	36.0
Long Planing Machines	-	57.6	41.1	40.9	67.5
Horizontal Shaping Machines	-	13.5	20.6	41.3	4.8
Vertical Shaping Machines	-	40.9	46.8	55.9	62.1
Broaching Machines	-	33.3	60.4	33.3	22.4
External Grinding Machines	-	30.1	33.5	45.3	56.4
Plane Grinding Machines	-	29.1	35.1	46.2	55.0
Internal Grinding Machines	-	67.1	58.1	62.7	55.5
Lapping and Honing Machines	-	60.0	63.4	37.3	45.2
Threading Machines	-	8.9	17.4	9.7	9.3
Circular Metal Saw Machines	-	11.6	36.2	16.1	24.1

Commodity	1950	1955	1959	1962	1963
Eccentric, Crank-drive and Toggle-lever Presses	-	51.4	47.7	51.8	47.4
Hydraulic Presses	-	41.3	46.7	78.6	93.3
Crank-drive lever Shears	-	42.7	54.0	72.4	76.2
Other Shears	-	10.3	10.3	11.7	12.0
Dropping Forges	-	3.1	10.6	6.2	3.8
Rolling Mill Machines	-	110.7	110.9	.	.

General Machinery

Fiber treating Machines	-	32.1	17.8	.	20.6
Weaving Machines	-	58.3	22.0	.	31.8
Knitting Machines	-	90.3	37.0	.	29.2
Industrial Sewing Machines	-	29.3	46.4	45.6	46.2
Tractor Ploughs	-	8.9	11.8	14.3	10.3
Tractor Harrows	-	10.1	5.7	5.8	10.5
Tractor Drilling and Sowing Machines	-	14.0	24.0	47.4†	46.4†
Tractor Cultivators	-	1.5	5.6	13.4	15.8
Grass Mowers	-	1.5	13.1	34.6	23.7
Combines	-	.5	15.8	3.4	.1
Threshing Machines	-	5.9	77.3	-	.
Hay and Straw Presses	-	2.2	45.8	58.4	61.2
Concrete Mixers	-	2.6	2.5	.	4.9
Potato Harvesters	-	-	2.0	74.0	85.8
Beet Harvesters	-	-	.7	11.7	48.9

Vehicles

Steam Locomotives	-	13.8	-	-	-
Electric Locomotives	-	84.4	50.3	43.7	50.8
Railroad Passenger Cars	-	80.5	84.6	83.8	90.8
Railroad Freight Cars	-	41.5	49.9	51.1	60.8
Passenger Automobiles	-	38.3	20.0	31.7	34.9
Trucks	-	38.4	37.4	16.3	23.1
Motor-scooters and cycles	-	10.8	25.2	15.7	24.6
Bicycles	4.2	20.9	33.8	2.9	16.2
Wheeled Tractors	-	7.6	20.7	23.7	19.5

Ships

Fishing "Seiner"	-	100.0	-	.	.
Fishing Luggers	-	100.0	-	.	.

Metalwares

Household Sewing Machines	-	34.0	49.5	62.2	64.9

Commodity	1950	1955	1959	1962	1963
Enamelwares	.	5.7	13.1	12.2	19.3

Electro-technical Products

Alternating Current Motors	-	4.4	7.8	28.3	26.5
Transformers	-	12.6	19.5	14.8	11.6
Radio Receivers	-	16.1	11.7	18.3	30.6
Large Light Bulbs	-	5.3	11.9	9.5	35.1
Small Light Bulbs	-	13.3	7.6	3.5	3.2
Vacuum Cleaners	.	.	.	14.0	37.3

Fine Mechanics and Optics

Standard Typewriters	-	82.8	75.1	93.7	97.5
Small and Portable Typewriters	-	68.7	62.7	97.2	93.6
Calculators and In-voicing Machines	30.9	73.1	67.7	83.7	81.7
Accounting Machines	-	69.4	72.1	95.1	100.7
Wrist Watches	-	24.4	53.3	42.5	33.5
Pocket Watches	-	21.0	8.9	10.1	3.2
Alarm Clocks	-	48.7	19.8	28.6	26.7
Mirror Reflex Cameras	-	70.1	55.2	66.2	59.0
Other Cameras	-	13.6	39.8	37.9	35.1

Wood and Cultural Products

Pianos	-	86.6	92.3	88.9	87.3
Accordions, Harmonicas	-	50.5	85.7	.	.
Hardwood (raw, sawn veneer)	-	1.4	3.0	3.2	4.3

Textiles

Artificial Silk	.1	.2	.6	.	.
Worsted-yarn Fabrics	-	4.4	20.3	18.6	19.6
Cotton Fabrics	-	2.7	4.7	1.2	2.8
Carded-yarn Fabrics (woolen)	-	-	4.2	12.3	19.1
Decorative and Curtain Fabrics	.	16.5	18.3	32.3	38.6
Artificial and semi-artificial silk Fabrics	.	3.2	3.2	7.2	18.2
Furniture Fabrics	-	30.4	31.3	40.5	44.4
Carpets and Rugs	-	29.9	29.8	25.3	43.4
Tulle and Curtains	-	23.5	44.1	45.4	49.3
Sleeping Blankets	-	41.1	52.1	55.8	51.7
Rope, twine, technical strings	-	2.5	3.3	2.6	3.4
Perlon Hose	-	34.4	44.3	43.9	55.9

Commodity	1950	1955	1959	1962	1963
Coarse Yarn Fabrics	.	14.1	9.9	9.5	2.6
Clothing					
Underwear	.	7.2	22.5	20.9	25.7
Overwear	.	2.3	12.8	13.3	24.2
Leather/Shoes/Furs					
Artificial Leather	-	3.9	7.1	6.8	17.4
Table, Floor, Wall Covering	.	6.7	11.8	12.2	54.8
Wax Cloth	.	21.5	22.8	24.5	24.8
Leather Shoes	-	.5	4.8	3.3	4.8
Cellulose and Paper					
Stationery	.	14.1	13.5	11.0	7.1
Newsprint	6.3	19.1	15.3	14.1	13.1
Writing and Printing Paper	9.8	9.6	11.2	7.8	8.7
Other Paper	-	2.1	1.2	.8	2.0
Cardboard and Pasteboard	9.6	6.3	2.5	3.4	3.5
Glass/Ceramics					
Sanitation Ceramics	.	19.7	15.0	12.6	10.2
Household and Restaurant Porcelain	.	23.8	25.1	31.1	.
Food/Drink/Tobacco					
White Beet Sugar	21.8	19.7	45.1	32.3	28.5
Forestry Products					
Mine Timber	33.8	19.1	22.8	15.6	16.6

Source:

> See Table 23

Notes:

> (see also Table 23)
> *Minimum figure, since export data, though not production data, exclude gas motors.
> †Minimum figure, since export, though not production data, exclude tractor drilling machines.

Table 23.   East German import ratios (imports
divided by the sum of production plus imports)
for selected commodities, in per cent,
selected years

Commodity	1950	1955	1959	1962	1963
Energy					
Electricity	.1	.7	.0	.1	.2
Gas	1.3	3.6	2.8	2.1	1.6
Mining					
Raw Lignite	2.8	2.0	2.7	2.3	2.2
Soft Coal	55.3	70.3	74.0	77.5	78.1
Soft Coal Coke	52.5	49.1	45.3	48.7	49.8
Iron Ore* (FE Content)	2.2	59.8	72.2	75.4	83.7
Pyrites† (S Content)	59.5	61.6	78.8	69.1	67.2
Metallurgy					
Foundry pig-iron	52.4[a]	24.4	28.8	22.2	23.4
Open-hearth pig-iron	90.6[a]	18.4	31.8	30.7	29.9
Rails	4.1[b]	33.1	52.1	52.8	58.6
Bar Iron	15.6[c]	26.2	32.8	31.6	26.0
Hot-rolled Hoop Iron	2.6[b]	4.5	14.0	13.4	9.2
Rolled Wire	11.6[b]	19.3	8.9	19.0	7.3
Coarse rolled sheets, 5 mm and above	23.9[b]	23.8	30.5	37.5	39.9
Medium rolled sheets	15.0[b]	23.9	46.2	64.3	65.9
Fine rolled sheets under 3 mm	18.2[b]	31.2	49.8	54.5	57.9
Bands and Discs	26.4[b]	18.7	28.2	33.6	40.3
Seamless Pipes	75.6	47.0	49.6	52.7	46.1
Welded Pipes	7.4[b]	19.3	38.1	46.9	43.4
Cold-rolled Hoop Iron	16.3[b]	21.2	25.5	27.6	25.1
Drawing die mill Products	4.4[b]	17.2	11.3	4.5	2.8
Chemicals					
Phosphorous Fertilizer	62.2	37.4	31.4	12.4	18.7
Organic Dyes	16.3[b]	21.2	42.9	14.9	30.6
Insulin	-	6.0	7.8	1.4	1.3
Animal Glues	.	-	2.8	8.3	1.4
Automobile Tires	.	4.3	1.2	2.1	2.7
Heavy Machinery					
Turret Lathes	.	.	.	7.9	6.8
Planing, shaping, broaching Machines	.	.	.	2.1	7.9

Commodity	1950	1955	1959	1962	1963
Grinding, lapping, honing machines	.	.	.	11.3	10.0
Drills, threading machines	.	.	.	1.2	.9
Vehicles					
Passenger Automobiles	1.3[b]	1.9	15.8	9.4	11.8
Trucks	-	.2	2.4	7.5	9.9
Motorcycles and scooters above 75 ccm	-	19.4	34.3	20.8	6.1
Bicycles	-	2.4	1.9	.0	.
Castings					
Gray cast-iron	-[a]	.5	6.7	2.9	2.8
Electro-technical Products					
Television sets	-	-	11.6	8.6	.
Wood and Cultural Products					
Hardwood (raw, sawn, veneer)	.3	7.3	19.6	28.2	34.0
Textiles					
Artificial silk and semi-artificial silk fabrics	-	1.5	6.2	7.3	4.3
Sack and packaging fabrics	.	-	21.6	28.1	29.9
Overwear	-	.3	.4	.4	.6
Processed plant fibers	14.7	29.0	36.3	36.2	32.0
Cotton yarns	-	6.3	10.9	6.9	8.5
Other yarns	.6	.3	.7	1.2	1.0
Worsted yarn fabrics	-[a]	11.4	12.4	7.5	4.1
Cotton fabrics	-	16.4	13.2	8.8	9.2
Wool, washed	64.6[c]	51.5	66.5	74.9	75.6
Leather/Shoes/Furs					
Soft Leather	-	.8	1.1	.4	.1
Leather Shoes	-[a]	5.6	15.8	9.4	5.8
Cellulose and Paper					.
Textile cellulose	-[b]	2.0	14.3	8.4	14.5
Sulfite cellulose	4.6[a]	6.3	12.7	11.6	21.0
Sulfate cellulose	3.5	5.8	12.5	37.0	41.5
Paper, all types	1.6	4.1	4.7	5.3	4.7
Cardboard, pasteboard	.	.5	2.5	3.2	3.1
Paper sacks	.	9.3	6.3	4.0	3.0

Commodity	1950	1955	1959	1962	1963
Food/Drink/Tobacco					
Meat and meat products	33.8	11.3	17.3	18.1	12.3
Animal fats, raw and processed	23.5	14.7	6.3	7.8	2.0
Vegetable oils, raw, refined, hardened	9.3	18.1	21.8	21.3	20.5
Butter	26.9	9.4	30.1	25.8	20.7
Fatty Cheese	-	31.6	29.1	30.3	27.6
Fresh Fish	5.3	63.8	46.1	32.5	23.3
Salted Fish	} 84.7	51.7	41.9	66.9	33.2
Canned Fish		65.2	45.9	40.8	26.3
Canned Fruits and Canned Vegetables	.	32.2	32.0	30.1	30.5
Fruit Juices	-	10.1	25.4	28.1	29.8
Wine and Champagne	47.0[a]	60.8	70.0	75.6	76.8
Beer	-[a]	1.2	.9	.6	.6
Other Liquor	.	.7	.4	2.5	.9
Cigarettes	-	5.0	1.8	6.2	3.3
Tobacco	53.4	87.7	91.6	91.3	93.2
Agriculture					
Wheat	17.8	31.4	49.3	48.5	44.4
Rye	-	7.4	8.8	20.6	14.4
Barley	22.4	32.3	7.4	10.8	6.9
Oats	11.6	2.9	6.1	.0	.
Corn	.	.	2.4	4.0	3.3
Legumes	5.9	30.8	37.3	14.2	19.8
Oil seeds (incl. seeds of fiber plants)	.3	52.0	57.0	35.7	48.5
Potatoes	.	.3	.4	1.0	1.0
Fresh Vegetables	.	5.9	16.7	10.7	14.4
Eggs	-	8.9	3.6	1.8	4.8

Source:

> Calculated by the author from production and trade data in physical units in the various issues of *SJDDR*.

Notes:

> *It was assumed that East German production figures given in effective tons have an iron content of 25 per cent, which is undoubtedly a high estimate for the low quality East German ores, and that imports had a content of

industry, which one normally would calculate from value statistics, has also increased. In studying the tables, the
reader should be reminded that they are based on commercial
export and import data only, hence the export ratios for 1950
are understatements, because they exclude uncompensated reparations exports. It will also be noted that import ratios for
items that cannot be produced in East Germany or are produced
in negligible amounts, such as natural rubber, crude oil, cotton, rice, citrus fruits, and coffee, have not been given.

A study of the export ratios is not conclusive. It suggests that most probably the export ratio of the metal-working
industries has risen between 1955 and 1963. Production, therefore, must have been expanded for the express purpose of increasing exports. This would be in line with CMEA goals.[27]
The increase in the export ratios of some light industries
seems to reflect the expansion in the western market. There
is no conclusive indication on the other hand, that there was
any increase in the chemical industry export ratio.

On the import side also the evidence is far from clear-
cut. If anything, the ratios suggest a general increase until
1963 in the foreign trade dependence in one major import
branch: metallurgy. There is no noticeable change in mining.
This is exactly what one should expect. In line with CMEA
policy (see CHAPTER 3), East Germany was to import less coke

---

50 per cent which is probably low.
          †It was assumed that imports had a content of 44 per
          cent.
        [a] - 1951
        [b] - 1952
        [c] - 1953
        Dash (-) means "ratio was zero."
        Dot (.) means "not ascertainable."
        Ratios above 100.0 per cent denote sales from inven-
        tory in addition to entire production.

Table 24. Percentage distribution of the
uses of East German real GNP

		1950	1951	1952	1953
1)	Individual Consumption	30.9	36.0	42.0	45.7
2)	Gross Domestic Investment	17.7	20.6	20.4	22.7
3)	"Other"	51.4	43.4	37.6	31.6
		100.0	100.0	100.0	100.0
Breakdown of "other" uses					
4)	Reparations Exports	28.6	25.1	23.2	18.4
5)	Government	25.5	17.7	17.5	14.9
6)	Net Foreign Investment	-2.7	0.6	-3.1	-1.7
	3) "Other" Uses	51.4	43.4	37.6	31.6
Breakdown of Net Foreign Investment					
7)	Commercial Exports	8.8	12.3	10.9	12.6
8)	Commercial Imports	11.5	11.7	14.0	14.3
	6) Net Foreign Investment	-2.7	0.6	-3.1	-1.7

Source:

Rows 1-3 based on absolute data in 1936 German prices
in W.F. Stolper, *op. cit.*, p. 436 and for 1959 on unpublished parts of the manuscript. These data were adjusted
to include uranium production *(Supplement,* p. 29*)* which was
first converted to 1938 prices (equal to 1936 prices) by the author. According to West German experts, prices in East Germany were practically identical with 1938 prices until 1946
inclusive. (This refers to legal prices in which the reparations data are expressed.) See Franz Rupp, *"Die Reparationsleistungen der sowjetischen Besatzungszone,"* BB (Bonn: BMfgF,
1951), p. 22, and Anonymous, *"Die Reparationen der sowjetischen Besatzungszone in den Jahren 1945 bis Ende 1953,"* BB
(Bonn: BMfgF, 1953), p. 6. The prices of the goods entering
reparations were 6.6 per cent above 1946 (or 1938) in 1947;
36.5 per cent above in 1948; 33.9 per cent higher in 1949;
33.3 per cent higher in 1950; and 60.0 per cent higher in 1953.
(Calculated by the author from West German estimates of repa-

Table 24.   continued

1954	1955	1956	1957	1958	1959
51.1	53.0	51.8	50.4	52.2	54.3
17.4	21.0	25.5	29.6	38.3	39.4
31.5	26.0	22.7	20.0	9.5	6.3
100.0	100.0	100.0	100.0	100.0	100.0
7.4	6.5	6.1	3.0	2.3	.6
23.3	19.0	16.5	16.8	7.3	5.8
0.8	0.5	0.1	0.2	-0.1	-0.1
31.5	26.0	22.7	20.0	9.5	6.3
13.8	11.9	11.9	12.9	13.0	10.1
13.0	11.4	11.8	12.7	13.1	10.2
0.8	0.5	0.1	0.2	-0.1	-0.1

rations expressed both in current and 1944 prices, based on classified East German statistics. See Franz Rupp, *op. cit.*, p. 22.) Since these are rough estimates and it is unlikely that legal prices actually declined somewhat after 1948, the author has assumed the following price index for legal intern- al East German prices of reparations goods:

1938	100	1948	133	1952	151
1945	100	1949	133	1953	160
1946	100	1950	133		
1947	107	1951	142		

The 1953 estimate is indirectly confirmed by a statement of Otto Grotewohl, then East Germany's Prime Minister *(Tägliche Rundschau,* 8-26-1953). In his 8-25-1953 report to the *Volks- kammer* he equated the $2.537 billion (at 1938 prices) of repa- rations "forgiven" by the Soviets with 10 billion DM-E at current prices. Since in 1938 $2.537 equalled RM 6.31713 bil-

and coal, but more finished metallurgical products. Data on
machinery imports are, unfortunately, not available for a long
enough period.

In general, there is little evidence that, since 1955,
East Germany has become more dependent on her foreign trade
partners, importing a larger proportion of her needs in raw
materials and fuels and other products assigned to other CMEA
nations and concentrating on the exports of the industries assigned to her by CMEA. This is not to deny, of course, that
she is in certain products extremely dependent on foreign
trade.

A second and more general answer to the question of foreign trade dependence can, however, also be given for the
years 1950-59. Using Professor Stolper's data on East German
GNP in 1936 prices, this author's estimate of reparations in
1938 prices (see Table 2 and the discussion pertaining thereto), and this author's study of East Germany's balance of
payments (see CHAPTER 6 below), it is possible to find the
percentage distribution of the uses of East German real GNP
for the above-mentioned years. This is shown in Table 24.[28]

---

lion, prices in 1953 must have been 58.3 per cent higher than
in 1938 or 1944 or 1946. Some sources indicate that prices
continued to rise somewhat after 1953, but by less, *VzW*, 4,
1957, pp. 398-99. The author has estimated the 1954-60 price
index roughly at 171-178-180-182-184-186-186. These price indices were then applied to the reparations data given in Table
1 to calculate 1938 RM equivalents.
     Row 4 was calculated from reparations data, as explained
     in Table 2.
     Row 5 was obtained by subtracting from row 3 the sum of
     rows 4 and 6.
     Row 7 and 8 were calculated from row 4 and the balance-
     of-payments information of CHAPTER 6, which contains,
in comparable rubles, reparations exports, commercial exports,
and commercial imports of commodities and services.
     Row 6 is the difference between rows 7 and 8.

As Table 24 clearly shows, in real terms the importance
of commercial exports and imports was practically unchanged
through the 1950's. If we include reparations exports, East
Germany is seen to have had a continuous, but steadily declining export surplus. There is no evidence in her total trade
of any increased integration with the rest of the world.

This indeed must be the final conclusion of our entire
chapter. Though there is no reason to doubt the sincerity of
the East German attempts at greater economic integration, from
an over-all standpoint the impact has so far been insignificant.[29] This is not to deny that there have been enormous
structural changes in production and trade compared to the
prewar era or that the trade structure with particular countries or the trade dependence for particular products has significantly changed. Nothing since the reparations era has
brought significant over-all economic change. Indeed, if anything, CMEA has preserved the status quo reached at the end
of that era.

FOOTNOTES

[1]Compare Gunnar Myrdal, *An International Economy*, (New York:
Harper and Brothers, 1956), pp. 2-13, 62-63, and 338-39.

[2]*"Der Aussenhandel mit Bulgarien,"* Der Aussenhandel der D.D.R.
(West Berlin: IWE - Informations- und Archivdienst, 1959),
IX, p. 4.

[3]Recent estimates of East German capital to output ratios for
1950-57 are as follows: for various basic industries from
2.3 to 9.5, for various metal-working industries from 2.0 to
5.4, for various consumer goods industries from .9 to 1.4.
See Wolfgang F. Stolper, and Karl W. Roskamp, "An Input-Output
Table for East Germany with Applications to Foreign Trade,"
Bulletin of the Oxford University Institute of Statistics,
November, 1961, Table V, p. 386.

[4]Compare the speech by Bruno Leuschner, Chairman of East Germany's State Planning Commission, in *ND,* 10-6-1953, p. 3.

[5]See Wolfgang F. Stolper and Karl W. Roskamp, *op. cit.* in footnote 3, Table IV.

[6]D. Lehmann, *"Die wichtigsten Investitionsvorhaben in unserer Republik seit 1949,"* PI, Nr. 99 (1782), 8-31-1959, pp. 3-5. His information refers to state investments, i.e., those of subgroups a) and b) above, while Stolper's estimates refer to investments by all groups. For industry, however, there is probably no difference between the two kinds of coverage, since cooperative, mixed, and private enterprises are almost exclusively found in agriculture, residential construction, and trade. All statements following in the text hereafter about State Planning Commission data have been taken from this source.

[7]See *Deutsches Institut für Wirtschaftsforschung, Institut für Konjunkturforschung, Wochenbericht,* (West Berlin: 6-12-1964), Nr. 24, p. 107. This will be referred to henceforth as *DIW* study.

[8]See *AH,* 4, 1965, pp. 21 and 22.

[9]See *PI* (32930), 5-6-1965, p. 12 and *AH,* 2, 1965, pp. 21 and 24.

[10]Compare *WW,* 3, 1959, p. 373.

[11]It will be recalled that structural changes prior to 1955 have been discussed in CHAPTER 1. The data here are also derived from basic data in W.F. Stolper, *op. cit.,* where they were expressed in constant 1950 West German prices. 1959 data are from unpublished parts of the manuscripts. 1944 data calculated by the author, as reported in CHAPTER 1.

[12]The shares of the individual basic industries in GNP originating in industry were in 1955 and 1959, respectively, 3.5 and 3.6 per cent for electricity, 9.6 and 8.4 per cent for mining and gas, 4.9 and 4.8 per cent for metallurgy, incl. castings, 14.1 and 14.1 per cent for chemicals, and 3.0 and 3.0 per cent for building materials.

[13]The technical possibility for this had been known for some time, but the process had never been regarded as economically profitable. See *Der Kohlenbergbau und die Energiewirtschaft in der sowjetischen Besatzungszone Deutschlands* (Bonn: BMfgF, 1957), Anlage 2.

[14]The shares of the individual metal-working industries in GNP originating in industry were in 1955 and 1959, respectively,

14.3 and 16.5 per cent for machinery, incl. shipbuilding, 1.8 and 2.2 per cent for road vehicles, 6.9 and 8.3 per cent for metalgoods, 5.9 and 6.1 per cent for electro-technical output, and 3.2 and 2.8 per cent for fine mechanics and optics.

[15]Individual changes were for woodworking from 2.4 to 2.5 per cent, for textiles, from 11.1 to 10.0 per cent, for leather/ shoes/furs from 2.1 to 2.3 per cent, for cellulose and paper as well as glass/ceramics from 1.7 to 1.6 per cent each. There were no changes in clothing (1.3 per cent) and printing (1.5 per cent).

[16]See *DIW-Wochenbericht* (West Berlin: 10-16-1964), Nr. 42, p. 182.

[17]Such as changing production to labor-intensive goods. See *AH*, 4/5, 1959, p. 11 and *VS*, 4, 1958, pp. 127-28. Compare also *Der Aussenhandel der D.D.R.* (West Berlin: IWE - Informations - und Archivdienst, 1959), II, p. 1.

[18]See *AH*, 2, 1965, pp. 13 and 18, and *ND*, 3-3-1965, p. 3, and 5-8-1965, p. 3.

[19]See *AH*, 12, 1964, p. 23.

[20]This mistake has even been made by East German economists who should know better; see *WW*, 1, 1958, p. 69 and *SJDDR 1955*, p. 243.

[21]See U.N., *Economic Survey of Europe in 1957* (Geneva: 1958) Chap. VI, pp. 8 and A 55, and Erich Klinkmüller and Elisabeth Ruban, *op. cit.*, p. 296.

[22]Consult, for instance, *Foreign Trade of the U.S.S.R. 1957* (New York: U.S. Joint Publications Research Service, 1959).

[23]East Germany, as was also pointed out in CHAPTER 3, is to import pig-iron in the future, rather than coal and iron ore. See *The New York Times*, 4-4-1960, p. 1. East Germany once hoped to abolish chemical imports altogether. See *ND*, 7-17-1957, p. 3. The low 1961 percentage is in line with such a plan, though it seems to run counter to CMEA plans of subdividing the production of types of given chemical products to achieve optimum plant sizes.

[24]For similar data for the other Communist countries not in CMEA consult the following sources: For China, *AH*, 4/5, 1957, p. 144; 13, 1957, p. 465; 2, 1958, p. 41; 10, 1958, p. 350; 7, 1960, p. 2; *VS*, 3/4, 1959, p. 121; *PI*, Nr. 117 (1653), 10-13-1958, p. 7; *DW*, 6-21-1956; *Tägliche Rundschau*, 10-11-

1950, and *Berliner Zeitung*, 6-19-1956. For North Vietnam, *ND*, 7-27-1957; *AH*, 4/5, 1960, p. 15. For North Korea, *AH*, 7, 1960, p. 3. For Yugoslavia, *AH*, 21, 1957, p. 764; *DW*, 6-21-1956; *Berliner Zeitung*, 6-19-1956.

[25]Calculated by the author from a sample of the most important goods traded, as given in *SHD*, pp. 410-11, 430, 437-38, and 441-43.

[26]This has been done in the west, for instance, by Erich Klinkmüller, *op. cit.*, pp. 103-104; and by Bruno Kiesewetter, *Der Ostblock: Aussenhandel des östlichen Wirtschaftsblockes einschliesslich China* (West Berlin: Safari-Verlag, 1960), p. 259. For an East German example see Gunther Kohlmey, *"Spaltungsdisproportionen und Aussenhandel,"* *WW*, 1, 1958, p. 70.

[27]There are, unfortunately, no sufficient data which would make it possible to calculate such ratios for trade with the bloc only. Conceivably such ratios might have increased even more than shown here for trade with all areas. This would reflect an increased dependence on the bloc and lesser dependence on the west.

[28]Previously published in the author's "On East Germany's Foreign Economic Relations," *Social Research*, Summer 1962, page 230.

[29]Indeed, Soviet bloc writers very frequently say so themselves. G. Hubert and P. Sydow, e.g., point out "that the socialist international specialization has not yet reached [a] significant magnitude." They also say that "the present status of the development of the international division of labor is not sufficient to further develop the economy of the CMEA countries at a high rate and to achieve, in the economic competition with the capitalist system, the most favorable results." See *AH*, 7, 1963, pp. 30-31. O. Bogomolov writes, "Despite the great efforts being made toward specialization, the results achieved so far are of limited significance. . ., international specialization of production turned out to be a much more complex matter than had been expected, . . . the share of specialization within the Comecon framework in the total volume of machinery and equipment production in separate countries is from 2 to 6 per cent." See *Planovoe khoziaistvo*, 4, 1964. I.O. Sobko, finally, notes that "the level of international specialization of production in machine building is still insufficient. As a proof let us note that the rate of growth of machinery production is greater than that of trade; machinery output in the member countries of CMEA increased to 152 per cent from 1955 to 1962, yet mutual deliveries (exports) in the same period only increased

to 133 per cent." In short, export ratios are declining rather than increasing in the very field in which specialization has been stressed most. See *DW*, 14, 1965, p. 25.

6

As students of Communist economies are well aware, Communist writings about the balance of payments are propagandistic and devoid of facts. The information gathered so far in pursuing the theme of the previous chapters makes it possible, however, to estimate the balance of payments for East Germany from 1950-1963. So far as the author knows, this is the first elaborate attempt at estimating any postwar East German balance of payments.[1] For reasons discussed in CHAPTER 2, the East German balance of payments will be estimated in terms of foreign trade rubles rather than German currency.

A. THE BALANCE OF TRADE

The balance of trade, the relation of commodity exports to commodity imports, holds the most important position within the balance of payments. In considering it, it is well to keep in mind the East German definition of commodity trade as discussed on page 59 above, which shows, among other things, that freight and other costs incurred while shipping imports from the selling country to the East German border appear in the balance of services rather than the balance of trade.

To set up the balance of trade, one cannot use the data on commercial exports and imports, as they appear above in Tables 3 and 4, without making at least two adjustments. The first one concerns the inclusion of reparations deliveries discussed in CHAPTER 1. These, furthermore, have to be translated from internal German DM values into foreign trade rubles to make them comparable with, and to add them to, commercial exports. This has been done as follows:

All reparations data in current internal prices were taken from Table 1. Services performed were excluded, since they do not enter the balance of trade. Since we are dealing with years since 1950 only, this leaves deliveries of commodi-

ties to the Soviet Union (row 2), to the Red Army, directly
and indirectly (rows 3 and 4), plus deliveries of SAG inventories and uncompensated uranium (rows 5 and 6). It will be
recalled that the uranium data were valued at cost and not at
official internal prices, which do not exist in this case.
Since we know from the statements of an escaped uranium mining
official, referred to in the *Supplement*, that the ruble value
of the paid-for portion of uranium deliveries was derived by
multiplying the costs to be carried by the Soviet Union with
the official exchange rate, the author has translated each
year's uranium reparations from cost data in DM to foreign
trade rubles at the official exchange rates, as given in AP-
PENDIX B.[2]

A similar procedure, however, cannot be followed in translating the DM values of all other reparations deliveries. Being expressed in internal prices, translation at the official
exchange rate into foreign trade rubles would be legitimate
only if internal prices were identical with the DM equivalent
of foreign trade rubles, i.e., if the PAG were zero. This is
hardly ever the case. In the case of commercial exports, as
is shown in APPENDIX B, the foreign trade enterprises sell in
foreign trade rubles, which are exchanged by the Central Bank
at the official rate into DM, which sum only by accident equals
the DM originally spent when buying the goods internally from
the producers. Therefore, whenever there is a positive or
negative PAG, the ratio between internal prices and foreign
trade rubles is not identical with the official exchange rate.
But it is this ratio that must be used to translate reparation
deliveries expressed at internal prices into foreign trade
rubles, or the ruble figures for reparations and commercial
exports would not be comparable.

An example shall emphasize this important point. Suppose
100 units of commodity A were exported commercially and 100

more units of it delivered as reparations. If the foreign
trade enterprises received 1,000 rubles for the commercial exports, one should value the reparations at 1,000 rubles also.
Suppose the official exchange rate were 2 rubles per DM and
the internal price of 100 units were 700 DM. Then translating the internal price of reparations at the official rate of
exchange would lead to an evaluation at 1,400 rubles, and the
importance of reparations relative to commercial exports in
the balance of payments would be exaggerated. The "correct"
rate of exchange applicable to reparations in internal prices
for purposes of comparability would have been, of course, foreign exchange receipts (1,000 rubles) divided by internal
price (700 DM), or 1.43 ruble/DM.

Though the value of commercial exports at internal prices
is in fact not officially published, it could be calculated,
if one knew the PAG's the foreign trade enterprises received
or made. In the above example, the foreign trade enterprises,
buying 100 units of A at 700 DM and receiving only 500 DM from
the Central Bank in exchange for 1,000 rubles, lost 200 DM,
which they would recover from the government budget. The correct rate of exchange between internal prices and foreign
trade rubles (1.43 ruble/DM) could, therefore, have been found
by deducting the PAG from the foreign-exchange equivalent of
the ruble figure, i.e., deducting negative DM 200 from DM 500,
which equals DM 700, and relating this figure (which is the
internal price of the good) to the foreign trade rubles.

This makes for a cumbersome way of comparing internal DM
values with foreign trade ruble values, but it is the only
meaningful one this author could find to translate internal DM
reparations data into rubles. Commercial export values are
known in rubles only. The ruble values can be translated at
the official exchange rate into a DM equivalent. For some
years at least PAG data are also known, hence the value of

commercial exports at internal prices can be calculated and
from it the real exchange rate from internal values for commercial exports to rubles. This rate, rather than the official one, can then be used to translate the reparation data in
such a fashion into rubles as to make them fully comparable to
the valuation of commercial exports.

Just as data on the balance of payments in general are a
closely guarded secret in East Germany, data on the PAG are
not easy to come by. They have never been published officially. The most detailed data on the PAG have been privately
circulated in West Germany by the Federal Ministry for All-
German Questions, which claims to have obtained them from
classified East German statistics. Unfortunately, they only
refer to the second half of 1951 and are given in columns 2
and 3 of Table 25. Subsequently absolute 1951 data at internal prices for deliveries to the Soviet Union and to the Red
Army (Table 1, rows 2 and 3) were broken down by industries
and each industry subtotal translated into rubles at the rates
shown in column 6 of Table 25, assuming them to be valid for
the entire year. This is shown in Table 26.

With this, only one more item remained to be translated
for 1951, viz., the small indirect deliveries to the Red Army
of DM 211.4 million. Since nothing is known about their composition except that they must have come from the light, food,
and possibly electro-technical, fine-mechanical, and optical
industries, this amount was translated at the average real exchange rate for these industries (weighted by reparations
values in internal prices), which was   .90 ruble/DM. This
amounted to 190.26 million rubles, giving total 1951 commodity
reparations of 5,398.34 million rubles, and a real exchange
rate of .99 ruble/DM. Hence, use of the official exchange
rate of 1.2 ruble/DM would have overstated greatly the importance of reparations compared to commercial exports.

Table 25. East German commercial exports by selected
industries, 2nd half-year 1951, at foreign trade DM
(FT DM), internal prices (IP DM), and foreign trade
rubles (FT Rubles), in millions. PAG and exchange
rate of foreign trade ruble values to internal price
values (Real R).

Industry (1)	FT DM (2)	PAG DM (3)	IP DM (4)	FT Rubles (5)	Real R (6)
Mining	108.62	-12.09	120.71	130.47	1.08
Chemical	143.69	-142.13	285.82	172.60	.60
Machinery[a]	726.23	-66.46	792.69	872.35	1.10
Electro-technical	210.64	-74.20	284.84	253.02	.89
Fine Mech./Optics	135.14	-22.78	157.92	162.33	1.03
Wood/Cultural	47.26	-37.45	84.71	56.77	.67
Textiles	42.14	-51.00	93.14	50.62	.54
Paper/Printing	51.53	-6.56	58.09	61.90	1.07
Glass/Ceramics	28.99	-3.65	32.64	34.82	1.07
Food/Drink/Tobacco	11.82	-.59	12.41	14.20	1.14

Sources:

Cols. 2 and 3 from material furnished to Professor W.F.
Stolper in West Germany and made available by him to
the author. All data in col. 2 represent the official DM
equivalent one would calculate by applying the official 1951
exchange rate of 1.2012 ruble/DM to trade figures in foreign
trade rubles. Col. 3 is the difference between the internal
price paid to the producer by the exporting enterprise of the
state and the amount of internal currency regained when selling the ruble receipts to the Central Bank at the official
rate. Col. 4 calculated by the author as col. 2 minus col. 3.
Col. 5 calculated by the author as col. 2 times 1951 exchange
rate. Col. 6 equals col. 5 divided by col. 4. It is seen
that this rate differs significantly from the official rate of
1.2012.

Note:

[a]Machinery is here defined as all metal-working industries excluding the two given separately.

Table 26.   Translation of 1951 reparations
from current internal prices (IP DM) into
foreign trade rubles (FT Rubles), in millions

Industry (1)	IP DM (2)	Real R (3)	FT Rubles (4)
Energy, Mining	84.64	1.08	91.41
Metallurgy	33.70	.74	24.94
Chemical	675.39	.60	405.23
Building Materials	53.92	.74	39.90
Machinery[a]	1,059.77	1.10	1,165.75
Electro-technical	615.10	.89	547.44
Fine Mech./Optics	220.36	1.03	226.97
Ceramics/Glass	249.64	1.07	267.11
Textile/Leather	155.85	.54	84.16
Other Light	386.46	.83	320.76
Food/Drink/Tobacco	105.00	1.14	119.70
Total	3,639.83	.90	3,293.37

Source:

     Col. 2 as for rows 2 and 3, Table 1. Col. 3 from Table 25, col. 6, assuming that the real exchange rate for energy equals that for mining, that for metallurgy and building materials equals the average of the other basic industries (weighted by export values at internal prices), that for leather equals that for textiles, that for other light industries is the weighted average of wood/cultural and paper/printing. Col. 4 equals col. 2 times col. 3.

Note:

    [a]Machinery is defined as all metal-working industries, excluding the two given separately.

Such detailed PAG data, unfortunately, are not available
for other years. It was possible, however, to gather reliable
data on the value of exports at internal prices as a whole
(rather than by industries) for the years 1950-1956. These,
together with the officially published export series in foreign trade rubles and the implied real exchange rate between
ruble data and internal values, are given in the first four
columns of Table 27.

It will be noted that the 1951 real exchange rate for
commodities delivered as reparations (excluding uranium), as
calculated in Table 26 from detailed data for the second half
of that year (.90) is different from the over-all 1951 rate,
given here as .81. This can be explained by the fact that
reparation deliveries were heavily weighted in favor of metal-
using industry products with a somewhat higher real rate of
exchange between internal prices and foreign trade rubles than
in the case of other products. Therefore, for all years other
than 1951, real rates as in Table 27, col. 5, have been used.
They are adjusted upward in the same relation as between the
1951 rates given in cols. 4 and 5 of Table 27. They have been
applied to all commodity deliveries of reparations other than
uranium as given in Table 1. For 1957 and 1958 the same rate
was used as for 1956.

The results of the calculations described so far are summarized in Table 28. It becomes immediately obvious that
simple use of official exchange rates would have had the result of vastly overstating the burden of reparations.

A second adjustment in the balance of trade concerns imports. It has been reported that East Germany, since the
early 1950's has been importing arms for the People's Police
and the National People's Army from Czechoslovakia, Poland,
Hungary, and primarily the Soviet Union. These imports cannot
originally have been included in the official statistics since

Table 27. East German commercial exports at
internal prices (IP DM) and foreign trade
rubles (FT Rubles), in billions, 1950-56,
and the implied real exchange rate (Real R)

| | | | Real R | |
Year (1)	IP DM (2)	FT Rubles (3)	Actual (commercial exports) (4)	Adjusted (reparations exports) (5)
1950	2.2	1.6241	.74	.82
1951	3.5	2.8508	.81	.90
1952	3.4	2.9547	.87	.97
1953	4.3	3.8700	.90	1.00
1954	6.8	5.1203	.75	.83
1955	5.7	5.1126	.90	1.00
1956	5.599814	5.5851	1.00	1.11

Sources:

    Col. 2, internal price data for 1950-55 from U.N., *Economic Survey of Europe in 1957* (Geneva: 1958), Chap. VI, p. 29. A high East German official, in an interview with Frederic L. Pryor, stated that these data, in contrast to many others circulating in the west, "are so close to the truth that they must have been stolen." 1956 figure calculated from information in *AH*, 23, 1958, p. 807, together with *SJDDR* 1956, p. 296. Col. 3, ruble data from *SJDDR* 1957, p. 514. They differ from data given in Table 3 because of corrections for trade with West Germany and uranium exports there. 1956 data here are for industrial exports only, which, however, were more than 99 per cent of total exports. (1956 agricultural exports were assumed to have been at the 1955 level, see *SJDDR* 1955, p. 243, and in this way a 1956 industrial export figure in rubles to match that in DM was calculated). Col. 4 equals col. 3 divided by col. 2. Col. 5, see text.

Table 28.   East Germany's commodity reparations
in foreign trade rubles and internal prices,
1950-60, and a comparison of the implied real
exchange rate with the official exchange rate

Year (1)	Million Foreign Trade Rubles			Million Internal DM (5)	Exchange Rates	
	Uranium[a] (2)	Other Goods (3)	Total[a] (4)		Ruble/DM	
					Real (6)	Official (7)
1950	1,720.52	3,390.73	5,111.25	5,216.04	.98	1.5916
1951	1,914.71	3,483.63	5,398.34	5,445.23	.99	1.2012
1952	1,722.52	4,122.79	5,845.31	5,684.30	1.03	1.2012
1953	1,531.53	3,737.31	5,268.84	5,012.31	1.05	1.2012
1954	1,576.80	1,195.20	2,772.00	2,316.00	1.20	1.80
1955	1,350.00	1,440.00	2,790.00	2,190.00	1.27	1.80
1956	1,276.20	1,598.40	2,874.60	2,149.00	1.34	1.80
1957	730.80	799.20	1,530.00	1,126.00	1.36	1.80
1958	630.00	599.40	1,229.40	890.00	1.38	1.80
1959	525.60	-	525.60	292.00	1.80	1.80
1960	450.00	-	450.00	250.00	1.80	1.80
Total	13,428.68	20,366.66	33,795.34	30,570.88	1.11	-

Source:

    See text.

Note:

[a]There is no doubt that uranium production and exports
are continuing to the present (mid-1965). In a tele-
gram to Walter Ulbricht, the leading German and Soviet officials of the uranium mining company Wismut reported to have
fulfilled the annual production plan by December 5, 1963. In
the first eleven months of that year, they reported to have
increased labor productivity by 14 per cent and decreased
prime costs by 1.6 per cent compared to the same period in
1962. They asserted that the planned quality of production
had been achieved and that they would "through exemplary deeds
in production continue to contribute to the strengthening of
the socialist camp and the maintenance of peace." See *ND*,
12-11-1963, p. 1. Again, in July of 1964, it was reported

the East German Statistical Yearbook *(SJDDR 1955, p. 244)*
lists negligible imports from the bloc under the appropriate
headings of heavy and general machinery. An escaped army of-
ficer, once employed by the Ministry of National Defense, has
reported, however, that armament imports from 1956 to early
1960 amounted to DM 1.2 billion.[3] If this is the equivalent
of foreign trade rubles, which is likely, this would correspond to a 1956-59 yearly average of about 540 million rubles.
Apparently imports of such magnitude were also made in earlier
years, since minimum imports of 527 million rubles were reported for 1954.[4] Because of the large burdens on the East
German economy prior to 1954, as well as Stalin's suspicions
of the Germans, however, it may be assumed that armament imports prior to 1954 were on the average much lower.

In general, the following facts about East German rearma-
ment are known: According to a Soviet military order of July
3, 1948, companies of "police troops" were established. The
"police troops" were officially designed to protect the borders and originally consisted of infantry, artillery, tank,

---

that the Wismut (uranium) industry will continue to develop
strongly. Praises were sung of the fact that once improvised
wooden shafts had been replaced with modern equipment, and
modern refrigeration equipment enabled workers to work in
Europe's deepest shaft where normal conditions would bring
about a temperature of 50°C. Indeed, a world record in productivity was cited for one brigade (10.5 cubic meters per
man and shift) and it was asserted that all uranium miners
would achieve this goal in the future. See *ND*, 7-5-1964,
p. 3.

The West German government estimated in January 1963
uranium mining employment at still about 50,000. See *S.B.Z.
von A bis Z* (Bonn: BMfgF, 1963), p. 487. Since this is only
slightly below the officially given figure for 1959 (see *Supplement*, Chap. I, p. 28), the author feels justified in estimating 1961-63 data in columns 2 and 4 as equal to 1960.

communications, and engineering companies. Ocean and air police companies were added later. By early 1950, their
strength was 60,000 men. The weapons used were Soviet trophies of the former German army, but were replaced by Soviet
weapons in 1952. In the same year, the strength was increased
to 85,000 men, by May, 1953, it reached 100,000, and was reduced to 95,000 by mid-1954. After a law of January, 1956,
the "police troops" were transferred into a National People's
Army. By early 1960, its total strength was 90,000 men, with
65,000 in land troops, 13,000 in the air force, and 12,000 in
the navy. In 1962, the East German military forces were reported to have a strength of 180,000 men, "double the strength
of a year ago," i.e., 1961. At the same time, East Germany's
Defense Minister announced that the National People's Army
would soon be further strengthened. However, in early 1964,
on the occasion of a visit to Berlin by the Soviet Defense Minister, Marshal Malinovsky, it was reported at a strength of
120,000 men, 80,000 of whom were in the army.

Beginning in 1957, there occurred a radical modernization
of equipment, leading to a peak in activity in 1959. By 1960,
they reportedly had available 2,000 pieces of artillery and
1,800 tanks, largely imported from the Soviet Union, partly
also from Czechoslovakia and Poland. The navy at the same
time had 150 ships, of which at least 30 were delivered by the
Soviet Union since 1957 and 120 were built in East Germany.
The air force, also after 1957, received at least 370 Soviet
planes.[5] On this basis the volume and distribution of armament imports was estimated roughly, from 1950-63, as 100, 100,
500, 200, 550, 200, 200, 200, 700, 1,050, 600, 1,200, 1,200,
300 million (old) rubles, respectively.[6]

Adding commodity reparations and armament data to those
given earlier for commercial trade, we can now arrive at an
estimate of the balance of trade. This is shown in the bal-

ance of payments, Table 41, rows 1-3. It is found that East
Germany has had a continuous and substantial export surplus in
commodity trade from 1950-58, growing deficits from 1959-62,
and again a surplus in 1963.[7] The surpluses were extremely
large at first, reflecting, of course, reparations deliveries,
and have diminished after 1951. In 1951, the export surplus
equalled 53.1 per cent of the commodity trade volume. This
percentage declined to 25.6 per cent by 1954 and to 8.4 per
cent by 1958. In 1959, there appeared a deficit of .05 per
cent of the trade volume, which percentage increased to 4.0
in 1962. The 1963 surplus was again equal to 8.2 per cent of
the trade volume. These are, of course, rough estimates only
in light of the tenuous estimates of armament imports, but
they undoubtedly reflect correctly the qualitative trend over
the period.

It is also possible to analyze these developments by looking at the regional distribution of the trade balance from
1950-63. This has been done in Table 29. It is not surprising to find that export surpluses existed with the Communist
bloc from 1950-60 and again in 1963, their magnitude being
considerable until 1958. But it is surprising that these surpluses were even larger than the total balance of trade for
all of these years, except 1950 and 1963, because East Germany
had import surpluses from western countries as a group from
1951 through 1960. In 1961 and 1962, this trend was reversed,
there were import surpluses with the bloc exceeding the negative balance of trade, i.e., there were (algebraically smaller) export surpluses to the west.

Looking at the detail, we find export surpluses for every
year, except 1961 and 1962, with Albania. These surpluses
were very large, considering the trade volume with that country, and they reflected the underdevelopment of Albania and
the East German capital exports to this area, as discussed be-

Table 29. Distribution of East Germany's
balance of trade by selected trading
areas, 1950-63, in 1,000 rubles[a]

Area	1950	1951	1952
Bloc	+4,693,300	+5,773,240	+5,243,510
Rest	+4,500	-54,445	-34,620
Total	+4,697,800	+5,718,795	+5,208,890
Albania	-	+5,958	+12,028
Bulgaria	-7,085	-4,531	+1,260
Czechoslovakia	-47,012	-1	-8,908
Hungary	-67,649	+32,482	+27,076
Poland	-33,424	+159,692	+41,656
Rumania	-1,005	+10,840	+23,709
U.S.S.R.	+4,849,157	+5,545,036	+5,098,646
Yugoslavia			
Communist Asia[d]	+318	+23,764	+48,043
"Anti-imperialist Areas"[d]	+2,792	+36,645	+70,498
West Germany and West Berlin	+15,100	-33,385	-51,060
Benelux, France, Italy	-17,251	-38,270	-59,289
All Others	+3,859	-19,435	+5,231

Source:

    Calculated from Tables 3 and 4. However, reparations
in terms of rubles were added to commercial exports to
the Soviet Union. They were taken from Table 28. No allow-
ance was made for the fact that allegedly some of these reparations were given by the U.S.S.R. to Poland. On this point
see *Polish Review*, Summer 1959, p. 24, U.N. *Economic Survey of
Europe in 1954*, p. 122, and R.P. Rochlin, *Die Wirtschaft Po-
lens von 1945 bis 1952* (West Berlin: Duncker und Humblot),
p. 139. Armament imports were added to imports from the
U.S.S.R., as discussed in the text.

Notes:

    [a]Blank space means "no trade," plus sign (+) means "ex-
port surplus," minus sign (-) means "import surplus."

Table 29   continued

1953	1954	1955	1956	1957
+5,120,497	+3,429,945	+3,408,867	+3,341,782	+2,142,532
-111,838	-39,260	-26,200	-23,008	-31,423
+5,008,659	+3,390,685	+3,382,667	+3,318,774	+2,111,109
+8,265	+6,216	+19,531	+10,578	+6,906
+7,635	-3,438	-38,985	-7,698	+12,765
-6,962	-15,592	+92,396	+17,632	+86,558
+33,075	-4,554	-63,944	+33,996	+64,669
-13,647	+88,238	+36,447	+136,666	+192,702
+65,305	+17,152	-52,413	-2,389	+51,378
+4,968,984	+3,174,893	+3,335,201	+3,073,536	+1,624,927
	-1,332	+739	-726	+10,528
+57,842	+168,362	+79,895	+80,187	+92,099
+3,000	+27,413	+33,599	+16,273	-28,734
+28,000	+4,400	+21,300	+31,300	+83,100
-80,309	-46,597	-82,583	-57,886	-25,926
-62,529	-24,476	+1,484	-12,695	-59,863

[b] old rubles

[c] new rubles

[d] for a definition see p. 55 above

Table 29   continued

Area	1958	1959	1960
Bloc	+1,565,962	+60,611	+64,557
Rest	-197,500	-68,850	-131,100
Total	+1,368,462	-8,239	-66,543
Albania	+13,171	+10,480	+2,631
Bulgaria	+24,209	+21,883	+58,187
Czechoslovakia	+35,078	+67,225	+33,847
Hungary	-37,589	+18,430	+4,887
Poland	+236,590	+286,889	+271,589
Rumania	+17,983	+60,065	-14,535
U.S.S.R.	+1,136,611	-436,780	-268,971
Yugoslavia	+4,978	+21,866	-39,847
Communist Asia[d]	+134,931	+10,553	+16,769
"Anti-imperialist Areas"[d]	-43,056	-23,107	-6,814
West Germany and West Berlin	+84,700	+4,576	+136,700
Benelux, France, Italy	-77,477	+18,134	-42,600
All Others	-161,667	-68,453	-218,386

Table 29 continued

1961[b]	1961[c]	1962[c]	1963[c]
-715,068	-160,890	-199,299	+336,612
+136,458	+30,700	+11,101	+49,878
-578,610	-130,190	-188,198	+386,490
-9,578.	-2,155	-1,710	+801
+71,218	+16,024	-11,021	+22,592
+44,040	+9,909	-6,647	+12,240
-17,667	-3,975	+12,565	+23,933
+423,738	+95,341	+112,292	+127,255
+33,969	+7,643	+10,534	+23,636
-1,384,307	-311,469	-306,660	+127,053
+50,133	+11,280	-1,158	+10,560
+73,386	+16,512	-7,494	-11,458
+153,508	+34,539	-10,876	+2,191
+88,900	+20,000	+16,400	+45,200
-104,964	-23,617	-227	+2,504
-986	-222	+5,804	-17

low. Interestingly, a deficit appeared exactly at the time of
Albania's break with the bloc.

In trade with Bulgaria, export and import surpluses have
alternated, with the former more frequent, however. Over the
period 1950-63 as a whole, there was an East German export surplus of 186.8 million (old) rubles. East German export surpluses have been particularly noticeable since the late 1950's.
This also reflects capital exports, as discussed below.

In trade with Czechoslovakia, trade deficits until 1954
have been followed by surpluses since (except for 1962), and
the over-all period (1950-63) showed a substantial East German
export surplus of 323.2 million (old) rubles. This can be explained by at least two factors. One is the necessity of purchasing certain Czechoslovak services, such as for freight in
transit to the South-East European nations, and the other is
the Czech ability to balance trade by the payment of hard western currencies. The East Germans are reported to be highly interested in this possibility.[8]

In trade with Hungary, deficits and surpluses have been
alternating, but East Germany had an over-all surplus of 185.4
million (old) rubles from 1950-63.

Trade with Poland, except for minor exceptions in 1950
and 1953, has been characterized by substantial export surpluses on the part of East Germany. From 1950-63, this total
surplus amounted to 2,891.8 million (old) rubles. A number of
considerations make this easily understandable. First, as has
been shown throughout this study, there has been a very large
and growing trade with the Soviet Union. This volume is largely being shipped by rail via Poland, and East Germany has to
pay transit costs by commodity exports. Frequently East Germany also has to rent Polish freight cars because a dispropor-
tionate amount of the trade volume travels in the last quarter
of the year, overburdening the East German transport system.

Secondly, East Germany is using other Polish services, such as
rail services for exports and imports with other, even Far
Eastern, Communist countries, and she is regularly chartering
Polish shipping space. In addition, there are charges for the
use of the Oder River, which is completely under Polish jurisdiction, as well as fees for various services performed in the
harbor of Szczecin.[9] Thirdly, some of the export surplus reflects the granting of credits to Poland in the 1950's and the
reduction by the Poles of their deliveries of coal and agricultural products since the Gomulka era.[10]

Trade with Rumania shows only one major deficit in 1955.
This was due to advance deliveries of Rumanian goods in partial payment for later East German capital goods exports on
credit. Over-all, East Germany had a surplus of 361.9 million
(old) rubles from 1950-63.

With the exception of the period 1959-1962, there have
been very large export surpluses in trade with the U.S.S.R.
for all years since 1950, and certainly also before that. The
total surplus from 1950-58 amounted to 32,806.991 million
(old) rubles. But there were 32,819.74 million (old) rubles
of reparation deliveries in the same period, hence there was
a slight import surplus ignoring reparations. Excluding also
armament imports of 2.75 billion (old) rubles, on the other
hand, there was a commercial export surplus of 2,737.251 million (old) rubles for the period.

From 1959-62, there were deficits totaling 3,452.989 million (old) rubles.[11] Reparations amounted to 1.8756 billion
and armament imports to 4.05 billion (old) rubles, hence without them there was now an import surplus of 1,278.589 million
(old) rubles. The tremendous magnitude of the reparations deliveries becomes clear, if one realizes that their size (from
1950-63) was equal to all commercial exports from 1950 to late
1957 and that reparations deliveries actually exceeded normal

commercial exports in size from at least 1950 to 1953. Commercially (i.e., ignoring reparations and armament imports), there was an over-all export surplus in trade with the U.S.S.R. of 1,873.34 million (old) rubles from 1950-63, but there were import surpluses in a few individual years, viz., 1950, 1952, 1953, and 1960-62.

Trade with Yugoslavia, which did not resume until after Stalin's death, also shows East German export surpluses of 88.1 million (old) rubles for the period 1954-63. Finally, trade with the Communist Asian countries has mostly (until 1961) been characterized by export surpluses, a total of 701.9 million (old) rubles from 1950-63.

With the Communist world as a whole, therefore, East Germany had a 34.74 billion (old) ruble surplus from 1950-63. Ignoring reparations and armament imports, there remained a (smaller) surplus of 6.665 billion (old) rubles.

There were export surpluses in trade with the "anti-imperialist" area until 1956, followed by deficits until 1960, a large surplus in 1961, and a small deficit and surplus, respectively, in the next two years. Over-all, however, there was still a 203.4 million (old) ruble surplus.

In trade with West Germany, surpluses were also typical, with a total of 687.4 million (old) rubles between 1950 and 1963. Trade with the other members of the Common Market, however, has been characterized by persistent deficits, except for 1959 and 1963, totaling for the 1950-63 period net 604.9 million (old) rubles. Hence there was, from 1950-63, with the Common Market as a whole a negligible surplus of 82.5 million (old) rubles. Trade with all other western nations shows deficits for all years, except 1950, 1952, 1955, and 1962, a total of 592.2 million (old) rubles. With the non-Communist world as a whole, therefore, East Germany had a 306.3 million ruble deficit from 1950-63. This, as will be shown below, has

frequently led to the need for Soviet assistance in terms of
hard currency loans.

It is also illuminating to analyze the commodity composition of the trade balance, as can be done with the data employed in CHAPTER 5 in connection with the discussion of the commodity structure of trade. Since we know now that there were
export surpluses with the bloc and import surpluses with the
rest of the world, what kind of goods did these trade balances
consist of? In the case of the bloc it is found that (for
1950-55) there actually were import surpluses in the basic industries (especially in mining and metallurgy, which deficits
overbalanced export surpluses in the energy, chemicals, and
building materials industries), in the light and food industries (especially textile raw materials), as well as in agriculture and forestry. All these deficits were then offset by
a very large export surplus in all the metal-using industries
(except castings and forgings). Data for 1960, so far as
available, suggest that the same situation prevailed then.

In the case of the western world, there actually were
export surpluses in the basic industries (especially in mining,
potassium salts, and chemicals, but an import surplus in metallurgy overbalanced by the others), the metal-using industries (except for heavy machinery), and the light industries.
All these surpluses were more than balanced, however, by
large import surpluses in the food industries and agriculture.

Hence we see again East Germany's basic foreign trade position. First and foremost, she is to provide the bloc with
the products of the metal-working industries and chemicals,
in exchange she receives raw materials and food. In addition,
more food is secured from the west, so are raw materials and
heavy machinery when possible, while goods the bloc shuns,
such as light industry products, are to be given preferably in
exchange.[12]

B.   THE SERVICE BALANCE

The first item that should enter this section of the balance of payments are the estimates of reparations services
performed for the Soviet Union. These have been given in
CHAPTER 1 in terms of current German marks. It seems appropriate to translate these amounts into foreign-exchange rubles at
the official exchange rates that have been established between
the East Germans and the U.S.S.R. for non-commercial transactions. Such rates are known to have been generally applied to
services. This is done in Table 30. Note that until a special agreement of 1957 these rates were identical with those
for commercial transactions.

The second and undoubtedly most important item to be considered are the costs related to commercial commodity trade,
such as freight, insurance, harbor fees, etc. Information on
this subject is sparse. Nothing has been published officially, but various articles contain hints which allow a reasonable estimate. The estimates were derived as follows: It is
generally acknowledged by the East Germans that they spend
more for freight and connected services than they earn. In
1957, 78.5 per cent of East Germany's foreign trade volume was
shipped by rail, 18.0 per cent by sea, the rest by inland shipping, truck, and air.[13] The main recipients of her expenditures for rail transit or renting of foreign railroad cars for
imports are said to be Poland and Czechoslovakia. These expenditures are in rubles and can be met with commodity export
surpluses.[14] Sea transport occurs on foreign ships for the
most part: 97.4 per cent in 1955, 94 per cent in 1957.[15] A
significant proportion also goes through foreign harbors, such
as Hamburg and Szczecin.[16] These expenditures usually cannot
be paid in rubles, but have to be paid in hard western currencies.[17] In 1956, 71.5 per cent of such currency earnings had
to be used for ship chartering.[18] This is highly distasteful

Table 30. East German service reparations
in millions of internal prices (IP DM)
and foreign trade rubles (FT Rubles),
1950-58, and exchange rates for
non-commercial transactions (Rn)

Year (1)	IP DM (2)	Rn FT Rubles/DM (3)	FT Rubles (4)
1950	477.42	1.5916	759.862
1951	497.14	1.2012	597.165
1952	519.86	1.2012	624.456
1953	456.00	1.2012	547.747
1954	160.00	1.80	288.000
1955	160.00	1.80	288.000
1956	160.00	1.80	288,000
1957	80.00	2.58	206.400
1958	60.00	2.58	154.800
Total	2,570.42		3,754.430

Source:

Col. 2 from Table 1, row 8.

Col. 3 from Table 44. See also footnote 2 to this
CHAPTER.

Col. 4 equals col. 2 times col. 3.

to the East German rulers. Hence, they have engaged in a number of efforts to reduce the expenditure of foreign exchange
for shipment by sea: 1) goods were shipped overland, even if
this cost more, but could be paid in rubles, e.g., we know
that the railroad via the other Communist countries is used in
trade with such countries as Greece, Turkey, Iran, and even
China.[19] 2) The Communist Party in East Germany declared the
building of its own merchant marine and the development of the
Baltic Sea harbors as the "third main task of the economy."[20]
The growth of the East German merchant marine has been rather
slow, however, which is not surprising given the small capacities of shipbuilding (created after the war only) and the very
large export quota in this branch of production. Even then,
it is reported, the low tonnage is often under-utilized due to
faulty planning.[21]

Absolute data on such expenditures by East Germany have
been given in a number of sources for 1956 and 1957. Foreign
exchange expended on railroad freights, transit fees, sea
freights, and harbor fees amounted to 372.3 million rubles in
1956 and 442.1 million in 1957.[22] Including also a number of
other services (in addition: truck freights, air freights,
storage fees, ship provisions, dispatcher services, controller
fees, insurance, assemblage costs, repairs, commissions, and
"others"), the expenditures amounted to 432.1269 million rubles in 1956 and 504.0282 million in 1957.[23] In terms of the
import data of CHAPTER 2, the import of these services amounted to 8.1 per cent of commodity imports in 1956 and 7.8 per
cent in 1957. It is at least possible that the decline in the
percentage is due to the gradual growth of the G.D.R. merchant
marine, but it could also be a coincidence.[24] Nevertheless,
to estimate the service imports in this category, somewhat
higher percentages were used for earlier years, when the East
German merchant marine was smaller or non-existent, and lower

percentages for years after 1957, when it was larger. But
since sea transport took only a small part of trade, as was
shown above, the differences in the percentage over the years
should not be too large. The author's estimates of the ruble
value of the above-named service imports, as well as their
relation to commodity imports, are given below in cols. 2 and
3 of Table 31.[25]

East German exports of the identical services are undoubtedly much smaller. The Czechs utilize mainly the Hamburg
and Szczecin ports for their overseas trade.[26] Though the
East Germans are hoping to divert this flow to their growing
harbors,[27] this is not so at the present. East Germany does
however, have some earnings from Czech, Polish and Soviet
transit trade, mainly via rail.[28] But such earnings are held
down by the Soviet and Polish use of the sea in trade with
Western Europe. Transit trade of the South-Eastern European
countries with Western Europe, on the other hand, goes via
Czechoslovakia. The same sources given above have reported
East German earnings from railroad and sea freights, transit
and harbor fees in 1956 as 59.8 million rubles and in 1957 as
67.1 million rubles. Including the other services given
above, the earnings were about the same in 1956, but were
101.402 million rubles in 1957. No further official information is available. It seems most reasonable to assume that
in every year earnings have a certain fixed relationship to
the magnitude of expenditures, i.e., earnings are always below expenditures but usually grow at the same rate. In 1956
and 1957, earnings equalled 13.8 and 20.1 per cent of expenditures, respectively. This might have to be adjusted only
for the effects of the growth of the G.D.R. merchant marine,
for at the same time when expenditures to foreigners drop relatively to total transport expenditures, earnings of the merchant marine through services rendered to foreigners increase

in relation to expenditures. The author has, therefore, assumed that foreign-exchange earnings prior to 1956 were 14 per
cent of such expenditures, 20 per cent for 1958-61, and 25 per
cent since, in rough accordance with the expansion rate of the
merchant marine.[29] The estimates appear in col. 4 of Table
31.

Third, a number of other services of lesser importance
are receipts and expenditures in connection with postal and
communications services, the foreign service, tourist travel,
fairs and exhibitions, and a variety of forms of "socialist
cooperation," such as the exchange of books, movies, specialists, students, patents, and technical documents. Nothing appears to have been published about the economic importance of
these items so far as the balance of payments is concerned.
Frequently it is reported, however, that no royalties are
charged for patents, technical documents and production li-
censes, and the only fees collected are those for copying and
postage.[30] Hence these items must be extremely small in value, even considering their stepped-up exchange in recent
years. Furthermore, there is ample reason to suspect that receipts and expenditures in this category would roughly balance
because such exchanges are mutual and about equal in quantity.[31] It was further estimated that foreign-exchange earnings
from and expenditures for fairs or exhibitions have been equal
throughout.[32] On the other hand, earnings and expenditures
involving the exchange of persons and tourism were probably
never of equal magnitude.[33] On the basis of such general considerations, the trade in services discussed here has been
estimated as in Table 32.

The balance-of-payments impact of postal and communications services and diplomatic missions has been estimated as
follows: Professor Wolfgang F. Stolper of the University of
Michigan has made available to the author a document of the

Table 31. East German commercial service
imports and exports 1950-63[a]

Year (1)	in per cent of commodity imports (2)	Imports in 1,000 rubles (3)	Exports (4)
1950	8.5	171,917	24,068
1951	8.5	206,578	28,921
1952	8.5	262,744	36,784
1953	8.5	334,063	46,769
1954	8.5	372,607	52,165
1955	8.2	384,655	53,852
1956	8.1	432,127	59,800
1957	7.8	504,028	101,402
1958	7.7	517,403	103,481
1959	7.6	605,678	121,136
1960	7.6	659,594	131,919
1961	7.6	678,655[b]	135,731[b]
1961		152,698[c]	30,540[c]
1962	7.5	161,687[c]	40,422[c]
1963	7.4	154,293[c]	38,573[c]

Sources:

Col. 2 estimated for 1950-55, and 1958-63. See text.
Col. 3 calculated from col. 2, and Table 4, col. 2.
Col. 4, see text.

Notes:

[a]For the coverage of the services see text.

[b]Old rubles

[c]New rubles

Table 32. East German exports and imports
of selected services (technical document
exchange, fairs and exhibitions, expert
and student exchange, tourism),
in 1,000 rubles, 1950-63

Year (1)	Exports (2)	Imports (3)
1950	35,700	37,000
1951	30,200	31,500
1952	25,100	26,600
1953	27,600	29,100
1954	42,000	43,600
1955	67,300	68,200
1956	79,600	79,200
1957	90,300	88,800
1958	112,700	108,200
1959	148,800	140,300
1960	181,600	170,300
1961	200,300	184,600
1962	215,400	195,000
1963	228,400	203,000

Source:

    See text.

U.S. High Commission for Germany (HICOG). This document is a
preliminary East German balance-of-payments plan for 1951.[34]
The commodity exports and imports therein are extremely close
to officially published realized figures, exports being in the
plan 2.6 million rubles larger (i.e., within 0.1 per cent of
realized exports) and imports 118.9 million smaller (i.e.,
within 4.9 per cent of realized imports). It was, therefore,
assumed that the other plan positions are also reliable. This
document lists exports of postal and communications services
in the 1951 Plan as 3.529 million rubles and imports as 0.578
million. It was assumed that in all years there has been an
export surplus in such services and that both exports and imports have grown as the volume of letters, packages, parcels,
and long-distance telephone calls handled by the East German
postal system.[35] The estimates appear in columns 2 and 3 of
Table 33.

According to the same document,[34] receipts from foreign
diplomatic missions were expected to be 31.82 million rubles
in 1951, the corresponding expenditures of the East German foreign service abroad were slated at 19.253 million rubles.
This is, in fact, quite understandable, because 1) the East
German foreign service abroad was just in its infancy, while
some foreign nations had had representatives in East Germany
for years, and 2) the East Germans have always been worried
about the passivity of their service balance and might on principle be more stringent in such expenditures. East Germany had
established two-way diplomatic relations with the seven European Communist countries, except Yugoslavia, and also with
China and North Korea, in 1949.[36] In 1950, Outer Mongolia
(two-ways) and CMEA (one-way) were added to the list. There
also were East German non-diplomatic trade offices in West Germany since that time (Frankfurt and Düsseldorf). In 1953,
trade missions were exchanged with Finland. In 1954, full two-

Table 33.   East German exports and imports
of postal and communications services and
of services connected with diplomatic
missions, in 1,000 rubles, 1950-63

Year (1)	Postal and Communications Services		Services for Diplomatic Missions	
	Exports (2)	Imports (3)	Exports (4)	Imports (5)
1950	3,557	583	31,820	19,253
1951	3,529	578	31,820	19,253
1952	3,533	579	31,820	20,052
1953	3,688	604	35,002	22,750
1954	3,960	649	38,184	27,450
1955	4,048	663	41,366	40,089
1956	4,065	666	44,548	85,527
1957	4,267	699	47,730	95,128
1958	4,372	716	54,094	111,696
1959	4,312	706	54,094	120,258
1960	4,457	730	54,094	131,499
1961	3,854	631	54,094	140,833
1962	3,921	642	63,640	160,290
1963	4,510	739	66,822	173,128

Source:

See text

way diplomatic relations were taken up with North Vietnam, and
East Germany established several trade missions in India (Bom-
bay, Calcutta, Madras) with no counterpart in East Germany.
The latter became typical procedure in the future. In 1955,
East Germany opened five trade missions (Egypt, Syria, Lebanon,
Burma, Uruguay) and one Chamber of Commerce office (Indonesia),
one mission was opened in East Germany (Syria). In 1956,
three more trade missions were established in the Sudan, Argentina, and Columbia, and the Chamber of Commerce gained recognition via permanent offices in eleven countries (Yugoslavia -
to be turned into a legation the next year - Austria, Belgium,
Chile, Denmark, France, Greece, Iceland, the Netherlands, Nor-
way, and Turkey). At the same time, permanent delegations
were dispatched to eight CMEA commissions. One such commission, on the other hand, was established in Berlin. In 1957,
a trade mission was established in Yemen, Chamber of Commerce
Offices in Italy and Sweden, a Yugoslav diplomatic mission in
East Germany. In 1958, three more trade missions were opened
(Brazil, Guinea, Iraq) and three more CMEA commissions joined.
An Egyptian trade mission and a CMEA commission came to East
Germany. In 1959, a trade mission in Ghana and a Chamber office in Great Britain were added, followed in 1960 by trade
missions in Cameroon and Cuba and one more CMEA commission.
In 1961, trade missions were established in Tunisia and Mali,
in 1962 in Algeria, Cambodia, Ceylon, and Morocco, with two
more CMEA commissions joined. On the other hand, in 1962, one
CMEA commission settled in Berlin and two countries opened
trade missions there (Iraq, Indonesia). In 1963, Cuba opened
an embassy in Berlin, East Germany the soon to be disputed one
in Zanzibar, while joining three new CMEA commissions. The
trade mission in Argentina was closed in late 1962.

On the basis of this information, the receipts and expenditures in this category have been estimated as in cols. 4 and

5 of Table 33. It was assumed that receipts and expenditures
bear a positive correlation to the number of countries with
which relations of this sort exist, that foreigners' expenditures per mission were always as in 1951, while East German
spending grew from roughly half that in 1951 to 80 per cent of
it in 1963. This can be justified for several reasons, e.g.,
the facts that the East Germans are extremely conscious about
balance-of-payments effects of spending abroad and that most
of their missions abroad are not full-fledged embassies as
most missions in East Germany are. On the other hand, each of
their missions abroad has taken on more and more activities,
frequently of diplomatic nature, as time went by.

Other services not considered so far are, finally, improvement, repair trade, etc., and interest paid on loans received from and received on loans extended to other countries.
So far as improvement, repair trade, etc., is concerned, it
should be noted that the data for bloc trade since 1961 (Tables 3, 4, 29, and 41) contain this item. Since, furthermore, data on these categories of trade are sparse and there
is no guide to their estimation, they were ignored for all other years. The information which does exist, however, suggests
that such trade is both insignificant and also fairly balanced.[37]

Interest receipts and payments, however, can be estimated
with much greater confidence, given the discussion below of
capital movements. The estimates are presented in Tables 34
and 35. For an explanation of how these data have been derived the reader is referred to the section on the capital accounts below.

The balance of services (row 6, Table 41) as a whole shows
an export surplus until 1953 and import surpluses of growing
dimensions since. But this result is easily misleading. The
export surplus up to 1953 and the low import surpluses until

1958 are due to the exports of reparations services. Such
service exports provided 88.9 per cent of all service exports
in 1950, still 82.9 per cent in 1953, 67.9 per cent in 1954,
and then fell to 35.9 per cent in 1958. Excluding such exports of services to the U.S.S.R., East Germany's service balance was considerably passive in all years, just as since
1959, when occupation costs had been abolished.[38]

In no year since 1950 were expenditures related to commodity imports less than 64 per cent of all service imports;
frequently they took a considerably higher percentage (e.g.,
86.4 per cent in 1953). Expenditures on the foreign service
and scientific-cultural exchange were the items next in importance throughout.

On the other hand, excluding reparations, earnings from
foreign diplomatic missions in East Germany, from services in
connection with the movement of commodities, and through scientific-cultural exchange have been just about equal to each
other until 1954, since then the latter two forms of service
export have become relatively more important, though still remaining roughly equal to each other.

C.   UNILATERAL TRANSFERS

At least three types of unilateral transfers ought to be
included in East Germany's balance of payments. The first one
concerns reparations, as discussed in the two preceding sections of this chapter. This would include the sum of commodity and service reparations, as given in Tables 28 and 30.

Secondly, an adjustment is in order for the gradual reduction of occupation costs and the Soviet assumption of the
costs of stationing her troops on East German territory under
the Warsaw Pact arrangements. It is probably safe to assume
that such costs were met entirely from German payments until
1956. It will be recalled from CHAPTER 1 that all forms of

Table 34. East Germany's interest
income, 1956-63, in 1,000 rubles[a]

Debtor[b]		1956	1957	1958
Albania	(1)	2,883	979	840
	(2)	-	-	-
	(3)	-	-	-
	(4)	-	-	-
	(5)	-	-	-
	(6)	-	-	-
	(7)	-	-	-
Bulgaria	(1)	-	-	-
Hungary	(1)	-	-	-
Poland	(1)	-	-	-
Rumania	(1)	-	-	-
North Korea	(1)	-	-	-
	(2)	-	3,278	624
North Vietnam	(1)	-	-	-
Egypt	(1)	-	-	-
Indonesia	(1)	-	-	-
Other Western countries	(1)	-	-	-
	(2)	-	-	-
Total		2,883	4,257	1,464

Source:

　　　See text

Notes:

　　　[a]There was no such income prior to 1956. Dash (-) means
　　　"amount was zero."

　　　[b]Number in parentheses refers to loan number as discus-
　　　sed below.

Table 34   continued

1959	1960	1961	1962	1963
700	600	500	400	300
-	225	25	20	15
-	1,120	167	133	100
-	450	83	67	50
200	40	-	-	-
747	170	-	-	-
-	-	635	219	188
-	-	-	-	4,214
-	-	5,400	960	720
-	-	-	10,875	2,775
-	-	-	-	8,512
-	4,947	324	-	-
312	-	-	-	-
-	-	4,787	960	720
-	-	-	6,460	1,615
-	-	-	7,540	804
-	-	5,000	1,000	750
-	-	-	3,938	-
1,959	7,552	16,921	32,572	20,763

Table 35.   East Germany's interest
payments, 1950-63, in 1,000 rubles[a]

Recipient[b]		1950	1951	1952	1955
Bulgaria	(1)	-	-	-	-
Č.S.S.R.	(1)	-	840	187	-
Hungary	(1)	-	900	-	-
	(2)	-	-	-	-
Poland	(1)	-	1,043	-	-
Rumania	(1)	-	-	-	-
U.S.S.R.	(1)	1,600	600	-	-
	(2)	-	4,470	-	-
	(3)	-	-	1,200	-
	(4)	-	-	-	20,750
	(5)	-	-	-	-
	(6)	-	-	-	-
	(7)	-	-	-	-
	(8)	-	-	-	-
	(9)	-	-	-	-
	(11)	-	-	-	-
Total		1,600	7,853	1,387	20,750

Source:

    See text

Notes:

[a]There were no such payments in 1953 and 1954.   Dash (-)
means "amount was zero."

[b]Number in parentheses refers to loan number as discussed below.

Table 35   continued

1956	1957	1958	1959	1960	1961	1962	1963
1,320	1,006	846	486	226	-	-	-
-	-	-	-	-	-	-	-
-	-	-	-	-	-	-	-
900	-	-	-	-	-	-	-
-	-	-	-	-	-	-	-
1,696	1,130	125	-	-	-	-	-
-	-	-	-	-	-	-	-
-	-	-	-	-	-	-	-
-	-	-	-	-	-	-	-
4,850	-	-	-	-	-	-	-
-	2,400	-	-	-	-	-	-
-	-	-	17,000	3,400	-	-	-
-	-	-	-	-	49,000	11,200	8,400
-	-	-	-	-	4,312	1,760	1,320
-	-	-	-	-	-	-	6,240
-	-	-	-	-	-	-	37,320
8,766	4,536	971	17,486	3,626	53,312	12,960	53,280

"reparations," excluding uranium, were abolished after 1953,
but East Germany was to continue taking care of Soviet troops.
The commodities and services represented by these costs have
been included above in the balance of trade and services, and
shown in the unilateral transfer account, as discussed in the
foregoing paragraph. According to Tables 28, col. 3, and 30,
col. 4, the relevant 1956 payments had been 1,886.4 million
rubles. They were cut to 1,005.6 million rubles in 1957, to
754.2 million in 1958, and then abolished. There was no corresponding reduction in Soviet troops, so far as is known.[39]
But it is conceivable, and has been frequently alleged in the
west, that part of the deliveries until 1956 actually had not
been used by the Soviet troops in Germany, but had been shipped to the Soviet Union instead. Hence, one might estimate
the needs of troop maintenance since 1956 at 1,000 million rubles per year. Probably, the goods and services this sum represents were bought in Germany. Hence the Russians may have
paid the East Germans nothing until 1957 inclusive, 245.8 million rubles in 1958, and 1,000 million rubles annually since
1959. This may explain in part the 1960-62 deficits in commercial trade (i.e., excluding reparations and armament imports) with the Soviet Union, while there had been surpluses
since 1954.[40]

Lastly, a number of governmental gifts should be considered here. Six such transfers, in all of which East Germany
was the donor, have become known, viz., to Hungary after the
revolution, to North Korea from 1950-54, to North Vietnam
first from 1954-55, and more thereafter, to Egypt during the
Suez crisis, to Algeria in 1962, and after a natural catas-
trophe, to Outer Mongolia in 1964.[41] These six items have,
however, not been included in the balance-of-payments estimate, because East German export statistics do not include
commodity exports, if they are gifts, and one would have to

adjust the balance of trade accordingly, and because many contradictory reports about the magnitudes involved are circulat-
ing. The result of those estimates included is seen in row 7
of Table 41.

D. THE CAPITAL BALANCE[42]

Establishment of the capital account of East Germany's
balance of payments is easier than a similar attempt would be
for a western country because private capital flows, difficult
to estimate under any circumstances, can with certainty be
ruled out as non-existent. On the other hand, Communist countries so far have never published systematic data on governmental capital flows, as would be the case in the west. There
are sufficient indications, nevertheless, to piece together a
reasonably correct picture of what has been happening in this
field.

1. Capital Movements with Albania

a. Drawings

East Germany has granted credits to Albania on seven occasions.

1) Agreement on a 50 million ruble loan was reached on
March 27, 1951. It was to be used in equal installments from
1951-55, carried a 2 per cent per annum (p.a.) interest rate,
and was repayable over ten years starting in 1956. The purpose was to finance Albanian imports of complete factories
from East Germany, such as a briquette factory and a fish cannery, costing 6 million rubles each, a .85 million ruble telephone exchange, and a number of other items (fishing cutters,
coast guard ships, and materials for the project of making
Durrës the main bloc harbor on the Adriatic Sea). The author's
estimates of actual drawings for commodity imports are 5.958
million rubles in 1951 (equal to the balance of trade), rather

than the slated 10 million.[43] In 1952, the briquette factory
and fish cannery were delivered; valued together at 12 million
rubles, and the balance of trade shows, indeed, 12.028 million
rubles in favor of East Germany. The author assumed this latter figure to have been the 1952 drawings. In 1953, drawings
under this credit arrangement were probably only 6.765 million
rubles. (The higher balance of trade is explained by another
1.5 million rubles credit delivery to be discussed shortly.)
Similarly, 1954 and 1955 drawings are estimated at 5.216 and
10.531 million rubles, since there were other known deliveries
on credit. The author assumed that the missing 9.502 million
rubles, to reach the promised 50 million total, were still delivered in 1956. This is most likely, since most deliveries
were complete factories that are known to have been almost
completed by the end of 1955 and certainly were not abandoned
in this state. (Another fish factory, for instance, was finally finished in November, 1956.) This is also corroborated
in another way, viz., by the fact that the balance of trade
was 10.578 million rubles in favor of East Germany in 1956,
while there was another credit of 5 million rubles granted
(discussed shortly), and the Albanians probably paid the first
installment of principal and interest on the 1951 loan. They
should have paid 5 million rubles, but probably did pay 3.924
million, since the gross credits used (9.502 plus 5 million
rubles) minus repayments usually can be expected to equal the
balance of trade (here of 10.578 million rubles). A systematic presentation of all estimates on the capital balance can
be found in Tables 37-40.

    2) A second credit agreement was signed in January,
1953. 1.5 million rubles were granted and used in 1953 for
general imports of Albania from East Germany. At a rate of 2
per cent p.a., they were to be repaid over 6 years starting
in 1960.

3) A third credit agreement for 10 million rubles was
reached in November, 1954. It was used also for Albanian imports from East Germany during 1954 and 1955. The interest
rate was reported as 2 per cent p.a., the terms of repayment
have not been revealed, but were assumed, as for the previous
loan, from 1960-65.

4) A 5 million ruble loan was arranged on February 15,
1956, and used during the same year for Albanian light industry imports from East Germany. The interest rate was 2 per
cent p.a., time of repayment was not revealed and assumed, as
for the above two loans, from 1960-65.

5) On February 21, 1957, a 4 million ruble loan was arranged. It was used by Albania during 1957 for the purchase
in East Germany of seed potatoes, agricultural machinery, fertilizer, and the services of East German specialists. This
credit was the outcome of a CMEA recommendation to make Albania the bloc's supplier of early potatoes. These had been imported by many bloc countries, including East Germany, from
southern Italy and Malta. The interest rate was 2 per cent
p.a., repayment was scheduled "by 1960." Presumably this
meant in equal installments in 1959 and 1960, as is implied
by the 1-6-1959 repayment protocol, which arranged for the Albanian cultivation of 700 hectares of early potatoes for East
Germany.

6) A sixth credit agreement was signed on March 13,
1957, for 17 million rubles. It reportedly was used mostly
during the same year for Albanian imports from East Germany of
complete factories, such as a heating plant, a hydro-electric
plant, a sugar and a cement factory. The interest rate was 2
per cent p.a., repayment scheduled "by 1960," assumed to mean
in 1959 and 1960. It is possible to guess the exact amount
used in 1957 as the difference between total gross credits for
commodities (which is the balance of trade plus Albanian repay-

ments of principal and interest on loan no. 1), or 14.865 million rubles, and other commodity credits used under loan no. 5. Since the fifth loan was partly to be used for services, the author assumed only 3 million to have been used for commodity imports. Hence 11.865 million rubles of loan no. 6 must have been used in 1957 and 5.135 million in 1958.

7) Finally, another credit agreement was signed on July 27, 1957. This credit was to be used from 1957-60 for imports into Albania from East Germany of complete factories, machinery, raw materials, and technical services. Information on amount, interest, and repayment conditions was not published, except that the loan was "long term." Since it has, however, been reported that East Germany from 1951-57 promised Albania a total of 100 million rubles in credit, the author estimates the amount of this loan as 12.5 million rubles. It was assumed that repayments occurred from 1961-67. Since a more detailed protocol was not signed until December 24, 1957, furthermore, the author has estimated the actual drawings as follows: 1958: 2.5 million rubles for services, 2 million rubles for commodities; 1959 and 1960 each 1 million rubles for services, 3 million rubles for commodities. It should be noted that given the preceding assumptions, the sum of credits received by Albania minus repayments of interest and principal exactly equals the balance of trade with East Germany for 1951 through 1957. For 1958-63, however, to carry through the (known) trade, credit, and (assumed) repayment programs with East Germany, Albania would have needed additional credits of 13.9, 24.6, 20.5, 1.1, 2.6, and 13.5 million (old) rubles, respectively, from somewhere else. This, of course, is quite conceivable. On the other hand, it has also been reported recently that East Germany "partially forgave" Albanian debts.[44]

b.   Repayments

Throughout this study, the author estimated interest payments and receipts by assuming that the given rate is to be
applied to the actual amount outstanding only and for the time
it is so outstanding. He also assumed for the purposes of
this calculation that drawings of principal were made on the
first day of the year, while repayments were made in the middle of the year, and, unless something to the contrary is
known, in equal installments. Furthermore, it was assumed
that the interest payments themselves were always made in such
a way as to wipe out all interest debt up to the date of payment, the first interest payment being made together with the
first payment on principal.[45] Only the relevant calculations
for the first Albanian loan are given in detail in Table 36.
For all others, only the results have been given in Tables 34
and 35 above.

2.   Capital Movements with Bulgaria

Agreement on a mutual loan was reached in August, 1955.
The East Germans extended a long term credit of 100 million
rubles that was to be used from 1955-69 for the Bulgarian import from East Germany of complete factories, especially for
the production of cement, cellulose (to be delivered by 1959),
sugar (to be sent in 1957), and textiles. The Bulgarians, on
the other hand, extended a smaller short-term credit to cover
the Bulgarian export surplus in 1955 and until the East German
deliveries would catch up with her imports. (The 1954 Bulgarian export surplus was reportedly offset multilaterally.) A
1963 report indicates that the cellulose plant in Bukjovzi was
started in 1955 and producing "now" 25,000 t of cellulose plus
27,500 t of paper annually. East Germany was being repaid
since 1963 in cellulose. Using this scanty information, the
author has estimated the total Bulgarian credit extension at

Table 36. Example of methodology for the
calculation of interest payments and
principal amortization, first Albanian
credit, in 1,000 rubles[a]

Year	Principal owed 1-1 to 6-30	Principal repaid[b] 7-1	Principal owed 7-1 to 12-31	Interest owed on 6-30	Interest paid on 7-1
1951	5,958.0	-	5,958.0	59.580	-
1952	17,986.0	-	17,986.0	299.020	-
1953	24,751.0	-	24,751.0	726.390	-
1954	29,967.0	-	29,967.0	1,273.570	-
1955	40,498.0	-	40,498.0	1,978.220	-
1956	50,000.0	1,040.8	48,959.2	2,883.200	2,883.200
1957	48,959.2	6,979.6	41,979.6	979.184	979.184
1958	41,979.6	6,979.6	35,000.0	839.592	839.592
1959	35,000.0	5,000.0	30,000.0	700.000	700.000
1960	30,000.0	5,000.0	25,000.0	600.000	600.000
1961	25,000.0	5,000.0	20,000.0	500.000	500.000
1962	20,000.0	5,000.0	15,000.0	400.000	400.000
1963	15,000.0	5,000.0	10,000.0	300.000	300.000

[a]Dash (-) means "amount zero."

[b]Since the 1956 total repayment of principal and interest has
been estimated above as 3.924 million rubles, this interest
calculation allowed an estimate of the 1956 principal repayment of 1.041 million rubles. It was then assumed that the
difference to the planned repayment of 5 million rubles was
paid together with the 1957 and 1958 repayments, and repayments were regular thereafter.

52 million rubles, East German repayment going from 1956-60.
The East German credit extension was estimated to have begun
in 1955, reaching scheduled annual deliveries only by 1961.
An interest charge of 2 per cent p.a. was assumed. It was assumed that Bulgarian repayments commenced in 1963 with a payment of 2.454 million rubles in principal and all interest
due.

3. Capital Movements with Czechoslovakia

1) On June 23, 1950, the Č.S.S.R. granted a 28 million
rubles short-term credit to East Germany for the purchase of
1.911 million pairs of shoes in the Č.S.S.R. It was repaid by
"the middle of 1952." Since, according to *SJDDR 1955*, p. 245,
East German imports of the industry "leather/shoes/furs" in
1950 from the bloc were 36.3 million rubles, but only 1.1 million in 1951, it was assumed that the entire amount actually
was drawn in 1950. It was also assumed that the interest rate
was 2 per cent p.a.

2) In September, 1959, the Č.S.S.R. granted a credit of
110 million rubles to East Germany for the purchase of potassium salt mining equipment. Drawings were assumed in equal
installments over five years starting in 1960.

4. Capital Movements with Hungary

Hungary has granted credits to East Germany in 1950 and
again in 1955, each being repaid in the year following their
use. In light of the knowledge about the balance of trade, it
was assumed that these credits amounted to 30 million rubles
each and were repaid with 2 per cent interest p.a.

East Germany granted a 60 million ruble credit to Hungary
immediately after the Hungarian Revolution. It was used in
the first quarter of 1957 for Hungarian imports from East Germany of 20 million rubles worth of chemicals and mining products, 12 million rubles worth of machinery, and 28 million

rubles worth of consumer goods. This credit was repayable, at
2 per cent p.a. interest, from 1961-65.

5. Capital Movements with Poland

Poland granted to East Germany a short term credit for
34.771 million rubles in 1950, according to a June 6 agreement.
Using this credit, East Germany imported in the same year
10,000 tons of meat, 2,400 tons of fish, and 9,000 tons of fat,
all from Poland. Full repayment at 2 per cent interest p.a.
was assumed for 1951.

On April 17, 1957, as the direct result of a CMEA recommendation, East Germany granted a long term credit for 400 million rubles to Poland. It was to be used from 1957-68 for
Polish imports from East Germany of commodities and services
for the development of five open-strip lignite mines (at Turov
and Konin). By 1958, already 100 million rubles had been
drawn. This credit carried only a 1.5 per cent p.a. rate of
interest, and was repayable always six years after drawings,
in the form of coal, coke, and electric energy. Repayment is
known to have started in 1962, full repayment being scheduled
by 1974. The 1963 repayment partly consisted of 5.6 million
tons of lignite out of a 10 million ton production.

A treaty was signed in January, 1961, for East German
participation in the construction on Polish territory of the
"Friendship" pipeline. East Germany, for the finance of labor, pipes, and other materials, granted to Poland a credit
of 257 million rubles at 1.5 per cent p.a. interest. It must
have been used up by 1963 when the pipeline was completed.
Repayment was to occur during the first ten years of the pipeline's operation by Polish crediting of East Germany for her
transit charges for Soviet oil deliveries to East Germany.

6. Capital Movements with Rumania

Rumania is known to have extended credits to East Germany in 1955 and 1956 amounting to 64.802 million rubles which were repaid in 1956-58. This credit was linked with another one East Germany granted to Rumania in July, 1956, but probably not drawn upon until 1958. The latter one was to be used from 1956-60, amounting to 110 million rubles, being repayable at 2 per cent p.a. interest from 1961-69. Just as utilization, actual repayment commenced in 1963, i.e., two years late. Both credits seem to be connected directly or indirectly with the development of the Danube delta region. East German scientists had been engaged in research since 1953 about the possibility of utilizing annually from 2 to 3 million tons of delta reeds for cellulose production. Originally it was planned that East Germany would deliver all the necessary equipment, being partly paid in advance by Rumanian export surpluses. After 1955, however, the East Germans declared themselves unable to carry the burden of the whole project by themselves. Hence the 1956 agreement provided for the inclusion of the Č.S.S.R. (30 million ruble credit) and Poland (10 million ruble credit) in the project. The project involved the creation at Braila of a cellulose production center. (See p. 138 above.)

7. Capital Movements with the U.S.S.R.

Until 1964, there have never been credits granted to the Soviet Union by East Germany, but the Soviet Union has extended "the helping hand of brotherly love" on eleven occasions.

1) A 100 million ruble credit was granted and used in 1949. With it East Germany imported from the Soviet Union a) 12,000 tons of fat and 40,000 tons of grain, and b) 800 agricultural machines plus 1,000 tractors and trucks. The interest rate was 2 per cent p.a. Part a) was repaid in late 1949

and in 1950, part b) in 1951. The value of part a) was probably 70 million rubles.[46]

2)   A 149 million ruble credit was granted and used in
1950. The G.D.R. imported from the U.S.S.R. 20,000 tons of
meat, 5,000 tons of butter, 15,000 tons of vegetable oils,
17,000 tons of fish, 8,000 tons of cotton, plus wool and grain.
The granted amount was repaid in 1951 at 2 per cent p.a. interest.

3)   The Soviet Union also gave 30 million rubles in credits for part of the 1950 and 1951 East German expenditures
on diplomatic missions. These were short term, repayable in
1952, assumed at 2 per cent p.a.

4)   In July and August, 1953, immediately after the East
German uprisings, the Soviet Union not only agreed to drastic
changes in her reparations policy, as discussed in CHAPTER 1,
but also granted 485 million rubles in credit, in effect con-
verting part of the 1953 reparations debt into a longer term
commercial debt.[47] 135 million of this credit was in hard
western currencies and used in 1953 for imports from the west.
350 million were used in 1953 and 1954 for commodity imports
from the U.S.S.R. and Poland. In particular, 231 million rubles were used, according to an additional trade agreement of
July 29, 1953, for the import of 27,000 tons of butter, 8,500
tons of animal fats, 11,000 tons of vegetable oils, 15,000
tons of oil seeds, 20,000 tons of meat, 1,500 tons of fatty
cheese, and 7,000 tons of cotton. The other 119 million rubles were used to pay part of the imports provided in another
additional trade agreement of August 25, 1953. This agreement, for 230 million rubles, covered the importation of 2
million tons of Polish soft coal, 239,000 tons of rolled steel,
6,000 tons of aluminum, 3,000 tons of rice, 3,000 tons of cotton yarn, 1,100 tons of flax. The entire credit of 485 million was repaid in 1955 and 1956 at 2 per cent p.a. interest.

5) In January, 1956, the Soviet Union granted an 80 million ruble credit in hard western currencies. It was used immediately, and repaid at 2 per cent p.a. interest in 1957.

6) On January 7, 1957, the Soviet Union granted another credit in hard western currencies for 340 million rubles. It was used immediately for imports from the west, and repaid at 2 per cent p.a. in 1959 and 1960.

7) On September 27, 1957, the Soviet Union granted a 700 million ruble credit which was drawn in 1958. 300 million of it consisted of hard western currencies, and, as the rest, were used for commodity imports. The credit was repayable in goods from 1961-65 at 2 per cent p.a.

8) On February 25, 1958, the Soviet Union, following a CMEA recommendation, agreed to extend credit to East Germany for the development of the chemical industry, with special emphasis on plastics production. The credit was to be used from 1958-60, the interest rate was 2 per cent, repayment scheduled for 1961-65 from the production to be initiated. All imports were to come from the Soviet Union. A ruble figure about the magnitude has been given in only one source as 110 million, but this might not be reliable, since various other sources publish DM-E figures of 110 million or 240 million or 300 million (divided into 16 for 1958, 130 each for 1959 and 1960, and 24 for 1961). Conceivably all figures are correct, depending on what kind of prices they are expressed in. The author assumed the minimum figure of 110 million rubles to be correct and that it was distributed over the years as the DM-E data given.

9) In August, 1959, for the finance of potassium salt mining investment, the Soviet Union granted a credit of 112 million rubles. It was assumed drawn by 1962 and repaid over 5 years thereafter at 2 per cent p.a. interest.

10) On May 30, 1961, an agreement was reached for a So-

viet long term credit of 2 billion DM, to be drawn during
1961-65. If the above amount referred to foreign trade DM, it
would correspond to 3.6 billion old rubles or 810 million new
rubles. This is, however, unlikely, since one source lists
the credit as "somewhat less than 2 billion (old) rubles." For
reasons given below, it was assumed at 1.914 billion (old)
rubles.

    11) On May 5, 1962, a treaty was signed at Leipzig con-
cerning an additional credit of 1.3 billion DM to be used in
1962 for commodity imports. The credit was "at the usual favorable terms" and to serve the acceleration of the socialist
reconstruction of the economy. Specifically, it was to finance investments designed to change rapidly the output structure towards chemicals, electro-technical production, second-
stage metallurgy and modern, labor-intensive machinery. The
amount of the credit was also listed as 280 million (new) rubles, i.e., 1.244 billion old rubles. It is on this basis
that the above (credit no. 10) DM figure was translated. A
repayment of 300 million rubles of principal was assumed for
1963.[48]

8. Capital Movements with Communist Asia

    It is known with certainty that East Germany has granted
three credits to North Korea and one to North Vietnam. The
first Korean credit was arranged on June 25, 1952, to be
"about 30 million rubles." It was used in 1952 and 1953 for
the Korean import from East Germany of machine tools and medical supplies. Nothing more is known, but in light of the magnitude of the trade balance (4.000 million rubles in 1952 and
28.449 million in 1953 in favor of East Germany), drawings
equal to the trade balance were assumed, with repayments at 2
per cent p.a. in 1960 and 1961.

    The second Korean credit was negotiated in 1953 and agreed
upon on September 19. It was used in 1954 and financed, among

other things, the import of a film studio and a hospital. The
author assumed it to have equalled the trade balance of 46.826
million rubles, and that repayments were made from 1957-59 at
2 per cent p.a. A third credit was granted to North Korea in
February, 1955, for 1955-64. It was to help finance the purchase of machinery and equipment equal to 462 million rubles.
Drawings have been estimated with the help of the trade balance and Korean repayments. No repayment of this loan before
1964 was assumed.

East Germany granted a 60 million ruble credit to North
Vietnam in 1955. It had apparently no time limit and was to
be used for imports from East Germany "over the following
years" of such items as steel cutters, hospitals, a film studio, a glass factory, "the most modern and largest printing
plant of Southeast Asia," and the Hanoi telephone exchange.
The author assumed that drawings from 1955-59 were equal to
the balance of trade, the rest was used in 1960, and that repayments at 2 per cent p.a. interest occurred in equal installments beginning in 1961 and lasting to 1965.

9. Capital Movements with Non-Communist Countries

On August 28, 1958, East Germany extended a long-term
credit of 7.5 million Egyptian pounds to the United Arab Republic. Complete factories were to be shipped to Egypt from
East Germany until 1961. At an interest rate of 2.5 per cent
p.a., repayment was scheduled thereafter, partly in cotton.
At the East German exchange rates, this amount equals 47.85
million DM or 86.13 million rubles. (The East German press
frequently has applied exchange rates for non-commercial transactions to this amount, thereby exaggerating vastly the importance of the loan.) The Egyptians have used it for the import
of a cotton textile plant, heating and refrigeration plants, a
cigarette factory, parts of the Heluan steel mill, and a
350 km Nile delta electric power grid. The author has esti-

mated equal yearly drawings until 1961 and equal repayments
from 1962-65. A Cairo treaty of January 31, 1965, provided
for the future shipment (partially on credit) of more machinery and equipment, valued at 17 million pounds.

On June 19, 1954, East Germany promised to deliver a cane
sugar factory on very long term credit to Indonesia. The value was "about 40 million rubles." The imports for this project began in 1955, the factory started to operate in 1958.
Drawings were estimated equal to the trade balance of 42.895
million rubles from 1955-57, with repayments assumed from
1962-65 at 2.5 per cent p.a. interest. A further treaty in
1965 promises the delivery by East Germany of a sunflower-oil
factory on credit.

Finally, it is known that other credits were granted to
other "anti-imperialist" nations, such as India and Burma.
(India received a textile plant, part of a steel mill, and a
roofing felt plant; Burma a cement factory, textile plant, and
an oil cracking installation.) India received a minimum of 10
million rubles on credit. The totals can be estimated from
the fact that "East Germany in 1957 and 1958 exported to the
capitalist area complete factories on long term credit of
about 75 million rubles." This would mean that about 50 million rubles of such credits have so far not been accounted for.
The author assigned, therefore, an equal amount of 25 million
rubles each to 1957 and 1958.[49] Repayment, at 2.5 per cent
p.a. interest was assumed for 1961-65.

Western sources report by March 1961 a total East German
credit extension to western underdeveloped countries of $56
million, i.e., 224 million (old) rubles. So far, only 179
million rubles have been accounted for. The difference of 45
million rubles was probably extended in 1959, since one source
directly states a figure of $9 million for that particular
year. Repayment was assumed for 1962 at 2.5 per cent interest.

Table 37. Capital exports (credits granted
by East Germany), annual drawings, 1951-63,
in 1,000 rubles[a]

Debtor		1951	1952	1953	1954
Albania	(1)	5,958	12,028	6,765	5,216
	(2)	-	-	1,500	-
	(3)	-	-	-	1,000
	(4)	-	-	-	-
	(5)	-	-	-	-
	(6)	-	-	-	-
	(7)	-	-	-	-
Bulgaria	(1)	-	-	-	-
Hungary	(1)	-	-	-	-
Poland	(1)	-	-	-	-
	(2)	-	-	-	-
Rumania	(1)	-	-	-	-
North Korea	(1)	-	4,000	28,449	-
	(2)	-	-	-	46,826
	(3)	-	-	-	-
North Vietnam	(1)	-	-	-	-
Egypt	(1)	-	-	-	-
Indonesia	(1)	-	-	-	-
Other Western (India, Burma, etc.)	(1)	-	-	-	-
	(2)	-	-	-	-
Total		5,958	16,028	36,714	53,042

[a]There were no credits extended in 1950.
 Dash (-) means "amount was zero."

Table 37   continued

Debtor		1955	1956	1957	1958
Albania	(1)	10,531	9,502	-	-
	(2)	-	-	-	-
	(3)	9,000	-	-	-
	(4)	-	5,000	-	-
	(5)	-	-	4,000	-
	(6)	-	-	11,865	5,135
	(7)	-	-	-	4,500
Bulgaria	(1)	1,015	1,302	3,759	5,363
Hungary	(1)	-	-	60,000	-
Poland	(1)	-	-	40,000	60,000
	(2)	-	-	-	-
Rumania	(1)	-	-	-	11,608
North Korea	(1)	-	-	-	-
	(2)	-	-	-	-
	(3)	30,014	26,530	35,993	26,905
North Vietnam	(1)	6,865	17,309	7,635	2,147
Egypt	(1)	-	-	-	21,533
Indonesia	(1)	24,549	16,593	1,753	-
Other Western (India, Burma, etc.)	(1)	-	-	25,000	25,000
	(2)	-	-	-	-
Total		81,974	76,236	190,005	162,191

Table 37 continued

1959	1960	1961	1962	1963
-	-	-	-	-
-	-	-	-	-
-	-	-	-	-
-	-	-	-	-
-	-	-	-	-
-	-	-	-	-
4,000	4,000	-	-	-
8,397	20,164	6,667	6,667	6,667
-	-	-	-	-
30,000	30,000	30,000	30,000	30,000
-	-	85,667	85,667	85,667
60,065	-	33,969	4,358	-
-	-	-	-	-
-	-	-	-	-
28,503	21,747	19,700	30,000	30,000
18,583	7,461	-	-	-
21,533	21,533	21,533	-	-
-	-	-	-	-
-	-	-	-	-
45,000	-	-	-	-
216,081	104,905	197,536	156,692	152,334

Table 38.   Capital exports (credits repaid
by East Germany), annual repayments,
1950-52, 1955-63, in 1,000 rubles[a]

Creditor		1950	1951	1952
Bulgaria	(1)	-	-	-
Č.S.S.R.	(1)	-	18,667	9,333
Hungary	(1)	-	30,000	-
	(2)	-	-	-
Poland	(1)	-	34,771	-
Rumania	(1)	-	-	-
U.S.S.R.	(1)	50,000	30,000	-
	(2)	-	149,000	-
	(3)	-	-	30,000
	(4)	-	-	-
	(5)	-	-	-
	(6)	-	-	-
	(7)	-	-	-
	(8)	-	-	-
	(9)	-	-	-
	(11)	-	-	-
Total		50,000	262,438	39,333

[a]There were no repayments in 1953 and 1954.
Dash (-) means "amount was zero."

Table 38 continued

1955	1956	1957	1958	1959	1960
-	1,680	8,000	18,000	13,000	11,320
-	-	-	-	-	-
-	-	-	-	-	-
-	30,000	-	-	-	-
-	-	-	-	-	-
-	8,304	50,248	6,250	-	-
-	-	-	-	-	-
-	-	-	-	-	-
-	-	-	-	-	-
242,500	242,500	-	-	-	-
-	-	80,000	-	-	-
-	-	-	-	170,000	170,000
-	-	-	-	-	-
-	-	-	-	-	-
-	-	-	-	-	-
-	-	-	-	-	-
242,500	282,484	138,248	24,250	183,000	181,320

Table 38   continued

Creditor		1961	1962	1963
Bulgaria	(1)	-	-	-
Č.S.S.R.	(1)	-	-	-
Hungary	(1)	-	-	-
	(2)	-	-	-
Poland	(1)	-	-	-
Rumania	(1)	-	-	-
U.S.S.R.	(1)	-	-	-
	(2)	-	-	-
	(3)	-	-	-
	(4)	-	-	-
	(5)	-	-	-
	(6)	-	-	-
	(7)	140,000	140,000	140,000
	(8)	22,000	22,000	22,000
	(9)	-	-	22,400
	(11)	-	-	300,000
Total		162,000	162,000	484,400

Table 39. Capital imports (credits granted
to East Germany), annual drawings,
1950-51, 1953-63, in 1,000 rubles[a]

Creditor		1950	1951	1953	1954
Bulgaria	(1)	-	-	-	-
Č.S.S.R.	(1)	28,000	-	-	-
	(2)	-	-	-	-
Hungary	(1)	30,000	-	-	-
	(2)	-	-	-	-
Poland	(1)	34,771	-	-	-
Rumania	(1)	-	-	-	-
U.S.S.R.	(2)	149,000	-	-	-
	(3)	15,000	15,000	-	-
	(4)	-	-	310,000*	175,000
	(5)	-	-	-	-
	(6)	-	-	-	-
	(7)	-	-	-	-
	(8)	-	-	-	-
	(9)	-	-	-	-
	(10)	-	-	-	-
	(11)	-	-	-	-
Total		256,771	15,000	310,000*	175,000

[a]There were no drawings in 1952.
 Dash (-) means "amount was zero."
*In part or wholly in western currencies.

Table 39   continued

Creditor		1955	1956	1957	1958
Bulgaria	(1)	40,000	12,000	-	-
Č.S.S.R.	(1)	-	-	-	-
	(2)	-	-	-	-
Hungary	(1)	-	-	-	-
	(2)	30,000	-	-	-
Poland	(1)	-	-	-	-
Rumania	(1)	52,413	12,389	-	-
U.S.S.R.	(2)	-	-	-	-
	(3)	-	-	-	-
	(4)	-	-	-	-
	(5)	-	80,000*	-	-
	(6)	-	-	340,000*	-
	(7)	-	-	-	700,000*
	(8)	-	-	-	5,867
	(9)	-	-	-	-
	(10)	-	-	-	-
	(11)	-	-	-	-
Total		122,413	104,389*	340,000*	705,867*

Table 39   continued

1959	1960	1961	1962	1963
-	-	-	-	-
-	-	-	-	-
-	22,000	22,000	22,000	22,000
-	-	-	-	-
-	-	-	-	-
-	-	-	-	-
-	-	-	-	-
-	-	-	-	-
-	-	-	-	-
-	-	-	-	-
-	-	-	-	-
-	-	-	-	-
-	-	-	-	-
47,667	47,667	8,800	-	-
16,000	32,000	32,000	32,000	-
-	-	382,800	382,800	382,800
-	-	-	1,244,000	-
63,667	101,667	445,600	1,680,800	404,800

Table 40. Capital imports (credits repaid
to East Germany), annual repayments,
1956-63, in 1,000 rubles[a]

Debtor		1956	1957	1958
Albania	(1)	1,041	6,980	6,980
	(2)	-	-	-
	(3)	-	-	-
	(4)	-	-	-
	(5)	-	-	-
	(6)	-	-	-
	(7)	-	-	-
Bulgaria	(1)	-	-	-
Hungary	(1)	-	-	-
Poland	(1)	-	-	-
Rumania	(1)	-	-	-
North Korea	(1)	-	-	-
	(2)	-	15,609	15,609
North Vietnam	(1)	-	-	-
Egypt	(1)	-	-	-
Indonesia	(1)	-	-	-
Other Western (India, Burma, etc.)	(1)	-	-	-
	(2)	-	-	-
Total		1,041	22,589	22,589

[a]There were no repayments prior to 1956.
Dash (-) means "amount was zero."

Table 40   continued

1959	1960	1961	1962	1963
5,000	5,000	5,000	5,000	5,000
-	250	250	250	250
-	1,667	1,667	1,667	1,667
-	833	833	833	833
2,000	2,000	-	-	-
8,500	8,500	-	-	-
-	-	1,563	1,563	1,563
-	-	-	-	2,454
-	-	12,000	12,000	12,000
-	-	-	40,000	60,000
-	-	-	-	1,488
-	16,225	16,225	-	-
15,609	-	-	-	-
-	-	12,000	12,000	12,000
-	-	-	21,533	21,533
-	-	-	10,724	10,724
-	-	10,000	10,000	10,000
-	-	-	45,000	-
31,109	34,475	59,538	160,570	139,512

Further credits are known to have been promised in 1964 to Cambodia (repayable in goods), Cuba, and Zanzibar (for machinery and equipment for the food industry). The Cuban credit was agreed upon in Berlin on July 20, 1964. It was to be used for the Cuban import of industrial equipment and other commodities from 1965-70 and worth 84 million DM. (A 1961 source had already mentioned the East German granting of a credit to Cuba covering 15 complete factories, as for the production of cans, radio parts, household china, photographic equipment, and machine tools. It was impossible to ascertain whether this referred to the same credit agreed upon 3 years later.) Finally, a February 22, 1965, treaty promised delivery of complete factories and other goods on long term credit by East Germany to Ceylon.

10. Summary

A summary picture of capital movements can be obtained from Tables 37-40, while interest data are summarized in Tables 34 and 35. It is seen that capital movements, even among the Communist countries, have never been of any appreciable magnitude when compared to the total volume of commodity trade. This underlines the basic difference of CMEA and the Marshall Plan organization. CMEA, though originally conceived as the counterpart to the Marshall Plan, has hardly been concerned at all with anything like the massive aid given by the U.S. to the West European nations.[50]

For the period 1950-63 as a whole, East Germany had a large import surplus on capital account (1,535.728 million rubles or over 30 per cent of the volume). Her actual credit extensions never surpassed 2.4 per cent of her commodity exports (and were below 1 per cent until 1956 inclusive). For 8 out of the 14 years, furthermore, her repayments exceeded her own credit extensions within the capital export category. (For the whole period they amounted to 60.4 per cent of capi-

tal exports.) On the other hand, credits granted to East Germany (covering over 90 per cent of capital imports) have on
three occasions reached or exceeded 9.5 per cent of her commodity import volume (12.1 per cent in 1950, 9.5 per cent in
1958, 15.6 per cent in 1962), while they were between 2.5 and
7.5 per cent in six years (1953-55, 1957, 1961, and 1963). Of
all the credits granted to her since 1950, 93.1 per cent have
come from the Soviet Union (exceeding total capital exports by
737 million rubles) and 19.4 per cent of this amount was in
western currencies. Hence one can, indeed, corroborate the
guesses advanced by some writers that East Germany's credits
to other Communist or "anti-imperialist" areas have ultimately
come from the Soviet Union.[51]

E.   THE BALANCE OF PAYMENTS AS A WHOLE, 1950-63

It is now possible to combine the various parts of the
balance of payments. The balance of payments as a whole is
presented in Table 41 below. The substantial export surplus
in the balance of trade has been discussed above. There also
has been a discussion of the service balance. We now see,
however, how enormous unilateral transfers in favor of the
Soviet Union, which were only slightly reversed after the Soviet Union started to take care of her own troops in Germany
in the late 1950's have cancelled most of the credit items
and created a rather precarious situation on current account.
The balance on current account has ranged from -879 to +1,644
million (old) rubles, was more often negative than positive
and showed a debit of 1,242.8 million (old) rubles for the
1950-63 period as a whole. As was shown above, capital imports for the 1950-63 period exceeded capital exports by some
1,535.7 million (old) rubles. Together this leaves a surplus
of 292.9 million (old) rubles for 1950-63 which is here listed
as covered by "errors and omissions."

Table 41.   East Germany's balance of
payments, 1950-63, in 1,000 rubles[a]

Item	1950	1951	1952
1. Commodity Exports	+6,820,350	+8,249,120	+8,799,990
2. Commodity Imports	-2,122,550	-2,530,325	-3,591,100
3. Trade Balance	+4,697,800	+5,718,795	+5,208,890
4. Service Exports	+855,007	+691,635	+721,693
5. Service Imports	-230,353	-265,762	-311,362
6. Service Balance	+624,654	+425,873	+410,331
7. Unilateral Trans- fers (net)	-5,871,112	-5,995,505	-6,469,766
8. Current Account	-548,658	+149,163	-850,545
9. Capital Exports	-50,000	-268,396	-55,361
10. Capital Imports	+256,771	+15,000	-
11. Capital Accounts	+206,771	-253,396	-55,361
12. Errors/Omissions	+341,887	+104,233	+905,906

Sources:

Row 1: Sum of col. 2, Table 3 and col. 4, Table 28.
As explained in note a) to Table 28, 1961-63 repara-
tions were estimated as equal to 1960.
Row 2: Sum of col. 2, Table 4 and corresponding data
for armament imports (p. 274 above).
Row 3: Sum of rows 1 and 2.
Row 4: Sum of Tables 30 (col. 4), 31 (col. 4), 32
(col. 2), 33 (cols. 2 and 4), and 34.
Row 5: Sum of Tables 31 (col. 3), 32 (col. 3), 33
(cols. 3 and 5), and 35.
Row 6: Sum of rows 4 and 5.
Row 7: Sum of col. 4, Table 28, col. 4, Table 30 minus
Soviet troop payments discussed on p. 300.
Row 8: Sum of rows 3, 6, and 7.
Row 9: Sum of totals from Tables 37 and 38.
Row 10: Sum of totals from Tables 39 and 40.
Row 11: Sum of rows 9 and 10.
Row 12: Sum of rows 8 and 11 multiplied by -1.

Table 41   continued

1953	1954	1955	1956	1957
+9,138,808	+8,324,297	+8,273,586	+8,853,625	+8,773,029
-4,130,149	-4,933,612	-4,890,919	-5,534,851	-6,661,920
+5,008,659	+3,390,685	+3,382,667	+3,318,774	+2,111,109
+660,806	+424,309	+454,566	+478,896	+454,356
-386,517	-444,306	-514,357	-606,286	-693,191
+274,289	-19,997	-59,791	-127,390	-238,835
-5,816,587	-3,060,000	-3,078,000	-3,162,600	-1,736,400
-533,639	+310,688	+244,876	+28,784	+135,874
-36,714	-53,042	-324,474	-358,720	-328,253
+310,000	+175,000	+122,413	+105,430	+362,589
+273,286	+121,958	-202,061	-253,290	+34,336
+260,353	-432,646	-42,815	+224,506	-170,210

Notes:

[a] Credit items are denoted by a plus sign (+), debits by a minus sign (-).

[b] Old rubles of .222168 g gold content.

[c] New rubles of .987412 g gold content.

Table 41   continued

Item	1958	1959	1960
1. Commodity Exports	+8,787,976	+9,011,211	+9,212,330
2. Commodity Imports	-7,419,514	-9,019,450	-9,278,873
3. Trade Balance	+1,368,462	-8,239	-66,543
4. Service Exports	+430,911	+330,301	+379,622
5. Service Imports	-738,986	-884,428	-965,749
6. Service Balance	-308,075	-554,127	-586,127
7. Unilateral Trans- fers (net)	-1,138,400	+474,400	+550,000
8. Current Account	-78,013	-87,966	-102,670
9. Capital Exports	-186,441	-399,081	-286,225
10. Capital Imports	+728,456	+94,776	+136,142
11. Capital Accounts	+542,015	-304,305	-150,083
12. Errors/Omissions	-464,002	+392,271	+252,753

It is, of course, not certain what this residual represents. It could, and we hope it does not, represent the uncan-
celled portion of huge errors that have crept into the estimate at various points. But supposing there are no errors anywhere in the balance of payments, then the residual would have
to present the extent of a type of capital movement that could
not be estimated separately, viz., the utilization or granting
of swing credits under the trade agreements[52] and the movement
of foreign-exchange reserves. The residual to be explained is
rather small for most years, hence this could be a legitimate
explanation. From the only bank statements ever published by
the East German Central Bank we know, for instance, that East
Germany, so far as the swing is concerned, was in a creditor

Table 41   continued

1961[b]	1961[c]	1962[c]	1963[c]
+9,551,065	+2,148,992	+2,237,631	+2,539,036
-10,129,675	-2,279,182	-2,425,829	-2,152,546
-578,610	-130,190	-188,198	+386,490
+410,900	+92,453	+111,417	+110,685
-1,058,031	-238,057	-244,687	-251,076
-647,131	-145,604	-133,270	-140,391
+550,000	+123,750	+123,750	+123,750
-675,741	-152,044	-197,718	+369,849
-359,536	-80,896	-71,706	-143,265
+505,138	+113,656	+414,309	+122,470
+145,602	+32,760	+342,603	-20,795
+530,139	+119,284	-144,885	-349,054

---

position as of December 31, 1949 (227.8 million rubles net
credit), but was a debtor as of December 31, 1950 (480 million rubles net debit).[53]   She also had other foreign-exchange debts of 229.5 million rubles on the last day of 1949,
while she had a slight (3.9 million rubles) surplus in this
other account at the end of 1950.   These data, for instance,
(suggesting a worsening of the swing-credit and foreign-ex-
change-reserve position by 474 million rubles during 1950)
fit very well into the balance of payments given above for
1950 (suggesting a worsening by 342 million rubles).   Pursuing further the possibility that the above balance of payments
is "correct" and errors and omissions represent primarily
short-term capital movements not included in the capital ac-

count, one could say the following:

East Germany has always been in an extremely precarious balance-of-payments position. She has had no appreciable foreign-exchange reserves to ride out any crisis.[54] Such a crisis existed in 1950, when the unfavorable balance on current account plus capital exports (credit repayments) created a 598.658 million ruble debit in the balance of payments. This gap was partially closed by special credits from Czechoslovakia, Hungary, Poland, and the Soviet Union, the rest probably by using the swing to the limit. What cannot be seen here is, of course, that imports might have been cut drastically below the desired magnitude.

By 1951, the balance on current account had become favorable, but the repayments of earlier credits created another minor crisis. Again, there must have been some relief via short-term capital imports. In 1952, the situation grew worse. Reparations increased, there was some repayment of credits, some granting of credit, and no capital imports, except, one presumes, via the swing. By 1953, the situation was still unfavorable. The current account plus capital exports were still of substantial (negative) magnitude. Now a large Soviet credit provided the rescue. Yet again swing credit must have been utilized.

The effect of the Soviet and other credits plus the decline in unilateral transfers (by considerably more than the decline of commodity exports) made itself felt in 1954 and 1955 in a somewhat improved position. East Germany could repay earlier swing indebtedness by almost 500 million rubles, yet might still have been indebted to over a billion. Events grew worse by 1956, however, when capital exports, especially credit repayments, were larger than the slightly favorable current account balance. Credits from various Communist countries bridged only part of the gap. Again there was need for further accommodating finance.

In 1957, a large Soviet credit more than covered East Germany's capital exports, and averted another potential crisis. Apparently, the East Germans had to cut imports drastically below plans in addition, however. The East Germans at least have hinted this on various occasions, pointing out that they would have liked a larger credit when negotiating in Moscow, but "the Soviet Union cannot carry the burdens of the whole socialist world by herself."[55] Slight repayment of swing indebtedness might have occurred. The East Germans did get a larger Soviet credit, finally, in 1958, thereby substantially overbalancing their debit items and enabling them to possibly reduce swing indebtedness by another 464 million rubles. Still, according to our estimate, there would have remained indebtedness of 727 million rubles in this category, discounting errors.

In 1959, the balance of trade turned negative for the first time and remained so through 1962. In fact, it worsened increasingly over the period. The balance on current account in spite of unilateral transfers in East Germany's favor after the abolition of occupation costs, reflected this development also. East German capital exports added to the problem. Substantial Soviet credits were needed. In fact, of all the credits granted by the Soviet Union to East Germany since 1950, 59.3 per cent were granted and used from 1959-63. Yet even this help was insufficient and did not prevent the renewed increase from 1959-61 of other indebtedness to a cumulative total of 1.9 billion (old) rubles.

In 1962, however, after receiving the largest (Soviet) credit ever, this debt could be reduced to 1.3 billion (old) rubles. At the fifth Plenum of East Germany's Communist Party, Walter Ulbricht announced that for the first time since 1958 East Germany had an active balance of trade and payments

in 1963.[56] This is, indeed, seen to be so. The balances of
trade and on current account improved so substantially that
East German swing indebtedness was completely wiped out. In
fact, East Germany, for the first time ever was in a creditor
position in this category equal to the amount of 292.9 million
(old) rubles given above.

All in all, there can be little doubt that the East Germans do have something like a continuous balance-of-payments
crisis, complete lack of flexibility, and are in major trouble
the moment imports grow a little bit too fast and exports too
slowly. They seem to be in no position to export capital to
the rest of the bloc without the help of the Soviet Union
which must refinance such loans almost immediately. According to the hints given by the East Germans about the constant
concern they have to give to their balance of payments, it
seems quite likely that the above analysis is substantially
correct. And given the huge unilateral transfers of the past,
it is quite understandable that the East German government
does not wish to publish its balance of payments. As the
reader will be aware, the above is only an estimate which can
and must be improved upon as more and better data become available.

FOOTNOTES

[1]The author is aware of two other estimates of the East German
balance of payments, but both are extremely sketchy and make
hardly any use of a wealth of information available. One of
these, for 1951-57, is by Erich Klinkmüller, *op. cit.*, pp. 21-
28, 92, and 174-75; the other can be found in *"Die Entwicklung
des Aussenhandels und der Auslandskreditverflechtung der Sowjetzone,"* Wochenbericht (West Berlin: Deutsches Institut für
Wirtschaftsforschung, 12-6-1957), Nr. 49, p. 197. The latter
contains a balance of payments for 1954-56, plus 1957 Plan,
but it excludes such items as trade with West Germany, reparations, uranium exports, armament imports, and services.

[2]That is, at a rate of 1.5916 rubles/DM for 1950, of 1.2012

for 1951-53, and of 1.8 for 1954-60. (See also note *a* to Table 1.) These are the rates at which official East German
trade data have been made comparable with each other. See
SJDDR 1955, p. 242. Commercial trade data in Tables 3 and 4
are also so expressed.

[3]Karl C. Thalheim, *Die Wirtschaftliche und Soziale Entwicklung
in Ostberlin und der sowjetischen Besatzungszone* (West Berlin:
Osteuropa Institut, Freie Universität Berlin, 1960), 6, p. 17.
Since 1962, however, government imports, i.e., presumably
arms, are said to be included in official statistics according
to DIW, *Wochenbericht*, 16/17, 1963, p. 75. This source bases
its conclusion on different official versions of the report on
the fulfillment of the national economic plan. Since such
discrepancies (670 and 700 million foreign trade DM for 1961
and 1962, respectively) do not appear in the Statistical Yearbooks, however, the data of which are used in this study, it
was assumed that armament imports are still excluded from the
post-1961 data of Table 4.

[4]According to *Informationsbüro-West* (West Berlin) daily bulletin of 9-20-1954.

[5]For the foregoing compare Helmut Bohn, *"Die Aufrüstung in der
sowjetischen Besatzungszone Deutschlands,"* BB (Bonn: BMfgF,
1960), pp. 102-05, 110, 113, 114, 121-24, 126; *SBZ von A bis Z*
(Bonn: BMfgF) *1958*, pp. 332-33, 337, and *1960*, pp. 286-88,
and *The New York Times*, 1-14-1962, p. 13, 4-2-1964, p. 3.

[6]For most recent estimates of East German governmental expendi-
tures at internal prices the reader may refer to Frederic L.
Pryor, *East and West German Governmental Expenditures* (New
Haven: Economic Growth Center, Yale University), mimeographed.

[7]This is acknowledged by the East Germans. See Fritz Fabian,
"Die Zahlungs-und Verrechnungsbilanz der D.D.R. (II)," AH, 11,
1957, p. 399 ("The balance of trade of the G.D.R. shows a surplus on principle"), and *DW*, A, 9, 1964, p. 23. The latter
source reports a statement of Walter Ulbricht to the fifth Plenum of the Central Committee of the Communist Party "that last
year for the first time since 1958 the balance of trade" of
the G.D.R. "has been active." Since the statement was made in
1964, there must have been deficits from 1959-62.

[8]*"Der Aussenhandel mit der tschechoslowakischen Republik,"* Der
Aussenhandel der D.D.R. (West Berlin: IWE--Informations-und
Archivdienst, 4-16-1959), VI, p. 2.

[9]On the chartering of Polish shipping, e.g., for imports from

India, Burma, and North Vietnam, compare *AH*, 10, 1957, p. 374.
On the use of Szczecin see *AH*, 1, 1962, p. 21. Recently it
was reported that "in the last years" Poland has earned annually more than 300 million foreign trade zlotys (i.e., 300
million old or 67.5 million new foreign trade rubles) from
services provided to the G.D.R. See *AH*, 7, 1964, p. 35. This
fits well, indeed, the data of Table 29.

[10]East Germany's former Foreign Trade Minister, Heinrich Rau,
had been quoted as saying that exports to Poland must be reduced, because less is imported from there: *AH*, 2, 1957, page
56. The official government yearbook, *JDDR 1957*, p. 123, also noted that "one cannot overlook" that Poland "did not fulfill her export obligations towards our republic in 1956,"
which caused temporary difficulties and the necessity to make
new arrangements.

[11]The West German government also has reported a passive balance in East German-Soviet trade for 1960 and 1961 due to armament imports. See *S.B.Z. von A bis Z* (Bonn: BMfgF, 1963),
8th revised and enlarged edition, p. 52.

[12]In 1956, 34 per cent of all western currencies were earned
via light industry exports. See *AH*, 10, 1957, p. 368. In
1963, 23 per cent of all exports to the west came from the
light industries, undoubtedly a much larger share than for exports as a whole. See *DW*, A, 36, 1964, p. 42, and Table 8
above.

[13]*AH*, 21, 1960, p. 11. According to a more recent source, the
foreign exchange expended in transport is roughly distributed
like the tonnage transported by the various means of transport.
See *DW*, A, 20, 1965, p. 2.

[14]There are open complaints, however, that these expenditures
are higher than they have to be, 1) because one would not have
to rent foreign railroad cars if the seasonal distribution of
transport were more even, and 2) because the U.S.S.R. sends
imports in cars half empty, the G.D.R. bearing full costs,
though the U.S.S.R. should bear them according to §67 of the
Allgemeine Bedingungen des RGW (General Rules of CMEA). See
AH, 10, 1957, p. 374, and 14, 1960, p. 13. More recently it
was pointed out, e.g., that transport towards East Germany's
east showed in 1963 the same weaknesses as in earlier years
"so that also during the last year it was not possible to carry through foreign trade transports according to the decisions
of CMEA with highest effectiveness." See *DW*, B, 1, 1964, page
11. The same source states that in 1962 the transport volume
fluctuated ± 10 per cent around the average for monthly data

and between +8 and -5 per cent for quarterly data. It stated
further that the contents of one large Soviet freight car is
moved at the Polish-Soviet border into three small cars of
which one "in many instances" remains from 70 - 90 per cent
empty. Another source, *DW*, A, 23, 1964, p. 9, reports the
development of the freight volume across the East German-Pol-
ish border from 1958-62 as follows (visually interpreting a
graph) 100, 114, 121, 127, 141.

[15]According to plan, 82 per cent in 1959, 76.4 per cent in
1960, and 55 per cent in 1965. See *AH*, 16/17, 1959, pp. 35-
36, and *WW*, 5, 1956, pp. 662 and 665. The announced ideal is
to transport half of the volume on own ships as this is the
"symbol of equality in trade relations with the socialist
world." A reduction in the above percentage means less, however, than one might be led to think, because since 1951 a
lower percentage of the foreign trade volume has been shipped
by sea every year. *AH*, 16/17, 1959, p. 33. In 1955, Polish
earnings from shipping services for East Germany amounted to
120 million rubles. See U.N., *Economic Bulletin for Europe*,
vol. 9, No. 1, p. 31. In addition, a significant portion
(50-60 per cent) of sea-going transport went via capitalist
ships still in the early 1960's. See *AH*, 8, 1964, p. 23.

[16]38.8 per cent of the sea volume via Hamburg in 1954, 31.1
per cent in 1957. See *AH*, 4/5, 1958, p. 146. In addition
some went via Szczecin. See *Polish Perspectives* (Warsaw:
Aug.-Sept., 1959), p. 87.

[17]90 per cent have to be paid so according to *AH*, 4/5, 1958,
pp. 145-46. See also *AH*, 12, 1957, p. 438. Foreign ship owners are generally accused of demanding higher rates from East
Germany than anyone else. See *AH*, 16/17, 1959, p. 33. It has
been urged to utilize Szczecin more to save western currencies.
Freight via Szczecin is paid partly in western currencies,
partly in rubles, but loading costs are in rubles. See *AH*, 11,
1961, p. 12.

[18]*AH*, 9, 1958, p. 333. However, the source also states that
East Germany really only lost 48.2 per cent of such currency
earnings, since China, in exchange for foreign trade rubles,
paid 23.3 per cent to facilitate Chinese exports to East Germany.

[19]See *AH*, 11, 1958, p. 394, and 14, 1958, p. 519.

[20]*AH*, 4/5, 1958, pp. 145-46. The first main task is to sur-
pass West Germany in per capita output. The "third main task"
has been vigorously promoted via the so-called *Steckenpferd-
aktion*. East German papers and magazines daily abound in the

"heroic" story of the *Steckenpferd*-workers: The workers of a
nationalized cosmetics and soap plant by that name, at the
time when the government abolished food rationing, "spontaneously met to discuss ways of expressing their gratitude."
Their solution: Work extra shifts, export the output, buy
freighters with the proceeds. This "splendid example of socialist consciousness" has been followed throughout the G.D.R.,
of course. Compare *AH*, 1, 1959, p. 6. In fact, the East German merchant marine has increased from 1 ship in 1951 (1,250
tdw) to 21 in 1957 (40,999 tdw), 82 in 1962 (439,895 tdw), 97
in 1963 (528,542 tdw), and 111 in 1965 (701,625 tdw). The
transport service accomplished rose from 5 million ton-km in
1951 (involving 9,000 tons) to 833 in 1957 (involving 370,000
tons), to 14,303 in 1962 (involving 2.745 million tons); and
to 20,435 in 1963 (involving 4.614 million tons). See *SJDDR
1963*, pp. 307 and 319, *1964*, pp. 323 and 337, and *ND*, 4-2-1964,
p. 8, 5-9-1965, p. 10. At the same time, the tonnage handled
in the Baltic Sea harbors rose from 2.3 million t in 1955
(41.4 per cent Wismar, 30.0 per cent Rostock, 28.6 per cent
Stralsund) to 3.8 million t in 1959 (56.1 per cent Wismar,
25.5 per cent Rostock, 18.3 per cent Stralsund), and to 7.6 million t in 1963 (24.5 per cent Wismar, 66.8 per cent Rostock,
8.6 per cent Stralsund). See *SJDDR 1963*, p. 312, and *1964*,
p. 328.

[21]*AH*, 3, 1960, p. 22.

[22]*AH*, 11, 1958, p. 394. The source also gives a detailed distribution of these figures by type of foreign exchange. (The
East German classification of foreign exchange into broad currency groups, as used in this article, is explained in *Deutsche Finanzwirtschaft*, 7, 1960, p. 216.) An earlier source
had also stated that foreign trade "expenditures for sea and
rail transport annually exceed 400 million rubles." *AH*, 24,
1957, p. 860.

[23]*AH*, 4/5, 1958, p. 145, and *SJDDR 1959*, p. 573. Percentage
figures in the article have been applied to absolute data in
the yearbook. These data are confirmed by *AH*, 24, 1957, page
860, 15, 1959, p. 25, and 18, 1958, p. 632.

[24]It has been reported that in 1956 international freights
were unusually high. See *AH*, 13, 1956, pp. 461-62, and 22,
1956, pp. 782-83.

[25]Since these service imports are directly related to the shipment of imports from the selling country's border to the G.D.R.
it is, of course, reasonable to relate their magnitude to that
of the commodity import volume. The percentages given in

Table 31 correspond almost exactly to the difference between
f.o.b. and c.i.f. imports in, e.g., West Germany's foreign
trade as related to the f.o.b. imports.

[26]See *AH*, 12, 1957, p. 425 and *Polish Perspectives*, Aug.-Sept.,
1959, p. 87.

[27]By engaging in a large scale program of building north-south
canals (to begin after 1965) and railroads (to be completed in
1967) to Rostock. See *AH*, 4/5, 1958, p. 146, *S.B.Z. von A bis
Z* (Bonn: BMfgF, 1965), ninth, revised, enlarged ed., p. 172.
See also p. 105 above.

[28]She is also known to have rented railroad cars to Bulgaria
during the harvest season. *AH*, 23, 1957, p. 835.

[29]See *SJDDR 1964*, p. 337. As to the use of East German harbors by foreign ships, only the following is known: 3,965, or
80.5 per cent of all ships entering East German harbors were
foreign in 1961, 4,018, or 79.6 per cent in 1962, 3,101, or
74.2 per cent in 1963. See *SJDDR 1962*, p. 502, *1963*, p. 318,
1964, p. 336. Hence earnings will hardly have increased on
that account between the three years. East Germany's merchant
marine, however, experienced its largest increases in history:
by 141,339 tdw from 1961 to 1962, by 89,000 tdw from 1962 to
1963.

[30]See *AH*, 16/17, 1957, p. 575, *ND*, 4-29-1959, p. 6, and *10
Jahre Rat für gegenseitige Wirtschaftshilfe* (West Berlin: Informationsdienst West, 5-22-1959), p. 3.

[31]See Erich Klinkmüller and Maria Elisabeth Ruban, *op. cit.*,
pp. 166 ff. See also footnote 15, Chap. 3 above, and Werner
Krause, *op. cit.*, p. 141 which lists annual data from 1949-57
on the exchange of technical-scientific documents. On the
average over the period, East Germany delivered about 25 per
cent more documents than she received. Hence she might have
a (small) export surplus in copying fees (assumed below as 40
rubles per document).

[32]On the basis of evidence given in *SJDDR 1964*, pp. 389-90 (on
the Leipzig fairs) and *JDDR 1958*, pp. 129-30; *1959*, p. 208;
1960, p. 244, and *1961*, p. 265 (on East German fairs abroad).
The magnitudes involved were estimated on the basis of the
number of foreign visitors at the Leipzig fair and the floor
space rented to foreigners. It was assumed that each foreign
visitor spent 400 rubles in East Germany and that each square
meter exhibiting space was rented for 400 rubles for the dura-
tion of the fair.

[33]On the average, till the end of 1957, 34 per cent more experts visited East Germany than went the other way to the bloc
countries. See Werner Krause, *op. cit.*, p. 144. On the other
hand, from 1951-57, on the average 48 per cent more East Germans were studying at bloc colleges than bloc nationals in
East Germany. See *SP*, 10, 1957, inside front cover. Assuming
that experts coming to East Germany and East Germans studying
abroad involve foreign-exchange expenditures by East Germany
and vice-versa for the reversal of direction, East Germany
would have import surpluses on both counts (a 15 per cent import surplus counting heads). It was assumed that each expert
sent or received earns or costs 4,000 rubles per year and the
same amount is involved in receiving or sending students. Foreign travel, on the other hand, was negligible until 1959.
(PI, Nr. 130 [1666], 11-12-1958, p. 8. The West German government estimates East German tourist expenditures abroad in 1958,
e.g., at 5.4 million rubles. See *S.B.Z. von A bis Z* [Bonn:
BMfgF, 1965], p. 436). After 1959, data for the number of
East German tourists travelling abroad were (in thousands) for
1960-63: 160, 215, 265, 290. See *SP*, 4, 1964, graph on front
cover, visually interpreted. Probably, the reverse flow of
foreign tourists to East Germany (including West Germans) has
always been larger. Each tourist was assumed to spend 400 rubles.

[34]This document expressed in 1,000 DM, is only identified as
"HICOG, Berlin 169, 9-10-1951, pp. 75-76." DM-E data have
been translated at the 1951 rate of 1.2 rubles/DM-E. DM-W da-
ta have first been translated into DM-E at the rate of 52.91
DM-E = 100 DM-W. This is also done with DM data in the East
German statistical yearbooks. Compare *SJDDR 1957*, p. 514.

[35]See *SJDDR 1959*, p. 526 and *1964*, p. 339. The East Germans
report having been a member of the Universal Postal Union
since 1952, but being hindered to participate fully because
of, among others, "illegal machinations of France." In 1961,
East Germany shipped 2.7 million kg of letters in transit and
in 1962, 172,540 packages in transit for 30 countries. See
WW, 4, 1964, p. 623.

[36]For this and the other information presented in this section
compare Archiv für gesamtdeutsche Fragen, *Zusammenstellung der
von der "Deutschen Demokratischen Republik" seit deren Grün-
dung (7.10.1949) abgeschlossenen Internationalen Verträge und
Vereinbarungen*, 2. Auflage, April 30, 1960; *S.B.Z. von A bis
Z* (Bonn: BMfgF), *1960*, p. 48, *1962*, p. 51, *1963*, pp. 54 and
113; *JDDR 1956*, pp. 44-45, *1957*, pp. 133-34, *1958*, pp. 106-
107, *1959*, pp. 99-101, *1961*, p. 259; *WW*, 4, 1964, p. 613; *AH*,
19, 1956, p. 687, 24, 1956, p. 867, 4/5, 1957, p. 178, 16/17,

1959, p. 62, 4/5, 1962, p. 78; and *The New York Times*, 5-4-1964, p. 11.   In considering East Germany's relations with other countries, not only *bona fide* diplomatic missions (such as embassies or consulates) have been considered, but also other permanent missions, like officially recognized trade missions, offices of the Chamber of Commerce, and delegations to the CMEA headquarters in Moscow and each of its Standing Commissions.   Sometimes, over the course of time, Chamber of Commerce offices were changed into official trade missions which then in turn took on regular diplomatic functions.

[37]Total exports and imports of improvement, repair trade, etc. (see p. 59 above and footnote 12, CHAPTER 2), but excluding such trade with West Germany, can be calculated for 1958-63 from official data in *SJDDR 1960/61*, p. 574, *1962*, pp. 547-48, and *1964*, pp. 381-82.   Exports were for these years 96.4, 78.2, 64.3, 70.5, 59.5, and 73.7 million (old) rubles, respectively, while imports were 78.7, 70.9, 69.4, 102.0, 114.7, and 110.5 million (old) rubles.   Detailed data for 1958-60 show that between 70 and 84 per cent of this trade was with bloc countries, Poland alone taking between 36 and 53 per cent of exports, Czechoslovakia between 14 and 29 per cent, Hungary between 4 and 17 per cent.   The Soviet Union delivered between 27 and 31 per cent of such imports, Czechoslovakia between 17 and 32 per cent, China up to 18 per cent.   No single capitalist country took ever more than 5.1 per cent of these exports, but Italy once delivered 20 per cent of imports.

[38]This is also generally acknowledged by the East Germans. See, for instance, a State Planning Commission Report in *AH*, 15, 1957, p. 558, or *AH*, 1, 1963, p. 11.

[39]There was reportedly a reduction of Soviet troops in East Germany by 91,000 men between 1955 and 1958, but their strength has ever since been reported at about 400,000.   See, for instance, *S.B.Z. von A bis Z* (Bonn: BMfgF) *1962*, p. 67, *1963*, p. 73, *1965*, p. 66, or *Europa Archiv*, 16, 1963, p. 626. Troops are now stationed in accordance with a treaty in force since May 9, 1957.

[40]Heinrich Rau, e.g., has reported that East Germany received in 1959 some free imports from the Soviet Union as payments for taking care of Soviet troops after occupation costs had been cancelled.   See *AH*, 1, 1959, p. 4.

[41]See *Osteuropa-Wirtschaft*, 2, 1958, p. 135, *JDDR 1957*, p. 119, *AH*, 20, 1957, p. 717, Karl C. Thalheim, *op. cit.*, 12, 1955, p. 23, 6, 1956, p. 27, 1/2, 1957, p. 68, 1/2, 1961, p. 63, and *ND*, 9-6-1962, p. 1, 3-26-1964, p. 1.

[42]The numerous sources to this section are given in the *Supplement*, Chap. II.

[43]The estimating procedure is discussed in detail only for the first Albanian loan, but a corresponding methodology has been employed throughout. In particular, the author has made use of the balance-of-trade data above, fitting total principal and interest payments in both directions to them. Though in the context of western economies it might not be legitimate to link up a favorable balance of trade with the granting of credits, it is roughly true for Communist foreign trade situations, where payment in gold or hard currencies is rare and even payment in rubles is not made, since rubles cannot be used freely in another bloc country due to the rigid bilateral set-up. The new CMEA bank is supposed to correct that latter shortcoming.

[44]See *ND*, 11-28-1964, p. 5.

[45]Naturally, one cannot be sure about this. Communist propaganda always stresses the low interest burden of socialist credit, hence the author has made the most favorable assumptions for the debtor. But it is also conceivable that 2 per cent interest is being charged on the total amount of credit agreed upon from the date of the agreement to the repayment of the last ruble. In this case the effective rate would be considerably higher.

[46]According to prices given in *Supplement*, Chap. II, source 1, Anlage 4, and *Vneshnyaya torgovlya SSSR za 1956 god* (Moscow: Vneshtorgizdat, 1957) p. 91.

[47]Note that the cancellation of state debts, agreed upon in the same set of agreements, did not concern commercial debts from previous special agreements discussed above or from the use of the swing. It concerned such items as payments for SAG discussed in CHAPTER 1. See Anonymous, *"Die Reparationen der sowjetischen Besatzungszone in den Jahren 1945 bis Ende 1953,"* BB (Bonn: BMfgF, not dated), p. 27.

[48]In his speech to the Central Committee of the Socialist Unity Party, Walter Ulbricht announced that no new foreign credits had been needed in 1963, while repayments on a large scale had begun. See *ND*, 2-5-1964, p. 3. Later it was even reported that East Germany in 1964 extended credits (as did Bulgaria, Czechoslovakia, and Hungary) to the Soviet Union for phosphorite mining. See *ND*, 4-24-1964, p. 5, and *WW*, 4, 1964, p. 532.

[49]In light of the prices of complete factories, this estimate
looks very reasonable. Among East Germany's favorite exports
in this branch are sugar and cement factories. A small sugar
factory (1,200 t/day) costs 19 million rubles, a medium one
(1,500 t/day) 20 million rubles, and a very large one (2,500
t/day) 50 million rubles. The Indonesian one had a 2,000
t/day capacity. A small cement factory costs 15 million rubles. See *IWE* of 12-10-1958 and *AH*, 21, 1956, p. 747.

[50]Heinrich Rau has in fact pointed out that the greatest help
countries can give each other in foreign trade comes through
stable prices and long-term, dependable contracts, not credits. See his speech in *ND*, 3-5-1961, p. 3.

[51]It should be pointed out that all credits discussed, including the ones in western currencies, were to be repaid in commodities, often from the production coming from the project to
which the credit was linked. This, as well as the low interest rates, has always been regarded by the Communists as the
chief attraction of "socialist credit." But it is also known
that some of the familiar claims, such as "no strings attached," are not true. The Soviet Union and East Germany, for instance, signed a treaty with Yugoslavia on August 1, 1956,
each granting 350 million rubles of credit, to be used from
1958-62 for the building of an aluminum refinery in Titograd.
It was repayable in not more than 50 per cent of the production, evaluated at world market prices, at 2 per cent interest p.a., over 20 years starting in 1961. Due to political
differences, however, the whole project was never started and
finally called off in the middle of 1958. See *ND*, 8-4-1956,
p. 1, U.N., *Economic Survey of Europe in 1957* (Geneva: 1958),
Chap. VI, p. 58, *Pravda*, 7-1-1958, pp. 2 and 4.

[52]"Apart from special long term loans, socialist countries
grant one another, under their trade agreements, practically
unlimited technical credit which facilitates the exchange of
goods." *Polish Perspectives*, Nov.-Dec., 1958, p. 5. Innumerable accounts in the East German magazine *Der Aussenhandel*
show that East German trade agreements with west and east typically provide for a non-interest bearing swing credit from
one to three quarter million dollars, but that larger interest
bearing swing use is possible. Having probably about 100 trading partners, full use of the swing might, therefore, imply
credit possibilities for 200 million rubles without and considerably more with interest. The new CMEA bank might further
increase the possibilities for such short term credit.

[53]Gerhard Abeken, *"Geld-und Bankwesen in der S.B.Z. seit der
Währungsreform,"* BB (Bonn: BMfgF, 1951), p. 19.

[54]This is also the opinion of a number of western experts. See U.N., *Economic Bulletin for Europe*, Vol. 8, No. 3, November, 1956, p. 83.

[55]See the speech by Prime Minister Grotewohl as quoted in *Osteuropa-Wirtschaft*, 1, 1957, p. 41.

[56]See *DW*, A, 9, 1964, p. 23.

CHAPTER **7** EAST
GERMANY'S
TERMS OF TRADE

East German writers consistently claim that in her trade
relations with East Germany the Soviet Union, because of her
economic and political strength, "has to a high degree been
the giving partner."[1] These writers usually mean by this that
the Soviet Union has favored East Germany in foreign trade
pricing compared to how East Germany would fare when trading
with the west; hence trade with the east is claimed to be
highly desirable for this reason alone. Furthermore, we are
assured, there have not been any economic or political strings
attached to this benevolence.

Western writers, on the other hand, have usually taken
quite the opposite stand. They have claimed that the Soviet
Union has misused her powers cruelly, also in the commercial
realm, that she has exploited East Germany, along with the other satellites, by setting export and import prices to her advantage.[2] Especially, it has been claimed by western writers
that as open reparation deliveries were reduced or abolished,
the terms of trade became more unfavorable, and the exploitation simply took on less obvious forms.

Recently a number of studies of this problem have been
made with the help of Soviet foreign trade statistics.[3] Using
quantity and value data for Soviet exports and imports from
1955 through 1959, various scholars have calculated unit values for various commodities traded by the Soviet Union, in order to see whether and how such unit values differ among different trading partners. It was possible to do this for a
significant portion of Soviet exports, but only for a much
smaller portion of Soviet imports. Assuming that commodities
of comparable type and quality were traded with the different
trading areas, and that the export and import samples were representative of total trade, it could be shown that satellite
countries were indeed the object of Soviet foreign trade price

discrimination. They had to pay more for Soviet exports than
western countries did, and they received less for Soviet imports than western exporters. East Germany, though treated
worse than western countries, was frequently treated better
than other satellites. However, to the extent that the above
assumptions do not hold, the results are less certain.

This chapter represents another and somewhat different
approach to the same problem. It is narrower in scope since
it deals only with East Germany, but is broader in the sense
that it is concerned with East Germany's terms of trade from
1950-63 in general, rather than with the Communist bloc or the
Soviet Union only. Since such a large proportion of East German trade is with the bloc and the Soviet Union, however,[4] the
terms of trade with the Communist areas certainly must strongly influence the over-all terms with the rest of the world as
a whole.

A. THE CALCULATION OF GROSS BARTER TERMS OF TRADE

1. Methodology

For the purposes of this study the gross barter terms of
trade are defined as the ratio of the quantity of commodity
imports to the quantity of commodity exports.[5] Algebraically
we have:

$$\text{Gross barter terms of trade} = \frac{\text{quantity index of imports}}{\text{quantity index of exports}} \cdot 100$$

Quantity indices of exports and imports have been calculated by the author according to the familiar formula of
Laspeyres:

$$\text{quantity index} = \frac{\Sigma p_0 \, q_1}{\Sigma p_0 \, q_0} \cdot 100$$

For this formula p_0 represents the price in the base period,
q_0 the quantity in the base period, and q_1 the quantity in the

current period. Hence it was necessary to evaluate each
year's quantitative export and import statistics (i.e., data
in physical units, such as tons and gallons) at constant
prices of any base period.

    In this instance, the year 1955 was chosen as the base
period. The quantitative export and import data used were
taken from various issues of *SJDDR*.[6] These data do not cover
every single export and import commodity, but were judged to
be a representative sample of the commodities flowing in East
Germany's foreign trade and to cover a very large portion of
the total foreign trade value.[7] The export sample used contained 176 commodities, the import sample 110. The author
made the assumption which is also being made by all Statistical Offices in west and east, that the quantity index derived
from the sample is identical with the index one would derive
with full coverage.

    The major problem for a calculation of terms of trade was
the choice of a price set to be used for evaluating the changing quantities exported and imported in the various years.
Since the author's choice has been West German foreign trade
prices, an explanation is in order. One could, of course, argue that the weighting system used for the construction of export and import quantity indices ought to reflect East German
scarcity-preference relations. Under these circumstances, the
use of West German relative prices could be considered a doubtful procedure, though there might be much in its favor on practical grounds, such as the general unavailability of East German price data or the fact that East German prices, even if
known, do not reflect the East German scarcity-preference relations. The procedure would be doubtful, because it would be
hard to believe that West German relative prices even approxi-
mately reflected the scarcity-preference relations which would
be embodied in the East German price system if it were ration-

al. Though one could argue that at the time of partition factor endowments, technology, and consumers' tastes were very
similar in the two parts of Germany and little time has passed
since, it would not follow that scarcity-preference relations
are still about the same today. For one thing, economic developments since the partition have not been the same in the
two Germanies and real rates of substitution must have diverged increasingly. More important, though individual consumers'
tastes might well be still the same in East and West Germany,
they do not count in East Germany's centrally planned economy.
The planners' preferences have been super-imposed upon those
of the consumers and are certainly very different from them.
If this author nevertheless uses West German prices, it is not
due to neglect of these conceptual problems involved. Rather
it arises from the fact that East German internal prices are
but one possible weighting system for the construction of export and import quantity indices. Scarcity-preference relations in the world at large, as reflected in world market prices, are another one. In fact, world market prices are usually used for purposes of terms of trade calculations, and the
East Germans, though they have never published anything systematically about actual prices paid and received in foreign
trade, have claimed again and again that they are trying to
trade at world market prices or, in the case of the intra-bloc
trade, at prices "closely based upon world market prices."
Hence, one might be justified in using a world market price
set for the purpose of adding physical quantities of diverse
goods. This would involve no assumption about the actual prices at which the East Germans trade, since only relative prices matter here and are needed for the index construction. As
long as intra-bloc trade is based upon world market prices,
this seems a particularly legitimate procedure, for it shows
an acceptance within the bloc for foreign trade purposes of a

weighting system based on world scarcity and preferences, regardless of the fact that scarcity-preference relations may
well be different in individual Communist countries, as well
as within the Communist world as a whole.[8]

The definition of "world market prices," however, is not
an easy task. This author has used 1955 prices of West German
foreign trade, not, as stated above, in the belief that such
prices reflect East German scarcity-preference relations, but
in the belief that West Germany traded at "world market" prices, which reflect world scarcity-preference relations.[9] This
choice was also best on practical grounds, since East and West
German foreign trade nomenclatures are still very much alike.
As a result, the technical problems of evaluation were kept to
a minimum.[10] The only major difficulty arose from the fact
that the West German statistics do not contain a detailed
breakdown of the machine tool category. Hence 1955 world market prices of East German machine tool exports were derived in
a different way: It was possible to assemble, with the help
of a once secret German government document, as well as occa-
sional East German articles, a complete collection of pictures
and technical specifications of the machine tools produced by
East Germany in the mid-1950's.[11] Two engineering experts on
tool and dye machines at the University of Michigan, who were
well acquainted with this type of machinery as well as their
prices, assessed the machinery items, found in East German
statistics, at 1956 world market prices in West German marks,
which were subsequently translated into 1955 prices by use of
separate price indices for cutting and non-cutting machine
tools. This completed the establishment of the price set
which was then used to evaluate the physical units for the
years from 1950 until 1963.[12]

2. Results

The results of the calculations are given in Table 42 be-

Table 42.   A sample of East German commodity
imports and exports in constant 1955 West
German foreign trade prices, quantity indices
of imports and exports, and gross barter
terms of trade,   1950-63

Year (1)	Imports[a] in million (2)	Exports DM-W (3)	Quantity Indices Imports (4)	Exports (5)	Gross Barter Terms of Trade (6)
1950	1,832	1,100	46.5	40.3	115.4
1951	2,014	1,386	51.2	50.8	100.8
1952	2,383	1,527	60.5	56.0	108.0
1953	3,203	1,729	81.4	63.4	128.4
1954	3,660	2,754	93.0	101.0	92.1
1955	3,937	2,726	100.0	100.0	100.0
1956	4,152	3,150	105.5	115.6	91.3
1957	4,832	3,458	122.7	126.8	96.8
1958	5,266	3,742	133.8	137.3	97.5
1959	6,322	4,275	160.6	156.8	102.4
1960	6,571	4,323	166.9	158.6	105.2
1961	6,372	4,538	161.9	166.5	97.2
1962	6,881	4,634	174.8	170.0	102.8
1963	6,495	5,245	165.0	192.4	85.8

Source:

    Cols. 2 and 3 calculated by the author (see preceding
section of text).   Cols. 4 and 5 calculated from un-
abbreviated data which appear in abbreviated form in cols. 2
and 3.   Col. 6 calculated from cols. 4 and 5.

Note:

    [a]It does not follow from these data that East Germany
had a continuous import surplus in real terms.   Rather,
the import sample covers a larger proportion of total imports
than does the export sample of total exports.

low. It seems quite plausible that the physical volumes of
imports and exports should have moved as is indicated by the
sample. We know that East German real GNP increased without
interruption until at least 1959, though by no means at an
even rate, and that East Germany, as a member of CMEA, has begun to abandon autarkic economic policies and to recognize the
advantages of an international division of labor. These factors alone should make one expect a growing trend of both exports and imports. Closer scrutiny reveals particularly
strong increases of imports in 1952, 1953, 1957, and 1959,
both in terms of index points and percentages. The 1953 increase almost certainly reflects the "New Course" in economic
policy after Stalin's death and the uprisings of that year
with the subsequent attempts by the government to placate the
populace. The 1957 upsurge can be explained by an improvement
in the net barter terms of trade, as discussed below, and the
1959 rise coincides with the appearance, for the first time,
of net unilateral transfers in favor of East Germany in East
Germany's balance of payments.[13] The growth rates of physical
commercial imports were smallest since 1960 (even negative in
1961 and 1963), exactly at a time when, as was shown above,
armament imports were probably highest.

The physical volume of exports, on the other hand, increased strongly in 1951, somewhat less in the next two years
and then spectacularly in 1954. It failed to grow at all in
1955, rose strongly in 1956, 1959, and 1963, moderately in
1957 and 1958, and hardly at all in the 1960-62 period. These
developments can all be explained by one or several of the
following factors: the uneven growth of real GNP, the gradual
reduction of real commodity reparation deliveries, and developments in connection with the bloc's economic integration projects. Real GNP, for instance, given the 1950-59 period, grew
strongest in 1951 (11.6 per cent), the growth rate fell in

each of the next two years (to 4.9 per cent in 1953) and rose
again in 1954 (to 5.5 per cent). The rate of growth thereafter averaged 3.7 per cent, but rose to 7.4 per cent in 1959.
It probably was very low in the early 1960's, if it was positive at all.

In particular, the East Germans have reported on many occasions that 1955 exports were held down intentionally with a
view to a faster increase in 1956. This was done allegedly in
order to make adjustment in the economy in line with plans for
international specialization within the bloc. As was pointed
out above, economic production plans of the CMEA nations
starting on January 1, 1956, were the first said to be "attuned" to each other. Though subsequent developments in Poland
and Hungary led to a breakdown of this first large-scale attempt at integration, the movement of 1955 and 1956 East German exports may well have been influenced by these events.
Finally, and certainly not least in importance, one must consider the fact that reparations in real terms were about constant from 1950 to 1952, fell somewhat in 1953 and were cut
drastically in 1954 (by 58 per cent compared to 1953). This
naturally left more to be exported commercially and, given the
enormous magnitude of reparations, can well explain the export
rise of 1954. Reparations were reduced again significantly in
1957 (by 48 per cent compared to 1956) and, except for some
portion of uranium deliveries, were abolished in 1959.

As a result of these developments, gross barter terms of
trade can be calculated as in column 6 of Table 42. In the
opinion of this author, however, one should not place too much
emphasis on the gross barter terms. As is well known, terms
of trade are unambiguous only if certain conditions are fulfilled. One of these would be the absence of productivity
changes. A decline in the terms, resulting from increased efficiency in the production of exports, need obviously not im-

ply an adverse change in real income. But this author is in
no position to conjecture how the factoral terms of trade may
have moved. Nor is he particularly distressed about the meaning of the results in the light of possible productivity
changes. After all, one can always argue that even though
real income may have gone up, as gross barter terms declined
(since productivity increased), it would have gone up by more
if one had not had to share part of the productivity gain with
the foreigner, and this represents an unfavorable movement. In
this sense then, the author would be prepared to argue, one
may neglect productivity changes.

    One may not neglect, however, the existence of other
items in the balance of payments besides commodity trade, unless the balance of trade is zero, i.e., commodity exports
equal commodity imports in value. Following this argument to
its conclusion, one can show that gross barter terms have no
separate meaningful existence apart from net barter terms.
Let us define net barter terms of trade in the usual way:

$$\text{Net barter terms of trade} = \frac{\text{price index of exports}}{\text{price index of imports}} \cdot 100$$

    1) If the trade balance is zero and remains so,

$$Q_x \cdot P_x = Q_m \cdot P_m \ ,$$

where Q_x and Q_m are quantity indices of exports and imports,
respectively, and P_x and P_m are price indices of exports and
imports. In this case net barter terms P_x/P_m, are always
identical with gross barter terms, as defined in this study,
Q_m/Q_x. A change in gross barter terms is in effect the same
thing as a change in net barter terms.

    2) If the trade balance is zero and then becomes posi-
tive because *ceteris paribus* the quantity of commodity imports
declines, the gross barter terms would decline, the net barter
terms be unchanged. But this decline in gross barter terms is
meaningless. The value of commodity exports exceeds that of
commodity imports because either services have been imported

(in which case the country is not really worse off, since the
type of payment for exports has only been shifted from commodities to services) or capital has been exported (in which case
the country is not really worse off except in the short run,
since the timing of payment for exports has only been shifted
to the future).[14] If one adjusted the export quantity downwards (to the extent that exports were already paid by service
imports or will be paid later), gross barter terms would again
equal net barter terms.

    3) If the trade balance is zero and then becomes nega-
tive, because *ceteris paribus* the quantity of commodity exports declines, the gross barter terms would increase, the net
barter terms be unchanged. But this improvement in gross barter terms would be equally meaningless. The value of commodity imports exceeds that of commodity exports, because either
services have been exported (in which case the country is not
really better off, since the type of payment for imports has
only been shifted from commodities to services) or capital has
been imported (in which case the country is not really better
off except in the short run, since the timing of payments for
imports has only been shifted to the future).[15] If one adjusted the import quantity downwards (to the extent that imports were already paid by service exports or will be paid
later), gross barter terms would again equal net barter terms.

    It can easily be shown that combinations of these cases,
and leaving aside the assumption of an initial zero trade balance, all yield the same result: either gross barter terms
move like net barter terms (if the balance of trade is zero)
or they are meaningless (if it is not). Since the above study
of East Germany's balance of payments has established that in
the East German case capital exports plus service imports did
not equal capital imports plus service exports, the gross barter terms as given in Table 42 are essentially meaningless,

unless one also looks at the balance of payments. One could
adjust them by adjusting the quantity indices of exports or
imports, respectively, depending on whether capital exports
plus service imports exceeded or fell short of capital imports
plus service exports. If this is done, one gets a result
which is identical with the net barter terms calculated below.

B.   THE CALCULATION OF NET BARTER TERMS OF TRADE

1. Methodology

Since the official East German Statistical Yearbooks contain data on the value of commercial exports and imports, it
is possible to calculate value indices of exports and imports.
Just as the value of exports or imports is the product of prices and quantities, such value indices can be thought of as
the product of price and quantity indices. This suggests the
possibility for using value indices calculated from the official data and quantity indices derived by the author for a
calculation of price indices of exports and imports. This is
all one needs for the calculation of the net barter terms of
trade, as defined above. If the quantity indices are reasonably "correct" the price indices calculated here would reflect
the prices actually paid and received by East Germany in her
trade with all countries.

2.   Results

The results of these further calculations are embodied
in Table 43. It shows that East German export prices rose
sharply from 1950 to 1951 with a slight downward readjustment
in 1952, while import prices rose throughout. This may well
reflect the impact of the Korean War. In 1953, very likely
as a result of the uprisings, East Germany's bargaining position (in the bloc) was enhanced. Export prices rose to an
all-time high, and import prices declined. Immediately in

Table 43.   Value and price indices of East German
commercial commodity exports and imports,
and net barter terms of trade, 1950-63

Year (1)	Exports Indices		Imports Indices		Net Barter Terms of Trade (6)
	Value (2)	Price (3)	Value (4)	Price (5)	
1950	31.8	78.9	40.0	86.0	91.7
1951	55.8	109.8	51.8	101.2	108.5
1952	57.8	103.2	65.9	108.9	94.8
1953	75.7	119.4	83.8	102.9	116.0
1954	100.2	99.2	93.4	100.4	98.8
1955	100.0	100.0	100.0	100.0	100.0
1956	110.1	95.2	113.7	107.8	88.3
1957	141.7	111.8	137.7	112.2	99.6
1958	147.8	107.6	143.2	107.0	100.6
1959	166.0	105.9	159.8[a]	99.5	106.4
1960	171.4	108.1	173.3[a]	103.8	104.1
1961	176.9	106.2	177.2[a]	109.5	97.0
1962	184.7	108.6	190.6[a]	109.0	99.6
1963	210.6	109.5	184.1[a]	111.6	98.1

Source:

    Cols. 2 and 4 calculated from *SJDDR 1960/61*, p. 573 and
1964, p. 381.   Col. 3 calculated from col. 2, Table 43
and col. 5, Table 42.   Col. 5 calculated from col. 4, Table 43
and col. 4, Table 42.   Col. 6 calculated from cols. 3 and 5.

Note:

    [a]Using the data of the author's estimate of the East
German balance of payments, which shows net unilateral
transfers in favor of East Germany, the author has recalcu-
lated the import value, by adjusting it downward to show, in
effect, some imports at a zero price.

1954, and further until 1956, however, export prices dropped
just as sharply. This may partly have been an adjustment to
the successful crushing of the revolt, making previous concessions unnecessary, but it is certainly also suggestive that
this should have coincided with the large reduction in reparations at that time. It is quite possible that here is reflected the East German inability to quickly find markets for
goods previously exported at a zero price. Possibly export
prices had to be lowered to get rid of production and the Soviet Union was happy to lend a helping hand. The alternative,
of stepping up in East Germany investments of machinery previously delivered to the Soviet Union does not seem to have
been considered favorably.[16] The upward drift of import prices between 1954 and 1957 may be due to a number of forces,
such as an adjustment to reparation reduction, or concessions
to areas of unrest (Hungary, Poland), or to the Suez crisis.

It has been claimed that in 1957 export prices of the
bloc countries to the Soviet Union were raised as a result of
intensive negotiations.[17] The data here are certainly consistent with such reports. But they also suggest that in
years since there has been a partial reversal till 1959 and a
return to about the 1957 position by 1963. Import prices declined similarly from 1957-59 and rose since. This might conceivably have been part of the 1957 price agreement among bloc
members.

C. CONCLUSIONS

East Germany's terms of trade with the rest of the world
improved early during the Korean conflict and deteriorated
near its end. The East German uprising resulted in a dramatic
and stronger improvement in the terms of trade. This improvement was subsequently more than reversed, and the 1953 level
was never reached again. By 1956, net barter terms of trade

were lower than at any time during the period considered.
Thereafter, a gradual improvement set in, which since 1959 has
been partially reversed. In 1963, the terms of trade were
considerably worse than in 1953, though better than in 1956
and about equal to the 1950-52 average.

Has the Soviet Union shifted exploitation from open reparations to the commercial realm? This is a question that
cannot be answered conclusively. The deterioration of the
terms of trade after 1953 (the time of the great reduction of
reparations) to a level below the 1952 mark, as well as the
1950-52 average, would certainly be suggestive of an affirma-
tive answer. One might similarly interpret the deterioration
of the terms of trade since 1959, when occupation costs were
finally abolished. But this observation would also be consistent with the hypothesis that East Germany's terms of trade
with the Soviet Union improved greatly, while those with other
Communist or western countries deteriorated even more, resulting in an over-all deterioration.

The reader will be well aware that, if for no other reason but the serious analytical difficulties embodied in the
use of index numbers, the results must be treated with caution
and only broad conclusions can be drawn. In light of a knowledge of all the relevant facts, however, such broad conclusions may be better than none at all. It is for this reason
only that the author has undertaken this study, for, as Professor Kindleberger once pointed out, if one really worried
about the statistical and conceptual difficulties in measuring the terms of trade, one would abandon the attempt. It
seems to this author, even cautiously interpreting the data,
that it is quite likely that the Soviet Union, between 1954
and 1956, has shifted exploitation to the commercial realm,
but that this extra burden was discontinued in 1957.[18] It is
similarly quite possible, but by no means certain, and in this

author's opinion less probable, that the Soviet Union has been compensated for the abolition of occupation costs after 1958 with price advantages in the commercial realm.

FOOTNOTES

[1] The East German literature abounds in such statements throughout the period considered here. To name just one, see Franz Heiduschat, *"Die Handelsbeziehungen der D.D.R. mit der Sowjetunion,"* *AH*, 21, 1957, p. 750.

[2] See Anonymous, *"Der Aussenhandel der sowjetischen Besatzungszone Deutschlands,"* *Mat.* (Bonn: BMfgF, not dated), p. 12, or Aleksandr Bilimovich, "The Common Market and Comecon," *Studies on the Soviet Union* (Munich), 2, 1962, p. 46: ("The Soviet Union concocts import and export prices to suit its own convenience, using methods of direct compulsion to impose them.")

[3] See, for instance, Jan Wszelaki, "Soviet Price Discrimination in Export to East-Central Europe," *Assembly of Captive European Nations*, 6-7, 1960, Document 207 (VI) Econ.; *idem*, "Economic Developments in East-Central Europe, 1954 until 1959," *Orbis: Quarterly Journal of World Affairs*, Vol. IV, No. 4, Winter 1961; Horst Mendershausen, "Terms of Trade between the Soviet Union and Smaller Communist Countries, 1955-1957," *The Review of Economics and Statistics*, May, 1959; and *idem*, "The Terms of Soviet-Satellite Trade: A Broadened Analysis," *ibid.*, May, 1960.

[4] Between 73 and 78 per cent of the trade volume since 1951 was with Communist bloc countries, 41-49 per cent with the Soviet Union alone. See Tables 3 and 4.

[5] Quite often the inverted form is found in the literature, but this definition has the advantage that, just as with net barter terms, an increase in the relative denotes an improvement in the terms of trade.

[6] *SJDDR 1956*, pp. 519-24, *1957*, pp. 515-20, *1958*, pp. 571-76, *1959*, pp. 480 and 575-80, *1960/61*, pp. 507 and 575-80, *1962*, pp. 483 and 549-54, *1963*, pp. 361-66, and *1964*, pp. 315 and 383-88.
    For a few commodities the author has estimated missing quantitative export or import data for individual years from (in the case of exports) production data (also available in physical units in the same sources) and trade data for previous or later years. Similarly, some data were estimated because they were combined with another series. If, for in-

stance, two types of imports were combined for three years,
but given separately for all other years, with one type always
holding 80 per cent of the combined total, the combined data
were split on the assumption that the make-up of the total
then was like that in the later years. All of these adjustments, however, are minor. Imports exclude armament imports,
exports exclude reparations.

[7]A breakdown by industries of the exports and imports in the
sample shows clearly, for instance, the characteristics of the
East German foreign trade commodity structure, i.e., in order
of decreasing importance we find the exports of the metalworking, basic, light, and food industries, and of agriculture, as
well as the imports of the basic industries, followed by agricultural imports, and imports of light, food, and metalworking
industries.

[8]This has led to the heated discussion in the Communist literature on whether or not intra-bloc trade should be based on
prices reflecting cost-demand conditions in the world at large
or within the Communist world only. See pp. 182-86 above.

[9]The prices were taken, with a few exceptions to be noted below, from the detailed West German foreign trade statistics
published in *Der Aussenhandel der Bundesrepublik Deutschland,
Teil 2, Der Spezialhandel nach Waren mit Angaben für die Her-
stellungs-und Verbrauchsländer, Dezember und Jahr 1955* (Wies-
baden: Statistisches Bundesamt; Stuttgart/Köln: W. Kohlham-
mer Verlag, 1956). "Prices" were arrived at by dividing the
quantity of a product group (such as square meters of all
types of furniture fabrics) into its value. Hence they are
really unit values and not true prices. As is immediately obvious, unit values could change over time without any change
occurring in any price, if the commodity composition of the
product group changes. But this disadvantage is of no concern
here, since only unit values for a given year, 1955, were used.
There is, however, in this case another and similar problem
connected with the use of unit values, viz., possible differences in the commodity composition of a product group not over
time, but over space, i.e., as between East German trade and
West German trade. In that case our evaluation of the East
German product group at the West German unit value might result in a different sum than that calculated from East German
products and West German prices individually. Except in the
case of machinery, where a different solution was found (see
text below), this was not regarded as an important problem,
since the product grouping was sufficiently narrow. The auth-
or has, however, devoted much attention to possible quality
differences between East and West German foreign trade commod-

ities, a problem not specifically connected with the use of unit values rather than prices. The East and West German literature was carefully screened on quality comparisons, and appropriate adjustments were made. The West German export price of gas, for instance, was adjusted downward, since East German gas exported is of lower caloric content.

[10]These were usually problems of conversion between different physical units, if, for instance, exports of cloth were given in terms of square meters, but the price in terms of kilograms. In such cases the author used technical handbooks to establish the correct conversion rate, as, in this case, between square meters and kilograms.

[11]The document, *Die Maschinenindustrie im Deutschen Reich 1943* (Berlin: 1944), contained detailed information (such as pictures of machines, their technical specifications, their places of production) on the 1943 German machinery industry. Since the East Germans, at least until the mid-1950's have constantly complained about the backwardness of their machinery industry, compared to West Germany, it was assumed that the 1955 machine tool production of East Germany was of about the same type and quality and certainly not better, than that of East Germany in 1943.

[12]The actual price set used as well as a list of the commodities included in the sample, can be found in *Supplement,* Chap. III.

[13]Due to the fact that the Russian assumption of the costs of stationing Soviet troops in Germany led to payments in favor of East Germany which exceeded unpaid uranium deliveries by East Germany. Compare Table 41 above.

[14]The third possibility, that unilateral transfers were made in favor of the foreigner, is ruled out by the *ceteris paribus* clause, for, strictly defined, this would amount to a fall of export prices (some exports being exported at the old price, others at a zero price). In this case net barter terms declined as much as gross barter terms.

[15]The third possibility, that unilateral transfers were made in the country's favor, is ruled out by the *ceteris paribus* clause, for, strictly defined, this would amount to a fall of import prices (some imports being imported at the old price, others at a zero price). In this case net barter terms increased as much as gross barter terms.

[16]See the speech by Heinrich Rau, at the 30th session of the Central Committee of the Communist Party, Jan. 30 - Feb. 1,

1957: *"Unsere ökonomischen Probleme und die Verbesserung der Wirtschaftsführung,"* *30. Tagung des ZK der SED* (East Berlin: Dietz Verlag), pp. 45-50. Heinrich Rau mentioned sudden increases in machinery inventories that could not be sold abroad. He contributed this, among other things, to sabotage, in particular to the "counter-revolutionary" ideas of Harich, an East Berlin lecturer and publisher. Harich had suggested to export fewer of the "hens that lay golden eggs," i.e., machinery, and to invest the machines in East Germany instead. Rau scathed the "stinking Harich eggs," and Harich was sentenced to ten years of hard labor in 1957. He was released, however, in December of 1964.

[17]See Heinrich Rau, *ibid.*

[18]It is, of course, still possible that East German terms of trade in 1957 were worse than they would have been if East Germany only traded with the west. But then the author would not believe that they were worse by more than in, say, 1952.

CONCLUSIONS

In this study we were interested in the Soviet bloc efforts at economic integration via the Council for Mutual Economic Aid, using developments in East Germany for illustrative purposes. The results of this inquiry can be summarized as follows.

1. The original and to date (1965) most forceful impetus to changes in the East German economy came in the form of Soviet demands for reparations. These were extracted from East Germany in all the forms envisaged at the Yalta Conference of the wartime Allies, and they exceeded in quantity the amount originally demanded by the Soviet Union. During World War II, the output of the metal-working industries in East Germany had been strongly expanded at the expense of the consumer goods industries. Dismantling drastically changed this abnormal economic structure, giving the consumer goods industries, being less affected by it, a preponderant position. Thereafter, however, in accordance with Soviet reparations demands, the structure of the economy was readjusted toward the wartime 1944, rather than its peacetime 1936 position. After 1946, just as during the war, the light industries were depressed, the metal-working and chemical industries emphatically developed. These internal structural changes can be regarded as the first step in economic integration with the newly formed Communist orbit. A by-product of the reparations policy was, furthermore, a serious retardation of the East German rate of economic growth as compared to West Germany.

2. While immediately after the war a large volume of reparations began to flow eastwards, regular commercial foreign trade relations resumed only slowly. By 1951, they were furthermore, under complete governmental control. In 1936, 17.8 per cent of East Germany's foreign trade volume had been with the later bloc area, and 82.2 per cent with the west. Until

1948, this regional distribution remained unchanged. Between
1948 and 1951, however, there occurred a significant and lasting trade reorientation towards the east, almost exactly re-
versing the previous relationships as to the relative importance of east and west trade. This change was the result of a
number of factors, such as the Berlin blockade, the western
trade embargo, the Korean crisis, and a basic policy decision
by the Communists to integrate East Germany into the bloc.
Since 1951, and in several cases earlier, the trade volume
with all European Communist countries and China has been absolutely and relatively more important than in 1936. (This however, even in 1963, was not true when comparing trade with Poland, defining 1936 "Poland" in present boundaries.) The
same statement can be made for all Communist countries since
1957 and for the "anti-imperialist" areas since 1961. Trade
with West Germany and Berlin, since 1948, has been absolutely
and relatively less significant than before the war. For all
other western countries trade was, since at least 1960, absolutely more, but relatively less important than in the prewar
era.

    3. Integration within the Communist bloc since the lat-
ter half of the 1950's was allegedly strongly promoted by the
Council for Mutual Economic Aid. Within this organization
East Germany, as well as the other bloc nations, were to participate in a grand scheme of international division of labor,
giving up their policy of national autarky and concentrating
on those productions for which there existed comparative advantage. East Germany, in particular, was to give up her emphasis on the mining, metallurgical, and heavy machinery industries, turning to chemicals, labor-intensive machinery,
electro-technical, and fine-mechanical-optical products. This
would require the same kind of economic structure as originally brought about by the Soviet reparations demands. On this

ground one should not expect further <u>drastic</u> changes in the
East German economy due to her involvement in CMEA. This expectation is reinforced by at least two considerations:

First, a study of CMEA history shows clearly a verbal re-
jection of an original emphasis on national autarky. The international output specialization decisions made (whether realized or not) are clearly based on the desire to reap the
benefits of either optimum plant sizes or a given area's comparative advantage. But CMEA history also shows a basic ideological commitment, strengthened by nationalism, to the full
and balanced economic development of each individual nation
(using the law of planned proportional development). This
sets definite limits on how far specialization is carried, if
it is attempted at all (using the law of value). Nothing can
better illustrate this point than the violent and quick reaction by all participants to the Valev proposal of 1964. In
an article in a Moscow University journal, he had proposed, as
a first step toward joint bloc-wide economic planning, the
creation of an integrated economy under CMEA direction in the
Danube-Black Sea area, covering 42 per cent of Rumanian, 34
per cent of Bulgarian, and .05 per cent of Soviet territory
and ignoring national boundaries. Just as the making of one
joint plan in the absence of factor movements has been rejected, the movement of labor and capital across national boundaries is negligible. National plans, separately made, but "attuned" to each other is as far as one is willing to go.

Characteristically, present policy is described as a "middle road" between autarky and complete one-sided specialization
(which <u>would</u> make for drastic structural changes in output and
input use), but that "middle road" is in fact not so much in
the middle and terribly close to autarky.

Second, a study of the methods used to derive at specialization decisions shows great theoretical problems, born out of

the Marxist teachings about value and price. As a result,
there is at present no rational way of making such decisions,
even if the willingness to make them should exist.

4) The study of the East German case then brings results
which are true to the expectation. Even if we do not doubt
the sincerity of attempts at greater economic cohesion within
the bloc, the impact of CMEA so far has been, from an over-all
standpoint, insignificant. Nothing since the reparations era
has brought significant change, regardless of whether we investigate the structure of the labor force, of investments, of
output, or of trade. Given the increasingly obvious growth of
nationalism in Eastern Europe, furthermore, this author does
not expect any significant general structural changes in the
near future. This is not to deny that in the production of
particular items and in trade of particular products or product groups with particular countries important changes have
occurred. They will continue to occur, but their aggregate impact can be expected to remain small.

5) The study of East Germany's balance of payments and
terms of trade finally suggests that East Germany's membership
in the Communist world has been costly. Continual balance-of-
payments trouble, presumably not entirely unrelated to the
east orientation of trade and the bilateral rigidities this
implies, has probably contributed to keeping the significance
of foreign trade in the economy below what it might have been,
reinforcing the slowness of the march away from autarky. Also,
there is considerable suggestion, though not certainty, that
the exploitations of the open reparations era might have been
continued in the middle 1950's via less obvious methods, viz.,
the manipulation of the terms of commercial trade.

This author is not prepared to say that economic integration in the Soviet bloc (as seen through East Germany's example) at this point is of truly great significance. Quite the

contrary is true. It is of marginal importance now, which is not to say that it always will remain so.

A) BASIC (OR HEAVY) INDUSTRIES

    1) Energy
    2) Mining
    3) Metallurgy
    4) Chemicals

        a) basic (inorganic and organic)
        b) pharmaceutical
        c) rubber-asbestos
        d) mineral oil and tar
        e) specialized products (e.g., film)
        f) technical-specialized products (e.g., soap)
        g) plastics
        h) synthetic fibers

    5) Building Materials

B) METAL-WORKING (OR INVESTMENT GOODS) INDUSTRIES

    1) Heavy Machinery
    2) General Machinery
    3) Vehicles
    4) Shipbuilding
    5) Castings and Forgings
    6) Metalgoods
    7) Electro-technical
    8) Fine Mechanics/Optics

C) LIGHT INDUSTRIES

    1) Woodworking and Cultural
    2) Textiles
    3) Clothing
    4) Leather/Shoes/Furs
    5) Cellulose and Paper
    6) Printing
    7) Glass and Ceramics

D) FOOD/DRINK/TOBACCO INDUSTRIES

Industries under (C) and (D) are also referred to as Consumer Goods Industries. For detail see *SJDDR 1959*, pp. 328 ff.

B

Until recently, Soviet bloc foreign trade plans determined as part of different national economic plans, were realized
by legally independent, state-owned foreign trade enterprises
(and in a few exceptional cases under their strict supervision
by producers).[1] They alone could enter into or license (bilateral) agreements with their foreign counterparts, specify-
ing the physical quantities of annual trade and assuring also
their bilateral equality in value terms. (On setting foreign
trade prices see pp. 182-86 above.) The New System of Economic Planning and Administration might change this, but that is
by no means certain and will be ignored in the following discussion.[2] Until recently, after the signing of trade agreements, the State Banks opened for each other accounts record-
ing all transactions in foreign trade rubles. Trade being
balanced bilaterally in the plan, debits and credits in such
accounts should balance at year's end. During the year, a
limited interest-free swing was granted from 5 to 20 per cent
of the trade volume. An imbalance at year's end was discouraged by an interest charge and delivery, within 3 months, of
commodities, gold or hard currencies. Multilateral offset-
ting was hardly practiced and required special agreements of
all involved. Since 1964, this technique has changed, each
member country having one foreign trade ruble account at the
CMEA bank, being credited or debited there for all exports and
imports with other members, receiving or paying continually
interest for imbalances, and receiving bi-weekly statements.
Any positive balance can be used to pay for imports from any
member (but see footnote 48, p. 155 above).

Internally, foreign trade enterprises pay producers or
charge buyers internal prices, while receiving from (or paying
to) the State Bank the internal currency equivalent of foreign
trade rubles. This gives rise to the PAG, as discussed above
(pp. 56, 57, 160-66, 265-70).[3] The payment relations between
foreign trade enterprises on the one hand and other domestic
firms or the government on the other involve, of course, only
a switching of demand deposits. Payment from or into the
State Bank, however, causes a change in the money supply. The
desire for annual equality of exports and imports in terms of
foreign trade rubles (or their domestic currency equivalent)
can thusly be equated with the desire to have no changes in
the money supply arising from foreign trade. Specifically (1)
In case of exports, requiring a PAG from (to) the budget, the
money supply will rise, but the increase in the hands of enterprises exceeds (falls short of) the over-all increase. (2)
In case of imports, requiring a PAG from (to) the budget, the
money supply will fall, but the fall in the hands of enterprises falls short of (exceeds) the over-all decrease.

As an integral part of the foreign trade monopoly, all
Communist countries have established a state monopoly in foreign exchange also. The volume and direction of foreign trade
is, however, independent of internal prices and exchange
rates. Is it true then that any exchange rate is as good as
another and that the frequent exchange rate changes in the Soviet bloc have been perfectly useless exercises?

In the western world, a change of an exchange rate would
certainly affect demand for exports and imports, internal prices, production, and employment. The Soviet-type economy
avoids these effects. The role of a "proper" exchange rate is
rather to assure internal monetary stability. Once the foreign trade program has been determined (i.e., trade quantities
and their foreign trade ruble prices), the official exchange
rate will determine the size of the local currency equivalent
of exports or imports, hence the size of the total money supply change. If exports and imports are always balanced in
terms of foreign trade rubles, any exchange rate would, of
course, be as good as another, since the local currency equivalents would be balanced (at whatever level), and the total
money supply unchanged. If there is temporary imbalance (say,
a seasonal export surplus) or if there is a long-term one
(say, a 10 year capital export), the size of the exchange rate
is not a matter of indifference. A higher rate, R (x rubles
per one unit of domestic currency), would cause in these cases a smaller temporary or long-term increase in the total money supply than the existing rate. These relationships can be
established systematically as follows, denoting exports and
imports in foreign trade rubles as X_F and M_F, their official
exchange rate equivalents as X_E and M_E, and their value in domestic wholesale prices as X_D and M_D. Then the change in the
total money supply resulting from foreign trade equals

$$1) \quad \Delta m_t \;=\; X_E \;-\; M_E \;=\; \frac{X_F}{R} \;-\; \frac{M_F}{R}$$

Assuming that all foreign trade enterprises earn a 10 per cent
profit margin on their trade volume at domestic prices, the
profit margin for exporting enterprises will be .1 X_D and for
import enterprises .1 M_D. The change in (producing and trading) enterprise money balances resulting from foreign trade
then equals

$$2) \quad \Delta m_e = X_D + .1X_D - M_D + .1M_D = 1.1X_D - .9M_D$$

The government budget will receive a PAG from exporting enter-
prises of $X_E - 1.1X_D$ and from importing enterprises of
$M_D - .1M_D - M_E$. These "receipts" can, of course, be negative.
The change in government money balances will, finally, equal

$$3) \quad \Delta m_g = X_E - 1.1X_D + .9M_D - M_E$$

The sum of equations 2) and 3) must equal 1). Using this
framework, let us investigate the consequence of an increase
of R, given domestic prices and a trade program in real terms
(i.e., dollar world market prices).[4]

   a)   the change in the total money supply due to foreign
trade:

   If $X_F = M_F$, Δm_t will be zero regardless of the size of R

   If $X_F > M_F$, Δm_t will be positive, but less so as R rises

   If $X_F < M_F$, Δm_t will be negative, but less so as R rises

   b)   the change in enterprise money balances due to foreign trade:

   If $X_D \geq M_D$, Δm_e will be positive

   If $X_D < M_D$, Δm_e could be positive, zero, or negative

In no case is Δm_e affected by a change in or the size of R.

   c)   the change in government money balances due to foreign trade:

   If $X_F = M_F$, Δm_g will equal - Δm_e. It will be unaffected
by R, be negative if $X_D \geq M_D$, and could be negative, zero, or
positive if $X_D < M_D$

   If $X_F > M_F$, regardless of the relative sizes of X_D and
M_D, Δm_g could be positive, zero, or negative, and any increase
in R would cause a fall in Δm_g

   If $X_F < M_F$ and $X_D \geq M_0$, Δm_g will be negative, but less so
as R rises. If $X_D < M_D$, Δm_g could be negative, zero, or positive, but rises as R rises.

   These considerations clearly establish the reason for
preferring one exchange rate over another: the level of the
exchange rate has internal monetary consequences, even if it
does not affect the trade program itself.[5]

   In practice the Soviet bloc economies have a double set
of exchange rates, for commercial and non-commercial transactions. The former set, based on gold parity, is by far the
most important but relates in no way the internal price levels
of various countries to each other.[6] It is applied to all
commercial exports and imports of commodities and some services (mostly commodity freights). The second set of rates has
been established by special agreements, mostly since 1957.[7]
They are supposed to reflect the purchasing power parity at
the retail price level. These rates are being applied to a)
travel expenses, b) expenditures of diplomatic and trade missions, etc., c) pensions, alimony, inheritances, gift remit-
tances and similar transactions of private character, d) copy-
right, patent fees, and fees for professional services, e) in-

Table 44.   East German exchange rates

Period	Commercial rate		Non-commercial rate[g]	
	$/DM	rubles/DM[b]	$/DM	rubles/DM
1/1/36- 3/31/36[a]	.4023	.4618		
4/1/36- 7/18/37[a]	.4000	2.0080		
7/19/37- 3/24/49[a]		2.1198[c]		
3/25/49- 2/28/50	.3003	1.5916		
3/1/50- 10/29/53		1.2012		
10/30/53- 12/31/60	.4505[d]	1.8000[d]	.2381[e]	2.5800[f]
1/1/61- at least 1/64		.4050[d]		.2580-.3125

Sources:

Bystrov, F.P. and Lopatin, G.S., eds., *International Clearing and Foreign Exchange Relations of the Countries of the Peoples Democracies* (Moscow: Foreign Trade Publishing House, 1956), in Russian, pp. 77, 83, 85; *Statistical Yearbook of the League of Nations 1937/8* (Geneva: 1938), page 231; *SJDDR 1957*, p. 532, *1958*, p. 248, *1959*, p. 248, *1960/61*, p. 246, *1962*, p. 60*, *1963*, p. 60*, *1964*, p. 68*; *Wochenbericht* (West Berlin: Deutsches Institut für Wirtschaftsforschung, 4-7-1961), pp. 59-60; Percy Stulz and Siegfried Thomas, *Quellen zur Geschichte: Die Deutsche Demokratische Republik auf dem Weg zum Sozialismus, Teil I (1945-1949)*, (East Berlin: Volk und Wissen VEB, 1959), pp. 165-69; "Der Aussenhandel der sowjetischen Besatzungszone im Jahre 1952 und Planziffern für 1953," *Mat.* (Bonn: BMfgF, 1953), p. 9; *AH*, 16, 1956, p. 593; 24, 1956, p. 870; 3, 1957, p. 102; 24, 1957, p. 888; and 15, 1961, p. 19.

Notes:

[a]currency unit until 7-23-1948 RM, since then DM

[b]in this book a time-weighted average exchange rate of 1.0983 rubles/RM was used for 1936, of 1.7117 and 1.2643 rubles/DM for 1949 and 1950, respectively.

[c]*Verrechnungseinheiten* VE (accounting units) used in

come from services and sale of property abroad (e.g., rentals)
f) dues to international organizations, g) postal, telegraph,
and telephone fees, h) taxes and similar payments (such as
court costs), i) passenger and freight transport services
abroad.

It is immediately clear that in these instances the exchange rate might well have a direct influence on the volume
of "trade." A depreciation, for instance, may attract tourists and increase foreign-exchange earnings. But probably
such types of demand are very inelastic, and such earnings are
certainly very insignificant.

Much more important is a warning that must be issued at
this point. The existence of the double set of exchange rates
has opened up new and unlimited possibilities for propaganda.
Since 1959, high East German officials, such as Heinrich Rau,
have frequently talked about a rubles/DM exchange rate of
about .96.[8] This rate was explained as a "purchasing power
parity" rate, derived from the fact that "really" 4.18 DM
equal \$1 (non-commercial rate) and each \$1 equals 4 rubles
(commercial rate). Obviously, one can in this fashion translate DM into rubles at any desired rate and then arrive at a
trade figure (for propaganda purposes) of any desired magnitude. For instance, translating DM at the non-commercial rate
into forint (3.733 ft/DM) and then into rubles at the old commercial Hungarian-Soviet rate (.341 rubles/forint), a ruble/DM
rate of 1.27 can be calculated. Doing the same via zlotys

East-West German trade were identical to RM until
6-17-1948 (West German currency reform), to DM-W since. The
exchange rate of rubles/VE used is 2.1198 till the West German currency reform, and 1.2619 since (DM-W gold content
.211588 g).

[d]equal to gold parity after East German definition of 1
DM equal to .399902 g pure gold.

[e]in effect since at least 12-10-1957.

[f]in effect since 4-15-1957

[g]On the occasion of the Leipzig Fair a special premium
is available for personal expenditures of visitors:
100 per cent of the non-commercial rate for suppliers of dollars, pound sterling, and Swiss francs, and between 80 and 95
per cent for all others. The non-commercial rates (xDM per
one foreign currency unit) with all western countries and Communist countries, except Poland, Yugoslavia, and (before 1961)
the U.S.S.R., are depreciated relative to commercial rates.

(non-commercial rate 3.931 zlotys/DM and old commercial rate 1 zloty/ruble), one derives a ruble/DM rate of 3.93.[9]

Exchange rates in force at various times in East Germany are given in Table 44.

FOOTNOTES

[1]Just as the rough material-balance-type planning is to be improved by elaborate input-output planning via electronic computers, experiments with more sophisticated foreign trade optimization models are now being carried out in several bloc countries. See *The American Review of Soviet and Eastern European Foreign Trade*, 1, 1965, pp. 19-25.

[2]"To further develop creatively the foreign trade monopoly," which in the past has isolated producers from foreign markets, exports in East Germany may, after 1-1-1965, also be carried out by producers without the supervision of the state's foreign trade enterprises, the optical firm Zeiss being the first one awarded the privilege. In Hungary, several firms have had this right for several years, in Poland it was just given to the Cegielski machinery plant. It is hoped that contact between producer and user can increase trade as well as improve production quality and servicing. See *WW*, 8, 1964, pp. 1233ff, Free Europe Committee, *Polish Press Survey*, 6-3-1965.

[3]This again is in the process of change. In East Germany, under the New System of Economic Planning and Administration, producers are to get amounts differing from the internal price after 3-5-1965, depending on the size of the DM equivalent of foreign trade rubles, the type and the destination of exports. The idea is to encourage and reward producers to take up contacts with ultimate buyers, improve quality and trade direction. Ultimately, the producer is to get paid the DM equivalent of the foreign price minus the foreign trade enterprise profit margin, abolishing the PAG completely. See *DW*, 17, 1965, p. 12, *AH*, 5, 1965, *Beilage "Recht im Aussenhandel."*

[4]In the case of the U.S.S.R., a rise of R would mean a rise in the $/ruble rate. For the other bloc countries the consequences shown appear only <u>given</u> foreign trade ruble prices, i.e., given the $/ruble rate. Hence a problem: As long as the $/ruble rate is unchanged, a change in any ruble/local currency rate (e.g., because <u>that</u> country changes the gold content of <u>its</u> currency), will affect money balances as indicated in the remainder of this section. If, however, a ruble/local currency rate changes because of a change in the ruble's relation to the dollar and all currencies (e.g., because the U.S.S.R. changes the gold content <u>of the ruble</u>), that coun-

try's money balances are normally unaffected (foreign trade
ruble prices might double, while the ruble/local currency
rate, just as the ruble/$ rate, doubles). One should there-
fore, consider a bloc country's exchange rate change only then
as relevant to money flows, if the new exchange rate, corrected for a change in the $/ruble rate, differs from the old
rate.

[5]It is, therefore, completely out of place to interpret the
depreciation of a Soviet bloc exchange rate as an attempt to
increase exports and domestic output and employment. An exchange rate revaluation has no effect on the volume, direction, and composition of foreign trade. It seems similarly
out of place to see in an exchange rate change the means to
exploiting the trading partners. Foreign settlements, i.e.,
the foreign trade ruble accounts, are in no way affected.
Therefore, foreigners are just as uninterested in the exchange
rate as are the domestic partners of the trade organizations,
i.e., producers of export goods or purchasers of import goods.
This statement must be qualified only for the case of non-commercial transactions and of future changes noted in footnote
3.

[6]There is, however, considerable confusion as to this matter
in the Soviet bloc literature. An East German writer, G.
Oehme, claimed, for instance, that "the gold content of one DM
was determined according to its purchasing power." See *AH*,
13, 1956, p. 465 (italics mine). Another writer, Hans Jürgen
Nitz, commented that "gold content and exchange rate have
nothing to do with purchasing power." See *AH*, 11, 1957, page
401 (italics mine). More recently L. Rouscik has reported
that CMEA's Commission for Economic Problems is working on Soviet bloc purchasing power parity rates. See *AH*, 15, 1960,
p. 24. They are reported to base such calculations on a sample of 2,000 consumer goods. See *Polish Perspectives*, 6,
1963, p. 7.

[7]On February 8, 1963, a multilateral treaty on non-commercial
transactions was signed in Prague by the Finance Ministers of
the 4 Asiatic Communist countries and of 8 European ones (only
Yugoslavia excluded, but including Albania).

[8]Rates of .9524, .9562, and .9843 were used in *ND* of 12-6-1959,
p. 1, and of 1-8-1960; in *DW* of 1-28-1960 and in the *Seven-
Year-Plan Law*. For the official rates see Table 44.

[9]Another problem might be mentioned at this point. Frequently
one encounters apparently equally official, but inconsistent
foreign trade statistics for a given country and a given year.
This derives from a unique practice in the Soviet bloc, viz.,

to revalue all previous foreign trade ruble (etc.) statistics
after each change in the gold content of the ruble (etc.).
This practice is rationalized as follows: foreign trade prices are "really" dollar world market prices, with some corrections, and expressed in rubles via the $/ruble gold parity. A
change in the gold content of the ruble does not change these
world market prices, but it does change their ruble equivalent. Hence trade in world market prices may be of constant
volume, yet there is a sharp discontinuity in the foreign
trade ruble series at the time of the ruble gold value change.
Hence all earlier trade values are revalued for comparability.
If, for instance, exports were $1 million for three consecu-
tive years and the ruble/$ exchange rate is 4 in year 1, 1 in
year 2, and 2 in year 3, an uncorrected foreign trade ruble
series would be 4, 1, and 2 million rubles, giving a totally
wrong impression. In actual practice the official statistics
would list exports in year 1 as 4, in year 2 for years 1 and 2
as 1 and in year 3 for years 1 through 3 as 2. Any one of
these sets is fine for intertemporal comparisons, but cannot
be used for international comparisons (here one should use 4
for year 1, 1 for year 2, and 2 for year 3), and one can use
neither the original nor the revalued data in the national income accounts without adjustments for the PAG gap.

APPENDIX C BASIC PRINCIPLES
OF THE INTERNATIONAL
SOCIALIST DIVISION OF LABOR*

RESOLUTION OF THE REPRESENTATIVES OF THE COUN-
TRIES OF THE COUNCIL FOR MUTUAL ECONOMIC AID

1. The Community of the Countries of Socialism and the International Socialist Division of Labor

The socialist world system is the social, economic, and
political community of free sovereign peoples advancing toward
Socialism and Communism, united by a community of interests
and goals and by inseparable links of international socialist
solidarity. The necessity of joining together closely the socialist countries in a system stems from objective laws of
economic and political development. The community of socialist nations is based on the same economic foundation created
in every country: the collective ownership of the means of
production; on the same type of state apparatus: the power of
the people with the working class at the top; and on a uniform
ideology: Marxism-Leninism. The united efforts of the peoples of the socialist community are directed toward the construction of Socialism and Communism, the vigorous development
of the economy of each country, and thereby of the system as a
whole, the defense of the revolutionary achievements against
the machinations of the imperialist reaction, and the securing
of a firm peace among peoples. The socialist world system has
entered a new phase of its development.

The joining together of the socialist nations in a united
camp and its ever increasing unity and continually growing
power will secure the full victory of Socialism and Communism
within the whole system. The community of the countries of Socialism realizes its goals by an all-embracing political, economic, and cultural cooperation. In this all socialist countries are strictly guided by the principles of full equality,
mutual respect of their independence and sovereignty, and of
brotherly mutual aid and mutual advantage. In the camp of Socialism nobody has, and nobody can have, any special rights
and privileges. Observation of the principles of Marxism-Leninism and of socialist internationalism is an indispensable
condition for the successful development of the socialist
world system.

---

*The following official statement has been translated by the
author from *Neues Deutschland* of June 17, 1962, pp. 5 and 6.

As V.I. Lenin predicted, the countries of victorious Socialism are exercising their decisive influence on the course of the social development in the world especially through their economic development. Thanks to the advantages of the new social order, to the active participation of the working masses in the construction of Socialism and Communism under the leadership of the Communist and Workers' Parties, and to their inseparable friendship and brotherly cooperation, the socialist countries have reached, in a historically short period, creative successes never heretofore experienced in the areas of production, science and technology, and the improvement of the living standard of the workers. In every socialist nation, national plans of economic development are being worked out. These are based on the concrete conditions of the country and its political and economic tasks set by the Communist and Workers' Parties. They also consider the needs and possibilities of all socialist countries. The new social order makes it possible to combine organically the development of the national economy with the development and strengthening of the socialist world economic system as a whole. The successes of the latter depend on the contribution of each single country.

The socialist countries consider it their international duty to direct their efforts toward the achievement of a high rate of growth of industrial and agricultural production of each country . . ., toward gradual equalization of the economic levels of development, and toward the successful solution of the task of surpassing the capitalist world system in the absolute volume of industrial and agricultural production, and then exceeding the economically highly developed capitalist countries in per capita production and the living standard of the workers. The solution of these tasks demands the maximum development of the creative abilities and initiative of the people of each socialist country; the industrial development of all socialist countries; increased productivity of social labor everywhere; uninterrupted technical progress; continual improvement in the practice of economic planning and in the utilization of collective experiences; and the enlarging and deepening of economic cooperation among socialist countries. The main road toward the further upswing of the socialist world economy lies in combining the efforts for the development of the national economy of each single country with the mutual efforts for the strengthening and widening of economic cooperation and mutual aid.

Among the countries of Socialism several forms of economic cooperation and mutual assistance have developed and are being perfected: coordination of national economic plans, specialization of and cooperation in production, international socialist trade, granting of credits, technical aid and scien-

tific-technical cooperation, cooperation in the construction
of economic objects, development of natural resources, and
others. The organizational bases of economic cooperation are
also being continually perfected: the collective organ for
the organization of this cooperation, the Council for Mutual
Economic Aid, has been strengthened. The strengthening and
widening of the economic relations of the countries of Socialism will favor the development of the objective tendency,
shown by V.I. Lenin, toward the future creation of a Communist
world economy, directed according to a uniform plan by the
victorious workers.

In the process of the economic and scientific-technical
cooperation of the countries of Socialism, a new type of international division of labor is being born. In contrast to
the international capitalist division of labor, which expres-
ses the relationship of exploitation of the weak by the strong
comes about spontaneously in the course of a bitter competi-
tive struggle and of the expansion of the capitalist monopo-
lies, deepens the unequal status of economic development, and
leads to a crippled one-sided structure of the economy of the
less developed countries, the international socialist division
of labor is being realized consciously and according to plan,
in accord with the life interests and tasks of the harmonic
and all-round development of all socialist countries, and it
leads to the strengthening of their unity. The planned international socialist division of labor contributes to the maximum utilization of the advantages of the socialist world system, to the determination of correct proportions in the national economy of each country, to the rational location of
productive factors with respect to the socialist world system,
to the effective utilization of labor and material resources,
and to the strengthening of the defensive power of the socialist camp. The division of labor must guarantee to each socialist country a dependable market for the specialized products and the supply of the necessary raw materials, semi-finished products, equipment, and other goods.

The aim of the international socialist division of labor
consists in increasing the effectiveness of social production
influencing the attainment of a high rate of growth of the
economy and of the welfare of the workers in all socialist
countries, in industrialization and the gradual overcoming of
the historically given differences in the economic levels of
development of the socialist countries, and in the creation of
a material basis for the more or less simultaneous transition
to Communism. The socialist international division of labor
contributes in every historic phase to the realization of the
main tasks faced by every single socialist country and by the
socialist world system as a whole. It is being built with
consideration of the world-wide division of labor. With the

development of the economic relations to all countries of the
world, the socialist countries are strengthening the material
basis of peaceful coexistence of the two social-economic world
systems. The Communist and Workers' Parties of the socialist
countries are functioning as the initiators and organizers of
the international socialist division of labor. The development and perfection of it is part of the scientifically founded economic policy of the Communist and Workers' Parties of
the socialist countries.

    The socialist countries have achieved significant pro-
gress in the development of the international division of labor. In accord with the recommendations of CMEA, the international specialization of and cooperation in production is being expanded in machine building, in the chemical industry, in
the production of some types of products of ferrous and non-
ferrous metallurgy, and in other branches of industry. The
volume of mutual deliveries of commodities among the socialist
countries is growing at a rapid rate; in 1960 it increased
relative to 1950 to more than threefold. After the consulta-
tion of representatives of the Communist and Workers' Parties
of the member countries of CMEA (May, 1958), the coordination
of the national economic plans was further developed as the
most important form of economic cooperation of the socialist
countries. At the same time, the socialist world system has
thereby at its disposal favorable possibilities of organizing
a far-reaching division of labor among the countries belonging
to it, especially in the areas of specialization of and cooperation in production and the better utilization of their advantages. Especially great possibilities in this context are
opened up in connection with the working out of long term development plans for the national economies of the socialist
countries.

    The socialist world system is promoting, in the practice
of international economic relations, actively the realization
of the principles of sovereignty and of equality, and of mutual advantage and of friendship among peoples. The expansion
of the economic cooperation of the socialist nations with the
countries of Asia, Africa, and Latin America, which is based
on these principles, is serving as an important factor in the
independent economic and political progress of the young nations. The socialist world system is exercising in the present time an enormous influence on the entire development in
the world. It is becoming the decisive factor of progress of
human society.

2.   Coordination of National Economic Plans - Basic
Instrument For the Successful Development and Deepening of the International Socialist Division of Labor

The experiences in the development of the socialist world
economic system show that the coordination of national economic plans is the basic instrument for the planned deepening of
the international socialist division of labor and for the ever
tighter unification of the productive efforts of the countries
of Socialism in the present era. The coordination of plans is
a voluntary, joint, and planned activity of the socialist nations. It is directed toward the maximum utilization of the
political and economic advantages of the socialist world system in the interest of securing the fastest possible victory
of Socialism and Communism. It facilitates the realization of
the policy of the Communist and Workers' Parties, which is
built upon the scientific principles of Marxism-Leninism and
the foundation of a thorough analysis of the possibilities for
and requirements of the development of the economy. As the
experiences of the economic cooperation of the member countries of CMEA show, the coordination of plans must be directed
toward the realization of the following interdependent objective principles of development of the international socialist
division of labor: _____ correct consideration of the objectively necessary proportions of the economic development of
each country and of the socialist world system as a whole,
which contributes to the balancing of the economy of each
country; _____ securing of a high economic effectiveness of
the international socialist division of labor, which finds expression in a fast growth rate of production and in the greatest possible fulfillment of the needs of the population in
each country with a minimum expenditure of social labor; _____
securing of the connection between international specialization of production and the complex (diversified) development
of the economy of the individual socialist countries in the interest of the fullest and most expedient utilization of the
natural and economic preconditions of production, inclusive of
labor reserves; _____ gradual overcoming of the historically
given differences in the economic levels of development of the
individual countries, especially through industrialization of
the countries with relatively low level of economic development on the basis of the maximum utilization of the internal
possibilities of each country as well as of the advantages of
the socialist world system.

The coordination of the national economic plans makes it
possible to guarantee continual agreement between the steeply
growing and structurally changing social needs and the development of material production in every country and the whole
socialist world system. It must be primarily concerned with

the most important branches of production, in which international specialization and cooperation is playing, and will continue to play, an increasing role . . . . It must also be concerned with the transport system, which mediates the international exchange of commodities.

The coordination of plans will gain ever-increasing importance for the expansion and strengthening of the relations
among the national economies of the socialist countries and
for the securing of the planned enlarged reproduction in the
individual countries and therewith in the socialist system as
a whole. The mutual relations among the economies of the individual countries, which follow from the division of labor,
must be strong and permanent, because their interruption, even
by only one country, leads inevitably to the impairment of the
economic rhythm in the other socialist countries. In the
course of coordinating the national economic plans, one must
consider to a maximum possible degree the necessity of guaran-
teeing, within the framework of the socialist world system,
the production of the most important products in those quantities which are necessary for the fulfillment of the needs of
the socialist countries and for the continual development of
their trade with other countries.

The proportions and the directions of the international
division of labor, through which the highest effectiveness of
social production is reached in each socialist country and in
the socialist world system as a whole, are changing under the
influence of numerous factors, primarily of technical progress.
A consideration of the basic trends of technical development
and their economic consequences constitutes the most important
part in the working out of long term plans by the countries
and in the coordination of these plans. An important method
of coordination of national economic plans, and of specialization of and cooperation in production among the socialist
countries consists in the joint collection of data on production and consumption of the most important types of products
in the whole socialist camp or in a group of interested countries. It also involves the working out of consolidated economic balances, analyses, and variants of the solution of individual economic problems. The necessity of equilibrating
the balance of payments also has to be considered, while coordinating the plans for the development of the national economy. . . . The continual improvement in the effectiveness of
the coordination requires that it _____ occurs bilaterally as
well as multilaterally. In this connection, it is considered
that in the future the importance of multilateral coordination
will grow; _____ is concerned primarily with long-term plans,
which makes possible to plan for necessary changes in structure, in production technology, etc., in the interest of deepening and perfecting the international socialist division of

labor; _____ occurs while the individual countries are drafting the plans; _____ entails measures which guarantee the fulfillment on the part of the countries of the coordinated obligations with respect to volume and timing of mutual deliveries, to the quality and technical level of the products to be
delivered, etc.; _____ considers common measures by a number
of countries for the solution of major economic and technical
problems.

The ever more comprehensive coordination of the national
economic plans of the socialist countries presupposes the attainment of uniformity in methodological principles of plan
index construction and of statistical data collection in these
countries, and, on this basis, of comparability of these indices.

3. The Main Direction of the Rational Division of Labor in the Most Important Branches of Production

Further perfection of the international socialist division of labor on the basis of the coordination of plans presupposes the accelerated development of such progressive forms
of the division of labor, as specialization of and cooperation
in production within the socialist camp. Specialization among
nations means: concentration of the production of similar
products in one or several socialist countries for the satisfaction of the needs of the interested countries, while simultaneously improving the technical level and organization of
production, as well as creating strong economic relations and
production cooperation among the countries. It leads to an
increase in the volume of production, to a decrease of prime
costs, to an increase in labor productivity, and to an improvement in the quality of the products and their technical characteristics. Because international specialization of and cooperation in production appear as active factors of technical
progress, they promote the fast industrial development of all
socialist countries. . . . They are of great economic importance for the development of all branches of the national economy, especially for the development of machine building, of
the chemical industry, and of ferrous and non-ferrous metallurgy. It is possible to achieve, on the basis of specialization,
a rapid initiation of production of the latest types of products corresponding to modern trends of technical progress.

A wide-spread program of establishing norms, types, and
standards within a country, as well as internationally, is a
very important precondition for the comprehensive deepening of
specialization and cooperation. This should primarily concern
materials, parts, components, and finished products, for which
it is expedient to organize mass production and production in
large series so as to fulfill the needs of several countries.

The most important conditions for the pursuit of the most rational directions of the international division of labor in the raw material, fuel and energy branches of industry, as well as for the attainment of a high rate of growth of these branches, are the following: _____ enlargement of the own raw material and energy basis, especially through intensifying geological prospecting efforts concerning places of deposits and improving the effectiveness of such efforts. They can, if necessary, occur through collaboration of several countries in large, long-term phases; _____ all-around intensification of production of the types of raw materials in deficit in the socialist camp in all countries under consideration of natural and economic conditions; _____ exchange of progressive technical experiences in the areas of producing and frugally using individual types of raw materials, of increasing the coefficient of extraction of natural resources where deposits are presently being mined, and of increasing the degree to which useful components are gained from the raw material mined; _____ mutual aid in enlarging the raw material branches of industry, especially through financial participation of those nations which are interested in the products of these branches; _____ development of technology in the areas of fuel and raw material production, and of the production of construction materials, with the goal of decreasing production costs, increasing the quality of already existing types, and introducing new, especially synthetic, types of fuels and materials; _____ complex utilization of the water resources of the countries for the development of the energy industry, of water transport, and of irrigation and melioration.

The effectiveness of utilizing raw material and energy resources depends to an important degree on the costs of transporting the raw materials to the place of use. A decrease of these costs can be achieved by: _____ preliminary processing of raw materials directly at the place where they are found; _____ processing of raw materials directly at the place where they are found up to such a degree that minimum costs are guaranteed for production and subsequent transport, according to the conditions and needs of the countries, and on the basis of agreements among them; _____ development of the most effective types of transportation, especially of electric energy transmission lines and pipeline transport, as well as continual improvement in the technical level and productivity of all types of transportation.

In coordinating the plans for the development of the most important branches of the national economy of the countries it is expedient to also consider the following:

a) The international socialist division of labor in the Fuel and Energy Branches will become ever deeper and will play

an increasing role for fulfilling the energy requirements of
the socialist countries. It presupposes: _____ development
of the production of electric energy in the socialist camp as
a whole at a rate which surpasses the rate of the development
of industry; _____ development of energy-intensive industrial
branches, especially in proximity to cheap energy sources, in
order to reduce losses of electric energy and to achieve sav-
ings in the construction of electric energy transmission
lines; _____ reduction of coal transport for energy purposes
to such a degree as appears profitable when replacing this
transport by direct transmission of electric energy via transmission lines; _____ gradual transition to unified energy systems of a group of countries as one of the important progressive directions of the division of labor and of the cooperation of social labor in the socialist camp. The unification
of energy systems of the socialist countries presupposes the
expansion of cooperation with respect to mutual deliveries of
electric energy and to the construction of large energy capacities and transmission lines.

The directions of the international socialist division of
labor in this area may change through the discovery of new
types of energy or energy sources, available to all countries,
as well as through a fundamental change in the way of utilizing the aforementioned classic sources of energy.

b) The development of the international socialist division of labor in the area of Metallurgy must contribute maximally to a rapid increase in the production of ferrous and
non-ferrous metals in the necessary assortment, in order to
satisfy the growing needs of the countries and to decrease the
production costs of metal. The division of labor in the metallurgical industry is determined by the necessity to develop
this branch in all socialist countries in accordance with existing raw materials, technological fuels and energy sources
or with the possibility of an expedient raw material import
from other countries. It is expedient to develop metallurgy
with all its production phases especially in those countries
which are fully, or at least substantially, endowed with ores
and technological fuels, or at least with one of these most
important types of raw material. As a result of the development of the international socialist division of labor in the
area of ferrous metallurgy (including the production of metallurgical raw materials), the proportion of semi-finished and
finished products (pig iron, rolled steel, pipes, etc.) in the
international exchange of commodities of this industrial
branch increases to an optimally possible size. The division
of labor in the metallurgical industry should expediently be
carried out in such a fashion as to promote an increase in the
concentration and an improvement in the technical-economic indices of labor of the metallurgical industry in the socialist

countries.

Because of the continual enlargement of the assortment of
finished products of ferrous and non-ferrous metallurgy, and
because of the unequal demands of modern industry for different rolled steel profiles, steel qualities, and individual
types of non-ferrous metals, it is, however, expedient to optimally combine large metallurgy combines with medium and small
capacity plants or departments, which correspond to the latest
technical level and produce smaller quantities of finished products. In order to achieve an optimum series of production and
thereby the most effective utilization of rolling mill equipment in all countries, it is expedient to specialize production
of rolled steel according to profiles and to then exchange the
appropriate rolled steel profiles. In order to create the conditions for the saving of metal in machine building and other
branches, the production of high quality steels, sheets, pipes,
and bent and other progressive rolled steel profiles should be
considerably enlarged on the basis of international specialization.

c) The production of Chemical Products, especially of
plastics and other synthetic materials, as of mineral fertilizers, is to be developed expediently in all socialist countries at an accelerated rate. Every socialist country devel-
ops the production of chemical products primarily from its own
raw materials. Further, the production of products is also developed from such raw materials, as are advantageously utilized
in spite of their transport over longer distances and the processing of which guarantees their complex utilization. The enlargement of the product assortment of the chemical industry
and the required creation of large units of production presuppose the deepening of the international specialization and economic cooperation in this branch, especially for productions
requiring large investments and special types of equipment, and
they presuppose exchange within the product assortments (dyes,
laboratory chemicals, pharmaceutical preparations, etc.).

d) The Machine Building Industry is developing in all socialist countries with utilization of the advantages of international specialization and cooperation. While realizing specialization, the necessity of an accelerated growth of the machine building industry in those countries in which it is still
relatively little developed, has to be considered. The increase of the volume of machinery production, with simultaneous
creation of new branches and types of production, continual
widening of the assortment, and improvement of the technical
level of the products, requires the continual deepening of international specialization and cooperation in this branch.
Specialization and cooperation are an important condition for
the more rapid introduction of progressive technologies, for

the complete mechanization and automation of production, and
for the production of the entire nomenclature of technically
modern types of machinery in the socialist camp and their continual technical perfection.

The specialization of production of machinery among the
socialist countries must not be restricted to a few individual
products or types of one product. In the long run, it is expedient to concentrate on the specialization according to major groups and types of machine building products (products
that are similar by construction and technology) as well as on
the specialization of and cooperation in production of complete factories and of equipment for entire assembly lines.
This creates better conditions for the concentration of production, the introduction of modern techniques and technology,
and also for the improvement of the organization of production
and the application of standardization, classification, and
unification. One of the long-term trends of the division of
labor in machine building consists in the specialization of
and cooperation in the production of component groups and individual parts. The production of all the parts necessary for
the complete product does, of course, not necessarily have to
occur in that country which is specializing in the production
of the finished product. The production of individual parts
and component groups should preferably occur in specialized
plants. In the case of specialization according to products,
the countries, which are producing certain types of products
for other countries, must guarantee to fully cover the demands
of the consuming countries, including the demand for products
needed for the completion of other products. They must also
guarantee a high technical quality of the produced machinery
and equipment and a supply with spare parts.

In countries with insufficient metallurgical basis it is
expedient to develop primarily the production of products that
are not metal-intensive and are relatively labor-intensive.
The metal-intensive, as well as also the labor-intensive types
of machinery products, should be developed in those countries
which have at their disposal a developed metallurgical basis.
In general, the specialization of the machinery industry of
each country, especially of the production of technological
equipment, is carried out with consideration of the existing
structure of the national economy of the countries and the
planned progressive change of this structure. . . . It is being carried out with consideration of the all-round increased
utilization of new construction materials, especially of materials produced by the chemicals industry.

e) The specialization of production of Industrial Consumer Goods is regarded as expedient, if the total demand for individual assortments or models in the particular country is

presently lying below the optimum for rational production at
the particular technical level and is expected to remain there
for the next years. The international specialization of the
production of consumer goods must occur on the basis of agreements among the interested countries with the goal of maximum
satisfaction of the needs of the population of these countries,
of increasing the size of production series, and of the all-
round increase in the exchange of these commodities for the en-
richment of the assortments on the internal markets.

The Food Industry of every country of the socialist camp
is being developed and specialized in such a way as to guarantee the most complete processing possible of local agricultural raw materials.

f) The further development of Agriculture in the socialist countries is determined by the necessity of reaching the
highest living standard of the workers in the world via the
all-round increase of production of food and raw materials of
agricultural origin. Because of the differences in agricultur-
ally usable area per head of population among the socialist
countries and the differing conditions of soil and climate,
the exchange of agricultural products among them is maintained
and undergoes further development. This requires, necessarily,
the coordination of plans with consideration of the possibilities of the further development of specialization among the socialist countries in the area of agricultural production,
starting from the interests and possibilities of these countries. The problem of specialization of agricultural production must, however, be solved in every socialist country with
consideration of the maximally possible increase in the production of grain and animal products. The increase of agricultural production and the increase of its effectiveness also presuppose coordination of plans and production cooperation of the
socialist countries in the areas of agricultural machine building, chemicals for agriculture, synthetic feeds, and of the expanded exchange of seeds, etc.

4. Guaranteeing a High Economic Effectiveness of the International Socialist Division of Labor

The international socialist division of labor guarantees
the increase of the effectiveness of social production and
thereby furthers the successful solution of the economic-polit-
ical tasks established by the Communist and Workers' Parties in
every historic phase of development. The effectiveness of social production shows itself in the socialist world system in a
high and steady rate of production increase, which makes it
possible to satisfy ever more completely the growing needs of
the peoples of all socialist countries and to overcome systematically the differences in their economic levels. One condi-

tion for a high economic effectiveness of the international division of labor in the socialist world system is the attainment
of rational proportions of production via coordination of the
plans of the countries, and thereby also via expedient distribution of productive capacities for the production of similar
or exchangeable products.

The growth of social labor productivity is the basic criterion for the economic effectiveness of the international socialist division of labor, i.e., the attainment of a minimum
input of material and labor for the production and transport
of a certain type of product. The decrease of inputs is being
attained in all countries through the deepening of the international socialist division of labor via specialization; optimum
concentration of production; improvement of its technical level; better utilization of equipment, raw materials, fuels, the
labor force, and the qualified cadres; more rational distribution of production factors; improvement of the quality of the
products, etc.

The increase of the effectiveness of social production,
based on the perfection of the international socialist division of labor, corresponds fully to the national as well as
the common interests of the countries of Socialism. The interest of every socialist country in the deepening of the international division of labor, which is effective from the
standpoint of the socialist world system as a whole, is, if
necessary, secured by appropriate forms of cooperation and assistance on the part of other socialist countries.

Calculations as to the comparable economic effectiveness
of investments and of production in the socialist countries,
as of the economic effectiveness of foreign trade, are being
utilized in the coordination of the plans of the countries as
an important, even though not as the sole criterion for establishing rational ways of deepening the international socialist
division of labor. One of the most important methods for
evaluating variants of specialization of production are calculations concerning the decrease of current inputs for production and transport of specialized products, as well as concerning the decrease of the specific investment required, considering the time factor and recoupment. The value indices
have to be supplemented by a system of comparable technical-
economic calculations and indices in natural units, which make
it possible to characterize in all-inclusive fashion the different variants of the international specialization of production from the standpoint of economic effectiveness. Considering the fact that measures concerning specialization of and cooperation in production are being worked out for a longer period, the comparison of the value indices and the technical-economic indices has to also take into account possible long-run

changes of these indices under the influence of technical progress.

Besides calculations of economic effectiveness, one also
has to consider, while perfecting the international socialist
division of labor, the necessity of assuring full employment
of labor and equilibrating the balance of payments. Further
to consider are the role of the particular production with respect to the increase of social labor productivity in the entire economy, the securing of an equalization of the economic
levels of development of the countries, the strengthening of
defense readiness; and other factors.

The continually expanding scientific-technical cooperation
of the socialist nations promotes the steady increase of the
economic advantage of social production in the socialist camp.
Specifically, this goal is also served by: _____ transmission
of progressive experiences and successes in all areas of production, science, and technology, as well as mutual assistance
in the training of cadres; _____ specialization and coordination of efforts in research, design and construction, as one of
the most important parts of the rational specialization of production itself; _____ common labors in research as well as design and construction; the perfection of organizational forms
of collective efforts; and the concentration of the scientific-
technical powers via specialization and coordination of efforts
directed toward the solution of the problems most important for
a more rapid economic development; _____ exchange of information in the areas of production organization and economic control in the plants and administrative organs.

5.   Connecting the International Specialization of
     Production with the Complex Development of the
     Economy of the Individual Socialist Countries

In the socialist world economic system there exist not only favorable conditions for the determined and planned deepening of the division of labor among the countries, but also for
the creation of a rational complex of economic branches, which
are interdependent with and supplementary to each other, within
every one of the countries. This signifies the creation of a
multi-branch structure of the national economy of the socialist
countries, which combines in an optimum complex industry and
agriculture, the extractive and the processing branches, and
the production of the means of production and of consumer
goods, and which contributes to an increase in the tempo and
the effectiveness of their economic development.

International specialization, as well as development of
national economic complexes in the individual socialist countries mutually determine each other. Only on the basis of

their harmonic connection, the most complete and most economical utilization of the productive factors of each socialist
country and of the socialist camp in its totality, can be guaranteed. The tendency to create a self-sufficient complex of
the national economy at the expense of the deepening of a rational international division of labor, or, vice versa, a one-
sided international specialization of the economy, may lead to
a decrease of the effectiveness and to a slowing down of the
tempo of the economic development in the individual socialist
countries as well as in the system as a whole. The national
economic complexes, as well as the international specialization
of production, are gradually coming about on the basis of the
most effective utilization, from the standpoint of the individual countries and the whole socialist system, of the following
basic factors: _____ existing and planned production capacities, labor resources, and possibilities for increase in the
number and qualification of cadres; _____ the present level of
national income, accumulation, and consumption in the economy,
the possibilities for increasing their levels and correspondingly the absorptive capacity of the internal market; _____
natural resources, as well as soil and climatic conditions;
_____ the geographic position of the country vis-a-vis other
countries, existing international transport routes, and the
possibilities for their further development; _____ existing
economic relations with socialist and other countries of the
world, and the possibilities for their future expansion and
for the inception of new relations.

The role of natural conditions and of historic traditions,
however, must not be overrated; their most effective and most
complete utilization must go hand in hand with the creation of
new conditions and traditions in accordance with the tasks of
socialist and communist construction. The national economic
complex should most expediently be developed in every country
in such a fashion that its economic level is continually increasing. This presupposes especially in every country the
greatest possible development of socialist industry as a leading branch of the national economy and the securing of the primacy of the growth of production of the means of production.
The creation of an optimum economic complex in every country
requires: _____ development of the local fuel, energy, and raw
material industry on the basis of the maximally possible utilization of internal resources, while considering the economic
effectiveness from the standpoint of the interests of the country and the whole socialist camp; _____ an increase in the importance of those economic branches which form the basis of
technical progress in the economy, especially of machine building and the chemicals industry; _____ development of the building materials industry as well as of the light and food industries, which are based on local raw materials and should cover

basic internal demand; _____ development of a modern transport
and communications system; _____ development of agriculture to
such a degree that the country's demand for food, feed, and
raw materials is covered to a maximally possible degree; any
necessary increase for this purpose of the intensity of cultivation of the basic types of agricultural production in all
countries; and the inclusion of not yet utilized agricultural
areas in production; _____ full employment of the employable
population; _____ accelerated industrial development of the
districts of the country with a low economic level; _____ all-
round utilization of the advantages of international specialization of production in the socialist camp and of the possibilities for increasing trade with the capitalist nations.

     In the branches of production, which are being developed
in all or in most socialist countries, it is expedient to deep-
en the international specialization according to individual
types of products. While developing specialization, one
should consider not only the needs of the socialist countries,
but also possibilities for export beyond the boundaries of the
socialist world system. Side by side with the complex development of the national economy of every country, the international socialist division of labor contributes to the formation of production complexes with participation of several socialist countries.

            6.   Overcoming the Historically Given Differences
               in the Economic Levels of Development of the
                           Socialist Countries

     The countries of the socialist world system have begun
the building of a socialist society from differing levels of
development of productive factors. The necessity for the
equalization of the economic levels of the countries stems from
the nature of Socialism itself. The highest living standard in
the whole world for all peoples of the socialist nations and
the more or less simultaneous transition of all countries to
Communism can only be guaranteed through the creation in every
country of the preconditions of production necessary thereto.
The material preconditions for the construction of Communism
are being created through the creative labors of the people of
every country and the steady increase of its contribution to
the strengthening of the socialist system. The overcoming of
the differences in the levels of economic development will
bring about a more complete utilization of the advantages of
the international socialist division of labor, and it is at the
same time one of the factors accelerating the rate of economic
development of the socialist system as a whole. It furthers
the creation of optimum proportions of enlarged reproduction
within the socialist world system. In the course of building

Socialism and Communism, the essential differences in the levels of development of the national productive powers are being
liquidated insofar as they are connected with the historic
conditions of economic development of the countries under capitalism. The socialist countries will approach each other
with respect to the size of the national income and industrial
production per capita, with respect to the effectiveness of
agricultural production, the level of labor productivity, and
the most important indices of the living standard of the population. This ultimately presupposes the more rapid development, relative to other socialist countries, of the countries
with a less high economic level.

The equalization of the levels of economic development of
the countries does, however, not mean the liquidation of all
differences arising from special endowment with natural resources, climatic conditions, and national peculiarities in
the structure of consumption and the way of life of the population. Conditions for the rapid upswing of the economies
and the living standards of the populations in the economically less developed countries are the all-round utilization of
the advantages of the socialist social order and the socialist
world system, and brotherly cooperation and mutual aid. This
presupposes the maximum mobilization of the internal resources
in the economically less developed socialist countries; a relatively higher level of accumulation in their economy; a
steady increase of the technical equipment of the national
economy and of the degree of employment of the employable population; and the assurance of a rapid growth of social labor
productivity. The other socialist countries contribute to the
increase of the effectiveness of the efforts of these countries, directed toward the rapid upswing of the national economy, in the following fashion: _____ through the transmission of the latest scientific-technical know-how; _____ through
assistance in the designing of technically progressive plants;
_____ through carrying out of geological prospecting; _____
through the training of qualified cadres; _____ through the
delivery of industrial equipment, especially of complete
equipment for industrial plants; _____ through aid in the assembly and during initial production runs of these plants;
_____ through the granting of credits and other types of aid.

The cooperation in the construction of industrial objects,
in the development of natural resources, and in satisfying the
demands for raw materials, fuels and electric energy also
serves these goals.

Socialist industrialization, directed toward the development of heavy industry and its core, machine building, is the
main road to overcoming technical-economic backwardness, as
has been proved by the experiences of the Soviet Union and oth-

er socialist nations. The realization of industrialization is
being accelerated manifold and made easier through the utilization of the advantages of the international socialist division of labor. The economic and scientific-technical cooperation among the socialist nations, their mutual aid, and the
organization of the division of labor among them, must contribute maximally to the strengthening of the national economic
complexes and to the expansion of production in the lesser developed countries. Every individual socialist country, and
the socialist world system as a whole, gain through this all-
round brotherly cooperation.

7.   Division of Labor and Commodity Exchange
Among the Socialist Countries

The international socialist division of labor is the basis for commodity exchange among the socialist countries,
which is based on the principle of equivalence. It is the
role of the appropriate organization of commodity deliveries
and currency relationships on the socialist world market to
contribute to the planned deepening of the division of labor
among the socialist countries. In accordance with the development of the division of labor, it is necessary to perfect
continually the forms of the commodity-money relationships
among the countries of Socialism. The practical realization
of the recommendations for international specialization and
cooperation, which have been accepted by the competent organs
of the countries, presupposes the signing of long-term bilateral and multilateral trade and other agreements. These must
specify the volume and conditions for delivery of specialized
products. They must also fix the responsibility of the partners for the fulfillment of the obligations for delivery of
said products, for their appropriate technical level, quality,
and dates of delivery. It is expedient to gradually introduce
the practice of multilateral trade and payments agreements.

The multilateral coordination of plans, and the recommendations for specialization of and cooperation in production
based thereon, must assure the balancing of payment relations
of every socialist country, especially on the basis of multilateral clearing, which is being used more and more. It
should be noted in this connection that balancing of the balance of payments is not equivalent with balancing of mutual
payments for individual groups of commodities and products.
The fulfillment of obligations taken on in trade and other
agreements, especially with respect to the agreed upon volumes,
commodity quality, and delivery dates, has to be regarded as a
primary duty of the socialist nations. It is necessary to perfect the system of price formation on the socialist world market continually in accordance with the requirements of a plan-

ned deepening of the international socialist division of labor,
a steady increase of commodity trade, and an acceleration of
the development of the socialist world economy. At the same
time the conditions must be created for a gradual transition
to an own price basis.

* * * * *

The basic principles of the international socialist division of labor are the expression of general laws of development of the socialist world system. They follow from the
character of the relationships among the socialist nations and
the levels of development of productive powers and of economic
cooperation reached by them. They take into account the concrete economic and political tasks standing before the individual countries and before the whole world system. In accord
with the further development and strengthening of the economic
cooperation of the countries of Socialism and the acquisition
of new experiences in the realization of the international
specialization of and cooperation in production, the aforementioned basic principles in the area of international socialist
division of labor will be perfected, supplemented, and spelled
out in detail.

SELECTED BIBLIOGRAPHY

A. EAST GERMAN PUBLICATIONS

1. Books and Pamphlets

Akademie der Wissenschaften der U.d.S.S.R., Institüt für Ökonomie, *Politische Ökonomie,* (Berlin: Dietz Verlag, 1955, and 3rd, rev. ed., 1961).

Behrens, Fritz, *Der Nutzeffekt der gesellschaftlichen Arbeit und der Struktureffekt bei der Messung der Arbeitsproduktivität* (Berlin: Akademie Verlag, 1961).

Brass, Heinz, *Aussenhandel und Nationaleinkommen im Sozialismus* (Berlin: Verlag Die Wirtschaft, 1961).

Brauer, Rudolf, ed., *Internationale sozialistische Arbeitsteilung und Perspektivplanung* (Berlin: Verlag Die Wirtschaft, 1961).

Brauer, Rudolf, *Probleme der Ermittlung des ökonomischen Nutzens der sozialistischen internationalen Arbeitsteilung und des Aussenhandels sozialistischer Staaten* (Berlin: Verlag Die Wirtschaft, 1962).

Domdey, Karl-Heinz, *"Entwicklungshilfe" oder echte sozialistische Hilfe* (Leipzig: Urania Verlag, 1961).

Gräbig, Gertrud, *Internationale Arbeitsteilung und Aussenhandel im sozialistischen Weltsystem* (Berlin: Verlag Die Wirtschaft, 1960).

Gräbig, Gertrud; and Held, Margarete, *Aufgaben des Aussenhandels in der sozialistischen Volkswirtschaft* (Berlin: Verlag Die Wirtschaft, 1961).

Grabley, Peter, *RGW Spezialisierung Chemie* (Berlin: Verlag Die Wirtschaft, 1963).

Illgen, Konrad, *Freundschaft in Aktion* (Berlin: Dietz Verlag, 1961).

Kindelberger, Albert, *Zahlen zeigen den Aufstieg der Deutschen Demokratischen Republik* (Berlin: VEB Deutscher Zentralverlag, 1956).

Kohlmey, Gunther, *Der demokratische Weltmarkt* (Berlin: Verlag Die Wirtschaft, 1955).

_____, *Entwicklungsprobleme des sozialistischen Weltwirtschaftssystems* (Berlin: 1958).

Krause, Werner, *Das Entwicklungstempo der sozialistischen Länder im ökonomischen Wettbewerb der beiden Weltsysteme* (Berlin:
Verlag Die Wirtschaft, 1960).

Kunz, Willi, *Grundfragen der Internationalen Wirtschaftszusam-
menarbeit der Länder des Rates für Gegenseitige Wirtschaftshilfe (RGW)* (Berlin: Akademie Verlag, 1964).

Liebsch, H.; Scholz, G.; and Streber, J., *Sozialistische Re-
konstruktion der Industrie und internationale Wirtschaftsbe-
ziehungen* (Berlin: Verlag Die Wirtschaft, 1960).

Luck, Herbert, *Schiffbau, Seehandelsschiffahrt und Seehafen-
wirtschaft der Deutschen Demokratischen Republik* (Berlin: Akademie Verlag, 1961).

Möse, Edith, *Das sozialistische Weltwirtschaftssystem* (Berlin:
Verlag Die Wirtschaft, 1961).

Nykryn, Jaroslav; Štěpán, Karel; Heřman, Karel; Sereghy, Jana;
and Heiduschat, Franz, *Der sozialistische Aussenhandel und der
Nutzeffekt der Aussenhandelsgeschäfte* (Berlin: Verlag Die
Wirtschaft, 1962).

Quellen zur Geschichte, *Die Deutsche Demokratische Republik
auf dem Wege zum Sozialismus I (1945-1949) and II (1950-1960)*
(Berlin: Volk und Wissen VEV).

Sowinski, Ulrich, *Die Preisermittlung im Handel mit kapitali-
stischen Ländern* (Berlin: Verlag Die Wirtschaft, 1960).

Stalin, Joseph, *Ökonomische Probleme des Sozialismus in der
U.d.S.S.R.* (Berlin: 1952).

Ulbricht, Walter, *Die Entwicklung des deutschen volksdemokra-
tischen Staates 1945-1958* (Berlin: Dietz Verlag, 1961).

Zehn Jahre Rat für Gegenseitige Wirtschaftshilfe (Berlin:
Dietz Verlag, 1960).

2.   Journals and Newspapers

a) *Der Aussenhandel und der innerdeutsche Handel.* Published
under the auspices of the Ministry for Foreign and Intra-German trade. Berlin: Verlag Die Wirtschaft, Bi-weekly journal
since 1950.

b) *Deutsche Finanzwirtschaft* (Berlin: Verlag Die Wirtschaft)
Monthly.

c) *Die Wirtschaft* (Berlin, weekly newspaper).

d) *Tägliche Rundschau* (Berlin, daily newspaper).

e) *Wirtschaftswissenschaft* (Berlin: Verlag Die Wirtschaft, monthly journal).

f) *Einheit* (Berlin, Dietz Verlag, monthly). Official organ of the Central Committee of the Communist Party.

g) *Neues Deutschland* (Berlin, daily newspaper). Official organ of the Communist Party.

h) *Sozialistische Planwirtschaft* (Berlin: Verlag Die Wirtschaft), esp. 8/9, 1962, a special international issue containing 16 articles on CMEA by member country experts.

3. Official East German Publications

a) *Statistische Praxis* (Berlin: VEB Deutscher Zentralverlag). Published by the Central Administration for Statistics. Monthly journal.

b) *Definitionen wichtiger Kennziffern und Begriffe für Planung und Statistik* (Berlin: Staatsverlag der D.D.R., 1965). Published by the Council of Ministers and the Central Administration for Statistics.

c) *Presse-Informationen* (Berlin). Published by the press office of the Prime Minister of the G.D.R.

d) *Statistisches Jahrbuch der D.D.R.* (Berlin: VEB Deutscher Zentralverlag, later Staatsverlag der D.D.R.).

e) *Vierteljahreshefte zur Statistik der D.D.R.* (Berlin, quarterly journal, now extinct).

f) *Jahrbuch der Deutschen Demokratischen Republik* (Berlin: Verlag Die Wirtschaft) issues of 1956-1961, now extinct and continued as *Handbuch der Deutschen Demokratischen Republik* (Berlin: Staatsverlag der D.D.R., 1964).

B. WEST GERMAN PUBLICATIONS

1. Books and Pamphlets

Am Abend der Demontage, Sechs Jahre Reparationspolitik, Mit Dokumentenanhang (Bremen: Friedrich Trüjen Verlag, 1951).

Jahn, Georg, ed., *Die Wirtschaftssysteme der Staaten Osteuro-*

pas und der Volksrepublik China (Berlin: Duncker und Humblot, 1962), II.

Jahn, Georg and v. Bissing, W.M., eds., Die Wirtschaftssysteme der Staaten Osteuropas und der Volksrepublik China (Berlin: Duncker and Humblot, 1961), I.

Kiesewetter, Bruno, Der Ostblock: Aussenhandel des östlichen Wirtschaftsblockes einschliesslich China (Berlin: Safari-Verlag, 1960).

Klinkmüller, Erich, Die gegenwärtige Aussenhandelsverflechtung der sowjetischen Besatzungszone Deutschland (Berlin: Duncker und Humblot, 1959).

Klinkmüller, Erich and Ruban, Elisabeth, Die wirtschaftliche Zusammenarbeit der Ostblockstaaten (Berlin: Duncker und Humblot, 1960).

Krüger, Karl, Der Ostblock: Die Produktion des östlichen Wirtschaftsblockes einschliesslich China nach dem Schwerpunktprogramm (Berlin: Safari- Verlag, 1960).

Sopade Informationsdienst, Denkschriften (Vorstand der SPD, Hannover and Bonn).

Statistisches Handbuch von Deutschland 1928-1944 (München: Franz Ehrenwirth-Verlag, 1949).

Zotschew, Theodor, "Der RGW als Instrument für die wirtschaftliche Integration und weltwirtschaftliche Expansion der Ostblockländer," ed. William Gülick, Südosteuropa Jahrbuch, 1958.

        2.   Official Publications of Bundesministerium
               für gesamtdeutsche Fragen (Bonn)

a) Bonner Berichte aus Mittel- und Ostdeutschland (irregular).

b) Materialien zur Wirtschaftslage in der sowjetischen Besatzungszone (irregular).

c) Others.

    S.B.Z. von A bis Z, various issues (latest 1965).

    Die sowjetische Besatzungszone Deutschlands 1945-1954, 1954, mimeographed. Bonn. I and II.

    S.B.Z. von 1945 bis 1954, Eine chronologische Übersicht, 1956.

3. Publications from Deutsches Institut
    für Wirtschaftsforschung (Berlin).

a) *Vierteljahreshefte zur Wirtschaftsforschung.*

b) *Wochenberichte* (weekly since 1950).

c) *Sonderhefte* (irregular).

d) Others.

Gleitze, Bruno, *Ostdeutsche Wirtschaft* (Duncker und Humblot, 1956).

Wirtschaftsprobleme der Besatzungszonen (Duncker und Humblot, 1948).

4. Miscellaneous

Der Aussenhandel der D.D.R. (Berlin: IWE- Informations- und Archivdienst, 1959), mimeographed.

Europa Archiv (Frankfurt).

10 Jahre Rat für gegenseitige Wirtschaftshilfe (Berlin: Informationsdienst West-Sonderdienst, 1959, mimeographed).

Osteuropa Wirtschaft (Bergisch Gladbach, quarterly).

Thalheim, Karl C., *Die wirtschaftliche und soziale Entwicklung in Ostberlin und der sowjetischen Besatzungszone,* (Berlin: Ost-europa Institut an der Freien Universität Berlin), mimeographed, irregular.

C.   OTHER PUBLICATIONS

1. Western

Eastern European Economics (International Arts and Sciences Press, New York).

Free Europe Committee, *Situation Reports, Press Surveys, Editorial Comments* (mimeographed, Research Department, Radio Free Europe).

Nettl, J. Peter, *The Eastern Zone and Soviet Policy in Germany 1945-1950* (London: Oxford University Press, 1951).

Problems of Economics (International Arts and Sciences Press, New York).

Pryor, Frederic L., *The Communist Foreign Trade System* (Cambridge: The M.I.T. Press, 1963).

Roustang, Guy, *Développement Économique de L'Allemagne Orientale* (Paris: Sedes, 1963).

Slusser, Robert, ed., *Soviet Economic Policy in Postwar Germany*, Research Program on the U.S.S.R. (New York: 1953).

Stolper, Wolfgang F., with the assistance of Roskamp, Karl W., *The Structure of the East German Economy* (Cambridge: Harvard University Press, 1960).

The American Review of Soviet and Eastern European Foreign Trade (International Arts and Sciences Press, New York).

The American Slavic and East European Review (New York: Columbia University Press), since 1962: *Slavic Review* (Seattle: University of Washington).

U.N., *Direction of International Trade*, Series T.

_____, *Economic Bulletin for Europe*, (monthly).

_____, *Economic Survey of Europe since the War* (Geneva: 1953).

_____, *Economic Survey of Europe* (Geneva, yearly).

2. Soviet Bloc

a) Books.

Bystrov, F.P., et. al., eds., *International Clearing and Foreign Exchange Relations Among the Countries of the Peoples Democracies* (Moscow: 1956).

Ivanov, N.I., *The Development of Economic Relations Among the European Countries of the Peoples Democracies* (Moscow: 1959), in Russian.

Kovrizhnikh, M.F., *Foreign Trade of the Countries of the Peoples Democracies* (Moscow: 1961), in Russian.

Lyubimov, N.N., *International Economic Relations* (Moscow: 1957), in Russian.

Semyenov, I.I., ed., *Problems of the Socialist International Division of Labor* (Moscow: 1960), in Russian.

Statistical Yearbooks (of all CMEA members).

b)   Journals

Czechoslovak Foreign Trade (Prague: Chamber of Commerce), in English.

Dyengi i kredit (Moscow).

Ekonomia Popullore (Tirana).

Ekonomika i organizacja pracy (Warsaw).

Ekonomicheskaya gazeta (Moscow).

Ekonomista (Warsaw).

Gospodarka Planowa (Warsaw).

Handel Zagraniczny (Warsaw).

Hungarian Foreign Trade (Budapest: Chamber of Commerce, in English).

Ikonomicheska Missl (Sofia).

Kommunist (Moscow).

Közgazdasági Szemle (Budapest).

Külkereskedelem (Budapest).

Mirovaya ekonomika i myezhdunarodniye ostnosheniya (Moscow).

Plánované Hospodářství (Prague).

Planovo stopanstvo i statistika (Sofia).

Planovoye Khozyaistvo (Moscow).

Polish Perspectives (Warsaw).

Politická Ekonomie (Prague).

Probleme Economice (Bucharest).

Przegląd Statystyczny (Warsaw).

Revista de Statistiká (Bucharest).

Soviet News (London: Press Department, Soviet Embassy).

Sprawy Miedzynarodowe (Warsaw).

Statistika (Sofia).

Statistika kontrola (Prague).

Statistický Obzor (Prague).

Statisztikai Szemle (Budapest).

Vestnik statistiki (Moscow).

Vneshnyaya torgovlya (Moscow).

Vnshna trgoviya (Sofia).

Voprosi Ekonomiki (Moscow).

Wiadomości Statystyczne (Warsaw).

Zahranicní Obchod (Prague).